CITIZEN-OFFICERS

Conflicting Worlds
New Dimensions of the American Civil War

T. Michael Parrish, Series Editor

CITIZEN-OFFICERS

The Union and Confederate Volunteer Junior Officer Corps IN THE American Civil War

ANDREW S. BLEDSOE

LOUISIANA STATE UNIVERSITY PRESS
BATON ROUGE

Published by Louisiana State University Press
Copyright © 2015 by Louisiana State University Press
All rights reserved
Manufactured in the United States of America
First printing

Designer: Laura Roubique Gleason
Typeface: Sentenel
Printer and binder: Maple Press

All graphs and charts are by Mary Lee Eggart.

Library of Congress Cataloging-in-Publication Data are available at the Library of Congress.

ISBN 978-0-8071-6070-1 (cloth: alk. paper) — ISBN 978-0-8071-6071-8 (pdf) — ISBN 978-0-8071-6072-5 (epub) — ISBN 978-0-8071-6073-2 (mobi)

The paper in this book meets the guidelines for permanence and durability of the Committee on Production Guidelines for Book Longevity of the Council on Library Resources. ∞

For Mom and Dad,
For my grandparents,
And especially for Trish

CONTENTS

	Preface	ix
	Acknowledgments	xv
1.	Ideological Origins of the Volunteer Junior Officer Corps	1
2.	Creation of the Civil War Junior Officer Corps	25
3.	The Challenges of Company Leadership	62
4.	Citizen-Officer Culture	102
5.	The Early War Combat Experience	135
6.	Maturation of the Volunteer Junior Officer Corps	178
	Epilogue	218
	Appendixes	223
	Notes	251
	Bibliography	275
	Index	313

Photographs follow page 134.

PREFACE

In 401 B.C. the Athenian citizen-general Xenophon and ten thousand of his fellow Greek soldiers entered the service of the Persian prince Cyrus the Younger, whose desire for the throne led him to rebel against his elder brother, Artaxerxes II. Despite the bravery of the "Ten Thousand," Cyrus's imperial ambitions died with him in battle. Friendless, stranded deep in enemy country, and surrounded by a hostile Persian army, the Greek citizen-soldiers undertook a desperate three-year journey home that Xenophon immortalized for posterity in his *Anabasis*. As the Ten Thousand prepared to return home, the general addressed his officers:

> Know, then, that being assembled in so great numbers you have the fairest of all opportunities; for all the soldiers fix their eyes on you: if they see you disheartened their courage will forsake them; but if you appear resolute yourselves and exhort them to do their duty, be assured they will follow you, and endeavour to imitate your example. It seems also reasonable that you should excel them in some degree, for you are their generals, their leaders, and their captains; and as in time of peace you have the advantage of them both in riches and honours, so now in time of war you ought to challenge the preeminence in courage, in counsel, and, if necessary, in labour. In the first place, then, it is my opinion that you will do great service to the army if you take care that generals and captains are immediately chosen in the room of those who are slain: since, without chiefs nothing either great or profitable can indeed be achieved on any occasion, but least of all in war; for as discipline preserves armies, so the want of it has already been fatal to many.[1]

Xenophon's appeal to his officers encompasses many of the indispensable values that military leaders had to exhibit to command citizen-soldiers successfully—convincing authority, leadership by example, decisiveness, resiliency, inspiration, competence, shared sacrifice, honor, moral excellence, conspicuous courage, fairness, empathy, and discipline. More than two millennia later, American citizen-officers, engaged in their own desperate struggle for survival, would no doubt have recognized the soundness of Xenophon's appeal. Civil War citizen-officers had ample opportunities to discover how useful these principles were in convincing their volunteers to obey orders and to risk death in battle for cause and country.

This study considers how Union and Confederate volunteer junior officers influenced, and how they were influenced by, the persistent citizen-soldier ethos of the republican tradition. It also considers how company-level military leadership developed in Civil War volunteer armies within the pliant margins of this ethos. Through an analysis of wartime writings, postwar reminiscences, company and regimental papers, census records, and demographic data, this study traces the origins, nature, and experiences of Union and Confederate citizen-officers and volunteers and assesses how their deeply held ideological expectations evolved under intense pressure, with important implications for the future.

Too often historians interpret the Civil War through the prism of a strict ideological dichotomy between North and South. Certainly, Northerners and Southerners fundamentally disagreed about a number of issues: slavery and freedom, race and identity, liberty and equality, federalism and states' rights, and the very meaning of union and the Constitution. Nevertheless, most who fought in the Civil War also shared a revolutionary heritage, a similar interpretation of the republican tradition, parallel assumptions about the obligations of citizenship, and a common understanding of the nature and limits of military service. These citizen-soldiers' conceptions of leadership and military service derived from venerable ideological antecedents, including the same classical political traditions that infused Xenophon's appeal to the officers of the Ten Thousand. The Civil War represents a shift in the ways Americans conceived of the citizen-soldier ethos, military service, and leadership. Volunteer junior officers played a crucial role in that process, and their wartime experiences provide us with a unique and valuable perspective on this important moment.

Oddly, the story of these men has yet to be told in full. Historians of the Civil War have lavished attention on the so-called "common soldier" in recent decades, constructing complex analytical amalgams of Johnny Reb and Billy Yank and then disassembling, transnationalizing, or historicizing these models even as they question their utility. Others assess common soldiers' combat motivation, their will to fight, their beliefs about death and religion, their understanding of nations and nationalism, their feelings about the home front and morale, and their attitudes toward victory and defeat, courage and cowardice, slavery and emancipation, race, sexuality, family, class, gender, manhood, honor, violence, and almost every other imaginable subject.[2] Yet for all the exceptional work done on the common soldier, scholars have given scant attention to citizen-officers' unique participation in the conflict. Modern Civil War historians do not typically evaluate volunteer officers as a distinctive group worthy of scholarly consideration. Moreover, historians have overlooked the ideological progression, leadership challenges, and avocational maturation citizen-officers experienced during the war. Only a few have examined citizen-officers as a distinct group.[3] Most approach the subject only obliquely, superficially, or from a limited analytical perspective.[4] This study is an attempt to remedy this oversight by exploring the nature, challenges, and evolution of company-grade volunteer military leadership during the Civil War.

The term "leadership" likely conjures a variety of mental images for modern minds. Military history aficionados might picture generals commanding armies, planning campaigns, managing subordinate commanders, and deciding the fate of nations in their battles; these are the men on horseback whose graven images now decorate—or clutter—national battlefield parks across the southeastern United States. Others might imagine corporate executives, institutional directors, managers of organizations, educators, religious figures, media personalities, or coaches; in short, leaders who inspire their followers to great achievements in business, the arts and sciences, public policy, humanitarian causes, or athletics. Still others see leadership in terms of authority and leaders as cultural or economic elites who, through ability, personality, influence, wealth, luck, or the unique advantages of their race, class, or gender, find themselves atop the power structures of society.

The junior officers at the heart of this study do not fit precisely into any of these categories, though they share traits with all of them. Their leadership occurred in a manner unlike that of generals, executives, or cultural elites. Company-grade citizen-officers, the captains and lieutenants who are the subjects of this study, were the lowest-ranking commanders in Civil War armies. The relationships between these volunteers and their men were at their most intimate, and the consequences for their failures or successes were immediate. Company officers lived among their enlisted volunteers, marched or rode beside them daily, led them into battle, and sustained casualties at an appalling rate, even by the shocking standards of the Civil War. These officers, like their enlisted charges, were products of the citizen-soldier ethos of their time; many were selected for command by their own men and through that most democratic of institutions, the vote. Before going off to war, citizen-officers were their volunteers' friends or neighbors, hailing from the same communities, attending the same churches, and sharing a mutual idiom of place, community, and purpose. But upon assuming their commissions, they were no longer the same as their enlisted soldiers. As military leaders, officers possessed an immense amount of authority over their men; in fact, Civil War captains and lieutenants held nothing less than the power of life and death over their soldiers and could, at least in theory, expect the institutional support of their armies to ensure they retained that essential component of command. Their struggle for authority, along with the delicate intellectual, psychological, and emotional balancing act necessary for maintaining it, is perhaps the least understood aspect of the volunteer officer experience; as such, it constitutes a significant component of this book.

Citizen-officers could not establish their authority without exercising effective military leadership. In its most basic sense, military leadership is a personal relationship that involves human interaction between commanders and subordinates. Certainly, senior commanders have been, and will continue to be, important subjects for historical examination: after all, generals direct battles, battles decide wars, and wars alter the course of history. Civil War military leadership occurred at all levels, however, not just at the highest echelons of authority; small command decisions and the personal relationships between junior officers and enlisted volunteers also had significant consequences for the outcome of the war, particularly when amplified across vast opposing citizen armies. As this study reveals, Civil War citizen-officers arrived at creative, often ingenious solutions to overcome the unique leadership challenges posed by the tension between antebellum democratic values and the demands of military necessity. Historians who choose to disregard the importance of interpersonal relationships in war risk losing sight of a pivotal facet of the Civil War experience.

Unfortunately, the study of military leadership is unfashionable in some academic circles. Perhaps historians are so eager to tell the stories of the overlooked, the powerless, the oppressed, or the otherwise ignored that they prefer to let officers speak for themselves. While it is true that many Civil War junior officers enjoyed antebellum economic and social privileges greater than those of their enlisted volunteers, and giving voice to the voiceless is a vital role for historians, it would be a mistake to disregard this group of men. Despite abundant untapped evidence available to historians, the complex challenges that volunteer junior officers faced is still one of the least understood aspects of the Civil War soldier experience and, potentially, one of the most fruitful areas for the future of Civil War soldier studies.

The terminology employed in this book necessitates some explanation. The term "citizen-officer" is in no way intended to diminish the citizenship, patriotism, or public-spiritedness of the professional officers who served in the regular U.S. Army during the Civil War, nor that of the regular-army officers who resigned their commissions to fight on behalf of the Confederacy. Obviously, professional officers were simultaneously citizens and soldiers, and in a sense the term "citizen-officer" is one of art. In the context of this study, citizen-officers are simply volunteer officers who held commissions in the Union or Confederate armies, who often had little or no professional training or antebellum military experience, and who served as commanders for a finite period. The term "volunteer" refers to soldiers of enlisted rank who, like citizen-officers, agreed to enlist for a specific period of service and who aspired to return to their civilian lives at its conclusion. For simplicity's sake, the term "volunteer" as used here is imprecise, even self-contradictory; it also includes the small minority of Civil War soldiers who were conscripts, paid substitutes, late enlisters, or otherwise might not have entered military service by choice. The terms "Northerner" and "Southerner" refer to Civil War participants who advocated the restoration of the Union or Confederate independence through secession, respectively. People from a multiplicity of origins fought in the Civil War, and they were motivated by a complex assortment of reasons transcending sectional affiliation. Labeling these participants by section is a reductive measure but necessary for the purposes of this study. Furthermore, volunteers were not all citizen-officers, though all citizen-officers were volunteers. Both citizen-officers and enlisted volunteers were citizen-soldiers, and both were shaped by the citizen-soldier ethos of the republican tradition in varying degrees.

By underscoring the ideological similarities between Union and Confederate volunteers and officers, the intent of this study is not to present a falsely reconciliationist account nor to minimize the fundamental differences between the two sides' respective causes. Union officers and men fought for something far different from their Confederate counterparts, and to claim otherwise does a disservice to both sides. Neither do I wish to advance a sacrificial or triumphalist narrative of the Civil War. The war was a bitter, divisive, bloody, and immensely destructive experience for those who participated in it, and many of the young men at the heart of this story both suffered and inflicted unimaginable hardships while engaging in astonishing acts of bravery and self-sacrifice. But some behaved quite badly, demonstrating cowardice, avarice, cruelty, selfishness, and worse. Those officers who survived often bore physical and emotional scars for the rest of their lives. While it is fitting that subsequent generations should appreciate the magnitude of these efforts, it is also imperative that Civil War citizen-officers' experiences serve as a warning, and their ordeal should give us pause. It presents us with an opportunity for sober reflection upon what war can and cannot accomplish and, I hope, can give us a deeper appreciation of the burdens that all soldiers are required to bear when their nations send them to fight.

ACKNOWLEDGMENTS

As with any challenging endeavor, this book would not exist without the kindness and support of others. I received essential support and assistance in my research and writing endeavors from Rice University, the Museum of the Confederacy, the Virginia Historical Society, the Tennessee State Library and Archives, the U.S. Army Heritage and Education Center, and the U.S. Army Military History Institute. Richard Sommers of the U.S. Army Military History Institute deserves special thanks and recognition for sharing with me his time and his thoughts on the nature and ancient Roman origins of Civil War citizen-officers. A conversation with Dr. Sommers in the Brochstein Pavilion at Rice University helped spark this project in the first place, and it was certainly the most productive cup of coffee I have shared with another historian in a long time. I also wish to express my deep gratitude to John L. Nau III for permitting me to explore his absolutely superb private collection of Civil War manuscripts and artifacts. I also thank Sally Anne Schmidt, a fellow Rice Owl and archivist of the Nau Civil War Collection, for her generosity and assistance. I am grateful to the staffs of the Alabama Department of Archives and History; the Arkansas History Commission; the Butler Center for Arkansas Studies; the Carter House and Carnton Plantation of Franklin, Tennessee; the Dawes Arboretum Collection on Ohio Memory; the Garland County Historical Society of Hot Springs, Arkansas; the Library of Congress; the Historical & Special Collections of the Harvard Law School Library; the William G. Squires Library at Lee University; the Ohio History Connection; the Library of Virginia; the University of Virginia Library; the Louis Round Wilson Special Collections Library at the University of North Carolina; the Woodson Research Center and Fondren Library at Rice University; and the rangers, archivists, and staffs of the Gettysburg, Chickamauga and Chattanooga, Fredericksburg and Spotsylvania, Kennesaw Mountain, Shiloh, and Stones River National Military and Battlefield Parks.

An amazing community of historians, scholars, editors, publishers, and archivists helped me in all phases of this book. T. Michael Parrish shepherded this project from the start, and his generosity, insights, encouragement, constructive criticism, and seemingly inexhaustible supply of new primary-source material made this book possible. Mike also presented me with the 1863 *U.S. Infantry Tactics* manual of a first lieutenant in the regular U.S. Army, which now occupies an exalted place in my collection. Rand Dotson and Lee Sioles at LSU Press made publication of this book possible, and I thank them for their friendly professionalism. I also thank Kevin Brock for his keen eye and his superb work as copyeditor and Mary Lee Eggart for her graphics expertise. I am also grateful to Peter S. Carmichael, Richard L. Dinardo, Gary W. Gallagher, Joseph T. Glatthaar, Luke E. Harlow, Andrew F. Lang, W. Caleb McDaniel, Kenneth W. Noe, Carl L. Paulus, Jason Phillips, Aaron Sheehan-Dean, Susannah J. Ural, Steve R. Waddell, and members of the Society of Civil War Historians for their kindness, observations, and suggestions. These and other historians have read and commented on elements of this work, and it is better for their assistance and insight.

I would like to single out several members of the community of scholars at Rice University and Lee University for my gratitude. In particular, I thank Lynda Crist, editor of *The Papers of Jefferson Davis,* for her support, interest, and generosity during my time at Rice. Randal Hall and Bethany Johnson of the *Journal of Southern History* always provided kind words and astute suggestions. W. Caleb McDaniel provided outstanding ideas on a variety of issues related to slavery and democracy in nineteenth-century America, and I am thankful for his ideas. My graduate-student colleagues at Rice also provided invaluable intellectual and moral support as I labored on this study. Each of them, scholars in their own right, encouraged me to engage the past with creativity and intellectual rigor, and I am grateful for the experience of learning alongside them. I would also like to thank the volunteers at Valhalla for their contributions, known and unknown, to this book. I owe a tremendous debt to John B. Boles, whose energy, sagacity, and unfailing support helped make this book possible. Ira D. Gruber's wisdom and deep understanding of Anglo-American military history and leadership encouraged me to pursue this project, and he has been a cheerful mentor and a steady warden throughout the entire process. My Lee University colleagues—Robert Barnett, John Coats, Aaron Johnson, Jason Ward, Jared Wielfaert, and Randy Wood—all provided intellectual and moral support as I finished this book.

Finally, I wish to thank the most significant people in my life. My parents, Bill and Pat Bledsoe, provided me with an abundance of love and support in ways I may never fully realize. Thank you for everything. My grandfather, A. E. Cheatham, who passed away during the writing of this book, and my grandmother, Irene, helped me love history. Most important, my wife, Trish, waited patiently in many ways, and I thank her most of all.

CITIZEN-OFFICERS

1

Ideological Origins of the Volunteer Junior Officer Corps

"When we assumed the Soldier, we did not lay aside the Citizen," George Washington avowed to the New York Provincial Congress in 1775, "& we shall most sincerely rejoice with you in that happy Hour, when the Establishment of American Liberty on the most firm, & solid Foundations, shall enable us to return to our private Stations in the bosom of a free, peaceful, & happy Country."[1] Washington's pronouncement set a profound precedent for military service in the fledgling American republic when he assumed command of the Continental Army in this fashion. By establishing a double identity for himself and for the American citizen-soldiers who would follow, Washington defined the duality of military service as an essential component of republican citizenship. The military-service aspect of this arrangement enabled soldiers to assert and affirm their citizenship through voluntary, temporary service, a "fatal, but necessary Operation of War," as Washington characterized it. American volunteers would assume the role of soldiers in times of war or national crisis, all the while preserving their identities as free citizens with all the rights and privileges due them.[2]

By the 1860s, however, Washington's vision of an American citizen army had undergone significant alterations. Antebellum white male Americans, from North and South alike, interpreted these concepts in different ways, and the ideological foundations of citizenship and military service faced stern challenges during the Civil War. By 1864, even more had changed about military service and the ideological tradition that defined it. "An army is an aristocracy, on a three-years' lease, supposing that [to be] the period of enlistment," wrote Union colonel Thomas Wentworth Higginson in that deadly year. "No mortal skill can make military power effective on democratic principles. A democratic people can perhaps carry on a war longer and better than any other; because no other can so well comprehend the object, raise the means, or bear the sacrifices. But these sacrifices include the surrender, for the time being, of the essential principle of the government."[3] Higginson, an abolitionist and a volunteer officer in the 51st Massachusetts Infantry, eventually commanded the Union army's first regiment of black volunteers. As such, he knew a good deal about leading citizen-soldiers in battle.[4] Arguing against the military practicality of the American citizen-soldier ethos, the colonel articulated the single greatest challenge facing the leadership of the Union and Confederate volunteer armies—that is, reconciling the demands of war with the ideological and cultural traditions of that very same philosophy.

This tension between ideology and necessity was not unique to the Union army, nor was it new in American life and thought. Despite their acrimony over section, secession, and slavery, Americans on both sides of the conflict possessed a common ideological heritage and a mutual understanding of citizenship and military service that, while crucial to their identities, was not always compatible with the necessary operations of war. The citizen-soldier ethos and the democratic prerogatives of the American republican tradition served as sources of frustration for Colonel Higginson and other Civil War officers seeking a more professional and systematic fighting force, but these twin values were part of the bedrock of the revolutionary heritage shared by Northerners and Southerners. Historian J. G. A. Pocock describes the central tenets of this tradition as "a civic and patriot ideal in which the personality was founded in property, perfected in citizenship but perpetually threatened by corruption; government figuring paradoxically as the principal source of corruption and operating through such means as patronage, faction, standing armies (opposed to the ideal of the militia), established churches (opposed to the Puritan and deist modes of American religion) and the promotion of a monied interest."[5] Within the vessel of the republican tradition, the citizen-soldier ethos involved civic virtue in the form of military service, a claim on the revolutionary heritage won by force of arms, suspicion of standing armies, and a sense of egalitarianism and political involvement that manifested as mutual dependence between soldiers, officers, and the state. Most importantly, the American citizen-soldier ethos shaped the nature of officer selection and leadership in both Union and Confederate armies for the entirety of the Civil War, and the democratic prerogatives of volunteers helped define the ways in which they performed their military service.[6]

Despite the sectional rift and the debates over union, slavery, and liberty at the heart of that disagreement, Americans of all persuasions drew upon the Revolution's lexicon to define and interpret their mutual civic heritage. Individual liberty, freedom, and self-government, according to republican tradition, provided a common identity and shared history that all Americans could, and did, claim. Northerners who fought to preserve the Union hearkened back to the Revolution's traditions of personal autonomy and moral citizenship tempered by the egalitarianism and a healthy resentment of elitism originating in the colonial upheaval. This primarily Northern interpretation of the republican tradition shaped the way that Union volunteers selected their commanders. Antebellum Northerners valued their right to participate in public life and government, and in so doing ensured the individual liberty necessary to preserve the potential for their upward economic, political, and social mobility.[7] The union of states, as the embodiment of the social compact, both contained and protected the rights of individual liberty, national integrity, and self-government, that their forefathers had shed blood to define and defend in the American Revolution.[8]

For many Northerners, to threaten the Union was to undermine majority rule and invite tyranny. As the *Philadelphia Public Ledger* put it on June 7, 1861: "[W]e are fighting for ... [a] great fundamental principle of republican Government—the right of the majority to rule. When the ballot-box was substituted for revolution, it was thought that all violent changes in established governments, all sudden overthrowing of political structures, would be obviated, for the will of the people could be peacefully known through the ballot." The rebellion of 1861, therefore, represented a repudiation of participatory government and political equality under the law, and military service was the obligation of every citizen invested in the survival of the Republic. "We are fighting to prove to the world, that the free Democratic spirit which established the government is equal to its protection and its maintenance. If this is not worth fighting for, then our revolt against England was a crime, and our republican Government a fraud."[9]

Southerners' conception of the republican tradition derived from the same sources as their Northern counterparts, though the secessionists interpreted that tradition quite differently. Their unique interpretation of their ideological heritage also shaped how Confederates viewed military service. Antebellum Southerners emphasized, to varying degrees, the independence of the individual, personal honor, the values and traditions of their community, private sacrifice for the public good, obedience to a Christian hierarchy, and preservation of the institution of slavery.[10] They professed to fight for the concept of self-government as defined and defended by the revolutionary generation, many of whom were also sons of the South. As the *Atlanta Southern Confederacy* opined on June 25, 1861: "We quit the Union only because we had to quit those who had quit the Constitution. We chose to adhere to the substance, and leave the form. . . . We have resolved to preserve and [Lincoln] to destroy self-government. If you are conquered, you are no more freemen, but slaves. If you conquer, you remain free. Confiscation and chains, is the openly declared policy of our enemies."[11]

Pro-secession Southerners saw the preservation of self-determination and the right to shape the destiny of the nation, not necessarily the preservation of the mechanism of union, as the key to individual liberty and detected no logical or moral contradiction between these principles and a vigorous defense of the longstanding and, to them, essential institution of slavery. Freedom, therefore, was based on choice; whether through choosing forms of government, by maintaining their membership in the union of states, or in selecting their political and military leaders, free citizens' right to choose transcended the very existence of the Union itself. Fearful of encroachments on individual liberty, these Southerners saw themselves as the true guardians of the revolutionary inheritance and the republican tradition. Secession, therefore, was the South's repudiation of a corrupted national union; it was the ultimate act of self-government, and they believed it to be perfectly consistent with the republican tradition and the ideological inheritance of the American Revolution.[12]

Though antebellum Northerners and Southerners were at loggerheads over their differing interpretations of the revolutionary heritage, their understanding of the American citizen-soldier ethos within the republican tradition tended to be quite similar. Antebellum militia companies were often analogous in form, function, and purpose irrespective of section, and militia companies North and South were often intimately involved in local affairs and politics. The citizen-soldier ethos that informed these militias remained a central part of antebellum society's social fabric until the Civil War, and militia companies and military service often reflected the shared values and political characteristics of their communities.[13] It derived from a sense of the civic-virtue ideal, and both sections professed reverence for the notion of military service for the common good. Civic virtue, a concept adopted and expanded upon by eighteenth-century Americans, was fundamental to this citizen-soldier ethos; full participation in antebellum public life for white male citizens required engagement in electoral politics as well as armed service in the militia, which in turn granted the individual a tangible stake in the national destiny.[14]

The essence of virtuous citizenship demanded that men put aside their selfish interests to engage in military service for the public good. The American citizen-soldier ethos, a practice epitomized by Washington's standard of selfless service to the public interest, partially originated in the English militia system and endured in part because of a fear of the evils of a standing army.[15] This ethos, deeply imbedded in the American psyche, had its roots in the radical Whig ideology of the American Revolution; this, in turn, was based on earlier English Opposition thought of men like James Harrington. In his "The Commonwealth of Oceana," Harrington linked the duties and privileges of citizenship to both the individual exercise of private power and personal economic autonomy. Historian Lawrence D. Cress observes of this relationship: "The exercise of private power was a prerequisite for public power, and the possession of property was the primary criterion for individual independence. Like the tests for citizenship in ancient Greece and Rome, Harrington's concept of citizenship rested on the possession of an inheritable landed freehold. A citizen lived on his own property, could hold public office, and had the right and responsibility to bear arms in the defense of the state."[16] The radical Whig twist on Harrington's conception introduced an almost primal fear of a standing army and military professionalism. Americans dreaded the use of mercenary forces because such an approach divorced citizens from their obligations to their nation, and antebellum Americans clung to the citizen-soldier ethos because they feared an abusive central government buttressed by the power of a peacetime army of professional soldiers. Having survived the War for Independence and the early crises of the young Republic, they distrusted efforts to establish and maintain a standing army as an uncontrollable institution and a corrupting influence on the public life. A peacetime military, they feared, would inevitably involve itself in politics, undermine civilian authority, subvert the relationship between citizens and the state, and produce a martial aristocracy based on power, not laws. Without a standing army to compel obedience, they believed, a corrupt government could be rendered impotent. Thus, the citizen-soldier ethos became an indispensable foil for Americans' anxieties about a tyrannical central government and the fragility of democracy, particularly in wartime.[17]

The concept of voluntariness was central to the republican tradition, and this concept is essential to understanding Civil War citizen-officers and citizen-soldiers. Voluntariness, or what has been called "volitional allegiance," was one of the central issues settled by the Revolution. "Americans came to see that citizenship must begin with an act of individual choice," writes historian James H. Kettner. "Every man had to have the right to decide whether to be a citizen or an alien. His power to make this choice was clearly acknowledged to be a matter of right, not of grace, for the American republics were to be legitimate governments firmly grounded on consent, not authoritarian states that ruled by force and fiat over involuntary and unwilling subjects." As free citizens, volunteers consented to serve the Republic; voluntary consent was the essence of civic virtue, and a citizen's choice whether or not to render military service was the difference between "subjectship and citizenship," or put another way, between liberty and tyranny.[18] Antebellum governments became so concerned that citizens would not volunteer to serve in the militias that they enacted laws requiring every free and able-bodied white male citizen between the ages of eighteen and forty-five to serve in a local company overseen by their state. Still, citizens who held certain offices or practiced particular professions were exempted from service. Furthermore, actual requirements depended a great deal on the organization, energy, and efficiency of militia officers and mustering authorities to enforce them. Though most white males accepted military service as a duty of their citizenship, the wealthy or the resourceful could circumvent this obligation and avoid militia service by hiring fit substitutes or paying fines.[19]

The democratic prerogatives, or the web of rights, customs, behaviors, traditions, and values that Alexis de Tocqueville refers to as the "manners of democracy," were ingrained into the public life of antebellum Americans by the time of the Civil War. Their instinctual belief in the moral rightness of government by consent of the governed was balanced against the interests of individual liberty and equality, at least for white male citizens. "The American learns to know the laws by participating in the act of legislation; and he takes a lesson in the forms of government from governing," Tocqueville observes. "The great work of society is ever going on beneath his eyes, and, as it were, under his hands." Even the least sophisticated frontiersman knew and defended his democratic prerogatives as a citizen. "He will inform you what his rights are," Tocqueville notes, "and by what means he exercises them; he will be able to point out the customs which obtain in the political world." Moreover, the instinct of democracy suffused the antebellum generation. "Americans ... transfuse the habits of public life into their manners in private; and in their country the jury is introduced into the games of schoolboys, and parliamentary forms are observed in the order of a feast."[20]

The manner of democracy, nurtured within the citizen-soldier ethos and celebrated by soldiers and civilians alike, has a long and distinguished pedigree in America's military tradition. Washington's explication of the citizen-soldier's dual nature, while a profound precedent, was by no means original to him. Revolutionary Americans knew and cherished the example of the mythical Roman consul Lucius Quinctius Cincinnatus, the ideal citizen-soldier for that generation. The Romans of the ancient republic, adapting the Greek concept of *areté,* or moral excellence, defined virtuous citizenship in terms of self-control, moral uprightness, and actual ability; in other words, "[citizenship] combines the ability and the willingness to act in good faith, regardless of circumstances, towards the right purpose."[21] The patrician Cincinnatus, as the story goes, was unjustly forced from his prestigious place in Rome, stripped of his wealth, and constrained to retire to the humble life of a subsistence farmer. When Rome faced the threat of invasion, Cincinnatus heeded the pleas of his fellow citizens, left his farm, and led the armies to victory as dictator. Once the crisis had been averted, the noble Cincinnatus resigned his military position in a supreme example of selflessness and civic virtue.[22] Americans of the revolutionary generation revered Cincinnatus's heroic example, enthusiastically incorporating his model of disinterested selflessness and temporary military service into their conception of republican citizenship during and after the War for Independence.[23]

For many Founders, Cincinnatus's name was a watchword for how citizens should serve a republic. "When a few mighty matters are accomplished here," John Adams wrote in 1776, "I retreat like Cincinnatus, to the Plough ..., and farewell Politicks."[24] "We have seen sons of Cincinnatus," declared Patrick Henry in 1788, "without splendid magnificence or parade, going, with the genius of their great progenitor, Cincinnatus, to the plough; men who served their country without ruining it—men who had served it to the destruction of their private patrimonies—their country owing them amazing amounts, for the payment of which no adequate provision was then made." Henry emphasized not only Cincinnatus's sacrifice of military service but also his selflessness and submission to the rule of laws inherent in the temporary nature of such service. "We have seen such men throw prostrate their arms at your feet. They did not call for those emoluments which ambition presents to some imaginations. The soldiers, who were able to command every thing, instead of trampling on those laws which they were instituted to defend, most strictly obeyed them."[25] Historian Carl J. Richard notes that Washington was often depicted either as a Roman citizen-soldier or as Cincinnatus himself in works of art by Antonio Canova, Giuseppe Ceracchi, John Trumbull, and Charles Wilson Peale. John J. Barralet's engraving *George Washington's Resignation* illustrates the general surrendering his authority to Columbia with the plow and pastures of Mount Vernon behind him, much like Cincinnatus's beloved fields in the Roman countryside. Poets from Charles Henry Wharton to Lord Byron likewise compared the two leaders in their paeans to the Virginian.[26]

The power of the Cincinnatus ideal, as embodied in Washington's example, lies in its vivid message of the moral excellence of virtuous citizenship over selfish ambition won through military service. While central to the citizen-soldier ethos of the revolutionary generation, the Cincinnatus ideal is only a part of a larger whole. That generation's conception of military service and citizen-officer leadership is perhaps best embodied in George Mason's "Remarks on Annual Elections for the Fairfax Independent Company," written in 1775 on the eve of war with Britain. Mason's observations are telling, clearly and cogently setting forth the democratic principles essential to the republican tradition. As a member of the Continental Congress, Mason chaired Fairfax County's Committee of Safety and was charged by the Virginia Convention of 1774 with organizing a county militia company independent of colonial forces. Officers of the colonial militia were appointed by the royal governor and served at his pleasure. Mason, however, was determined to organize this new company based on democratic principles, pressing for election of officers with one-year terms and precluding them from succeeding themselves in command.[27] "This company is essentially different from a common collection of mercenary soldiers," he explains, drawing a distinction between the free citizen-soldiers of Virginia and the self-serving professionals and European conscripts of King George III. "It was formed upon the liberal sentiments of public good, for the great and useful purposes of defending our country, and preserving those inestimable rights which we inherit from our ancestors," thus delineating the fundamental purpose of military service in the republican tradition. Moreover, emphasizes Mason, citizen-soldier and citizen-officer service had to be temporary in nature, "intended in these times of extreme danger, when we are threatened with the ruin of that constitution under which we were born, and the destruction of all that is dear to us, to rouse the attention of the public, to introduce the use of arms and discipline, to infuse a martial spirit of emulation, and to provide a fund of officers." Citizens' temporary military service was a matter of survival, "that in case of absolute necessity, the people might be the better enabled to act in defence of their invaded liberty."[28]

Mason places particular emphasis on the service element of the citizen-soldier ethos, declaring that military service required noble submission to the authority of fellow citizens, an unnatural position of voluntary vulnerability that deserved respect. "Upon this generous and public-spirited plan, gentlemen of the first fortune and character among us have become members of the Fairfax Independent Company, have submitted to stand in the ranks as common soldiers," he maintains, "and to pay due obedience to the officers of their own choice." Such a sacrifice should never be exploited for selfish or ambitious reasons and should stand as a shining model for the other colonies. "This part of the country has the glory of setting so laudable an example: let us not tarnish it by any little dirty views of party, of mean self-interest or of low ambition." Mason then reminds his audience that citizens' military service must always be for the benefit of the whole, and the aim of those few who sacrifice their freedoms and comfort should be to secure the rights and liberties of all. "We came equals into this world, and equals shall we go out of it," he proclaims. "All men are by nature born equally free and independent. To protect the weaker from the injuries and insults of the stronger were societies first formed; when men entered into compacts to give up some of their natural rights, that by union and mutual assistance they might secure the rest; but they gave up no more than the nature of the thing required." Throughout Mason's appeal is the principle of *areté,* with its demand for moral excellence and ability employed for the greater good. "Every society, all government, and every kind of civil compact therefore, is or ought to be, calculated for the general good and safety of the community," he writes. "Every power, every authority vested in particular men is, or ought to be, ultimately directed to this sole end; and whenever any power or authority whatever extends further, or is of longer duration than is in its nature necessary for these purposes, it may be called government, but it is in fact oppression." If this ultimate goal was ever subverted, Mason argues, the inevitable result would be corruption and tyranny. "Whenever this is neglected or evaded, or the free voice of the people is suppressed or corrupted; or whenever any military establishment or authority is not, by some certain mode of rotation, dissolved into and blended with that mass from which it was taken, inevitable destruction to the state follows."[29]

Mason believed that military service had to be temporary to ward against corruption. And like his contemporaries in the revolutionary generation, he here draws upon the example of the Roman Republic for inspiration: "While the Roman Commonwealth preserved its vigour, new consuls were annually elected, new levies made, and new officers appointed." And far from impeding the military effectiveness of the Roman armies, he argues, this practice ensured virtue and excellence in its commanders. "A long and almost constant series of success proved the wisdom and utility of measures which carried victory through the world, and at the same time secured the public safety and liberty at home; for by these means the people had always an inexhaustible fund of experienced officers, upon every emergency, untainted with the dangerous impressions which continued command naturally makes." Mason again warns of the dangers of ignoring these principles, describing the perils of corruption in an army not subject to the will of the people it was charged with defending. "But when by degrees these essential maxims of the state were undermined, and pretences were found to continue commanders beyond the stated times, their army no longer considered themselves the soldiers of the Republic, but as the troops of Marius or of Sylla, of Pompey or of Ceasar, of Marc Antony or of Octavius." He concludes from this: "The dissolution of that once glorious and happy commonwealth was the natural consequence, and has afforded a useful lesson to succeeding generations." Mason's ideals, substantiated in the citizen-soldier ethos of the revolutionary generation, depend upon a single simple principle. "In all our associations; in all our agreements let us never lose sight of this fundamental maxim—that all power was originally lodged in, and consequently is derived from, the people. We should wear it as a breastplate, and buckle it on as our armour."[30]

The experience of the Revolution inscribed these values on the hearts and minds of antebellum Americans. Veteran officers of the War for Independence were among the first to learn of the power of the citizen-soldier ideal. Indignant at not receiving pay for several years, at the dissolution of the Continental Army, a number of officers organized to protest what they considered the ingratitude and injustice of their treatment by the Continental Congress. Though they, like their soldiers, had sacrificed a great deal during the war, these men misjudged the sentiments of the American public when they made their demands. With a mixture of resentment, entitlement, and superiority, many of the aggrieved officers found themselves adrift, at odds with the Congress that represented the public they had sworn to defend, and alienated from the yeoman amateurs in the rank and file.[31] Though organizing themselves into a society called the Cincinnati, they had begun to lose touch with the *areté* of the ancients and the Cincinnatus ideal. As historian Charles Royster writes, "The public wanted the officers, like the privates, to return to civilian life inconspicuously, not only laying aside their military character for the safety of republicanism but also forgoing invidious claims to have done more for independence than civilians had done."[32]

Washington's charismatic leadership and selfless example defused the Newburgh conspiracy of 1783, setting the critical precedent that American citizen-soldiers and their officers would remain subject to the ultimate authority of Congress, and thus to the people. During the War for Independence, Washington had been careful to recruit and employ talent based on merit, with a special emphasis on personal excellence over pedigree or connections. Through these actions, he set the tone for future American soldiers by subordinating the army to the Republic and by ensuring that the American military tradition would be one based on merit. And like Cincinnatus returning to his plow, citizen-officers were reminded by Washington's example that they could not claim social or political superiority due to their military service, no matter how selfless and noble they might think it; they were servants of the Republic first, subject to the will of the people. That is not to say that Washington favored entirely disbanding the regular army in favor of a militia system. The same year as the Newburgh affair, the general put his thoughts on military policy to paper in his "Sentiments on a Peace Establishment," formally calling for an effective and well-organized militia as well as a capable regular army trained and equipped to defend the frontier. Washington further called for the flowering of a professional officer corps, advocating military education, technical specialization, and a rudimentary expansible army necessary to secure the new republic's vast borders. Yet he never lost sight of the purpose of this army—to defend the nation, not to dominate it.[33]

A professional standing army would take a great deal of time and effort to develop, while the volunteer militia system remained intact after the war. In the meantime, their imaginations fired by images of Cincinnatus, the Revolution's citizen-soldier ethos, and the peerless example of Washington, militiamen clung fiercely to their democratic prerogatives when they stepped onto the mustering field. As good republicans, American volunteers of the early republic and the antebellum eras believed in the duty and right to govern themselves, and they expected to choose their own officers and shape the terms and nature of their military service in the same ways that their fathers and grandfathers had done. By long tradition and by virtue of company constitutions, militias perpetuated an element of exclusivity, yet the manner of democracy and majority rule so fundamental to American public life permeated these associations. Volunteer military service not only represented a colloquy for like-minded members of the Republic but also served as a forum for the expression of civic virtue, manhood, honor, meritocracy, and service to the community and the body politic. Discipline and military effectiveness were often secondary considerations.[34]

As the radical Whig anti-aristocratic ideas of the Revolution took hold in antebellum public life, Americans' understanding of the citizen-soldier ethos evolved, adapting Mason's conceptions of service to an even more egalitarian framework. American political culture further deemphasized officeholders' backgrounds, wealth, family, and social standing, instead proclaiming forcefully that no man should be entitled to power or status simply by accident of birth, fortune, or service. President Andrew Jackson's first annual message illustrates this point: "In a country where offices are created solely for the benefit of the people no one man has any more intrinsic right to official station than another."[35] The old system of enlightened paternalism, in which the "better sort" led the "mob" out of a sense of civic virtue, came under intense pressure as Americans of the Jacksonian era adopted new ways of imagining public and military leadership. Ordinary citizens had the same claim to the privilege of office holding as the "gentlemen" of the Founders' generation. Nevertheless, the educated and the elite continued to hold most public and militia offices in antebellum America, and the militia system entered a long and steady declension after the Revolution. But the citizen-soldier ethos remained, and powerful changes in public conceptions about the nature of power began to take root. Merit in times of war, volunteers learned, meant just as much for yeomen as it did for gentlemen. Voluntary military service gave non-elite men a tangible stake in their claim to republican citizenship and highlighted the social changes that had been taking place since the Revolution; namely, the decline of deference, an emphasis on individual liberty, and the presumed equality of all white men.[36]

Officers were a necessary evil to antebellum volunteers, and these men were to be tolerated but distrusted. As Mason advocated, to temper the tyrannical or aristocratic pretensions of ambitious officers, the citizen-soldier ethos required that these leaders be held in check by the democratic process. Though the idea of electing military officers seems alien, even illogical, to the modern mind, for Civil War volunteers, choosing commanders from among their peers was as natural as choosing one's justice of the peace, sheriff, or mayor. As early as the Seven Years' War (1756–63), American volunteers traditionally conceived of their service along contractual principles; citizen-soldiers served, citizen-officers led, and the former reserved the right to choose the latter through the democratic process. In this way officers were beholden to their men, who were most often their neighbors and colleagues in civilian life. This election tradition served as an endless source of frustration for British regulars and later for U.S. Army regulars. But under the strictures of the citizen-soldier ethos, neither citizen-officers nor volunteers were professional soldiers, and as Mason had hoped in 1775, their positions were never meant to be permanent. The arrangement of mutual dependence in militia elections carried through from war to peace and became a time-honored fixture of the American volunteer system.[37]

Despite its problems, the election system served an important purpose for antebellum volunteers. It was a reminder to both officers and men that Americans, regardless of social, military, or political rank, were citizens first. As Mexican War volunteer Thomas Barclay wrote in January 1848, "The volunteer officers chosen from the ranks by their men should never forget the obligations they owe their companies and indeed in general they act right and their treatment of the men is very different from that of many of the Regular officers."[38] Civil War volunteers, like their antebellum forebears, upheld a tradition of serving their nation and obeying orders on their own terms as much as possible. When the contract between officers and men had been breached for whatever reason, volunteers protested by electing new officers, disobeying bad ones, or by simply deserting. Confederate president Jefferson Davis, a West Pointer, a former volunteer officer, and a former U.S. secretary of war, believed that "[t]he citizens of the several States volunteered to defend their homes and inherited rights. . . . [T]he troops were drawn from the pursuits of civil life. Who so capable to judge of fitness to command a company, a battalion or a regiment as the men composing it?"[39] As Davis told Southerners in 1862, ordinary white male Americans had the same claim to the privilege of office holding as the gentlemen of the Founders' generation. Further, many of these citizens could claim the revolutionary birthright for their own by virtue of the blood, sweat, and treasure of prior generations.[40]

Northerners and Southerners were proud of their revolutionary tradition of self-government and boasted loudly of its perfection to anyone willing to listen. White men were, under the republican tradition, equal under the eyes of the law, a condition that Europeans could not likewise claim on so universal a scale. Citizens of the Republic could claim the right to be treated the same as any other citizen by their government; moreover, that very government was subject to their wishes. A representative government, its institutions constituted by law and overseen through an electoral process, formed the core of the republican tradition. This was a source for America's exceptional nature and a reason for its citizens to boast, they believed; in no other nation could citizens claim such political and social equality. That is not to say that the antebellum United States was an equal society. Women, children, people of color, and slaves did not share the fruits of liberty and equality. Even among white men, a definite hierarchy conditioned by generations of habit and institutional, social, religious, and political reinforcement remained in place. Nevertheless, liberty and equality ensured by the franchise, and a sense that one American was as good as the next, were fundamental to the republican tradition.[41]

The egalitarianism of the Jacksonian era altered Americans' faith in the natural aristocracy of Washington and Jefferson's generation and reconfigured their views toward leadership. Though the educated and the elite continued to hold most public and militia offices in the antebellum United States and old social and political hierarchies persisted, powerful changes in public conceptions about the nature of power in American society had taken root. Ability, particularly in times of war, was no respecter of persons, and positions of leadership and prosperity were open to any who had the wherewithal to claim them. Frontier farmers and neophyte cotton planters pushed west, secure in the knowledge that they could market their crops on steamboats, trains, or good roads. Likewise, manufactured goods, supplies, and fresh settlers took advantage of the developing transportation infrastructure to spread the nation's influence westward. Railroads and steamboats regularized time, as they were dependent on precise schedules, and further encouraged westward migration for profit and opportunity. National expansion demanded new territory, and with a spirit of Manifest Destiny in mind as well as the South's desire for new lands for slavery, the United States eyed Mexican territories north of the Rio Grande with covetous eyes. Amid all this dynamism and opportunity, political equality among white men had become a fundamental tenant of the American Republic. Equality required faith in the wisdom of the majority. This transformation did not do away with social hierarchy or elitism; most politicians came from or aspired to join the elite, and militia officers were mostly drawn from the "better sort" of society.[42] But the impulse from elitism to egalitarianism freed common white men from many of the older social customs and forms, including deference to one's superiors and the habit of obedience or allegiance based on status. Egalitarian rhetoric permeated antebellum public life, and the mindset of equality seeped into the public consciousness.[43] The self-made man thus became the ideal citizen and the early model for the citizen-officer in the volunteer armies of the Civil War.

The early American ideal of the citizen army, filtered through the republican tradition of the citizen-soldier ethos and democratic prerogatives, served a valuable purpose in helping connect the men to the state. Invested in the health and survival of their version of the nation, volunteers did not merely serve the state or carry out the designs of a distant authority. Not only did Americans represent their nation in public and private life, but they also believed that they had a civic duty as well as a vested private interest in protecting the wellspring of their personal liberty. As free citizens, volunteers fought for their individual rights as well as for the collective good of their community, defending its values, freedoms, and traditions through their service.[44] As George Mason argued in 1775, liberty meant that no citizen should be subject to the arbitrary rule of another, and no citizen-soldier should be subject to the tyranny of an officer. Temporary subordination might be militarily necessary, but the community otherwise ensured this equilibrium through law and tradition, the community itself being subject to majority rule while defending the rights of the minority.[45]

As antebellum Americans reshaped their conceptions of the citizen-soldier ethos and their democratic prerogatives, a different sort of evolution was taking place in the U.S. Army's officer corps. From the War of 1812 to the Mexican War (1846–48), the regular army developed into a professional force with standards of discipline, doctrine, practice, and continuity. Under the umbrella of professionalization, this process faced numerous obstacles from the general political and social environment of the young Republic. Nonmilitary professions such as doctors and lawyers remained loosely organized, if at all, into the late eighteenth century; only through persistence and ingenuity were antebellum military planners and the army's officer corps able to refine military culture toward a more professional model.[46] A succession of influential civilian administrators, including Alexander Hamilton, William Harris Crawford, and John C. Calhoun, took the challenge of professionalizing the army seriously. Given the generally poor performance of undisciplined volunteer militia troops during the War of 1812, along with the pressing need for a vigorous, efficient, and flexible force to police the vast U.S. frontier, these architects determined that a permanent peacetime army was essential to the Republic's security. A skilled, dedicated professional officer corps with the authority to implement discipline was the key to maintaining that force. By the outbreak of the Civil War, however, their vision had not yet fully come to pass.[47]

The road to officer professionalization in the American military was a long and sometimes torturous one. Contending with public apathy, republican antimilitarism, antipathy toward a standing army, and charges of aristocratic or European pretensions, antebellum advocates of a professional officer corps faced long odds in the years following the War of 1812. Further, those who dared criticize the citizen-soldier model in favor of a well-trained, disciplined, and effective professional army had to contend with the public's delight at the victory won by Jackson's rough-and-tumble militia over disciplined British regulars at the Battle of New Orleans in 1815. Then in the 1840s the end of the Second Seminole War (1835–42), an extended economic depression, and public pressure caused antimilitarism in the government to reach a fever pitch. So anemic was congressional support for a regular army in the years before the Mexican War that by 1845 the entire U.S. Army numbered just 8,509 men, only 826 of whom were officers.[48] With such a small force and with promotion based on seniority, officers faced poor prospects for professional advancement in peacetime. An elaborate system of brevet promotions based on the British army's system recognized merit or gallantry but added an element of confusion and rivalry among ambitious men trapped in their grade by the glacial seniority arrangement.[49]

Nevertheless, the antebellum regular-army officer corps modeled itself on Washington's example, seeing itself as an apolitical instrument of the state and recruiting and promoting based on merit while maintaining a strict authoritarian hierarchy. Cadets lived, worked, and studied together at West Point, then served together as officers on the frontier and in cities. This sense of unity and shared experience, no matter what one's wealth, background, or section of origin, helped produce a corporate feeling in the officer corps essential to professionalization. Held to uniform standards, meticulously educated, provided with a stable, lifelong career, and entrusted by the public with a degree of autonomy, regular officers began to view their service as a career commitment. Historian William B. Skelton finds that between 1830 and 1860, over half of the officers in the antebellum U.S. Army served for a period of at least twenty years. By 1860 nearly a quarter of regular-army officers had careers spanning forty years or more.[50] The relative permanence of regular officers' term of service in comparison to militia officers, coupled with the regulation of procedures and the systematization of training and education at West Point, worked a gradual transformation in the antebellum officer corps. These men developed an intellectual approach to their duties, studying European models and generating professional literature, all with the intent of improving the technical and practical effectiveness of the army.[51]

Unfortunately, antebellum regular officers cultivated a sense of aristocracy that distinguished them from civilian society and sometimes led to a sense of alienation, not only from the American public but also from the citizen-soldiers they sometimes led. These men followed the European model for professional behavior, assuming airs and traditions of gentility at odds with the egalitarian impulse of the Jacksonian era. From the War of 1812 into the immediate antebellum era, the U.S. Army was, as historian J. C. A. Stagg describes it, necessarily "not much more than a pastiche of European precedents and a pale imitation of European institutions and practices that had too many of their vices and too few of their virtues."[52] That is not to say that the army's officer corps abandoned its American identity for a European one; in fact, American officers came to resent unfavorable comparisons with their European counterparts, even as they both admired and emulated the Old World's military thinkers.[53] Antebellum officers also hewed to many of the aristocratic attributes of eighteenth-century European officers in developing their conception of command. These men valued social and personal respectability, honor, courage, and physical presence combined with sophistication, gentility, and a "liberal education" in themselves and their brother officers. Professional educational institutions like West Point perpetuated this mindset in the decades prior to the Mexican War, while increasingly elaborate and systematic regulations and the culture of garrison life served to shape the officer corps into a distinctive body in which professional excellence, political neutrality, and personal gentility were, in theory, the standard.[54]

By the advent of the Mexican War, this sense of professional distinctiveness and occupational competence made for an effective officer corps. But these changes also served to emphasize the disparity in quality, outlook, and training between regulars and volunteers, much to the consternation of regular officers. The persistence of the citizen-soldier ethos and the democratic prerogatives among American volunteers came with a price, and consent-based service, amateurism, and individualism based on inherent egalitarianism presented great difficulties for military leadership and discipline. The U.S. Army was designed to be expansible in times of war and depended heavily on volunteers with temporary terms of service. Conflict between regulars and volunteers was therefore inevitable, and the problems associated with commanding headstrong, untrained citizen-soldiers bedeviled professional officers throughout the war with Mexico.[55]

Lieutenant George Gordon Meade, later a Union major general, formed his opinions of volunteer troops and their officers early in the Mexican War; he would hardly budge from this position nearly two decades later. "The volunteers have in this war, on the whole, behaved better than I had believed they would, and infinitely better than they did in the Florida war, under my own eye," Meade wrote to his wife in 1846. "Still, without a modification of the manner in which they are officered, they are almost useless in an offensive war. They are sufficiently well-drilled for practical purposes, and are, I believe, brave, and will fight as gallantly as any men, but they are a set of Goths and Vandals, without discipline, laying waste the country wherever we go, making us a terror to innocent people, and if there is any spirit or energy in the Mexicans, will finally rouse the people against us, who now are perfectly neutral." The regular officer saw volunteers' indiscipline as their most serious drawback, not only because it interfered with effective leadership but also because it contributed to the overall inefficiency of the army. "[Volunteers] add immensely to the expenses of the war," he decided. "They cannot take any care of themselves; the hospitals are crowded with them, they die like sheep; they waste their provisions, requiring twice as much to supply them as regulars do." Meade pitied the untrained and poorly led militia, yet he found their excesses toward Mexican civilians reprehensible. "They plunder the poor inhabitants of everything they can lay their hands on, and shoot them when they remonstrate," he reported, "and if one of their number happens to get into a drunken brawl and is killed, they run over the country, killing all the poor innocent people they find in their way, to avenge, as they say, the murder of their brother."[56]

For regulars like Meade, the volunteers were not necessarily to blame for their indiscipline and inefficiency; as citizen-soldiers it would be illogical to expect them to behave with all the hard-won discipline and skill of regulars. Yet he believed that the root of much of the difficulty could be placed at the feet of citizen-officers' inability to keep control over their men. "This is a true picture, and the cause is the utter incapacity of their officers to control them or command respect," he complained. "The officers (many of whom are gentlemen and clever fellows) have no command over their men. They know they are in service for only twelve months; at the end of that time they will return to their homes, when these men will be their equals and their companions, as they had been before, and in consequence they dare not attempt to exercise any control over them." With this declaration, Meade struck at the essence of the citizen-officer dilemma. Volunteer officers were drawn from the pool of citizen-soldiers by the very men they were expected to discipline, command, and lead in battle. Furthermore, their term of service was not indefinite, and like their men, they intended to return to civilian life as equal citizens. These officers, to Meade, also suffered from gross incompetence that undermined what little authority they could eke out among their volunteers. "[F]or the most part," he concluded, "they are as ignorant of their duties as the men, and conscious of their ignorance, they feel they cannot have the command over their people that the regular officers do over their soldiers."[57]

As these peevish accounts indicate, the ordeal of the Mexican War revealed significant problems in the volunteer system as well as tensions between the professionals of the regular army and the amateurs of the militia. Not only did the citizen-soldier ethos and the republican traditions of volunteers impede discipline, but the perceived amateurishness and inexperience of volunteer troops also mortified many regular officers. They widely panned the discipline, efficiency, and effectiveness of volunteers and routinely criticized their resistance to military authority and savage behavior toward Mexican civilians.[58] Regular-army lieutenant and future Confederate lieutenant general Daniel Harvey Hill complained about the volunteers' sheer lawlessness and ungovernability while in Mexico. "Murder, rape and robbery were committed by the Volunteers in broad light of day," Hill wrote in 1847 from Monterey. "They would have burned the City but nine-tenths of the houses are fireproof. They, however, burnt the thatched huts of the miserable peasants." Hill tempered his anger by clarifying that most of the crimes had been committed by just a small group of unruly men. "In justice to the Volunteers it must be acknowledged that these atrocities were committed principally by Col. Hays' Regiment of Texans, quartered in town, the other Volunteers were in Camp at too great distance from the City to do much mischief in the City." The Texans alone were apparently more than capable of causing mayhem among the Mexican civilians. "'Tis thought that at least one hundred of the inhabitants were murdered in cold blood by the Volunteers," Hill added.[59]

Lieutenant and future Union major general George B. McClellan wrote from Camargo, Mexico, in 1846, "The people are very polite to the Regulars (Soldados spéciales de la leina) but they hate the Volunteers as they do Old Scratch himself." He attributed the army's difficulties with the Mexican population to the behavior of American volunteers. "The people were rather sulky—probably because the volunteers are very troublesome to them. A Mexican was shot a mile or two from here by some volunteers yesterday afternoon. This is by no means an uncommon occurrence. The worst thing we will hear will be that a volunteer is shot by way of retribution." McClellan could not help but contrast this behavior with the restraint and discipline of regular troops. "You never hear of a Mexican being murdered by a regular or a regular by a Mexican," he added. "The volunteers carry on in a most shameful and disgraceful manner."[60] McClellan also decried the incompetence with which the volunteers were led, organized, and cared for by their citizen-officers. "I have seen more suffering since I came out here than I could have imagined to exist," he wrote to his mother in disgust. "It is really awful. I allude to the sufferings of the Volunteers. They literally die like dogs." McClellan believed that the true story of the volunteers' plight would bring a swift end to the entire militia system in favor of a professional standing army. "Were it all known in the States, there would be no more hue and cry against the Army, all would be willing to have so large a regular army that we could dispense entirely with the volunteer system. The suffering among the Regulars is comparatively trifling, for their officers know their duty and take good care of the men."[61]

Regular-army lieutenant Theodore Laidley feared the slovenly practices of volunteers would lead to an outbreak of illness and endanger the entire war effort. Concerned about yellow fever during the occupation of

Vera Cruz in 1847, he wrote: "It is about time we were leaving the 'tierras calientes,' as they call it. . . . The volunteers, not knowing how to take care of them[selves], thus suffer the most and deaths among them are becoming more common."[62] Laidley also criticized what he saw as the vainglorious self-promotion of incompetent volunteer troops at the expense of the regulars. "These Penn. volunteers are trying to make the people of the U.S. believe that the siege of Puebla is the greatest on record; that the deeds of valor performed by them have not been equalled since the days of Napolean," he complained to his father. "They have established a paper and are heralding their daring exploits to the world, as well as some they did not perform, and anything complimentary to officers of the regular army cannot find admission," the lieutenant somewhat jealously added. Laidley preferred the unassuming professionalism of the regular army to the crassness and self-aggrandizement of the volunteers and took pains to draw the distinction between their behavior. "The regulars do not act thus," he insisted. "If others do not publish their merits, their exploits they do not do it themselves, and they are ready to give the volunteers the credit they deserve. No wonder the people should think highly of the volunteers when they fill the newspapers with their own stories exaggerated so that they would not be known by those who were participators in their glorious actions." Even worse, according to Laidley, was the hypocrisy, even barbarity, of the undisciplined volunteers. "But the other side of the story is not heard," he vented. "How they rob houses, steal, sack churches, ruin families, plunder and pillage. No, this is not heard of. But the poor sufferers know and hear it. The outrages they have committed, here, will never be known by the people of the U.S. They would not believe it if they did hear of it—But enough."[63]

Citizen-officers themselves occasionally faced resistance from both their volunteers and their fellow officers when they tried to follow the regular-army example. Captain Stanislaus Lasselle of Indiana believed that his hometown newspaper had written unfavorably of his Mexican War service because he was the only officer in his regiment who lived in camp and drilled the men daily. He blamed his fellow citizen-officers for setting a poor example for the men and, apparently, for staining his reputation at home.[64] Captain John R. Kenly of the 1st Battalion of Baltimore and Maryland Volunteers believed his unit's reputation for indiscipline was undeserved, though he conceded that because "nearly every man in it was from the cities of Washington and Baltimore, many of whom had been sailors, others members of fire-companies, fishing-clubs, etc. . . . , they were a wild, frolicksome, reckless set, full of fun and hard to keep in camp." He and other citizen-officers chronicled a growing sense of disillusionment with the hardships of extended military service and stern discipline among their volunteers. Kenly later wrote, "Our volunteers are pretty generally disgusted with volunteering, for it is no child's play, the daily labor now being done in earnest."[65]

Despite the efforts of citizen-officers like Lasselle and Kenly to discipline their volunteers, regular officers frequently expressed disdain at the men's undisciplined and unprofessional behavior. Captain Robert Anderson of the 3rd U.S. Artillery noted one such incident in his diary. "To-day I dined with Maj. Morris, *Chef de police de Tampico,*" he wrote in January 1847. "Yesterday he [Morris] sent a Capt. and Lt. of Volunteers to the guardhouse. He orders any house where there is rioting or unnecessary noise to be instantly closed, and his authority is undisputed." Anderson, while admiring Morris's stern authoritarianism, decided to take a different approach to maintaining order among the citizen-officers. "Today I am Officer of the Day, and have the right of exercising nearly all the above mentioned authority, but as my plan and desire is, to prevent rather than to suppress, I have already stopped by timely advice one or two incipient cases of riotous conduct."[66]

George Meade, as was his custom, showed little restraint in his expressions of vitriol about the scant value of volunteer troops and their officers. "I believe with fifteen thousand regulars, we could go to the City of Mexico, but with thirty thousand volunteers the whole nature and policy of the war will be changed," he asserted in the summer of 1846. "Already are the injurious influences of their presence perceptible, and you will hear any Mexican in the street descanting on the good conduct of the 'tropas de ligna,' as they call us, and the dread of the 'volontarios.'" This was due, Meade believed, to the savage and undisciplined behavior of the volunteers. "[T]hey [the volunteers] have killed five or six innocent people walking in the streets, for no other object than their own amusement; to-be-sure, they are always drunk, and are in a measure irresponsible for their conduct. They rob and steal the cattle and corn of the poor farmers, and in fact act more like a body of hostile Indians than of civilized whites." Repeating a familiar refrain, he blamed the volunteers' loutish behavior on the incompetence or laziness of their leadership. "Their own officers have no command or control over them, and the General has given up in despair any hope of keeping them in order. The consequence is they are exciting a feeling among the people which will induce them to rise *en masse* to obstruct our progress, and if, when we reach the mountains, we have to fight the people as well as the soldiers, the game will be up with us." Meade believed that the only practical solution to the problem was to put as much distance between volunteers and temptation as was possible. "I have some hope, however, that when we leave this place, which has become a mass of grog-shops and gambling-houses, and march to meet the enemy, the absence of liquor, and the fear of the enemy, may induce a little order among them and bring them to a better state of discipline."[67]

The citizen-soldier ethos and the democratic prerogatives of the republican tradition account for the persistence of the volunteer system in the antebellum American military. Civil War volunteers maintained the dual nature of temporary soldiers and permanent citizens throughout that conflict, following George Washington's model of the republican citizen-soldier. Northerners and Southerners understood these concepts in different ways, and their expectations of military service encountered significant pressures during the Civil War. But the shared beliefs at the heart of the republican tradition remained a fixture of white male Americans' conception of military service; civic virtue required their participation as citizen-soldiers, thus protecting their individual rights and liberties against the encroachments of central government and a powerful, professional standing army. Military service also helped Americans define their virtuous citizenship in terms of voluntariness, moral excellence, self-control, and ability. Like Cincinnatus, these volunteers imagined themselves as temporary soldiers motivated by disinterested selflessness in pursuit of a greater good. The evolving manner of democracy, the emphasis on majority rule, and the opportunity to rise based on ability rather than status encouraged ordinary men to invest themselves in their republican citizenship through military service. Citizen-soldiers' contractual, egalitarian, and informal approach to military service also created significant problems for the antebellum U.S. Army in attempting to employ volunteers in the field. Despite an overall decline in the militia system, a growing impulse toward professionalization in the regular army, and the myriad problems and shortcomings of the volunteer system revealed during the Mexican War, the citizen-soldier traditions of electioneering, voluntariness, indiscipline, contests of popularity, egalitarianism, and negotiated service all endured throughout the antebellum period. Since the citizen-soldier ethos encouraged volunteers to guard their democratic prerogatives jealously, Civil War commanders were, like their antebellum antecedents, bound by the limits imposed upon them by their men. These ideological traditions served as powerful and consistent guides for volunteers from the American Revolution through the Mexican War and shaped the creation and evolution of the citizen-officer corps in both the Union and Confederate armies.

2

Creation of the Civil War Junior Officer Corps

In 1861 Confederate private Taliaferro N. Simpson of the 3rd South Carolina Infantry seemed a natural candidate for a junior officer's commission. Raised in a prominent family and educated at Wofford College in Spartanburg, South Carolina, "Tally" Simpson decided to forgo his final year at school after the surrender of Fort Sumter and enlisted in a volunteer infantry company with his brother, Richard. Tally and Richard, called "Buddie" by his family, both knew something about military matters even before they entered Confederate service. In February 1860 Tally was elected to a lieutenancy in a student militia unit at his college; Buddie was elected sergeant in the same unit. "I suppose Buddie has informed you," Tally wrote to his father soon after his election, "that we students have formed a military company and are now in the [process] of organizing it. I am now Lieutenant Taliaferro Simpson, quite an honorable title for an unworthy junior." His letters burst with pride at this honor. "Since Buddie wrote last, he has been elected sergeant and is prouder of it than a peacock is of its feathers and struts similar to a turkey gobbler. But you ought to see me looking down on the little fellow."[1] In a new Confederate army thirsting for leaders with any modicum of military experience, Tally Simpson seemed destined for a bright future as a volunteer officer.

By early 1863, however, things had gone wrong for twenty-three-year-old Tally Simpson's grand ambitions for glory. Despite his education, prominent family connections, and antebellum military experience, after two years of war Simpson was still a mere private in the 3rd South Carolina

Infantry. To make matters worse, for unknown reasons his fellow volunteers seemed to have little regard for his potential as an officer. "We had an election in our company the other day for Third Lieutenant," Simpson dejectedly told his family in January of that year. "Several of the members intimated that they wished me to run for the office. I thought I would try, whether I was beaten or not, but party spirit was too strong against me." Embittered and humiliated by the experience, he viewed the defeat as a personal betrayal. "I must confess that there are some of the most consummate villains in this co[mpany] I ever knew," the young man informed his parents after his failure. "They actually told me flatly that they intended to vote for me, and when the election came off, they voted for some one else. Some, without doubt, promised each one of the candidates to vote for them. Such liars I did not believe were in the 3d Regt. We live and learn, and each day I lose confidence in mankind." Tally Simpson was killed at the Battle of Chickamauga in September 1863, having never risen higher in rank than corporal.[2]

Volunteer soldiers like Tally and Buddie Simpson composed more than 90 percent of the Union army and virtually all of the Confederate army. The overwhelming majority of company-grade junior officers on both sides, whether elected, promoted, or appointed, were selected from within their own company's ranks.[3] Elected citizen-officers were chosen by their peers, the very men they led, lived with, and were expected to potentially order to their deaths. Although the election of officers is a foreign concept to modern Americans accustomed to a professional officer corps, for Union and Confederate citizen-soldiers, it was a cherished element of their deeply ingrained republican beliefs. Volunteers operated within the confines of that ideological universe, defining the essence of service for millions of Confederate and Union citizen-soldiers. These men learned, as Union colonel Thomas Higginson observed, that they had to alter their expectations to fit the hard realities of war. For many this meant modifying their understanding of what the democratic prerogatives and the American citizen-soldier ethos meant, not only to themselves and their comrades but also to their fellow citizens at home. "Personal independence in the soldier, like personal liberty in the civilian, must be waived for the preservation of the nation," Higginson wrote in 1864, after enduring three grueling years of war. "With shipwreck staring men in the face, the choice lies between despotism and anarchy, trusting to the common sense of those concerned, when the danger is over, to revert to the old safeguards."[4] The manner in which citizen-officers were created, and the ways in which that process changed under the stresses of war, are critical to a more complete understanding of the nature of Civil War service and of the evolution of the American citizen-soldier ethos.

The Union and Confederate officer-election systems were enshrined in law and regulations from the first volunteer mobilizations of the war. On April 15, 1861, President Lincoln called on the Northern states to provide 75,000 ninety-day troops to suppress the growing rebellion in the slave states. By July Congress had authorized another 500,000 volunteers. Over the next four years, approximately 2.7 million men would serve in the Union army, a sixty-two-fold increase over antebellum regular-army levels.[5] The Confederacy lacked the Union's advantages in raw manpower and resources but still managed to field between 1.2 million and 1.4 million men; it faced similar challenges in staffing and leading its volunteer armies.[6] In 1861 both sides were largely unprepared to organize, equip, train, and lead such vast numbers of inexperienced troops. To illustrate the magnitude of the leadership deficit, regulations mandated that the nearly 750,000 Union volunteers in the initial mobilizations be led by something on the order of 24,000 officers. The regular army could claim barely 1,100 officers of all grades; the Confederate army, of course, had none save the 300 or so officers who had resigned from the U.S. Army to join the Southern cause.[7]

At the outbreak of hostilities, the Federal and Confederate governments modeled the legal and regulatory frameworks for their respective volunteer armies using the organizational structure of the antebellum U.S. Army. Initially, both sets of regulations followed similar lines, requiring that volunteer junior officers of company grade be nominated by the governors of their respective states or, less commonly, by the president. Confederate officers between the ranks of second lieutenant and colonel received their commissions directly from the national government and, whether elected or appointed, were confirmed by the Confederate Senate. Union officers of equivalent rank, however, could be appointed directly by the governor of their respective state, an arrangement that often led to political jockeying and intrigue among ambitious candidates in Northern companies and regiments.[8]

Companies, the most basic units of organization in Civil War armies, were intended to have a nominal strength of around one hundred men. Union infantry companies were allotted a maximum strength of nineteen commissioned and noncommissioned officers and between sixty-four and eighty-three privates, all commanded by a captain, a first lieutenant, and a second lieutenant. Union infantry regiments were to consist of ten companies, cavalry regiments of twelve companies, and field-artillery batteries of four to six guns.[9] The Confederate army followed a similar organizational model and regulatory structure; in fact, on March 6, 1861, the Provisional Confederate Congress adopted the *Revised Regulations for the Army of the United States* largely verbatim, simply replacing the words "United States" with "Confederate States" in the text.[10] In reality, unit strengths were hardly standardized, and companies rarely reached the numbers mandated by regulations. The policy of both sides was to organize recruits into new regiments rather than incorporate replacements into existing units; consequently, company strength declined steadily throughout the war. Consolidation and occasional infusions of conscripts or new recruits bolstered numbers in existing units, but by the time of the Confederate surrenders at Appomattox Court House, Virginia, and Durham Station, North Carolina, in April 1865, many devastated Union and Confederate companies could muster only a handful of men.[11]

Before the armies could field their troops, however, they had to solve the difficult issue of placing officers over them. During the chaotic mobilizations of 1861, Union authorities disagreed as to the best way to integrate their volunteers into national service. Leaders in the army and the War Department favored staffing volunteer units with regular-army officers, while state authorities pressed for acceptance of volunteer regiments and their self-selected citizen-officers en masse. Neither solution was entirely satisfactory, and both sides issued a tangled web of acts, orders, and regulations to solve the problem. After a good deal of internal debate, in May 1861 Congress authorized the acceptance of volunteer companies into national service and granted both the president and state governors the authority to appoint volunteer officers; the War Department implemented the act as General Orders No. 15.[12] On July 22 Congress altered the May act by allowing volunteer regiments to fill junior-officer vacancies by election upon reenlistment; field officers, or those with the ranks of major, lieutenant colonel, and colonel, were to be elected by the officers of their respective regiments.[13] Lawmakers eventually amended the July act to give states the authority to appoint citizen-officers to vacancies in engineering and topographical units but retained the officer-election system in volunteer units.[14] The Confederacy faced the same problems in providing enough citizen-officers for its volunteer armies and adopted similar solutions. On

February 28, 1861, the Provisional Congress authorized President Davis to take state volunteer troops into Confederate service for a twelve-month period of service.[15] A December 11 act granted a bounty of fifty dollars and a furlough to volunteers who agreed to reenlist for a term of three years or the duration of the war when their initial enlistments expired. The law also permitted reenlisting Confederates, like their Union foes, to hold new officer elections upon reorganization.[16]

Almost as soon as Union and Confederate planners had worked out the difficulties of fielding and leading their armies, another crisis presented itself. Leaders on both sides feared a manpower shortage in the spring of 1862; the enlistments of the twelve-month volunteers who had rushed to enlist in April 1861 were soon expiring, and the war showed no sign of coming to an early conclusion. Consequently, in April 1862 the Confederate Congress took the drastic step of conscripting all white males between the ages of eighteen and thirty-five. The Confederate Conscription Act, the first measure of its kind in American history, was actually a series of laws, the first of which was passed on April 16, and sparked widespread resistance among Southerners.[17] The legislation permitted volunteer units to keep their organizational integrity as much as possible, and troops whose original term of enlistment had not yet expired would have the right to reorganize into companies and elect new officers at reenlistment. After this initial vote, all company-grade-officer vacancies were to be filled by promotion by seniority, except for vacancies among the most junior lieutenants, whose positions would still be filled by election. On April 21 the Confederate Congress passed an additional act authorizing the president to fill vacancies through appointment or as a special reward for "valor and skill" displayed in action.[18] Union conscription came a year later, in March 1863. The Enrollment Act, complete with its accompanying bureaucracy and a lengthy and controversial list of exemptions that often benefited the wealthy, imposed draft quotas and stoked Northerners' anger, convincing some that the conflict had become a rich man's war but a poor man's fight.[19] Volunteerism in the Union army was in steep decline by the end of 1862; early military reversals, a waning of the initial *rage militaire* among Northerners, and a dawning realization that the war would require a substantial national commitment even greater than previously thought convinced Congress that a manpower crisis was imminent. Conscription, though distasteful to a people steeped in the citizen-soldier ethos, helped bolster both armies' ranks at these critical junctures.[20]

Conscription was ideologically problematic for Union and Confederate volunteers. Such policies for each side contained several clear concessions to the citizen-soldier ethos, concessions that Union general and postwar military theorist Emory Upton characterized as "subversive to all discipline and subordination."[21] With a desperate need to field and lead massive, untrained armies, why were Union and Confederate volunteers allowed to retain the rights to reorganize themselves as they pleased and to elect their own amateur officers? The simple answer is that sheer necessity overrode other concerns. The officer-election system was intended as a pragmatic acquiescence to the democratic prerogatives of volunteers and to the citizen-soldier ethos that informed and motivated their service. Conscription, in one fell swoop, would have removed the very essence and identity of the volunteer citizen-soldier by making his service compulsory. Threatened with the shame of conscription, Union and Confederate troops would choose to reenlist, authorities hoped, particularly if their cherished prerogative to choose their own officers was preserved. Furthermore, the only way to provide a sufficient number of junior officers to lead and manage the hundreds of thousands of volunteers entering military service was to maintain the tradition of electing officers that American citizen-soldiers were accustomed to and expected.

Upton suspected that the Confederacy, in particular, preserved volunteers' rights to elect their own officers out of fear of the alternative. "[I]n making independent of the States the first experiment of conscription ever tried on the continent," he wrote after the war, "the Confederate Congress did not dare to repudiate the promise made to the soldiers by the Provisional Congress. Had the soldiers revolted, the Rebellion would have instantly collapsed. It was therefore of vital importance to appease and pacify the army, and to this end every soldier coming under the operation of the law was given not only a voice in the selection of his commanders, but a furlough for two months and a bounty of $50." Upton believed that the Confederate Congress did not act out of principle or of altruism, but rather out of the pragmatic necessity of preserving its fledgling volunteer army under trying conditions. "This feature of the law was not dictated *by* any regard for the sovereignty of the States, for by the terms of the law all appointments were to be made by the Confederate President. It is rather to be explained by the inability of civilians to appreciate the proper qualifications of officers, and the relations which must exist between them and the soldier to attain the highest degree of efficiency and discipline."[22]

Civil War volunteers demanded such concessions in exchange for their service, carrying their expectations about military service with them into the conflict. Among these expectations, those who volunteered to fight resented fellow citizens who did not demonstrate similar patriotism and dedication to the republican tradition. For company-grade citizen-officers like Lieutenant John H. Black of the 12th Pennsylvania Cavalry, his neighbors' reluctance to sacrifice their comfort in service of the national cause was tantamount to treason. "There are any amount of young men in Blair Co. that I would love to hear of being made to go and handle the musket to quell the rebellion," he wrote in the summer of 1862, "for the more soldiers we have the sooner the war will be over, and if Skyles shrinks from the present call I will regard him as one who is not a true loyal citizen at heart, for I cannot see why under the Sun any young man can stay at home, when his country is all the time calling with might and main for his help." Black and other likeminded Union citizen-officers saw such shirking as evidence of the Republic's growing corruption, believing that blood must be shed to preserve their revolutionary inheritance. "Shame! Shame!! Shame!!! on all young men who will stay at home and think that life is dearer than a land of Liberty," the lieutenant declared. "My motto is give me freedom though it costs many lives, and if I should not be spared to enjoy it after the war is over, I still have the blessed consolation of being one among the number who so nobly volunteered to gain it." Black acknowledged the cost of such a commitment and believed that freedom was worth the price. "To crush this rebellion it will yet cost the blood of many, and many to who will not be forgotten for many years after," he added. "But far better for those who are at home to lose friends and relatives in battling for freedom than to have tyranny with its destroying hand to rule over such a heaven favored country like this."[23]

In February 1862 Lieutenant Robert H. Miller of the 14th Louisiana Infantry expressed similar fears about his comrades' patriotism in a letter to his mother. "The several severe losses we have suffered in Tenisee and on the Carolina Coast have thrown a feeling of gloom over the soldiers here," Miller wrote from Virginia, "and the fear that the twelve-months-men will be so mean as to quit the cause adds to it. As to the latter class of men, I do not feel so much afraid—for I think there is yet enough Patriotism left in them to dictate to him their duty." The officer had faith in his fellow volunteers but reserved grave doubts about the patriotic spirit of citizens who had not enlisted at the outset of the war. "[T]here are those at home who seem to be a less reliable class," he mused. "They are those who remain quietly by their firesides, with no intention of aiding the cause at all."[24] Apparently, the sense of civic virtue forged in the Revolution and shared by American citizens of all sections had, in the years since that war, lost a great deal of its remaining potency.[25]

Even so, the citizen-soldier ethos among the surge of new recruits was strong enough to present significant problems to leaders on both sides tasked with incorporating volunteers into Civil War armies and placing officers over them. Early in the war, few concerns preoccupied both the Union and Confederate high commands more than that of volunteers and their troublesome tradition of choosing their own officers. At the time of the great mobilizations of 1861, the American volunteer system, including officer elections, was largely unchanged from the Mexican War; it would remain intact, albeit with significant modifications, throughout most of the Civil War. "Congress may understand the pernicious effect of elections," Confederate assistant adjutant general Samuel W. Melton wrote to Secretary of War James A. Seddon in the fall of 1863. "Every one—the soldier himself—appreciates the truth. But they will yield because the demand is made, as it will be, by our heroic and self-sacrificing soldiery. It will be achieving much if the Department can confine this reorganization to companies and the elections to company officers." In making this recommendation, Melton hoped to limit the damage he believed officer elections created in the army. "This will not, indeed, work serious injury, if a more liberal authority be given to the Executive to make appointments for merit," he believed. "The appointment of all field officers should be insisted upon pertinaciously of course, and the law should permit the President to fill all vacancies by appointment, restricting the choice only to persons from the same State." To Melton, the experience of war reinforced his conviction that this system undermined discipline, particularly among junior and noncommissioned officers. "The evils of elections are most trying and most pernicious when held to fill vacancies 'in the lowest grade,'" he argued. "This [election] system has almost utterly destroyed the efficiency of non-commissioned officers, whose services in the work of discipline are incalculably important, while it perpetuates day after day all the derelictions of duty winked at by successful aspirants." Dismayed by the indiscipline that officer elections seemed to encourage, Melton advocated one final, comprehensive election followed by an outright abolition of the system in the Confederate army. "Far better to allow once for all a full election of company officers," he reasoned, "if with it can be obtained a power of appointment by which further elections may be prevented when advisable."[26]

"I fear no amount of personal energy or efforts to do what is right will ever make these volunteers into soldiers," George Meade lamented in 1861, rehashing old Mexican War criticisms of volunteers' citizen-soldier ethos (and unwittingly Melton's concerns). "The radical error is in their organization and the election of officers, in most cases more ignorant than the men. It is most unsatisfactory and trying to find all your efforts unsuccessful, and the consciousness of knowing that matters grow daily worse instead of better is very hard to bear." Meade still did not blame the soldiers for thinking and behaving like volunteers; rather, like the citizen-officers he deplored decades earlier, the general placed the blame for volunteers' ineptitude at their officers' feet. "The men are good material, and with good officers might readily be moulded into soldiers; but the officers, as a rule, with but very few exceptions, are ignorant, inefficient and worthless. They have not control or command over the men, and if they had, they do not know what to do with them." Meade believed the officer-election system remained the primary source of the problem with his volunteer troops. "We have been weeding out some of the worst [volunteer officers], but owing to the vicious system of electing successors which prevails, those who take their places are no better."[27]

The Confederate high command immediately recognized the flaws in officer elections and criticized the practice in similar language. Secretary of War Seddon believed that "the policy of elections . . . may be well questioned, since inseparable from it [arises] an undue regard to popularity, especially among the non-commissioned officers, and a spirit of electioneering subversive of subordination and discipline."[28] In a December 1861 letter, General Robert E. Lee expressed his misgivings in tactful terms. "The best troops are ineffectual without good officers. Our volunteers, more than any others, require officers whom they can respect and trust," he wrote. "It would be safe to trust men of the intelligence and character of our volunteers to elect their officers, could they at the time of election realize their dependent condition in the day of battle. But this they cannot do, and I have known them in the hour of danger repudiate and disown officers of their choice and beg for others." Lee, who knew from Mexican War experience the perilous consequences of poor military leadership, had little confidence in the raw abilities of citizen-officers. While expressing faith in the instincts of his men to make appropriate choices given their limited experience, he also knew that green volunteers were unlikely to comprehend the heavy burdens that combat and campaigning placed upon themselves and on amateur officers. To expect otherwise, Lee reasoned, would be a grave injustice to volunteers innocent of the hard realities of war. "Is it right, then," the general continued, "for a State to throw upon its citizens a responsibility which they do not feel and cannot properly exercise?" While Lee did not specifically address the election of junior officers, he clearly preferred that line officers be appointed by their superiors rather than be elected by their men. "The colonel of a regiment has an important trust, and is a guardian of the honor of the State as well as of the lives of the citizens. I think it better for the field officers of the regiment in the State service to be appointed by the governor, with the advice and consent of its legislature, and those in the Confederate service by the President and Congress."[29]

State governors, North and South, also questioned the wisdom of the officer-election system from the start. Governor John A. Andrew of Massachusetts expressed his doubts about it in a telegram to Senators Charles Sumner and Henry Wilson on August 3, 1861. "Can it be intended by Congress," he wondered, "that volunteers in the field shall fill vacancies by election? Where is to be the source of discipline, when every candidate is seeking personal favor from the men?"[30] The criticisms persisted into the war, and as late as 1864 Pennsylvania governor Andrew G. Curtin expressed his fears of the "angry dissensions and too often political jealousies which divide military organizations by the election of officers, and to secure the services of the most deserving and competent men." He concluded that "[t]he election of officers in the volunteer forces in the field has been found to be injurious to the service, while promotions by seniority and appointments of meritorious privates have produced harmony and stimulated to faithfulness."[31] Politicians and community leaders joined the chorus of concern, both early and often. On August 1, 1861, for example, the editors of the *New York Times* protested the practice of permitting volunteers to elect their officers. In an open letter to President Lincoln, a group of unnamed New York "property-holders" complained:

That a suitable supervision has not been extended by Government to the officering of the volunteer forces; that the principle of allowing companies to choose their own officers, or officers their own colonels, is fatal to military discipline; that political, local, and personal interests have had far too much sway in the selection of officers; that undue laxity prevails in the control of volunteer officers by their military superiors, and that an ill-grounded apprehension of local or political censure has prevented the proper authorities from removing incompetent commanders and from placing in responsible military positions those most capable of filling them without regard to anything but their qualifications.[32]

While the majority of Union and Confederate planners were firmly against the officer-election system, this opinion was not universal. Disagreements over the system provoked a minor states' rights controversy between the Confederate War Department and the governor of Georgia in 1863. In a heated correspondence with Secretary of War Seddon, Governor Joseph E. Brown laid out the constitutional and moral case for the officer-election system in great detail when the War Department denied a Georgia regiment the right to elect a new colonel. Brown argued that "the right of election is too plain to be questioned" and that all volunteer regiments must have the right under law "to elect their own officers to fill all vacancies which have or may occur."[33] He considered Georgia troops to be militia and thus, under the Confederate Constitution, subject only to the laws of their state. The War Department ruled that state volunteers were in fact part of the Provisional Army of the Confederacy, governed by the laws of the Confederate States as a whole. Brown eventually swallowed his objections, but the controversy emphasizes one of the ironies of Confederate military policy. While advocating state sovereignty and a federal model of government, Richmond officials circumvented governors' authority by removing their exclusive power to appoint commissioned officers and placing that power in the hands of the national executive. The Union government, on the other hand, recognized governors' authority to appoint officers independently from the president and preserved that prerogative throughout the war.[34]

Field and company officers on both sides recognized the limitations of the election system, and their letters and diaries reflect their frustrations at the indiscipline and incompetence they believed the policy fomented in their troops. Major Wilder Dwight, a citizen-officer of the 2nd Massachusetts Infantry, wrote in September 1861 of the threat to military discipline and order he believed his volunteers' democratic notions posed. "American soldiers will only become efficient in proportion as they abandon their national theories and give themselves up obediently to the *military laws* which have always governed the successful prosecution of war," he chafed. "To-day our army is crippled by the ideas of equality and independence which have colored the whole life of our people. Men elect their officers, and then expect them *to behave themselves!* Obedience is permissive, not compelled, and the radical basis is wrong." Dwight saw the democratic prerogatives of American volunteers as a malady and believed that the only real cure was abolition of the election system and the imposition of regular-army discipline, by force if necessary. "We have to struggle against the evil tendencies of this contagion. When this defect is cured, and men recognize authority and obey without knowing why,—obey from habit and instinct, not from any process of reasoning or presumed consent,—we shall begin to get an army," the major declared. "It is only necessary to appreciate the fact that, in war, *one will* must act through all the others, to see that American soldiers, with all their presumed intelligence and skill, have *the one lesson* yet to learn."[35]

Though the regulations of both the Union and Confederate armies specified otherwise, officer elections were usually held at the discretion of regimental, brigade, or division commanders. Confirmation of voting results by state governors was usually a mere formality. If a commander wished to fill a company officer vacancy by appointment, he sometimes did so on his own authority, though only if he felt his leadership was strong enough to withstand the potential resentment of his volunteers. Nevertheless, circumventing officer elections, particularly early in the war, risked incurring the displeasure of the enlisted men. Thus, commanding officers had to gauge the sentiments of their volunteers with care, for a miscalculation could result in anger, loss of morale, or in extreme cases, outright rebellion. The "'Madison Guards' rebelled and disbanded on account of the election of regimental officers," Mississippi volunteer Ruffin Thomson informed his father in 1861.[36] "We have a first lieutenant appointed over us by the Col.," wrote Joseph J. Hoyle of the 55th North Carolina Infantry in the fall of 1862. "He is a perfect stranger to us, and every body is perfectly mad this evening."[37] Rebellion against duly elected officers proved to be the exception rather than the rule, though volunteers occasionally refused to obey officers of whom they did not approve. Nevertheless, while citizen-soldiers may have resented results they did not like, ultimately they had no official recourse once a new officer had been installed. As Union volunteer Albert O. Marshall remembered of the 1862 officer elections in his company: "The result of the vote was sent off to the Governor of Illinois. It was of course of no binding force, but was supposed to be a recommendation that would be complied with."[38]

When volunteers realized they had made a mistake in their selection, they could do little else besides nurse their regrets until the undesirable officer left the unit, though they could drive him away by making his life miserable. "Mr. John Wade is an excellent man, but he makes a much worse Capt. than I had any idea he would," chafed Lieutenant James Henry Langhorne of the 4th Virginia Infantry in October 1861. "[T]he men do not fear to violate his orders, and the Company has lost more than I had any idea it would in discipline & moral[e] since Capt Trigg left it, but in fact our whole Reg. has lost in discipline since the battle of 21st July [First Bull Run]." Langhorne, who had challenged Wade for the captaincy and lost, could only salve his bruised pride and bide his time. "The men all regret having elected Capt Wade (when I say all I mean a majority).... I got 11 votes in the election, and many of the men did not vote at all. If the election was to be held to day I could beat him two to one."[39] Occasionally, an officer's incompetence or lack of courage influenced his chances of securing reelection, but units that did not participate in any battles before the 1862 reorganizations could not judge candidates for company-grade leadership based on their combat record.[40]

By many volunteers' accounts, early war officer elections were often messy affairs, riddled with intrigue and destructive to morale. During the reorganization elections in the spring of 1862, Union volunteer Henry Perkins Goddard was candid about the corruption and incompetence of the candidates in Company G of his 14th Connecticut Infantry. That unit, Goddard explained to his sister, "is composed of three united squads under [current] Capt. [James B.] Coit and they have not enough men to elect more than two officers, and all are too much afraid of the others to hold an election, and the consolidation has not been approved by its Colonel." Goddard's observations show the venomous atmosphere that pervaded some volunteer companies. "There are five candidates [for captain]; Coit is one. He is very fair spoken and has promised some six lieutenants, and curses them all behind their backs. He makes outrageous mistakes whenever on duty and usurps authority everywhere." Another candidate, "Hill of New Haven[,] is a little fool who doesn't know beans about the military, and his lieutenant says [Hill] was in jail once for passing counterfeit money." Goddard also declared, "Stone of Putnam is a country bumpkin discharged as a private from the 5th C.V. [Connecticut Volunteers] as much for worthlessness as anything else having a cross-eye." In his opinion, Stone was immature and undisciplined, maintaining an inappropriate level of familiarity with the enlisted men and even bribing them for support in the company elections. "He plays leap-frog with the privates, and offers fifty-cents a piece for a vote; these men recruited about twenty apiece and then united," Goddard reported. "They have about sixty-two mustered in and it is the most insubordinate street in the camp." He then turned his attention to another of Hill's supposed cronies. "Then there is Hotchkiss, whom Hill promised to make 1st Lieut., a black leg and gambler of New Haven, who swears Hill shall never have an election." Hotchkiss's lack of character and immoral lifestyle were more than enough to disqualify him in Goddard's eyes. Hill's agreement to secure a commission without an election only emphasized the corruption of both the candidate and the election process. "Fifth," Goddard continued, "there is Len Robinson of Norwich whom Coit is working to make 1st Lieut. If I were a civilian and they should come into my office, I would not make one of them a printer's devil. I am disgusted with such men and feel as if I wish I could be shot in the first action rather than endure it much longer." He concluded: "It is unbearable. . . . I never want to be adjutant of a regiment—I have seen too much of it."[41] Despite his disdain for the process, Goddard eventually won a captain's commission in his regiment.[42]

Sergeant Charles Frederic Bahnson of the 2nd North Carolina Battalion was more circumspect than Goddard in describing his unit's raucous 1862 reorganization elections. In a letter to his father that fall, Bahnson explained that "[t]he election is over, & I am still Orderly Sergeant. There was a great deal of wire pulling, & underground working, & I concluded not to run for the present. I think the way the wind is blowing, I may possibly find some seat more pleasant than any I missed this afternoon. Everything is still uncertain, but still I have every reason to hope for the best." Bahnson was concerned about the damage that failure to win a commission might do to his reputation back home. "If anyone wants to know anything about it, please say I did not want to run for any office," he urged his father. The sergeant's political instincts paid off, as did his discretion. Three days later the regiment elected a new colonel, who promptly appointed Bahnson to his staff as a lieutenant.[43]

Enlisted men and officers alike commonly expressed their contempt for corrupt "wire-pulling" or electioneering even as they fully participated in the practice. "Our election has not yet come off, and to one who like myself is not a candidate it is a time replete with feelings of disgust and contempt," wrote Confederate private Henry L. Graves during the May 1862 reorganizations in his 2nd Georgia Infantry Battalion. "The candidates of course are interested and busy. I could start out here now and eat myself dead on 'election cake,' be hugged into a perfect 'squ[i]sh' by most particular, eternal, disinterested, affectionate friends," he bitterly reported. "A man is perfectly bewildered by the intensity of the affection that is lavished upon him. I never dreamed before that I was half as popular, fine looking, and talented as I found out I am during the past few days."[44] Sergeant Major Stephen F. Fleharty of the 102nd Illinois Infantry remembered the unseemly displays of ambition that the 1862 officer elections excited among his comrades. "[T]he patriotism of many was of such a character that it led them to believe they could best serve their country in some exalted position," he recalled in 1865. "Hence there was much wire-pulling, and many who had expected to wear what the boys called 'pumpkin rinds,' were compelled to march by the side of those who were lured into the service by pure patriotism, and thirteen dollars a month, with allowances." For some, the lure of "chicken guts" and "pumpkin rinds," an officer's gilded braids or shoulder straps, paled in comparison to the appeal of the privileges that accompanied an officer's authority. These rewards, and the corruptible election system, Fleharty believed, created an incentive for the self-interested and the incompetent to win commissions over better candidates. Men of talent who did not have the political acumen or gregarious personality required to win election were shunted aside, with dire consequences for themselves and for the men they rightfully should have led. "The wonder with us was, that amid so much contention, so many good and faithful men received commissions," Fleharty recalled. "There were some who afterwards proved failures. I need not mention their names here. They are fixed in the minds of the men of the regiment, indelibly."[45]

Though they often bitterly criticized the "wire-pulling" that preceded these votes, electioneering fulfilled important functions for Civil War volunteers. First, it ensured that officers possessed certain abilities critical to the command of citizen-soldiers. Successful candidates had to win the trust and acceptance of a majority of the men under their leadership and do so quickly. They had to be on good terms, affable, at least somewhat charismatic, and project, if not necessarily possess, an air of competence and confidence. Second, electioneering fulfilled an essential element of the citizen-soldier ethos in that volunteers reserved the right to define the terms of their service, including selecting the leaders placed over them. It also broke down social and economic divisions among classes, at least in the days and hours prior to the actual vote. Potential officers, no matter what their backgrounds or origins, were required to go out among their comrades to seek their support. In this sense these elections mirrored the American electoral tradition and emphasized the sense of mutual, personal obligation between officers and men that citizen-soldiers valued so highly. On the other hand, such displays could lead to popularity contests, corruption, or outright demagoguery.[46] On the whole, however, electioneering ensured that the men chosen for command by their peers reflected the values and characteristics they deemed essential for leaders who would respect and preserve their identities as citizen-soldiers. Electioneering also required citizen-officers to prove their worth to their men and thereby justify the surrender of authority and independence they would demand of volunteers.

The election system tended to produce citizen-officers who were, on average, slightly older than enlisted men; volunteers tended to choose their officers from the more prominent, mature, or experienced members of their companies, and these men therefore tended to be slightly older than the typical soldier.[47] In the research sample of Union and Confederate volunteer junior officers, Union officers' average age in 1861 was 26.76 years old, while Confederate officers' average 1861 age was 27.8. Junior officers, on average, were about one year older than the average of all Union and Confederate volunteers, whose overall average ages at enlistment were 25.8 and 26.5, respectively.[48] Union junior officers were mostly unmarried: 45 percent of the Union sample were married in 1860, and 32 percent had at least one dependent child. A slight majority of Confederate junior officers in the sample, 53 percent, were married in 1860; 45 percent had at least one dependent child.[49] Junior officers usually came from middle- and upper-class economic backgrounds before the war, practiced a trade or a profession, and owned land or had a notable amount of family wealth. Union junior officers' family wealth varied significantly in the 1860 census but averaged a substantial $6,263.08 per household. Their median family wealth was $2,500.00 in 1860. Confederate junior officers' average family wealth also varied but, at $11,245.09 per household, was nearly double that of their Union counterparts. At $4,300.00, their median family wealth was also greater than that of their Union counterparts.[50]

Citizen-officers of company grade tended to come from "gentlemanly" occupations prior to the Civil War, with both Union and Confederate junior officers usually coming from professional, white-collar, farming, or skilled-artisan occupations in far greater proportions than enlisted men. Of Union junior officers, 89 percent reported professional, white-collar, agricultural, or skilled-artisan occupations in the 1860 census. Of these, 36 percent were skilled artisans such as jewelers, carpenters, or printers; 19 percent were farmers; 16 percent were white-collar workers such as clerks or merchants; 9 percent were professionals such as physicians, lawyers, or teachers; and 9 percent were students. Just 11 percent of the sample were unskilled laborers before the war. Confederate junior officers came heavily from professional and agricultural occupations. In the 1860 census 94 percent were farmers, planters, professionals, white-collar workers, or skilled artisans. Of the sample around 48 percent were farmers or planters, 23 percent were professionals, 6 percent were white-collar workers, 9 percent were students, and 8 percent were skilled artisans. Only 6 percent of Confederate junior officers were unskilled laborers prior to enlistment in 1861. These men also tended to come from slaveholding households prior to the Civil War; 40 percent reported owning slaves or residing in slaveholding households in the 1860 census slave schedules, much higher than the 24.9 percent slaveholding rate of all Confederate households. Of the junior-officer slaveholders and slaveholding households in the sample, 50 percent reported owning either one or two slaves, 25 percent owned between three and ten slaves, and 25 percent owned more than ten slaves.[51]

Citizen-soldiers expected their officers to be men of ability, status, and prestige in civilian life, which translated into an officer corps that tended to be drawn from certain antebellum classes, occupations, and occupations. Nevertheless, some potential officers who seemed to possess all of these essential characteristics resisted their comrades' entreaties to seek positions of leadership in the armies. Confederate William Thomas Poague felt unworthy for the honor when nominated for a lieutenancy in the Rockbridge Artillery in April 1861. Poague was a prominent young lawyer prior to enlisting in the army, and his comrades considered him a natural fit for command. The Virginian, however, disagreed. "I did not want an office in the company," Poague recalled, "simply because I was not qualified for it." Even so, his allies nominated him for both the first and second lieutenant's posts in the company's officer elections. Poague refused to stand for first lieutenant and only reluctantly allowed his name to go forward for second lieutenant. His competitors for the position were John B. Craig, a "noted bully and street fighter," and James Cole Davis, a lawyer like Poague. "In the election, which was *viva voce*," Poague related, "Davis voted for Craig and I voted for Davis." He estimated that Davis was "a gallant soldier, brave as the bravest, though not very popular," and that Craig "could not stand the racket of battle" as an officer should. Despite his doubts, Poague possessed the essential prestige, popularity, and charisma necessary to win the election and prevailed over both candidates.[52]

Some citizen-officers were openly contemptuous of elections, even though they owed their commissions to that very system. "We are all very much disgusted at the law lately passed," wrote Lieutenant Robert Gould Shaw of the 2nd Massachusetts Infantry in August 1861, "which provides that vacancies among volunteer officers shall be filled by an election in the company. The very reason that, in most volunteer regiments, the officers have so little control over their men, is because they owe their places to them." Shaw, who had received his own commission as lieutenant in no small part because of his eminent family's social and political connections, roundly condemned the system as detrimental to discipline. "It upsets the line of promotion with us entirely, and I believe that, in the end, it will be found to be a mistake. If every officer, so elected, were obliged by law to pass an examination, that it would do well enough, but they are not." Like many critics, Shaw distrusted the motives and abilities of his men to elect competent leaders. "If the captain of a company is killed, they can vote a private into his place, and he needn't be examined, unless some one reports to the Board that it is necessary."[53]

Some citizen-officers did their best to subvert elections whenever possible. During the 1862 reorganizations, a lieutenancy opened in Company G, 3rd North Carolina Infantry. Brigade headquarters ordered that an election be held to fill the vacancy, to the irritation of the regiment's officers, who did not think much of the election system. The 3rd North Carolina's commanding officer, Colonel Gaston Meares, read the order to hold the election and passed it on to his second in command, Lieutenant Colonel William Lord DeRosset. "Not seeing his way clear, but knowing the feelings of Colonel Meares as to permitting elections," DeRosset remembered, "[I] walked off in the direction of the camp of that company, hoping for some solution of the problem. Fortunately [I] found Lieutenant [William H.] Quince of that company in charge, the captain being absent from camp." Lieutenant Quince, he explained, had risen to his commission from the ranks of the Wilmington Light Infantry, "and [I] knew he could be depended upon. At once handing the order to Quince, he . . . threw up his hands with horror at being called upon to be the instrument in carrying out such an order." DeRosset reassured the lieutenant that "the opinions of all the regimental, field and staff, as well as most of the line officers, were well known to be against such a system, but the order was imperative, and must be obeyed." Quince was a canny officer and could take the hint that elections were not to be taken seriously. DeRosset reported the following exchange between the lieutenant and his company: "'Sergeant, make the men fall in with arms.' This was done quickly, and, addressing the men, [Quince] read the order, and remarked: 'Men, there are two candidates for the office,' naming them, 'and there is but one of them worth a d——n, and I nominate him. All who are in favor of electing Sergeant ——, come to a shoulder. Company, shoulder arms!' Then, turning to the Orderly Sergeant, [Quince] remarked: 'Sergeant, take charge of the company and dismiss them.'" In a matter of minutes Quince reported that "an election had been held in accordance with Special Order No. ——, and that Sergeant —— had been unanimously elected." The exercise "put a stop to all talk about elections for some time," according to DeRosset.[54]

Private Albert O. Marshall of the 33rd Illinois Infantry remembered the indignation that he and his comrades felt when company officers interfered with their democratic prerogatives by meddling with elections. In March 1862, after dispensing with an unpopular officer who had been appointed to the regiment, Marshall recalled, "as a vote had never been taken for that office, that the men of the regiment [believed they] had a right to take a vote for his successor and ignore all questions of regular promotion." When the winning candidate, Captain Isaac H. Elliot, was selected, Marshall recited the flimsy qualifications he believed had ensured Elliot's success. "Among them were his supposed military experience, he having had a fight with, and been whipped and taken prisoner by [Confederate brigadier general] Jeff Thompson and afterward been exchanged, his very pleasant and social way among the soldiers, he having in a short time formed the personal acquaintance of every member of the regiment, and last, but not least, his good looks, he being the handsomest officer in the Normal Regiment." Marshall also explained why the regiment's second in command, Major Edward R. Roe, was unsuccessful in the election. "Major Roe got a light vote because he was, as you know, the orator of the regiment. The only proper office for a regimental orator to hold is that of major of the regiment or a second lieutenant of a company—those with the least duties attached."[55] In an 1862 diary entry, Private Henry A. Buck of the 51st Illinois Infantry expressed his fury at the corruption he saw in his regiment's officer elections. "In the evening Col. Cumming meets us in our barracks and tells us that Adj. Gen. Fuller insisted on hurrying up our regimental organization—that he (Col. C) not knowing of any objection on our part (?) (!) had our acting officers ... mustered into the U.S. Service ..., that an election was only a matter of form (!) then put it to us by word of mouth, whether or not we would sustain him, and no one daring to object, he was sustained—this is called an election! What a farce!"[56]

Just as volunteers resented officers who tried to disrupt elections, the persistent democratic prerogatives remained a constant source of irritation for many junior officers with a mind to make proper soldiers out of their volunteers. In an 1861 letter to his sister, Lieutenant Shaw lamented the indiscipline he believed the citizen-soldier ethos had instilled in his Massachusetts volunteers, particularly when compared to that of regular-army troops. "Phil. Schulyer is fortunate in being in the regular service," Shaw wrote of a friend, an officer serving in the U.S. Army. "I see more clearly, every day, that the volunteer system is a perfectly rotten one, at least as it is organized in this country; and Congress, instead of trying to put the whole of us under real military regulations, makes us more and more militia-like. They seem to be transformed into a set of muttonheads, as soon as they begin to legislate on military matters." Shaw was referring to a letter published in the *New York Daily Tribune* by Frederick Law Olmsted, in which Olmsted condemned the purported slovenliness of Union company-grade volunteer officers. "Like everyone else who writes about it," Shaw reflected, "[Olmsted] pitched into the Captains but never said a word about the government having appointed 3000 officers without requiring them to pass any examination, and everyone of whom may be, for all the govt knows, as unfit for his place as the most ignorant private in the ranks." The election system, combined with the inconsistent application of a rigorous examination system, in Shaw's view virtually ensured that incompetent junior officers would find a "place" in command. "Certainly the Govt is to blame for such things for it is natural for a man to take a good position when it is offered," he concluded, "& they often think themselves competent when they are not." Shaw reiterated his disdain for the election system and blessed his good fortune that he had not been subjected to the indignities of a simple vote to win his place. "Thank Heaven *we* weren't elected by our men—when men are all good perhaps it will do to make the army democratic but until then I am certain it is a great mistake. But in spite of the ridiculous, rotten volunteer system, the army in and around Washington has improved greatly."[57] General Upton agreed with this sentiment and believed the officer-election system was "the worst vice known in the military system of any of the States," advocating instead strict boards of examination for officers in the Union army.[58] Many in the War Department and Congress concurred. In 1862 the United States granted generals the authority to appoint military boards of examination; in 1864 Congress reaffirmed generals' authority to test the "capacity, qualifications, propriety of conduct, and efficiency of any officer of volunteers" to do their job properly.[59]

The Union's officer-examination system evolved in fits and starts, and only later was it supplemented by officers' schools and training programs, though even these were of varying quality and application. More often, commanders assessed new junior officers' qualifications based on observation, intuition, and experience rather than any plan or method. The 1862 example of Captain Levi Bird Duff is emblematic of this slapdash approach to early officer examinations. Duff, an educated and articulate lawyer before the war, enlisted in a Pennsylvania regiment in 1861 and served for some time as a private in the ranks. His leadership potential attracted the notice of the regiment's commanding officer, Colonel McKnight, who summoned Duff to his tent one evening and subjected him to an impromptu examination. After questioning him on matters of moral character and military service, McKnight called for a musket and began barking orders at Duff, walking him through the manual of arms. The examination did not seem to be going well to the nervous private. "I started, the first shift was wrong, the second ditto & my spirit sunk so rapidly that I was almost afraid to open my mouth," he explained to his fiancée soon after the encounter. "But on he went into the School of the Company. In this I was better posted than in the manual of arms & I began to get a little confidence. He asked me the position of the rear rank in the oblique firings. I described it for I knew it perfectly. He sort of intimated that I was wrong but he did not say so. I appealed to the book, & after some hesitation he opened it. I was right, & this little victory straightened me right up." After an intense hour of this sort of testing, "[McKnight] rose from his seat, & said 'Mr. Duff we will give you a position here, your examination is very satisfactory.'" Without further comment the colonel ordered his clerk to draw up Duff's paperwork for a captain's commission, and soon the new officer was a company commander in the regiment. "This was a great surprise to me," Duff confessed, "for I thought [my examination] a miserable failure."[60] By 1862 the Army of the Potomac and the Army of the Cumberland had instituted systematic examinations and inspections, and most regiments required junior officers to meet several times a week for instruction in tactics and the recitation of regulations.

Soon other armies followed suit. Coupled with the benefits of practical experience in the field, junior-officer quality and training showed a gradual improvement in the Union army starting in early 1863.[61]

The Confederacy faced a similar predicament in ensuring quality junior leadership in its armies. Colonel William Preston Johnston, special inspector for the War Department and the son of ill-fated general Albert Sidney Johnston, visited the Army of Mississippi soon after the Battle of Shiloh in April 1862. The colonel was dismayed by the citizen-soldier ethos run amok among the volunteers, reporting that "[t]he present organization of the army is anomalous and not in accordance with the law, and will require Executive and perhaps Congressional action to remedy its evils." Johnston placed much of the blame for indiscipline in the army upon the election provisions included in the Conscription Act. "The conscript act (so called), perpetuating the organization of twelve-months men and prescribing a new election of officers, has worked most disastrously in this army," he declared. Johnston concluded that granting conscripts the same rights as volunteers to choose their own officers had caused division, corruption, and a breakdown of discipline. Conscripts, he reasoned, neither understood nor followed the citizen-soldier ethos, the key element of voluntariness being entirely absent from their ideology, which Johnston believed compromised the entire officer-election system. "A right to reorganize at will might have satisfied all of those whom an imperious necessity did not call to their homes; but to be drafted for the war into companies, which experience had proved distasteful to them, engendered a spirit of bitter discontent, which in many instances was fanned by designing men." Conscripts, in the colonel's opinion, were especially ill equipped to select suitable company officers, and units that conducted their reorganization elections in this dysfunctional environment made disastrous choices in leaders. "While the spirit of insubordination was rife the election of new officers took place, and a large number of valuable and experienced officers were replaced by men grossly incompetent and unable to pass an examination on their duties before the most indulgent boards," Johnston observed. "Their legal successors were equally unfit, and some regiments seemed tending toward disorganization and anarchy. Temporary appointments were made by the commanding general which in some instances have been ratified by the soldiers, but in others are still contested by rival claimants."[62]

Later, Confederate commanders resorted to general courts-martial to cull incompetent officers from companies, and Robert E. Lee encouraged subordinates to petition state governors for the removal of incompetent or unfit citizen-officers. Eventually, the War Department implemented formal boards of examination for officers, though their efforts were hardly systematic or universal. In 1862, General Orders No. 36 and No. 39 granted generals the authority to convene boards of examination to scrutinize newly promoted officers or officers of "questionable" competency. The criteria for these reviews were vague; boards were directed to "determine the candidates' capabilities of instructing and controlling their commands commensurate to the grade which promotion is expected, as also their efficiency and perfect sobriety."[63] In October 1863 the Confederate Congress enacted additional legislation requiring generals to periodically review their subordinate officers' performances and to subject them to boards of examination to determine their fitness when "the good of the service and the efficiency of his command" required it.[64]

Such review boards were never fully or consistently implemented in either army, though the system, along with attrition, did manage to weed out a large portion of unfit or incompetent junior officers. Colonel Johnston reiterated the importance of maintaining rigorous boards of examination in early 1862, having seen their benefit firsthand in the field. He also favored consistency in the rules and regulations for officer standards. "The more intelligent opinion of the army seems to be that the purging power of the examining boards and the arbitrary action of the commanding general had improved the organization of the army. It would be well if the organization could be conformed to the law or the law to the organization."[65] President Davis in particular favored the republican principles undergirding the officer-election system, though he also feared incompetence among citizen-officers and pressed for the systematic use of the boards of examination as advocated by officers like Johnston. "In the election and appointment of officers for the Provisional Army it was to be anticipated that mistakes would be made and incompetent officers of all grades introduced into the service," he admitted in 1862. "In the absence of experience, and with no reliable guide for selection, executive appointments as well as elections have been sometimes unfortunate." For Davis, the potential cost for ignoring the problem of incompetence was too great to bear; even greater than the risk of offending the personal honor of certain citizen-officers. "The good of the service, the interests of our country," he informed Congress, "require that some means be devised for withdrawing the commissions of officers who are incompetent for the duties required by their position, and I trust you will find means for relieving the Army of such officers by some mode more prompt and less wounding to their sensibility than the judgment of a court-martial."[66]

It was President Davis's custom to involve himself in the details of army administration whenever he felt it necessary; as a military man himself, Davis believed he was particularly well suited to weigh in on these matters. "An army without discipline and instruction cannot be relied on for purposes of defense, still less for operations in an enemy's country," he informed the Confederate Senate in 1862. "It is in vain to add men and munitions, unless we can at the same time give to the aggregated mass the character and capacity of soldiers. The discipline and instruction required for its efficiency cannot be imparted without competent officers. . . . Extreme cases ought not to furnish a rule, yet some provision should be made to meet evils, even exceptional, in a matter so vitally affecting the safety of our troops." Echoing General Lee's concerns about the wisdom of subjecting untrained troops to incompetent or inexperienced citizen-officers, Davis reminded Congress that inept commanders could lead to disaster in combat. "Tender consideration for worthless and incompetent officers is but another name for cruelty toward the brave men who fall sacrifices to these defects of their leaders," he added. Ever mindful of volunteers' desire to serve with other troops from their states, the president believed that giving the executive branch the authority to require examination boards was the logical solution. "It is not difficult to devise a proper mode of obviating this evil. The law authorizes the refusal to promote officers who are found incompetent to fill vacancies, and the promotion of their juniors in their stead; but instances occur in which no officer remaining in a regiment is fit to be promoted to the grade of colonel, and no officer remaining in a company is competent to command it as captain. Legislation providing for the selection in such cases of competent officers from other regiments of the same State affords a ready remedy for this evil, as well as for the case when officers elected are found unfit for the positions to which they may be chosen."[67]

Assistant Adjutant General Melton was, like President Davis, an enthusiastic advocate for boards of examination. In November 1863 Melton wrote to Secretary of War Seddon: "[Boards of examination] should be made imperative in every instance of promotion. It will not do to leave it to general officers to determine when boards shall be convened, and whether an officer does or does not deserve to appear before them. I know that this privilege is grossly abused, and a field open which is fully occupied for the exhibition of personal partialities and intrigues for personal popularity." Melton, a meticulous professional and a West Point graduate, distrusted the judgment of generals when it came to upholding the highest standards for their volunteer junior officers. "Very many, if not all, general officers are politicians in their way," he opined to Seddon. "[T]he routine of duty very soon dulls their quantum of earnestness, and they are perhaps not more infallible than other men. To this the fact that they command troops from their own State contributes in a large degree." Melton believed impartial and rigorous examination boards were the best solution to avoiding favoritism or corruption in the commissioning process. "To sum up, where seniority accords priority of right, the aspirant should in every instance be made to show not only his competency, but his superiority," Melton argued. "The whole sum and substance of the inefficiency in our armies is due to indifferent leadership; this without qualification is the truth. The men are brave, true, patient, unmurmuring, obedient, exceedingly tractable, and they need only be taught and led to achieve everything."[68]

Despite the good intentions behind them, boards of examination sometimes had unintended and unfortunate effects. Otherwise competent citizen-officers could have their confidence in themselves and in their comrades eroded by the prospect of review, as Captain James C. Bates of the 9th Texas Cavalry discovered in May 1862. While still growing accustomed to his leadership role, Bates struggled with his misgivings about the abilities and qualifications of his fellow officers as rumors about the draconian practices of the examination boards made the rounds in his mess. "I think it doubtful," he detailed in his diary, "whether our Col elect will be able to stand an examination by the Military board of examiners or not. All officers elected in the reorganization have to undergo a rigid examination and if found incompetent are rejected. I have been told that *sixteen* were rejected from [Samuel B.] Maxeys old [9th Texas Infantry] Regiment." Bates expressed his own concerns about facing examination in candid terms but believed that his victorious election and the bond of loyalty with his men would protect him from dismissal, if necessary. "Whether I will be able to stand the test or not is yet to be tried. In fact I am not very particular as to whether I am passed or not as officers not *reelected* & passed will be relieved from duty for the remainder of our twelve months or long enough to go home for a time." For Bates and others, the examination system introduced a level of anxiety that unnecessarily eroded their morale. "If it were not for the members of the company I would procure a transfer to some other Regiment," the captain complained. "The boys say if I leave I will have to take them with me, or they will desert.... I am heartily tired of this Regiment."[69]

The election system and the uncertainty of examination was not the only path to an officer's commission for Union and Confederate volunteers. Staff commissions such as aides-de-camp or adjutants, were not elected positions and were only available through appointment or by promotion from a lower grade. Personal staff officers such as aides-de-camp served at the pleasure of their commanders, and if their appointment expired or was terminated, or if their commander was killed or relieved, these officers could find themselves back in the ranks as enlisted men. Both sides made efforts to curtail the expansion of personal staffs, which continued to balloon throughout the war as generals added more junior officers to their entourages. Major General George B. McClellan, for instance, habitually trailed a glittering procession of young staff officers during the Peninsula Campaign in 1862, among them a pair of French aristocrats boasting captains' commissions.[70] Specialized staff positions requiring men with exceptional technical abilities, such as officers in the topographical, ordnance, medical, or engineering departments, were also filled by appointment or promotion rather than by election. Vacancies among line officers were not exclusively filled by election either, and elections in both the Union and Confederate armies declined after the reorganizations of mid-1862. Furthermore, generals in both armies could, at their discretion, recommend candidates for commissions; often these new officers were drawn from among the senior noncommissioned officers in companies. Nevertheless, the majority of Union and Confederate junior officers commissioned before 1864 began their careers through the election system, which ensured that volunteers maintained their democratic prerogative to define the terms of their service, though doubtless denied many qualified enlisted men the chance to serve as officers.

Citizen-officers who rose quickest usually did so through appointments and promotions rather than elections. Appointments in particular often depended upon patronage, either through personal favors or influence secured by family connections at home. Union volunteer Augustus D. Ayling of the 29th Massachusetts Infantry could thank his elite Boston family's patronage for his elevation in January 1862. "I received today a nice letter from Uncle Henry saying I was to be commissioned as 2nd Lieutenant in the 29th Massachusetts Volunteers," he recorded in his diary. "I was, of course, delighted, and felt very grateful to him for it was to his efforts I was indebted for my promotion." Ayling, like many other citizen-officers plucked from the ranks, worried that facing a hostile board of examination might derail his new commission. "I supposed I should have to be examined before muster-in as an officer, and immediately commenced to 'cram' on tactics," he wrote. "Fortunately, however, no examination was required, but the hard study I put in for several days and nights was of considerable benefit to me, as I found out later, when I joined the regiment." Relieved at having evaded the rigors of a formal examination, Ayling could boast of his newly acquired technical competence as a result of his scare. By the time he assumed his new post, the young lieutenant believed that he "knew fully as much, and perhaps a little more than the other officers in my company."[71]

When the election process did not yield the results that volunteers or candidates hoped for, they occasionally felt compelled to resort to personal pleas for intervention from the highest authorities. In June 1864 President Lincoln received one such request from an angry mother in Chicago, Illinois. Juliette Kinzie's son Arthur, a lieutenant serving in the Mississippi valley, had recently gone on furlough from his regiment. When the young officer rejoined his unit, an unpleasant surprise awaited him. "He returned to his Regiment to find that he had been passed by—(we at the west would say '*jumped*') in the routine of promotion," Kinzie wrote to the president. Bristling with outrage, she protested that "one of his former sergeants was now his Captain. His regiment came north this spring to recruit and re-enlist[.] After their return to Mississippi [the men] claimed, in virtue of a promise that had been made them, the right of a new election of officers, and, to show their disapprobation of regular discipline, and subordination in the service, *elected Arthur out*."[72] Lincoln declined to overturn the voting results. Lieutenant Kinzie never returned to his regiment, though he presumably recovered from the ignominy of his mother's intervention.

When he joined the North Carolina volunteers in 1862, sixteen-year-old Confederate William H. S. Burgwyn hoped that his brother Henry, lieutenant colonel of the 26th North Carolina Infantry, would secure him a lieutenant's commission and an adjutant's post in that regiment. Henry Burgwyn harbored reservations about his younger brother's temperament, however, and confided his doubts to his mother: "If . . . the adjutancy of my regiment will be vacant Willie will want me to appoint him but I know we will not get along well together, and am really too afraid of his disposition to appoint him. . . . [U]nder the circumstances in which we would be placed there would be difficulties and disagreements which would make us both unhappy." Henry spoke to a friend and fellow officer, Colonel Matthew W. Ransom of the 35th North Carolina Infantry, who assured him that "he would have William elected to a lieutenancy in a few days." William's disappointment in losing the adjutancy in his brother's regiment was outweighed by his confidence in his prospects with Ransom's unit. "As the Lieutenant Colonel and Major are ... particular friends of mine and a great many of the officers also being my friends I think I will probably get it," William wrote to his parents. Ransom was as good as his word and conveniently arranged for William to be elected lieutenant in the 35th North Carolina.[73] Burgwyn framed his appointment in terms of friendship; in this sense his approach reflects one of the methods that nineteenth-century Americans used to mitigate their reservations about partisanship and electioneering. By casting his appointment as a favor between friends, Burgwyn was able to reconcile the hierarchical, influence-based benefits of patronage with the democratic, egalitarian demands of honor, mutual obligation, and fairness among the volunteers.[74]

Nevertheless, the advancement of citizen-officers through patronage or favoritism could be caustic to morale. Josiah Marshall Favill, an intelligent and competent young lieutenant in the 57th New York Infantry with antebellum military experience, enumerated his frustrations about perceived favoritism in September 1862. "Another difficulty with the service is the lack of system in promotion," Favill wrote in his diary. "Excepting subaltern commissions, nearly all are obtained through influence at home. There are notable instances in my own regiment, where officers have been commissioned, directly in opposition to the colonel's recommendation, and the seniority and rights of other officers."[75] Confederate citizen-officers also objected to such practices, as demonstrated by Captain John W. Harris's observations about the crass nepotism among staff appointments in the Army of Mississippi in early 1862. Writing from Corinth, Mississippi, in February of that year, the young staff officer told his mother that he had "very little confidence though in [Brigadier] General [Daniel] Ruggles who is in command here, for I do not think that he is the right sort of man to be over a brigade, he is too timid and childish, his staff is composed of mere boys, only one being on it who is over twenty years old, they are all either his sons or nephews, and know nothing at all about business."[76] Lieutenant Robert H. Miller was deeply upset that his 14th Louisiana Infantry's acting commander, Colonel Valery Sulokowski, was demoted in February 1862 in favor of a political appointee, Georgia politician Howell Cobb. Cobb was, Miller fumed, "a politician who has not spent two weeks of his time in camp since he was made a Colonel, but has been in Richmond electioneering for this very office, which he is, not competent to fill but which in the opinion of those who know him, it is really criminal to accept, with his Egyptian ignorance of every item of knowledge that one in the position he now holds should have." The volunteers in Miller's unit were similarly enraged by Cobb's appointment. "[T]o see a cotton politician placed over [Sulokowski's] head in the very time our Cause suffers most from this species of acting on the part of the Government was too much for him and he left us," the lieutenant lamented. "[L]eft the finest Regiment in the whole world—and left it too to destruction and ruin, for upon the very night of his departure the Regiment became wild and uncontrollable, they tore down the Sutlers Shop in their fury, and threatened the gallant Col. Jones, who in the pride of his glory betook himself to the Surgeons quarters for safety leaving Dr. Henry Villiers (the Sutler) and myself to keep back the mob that a knowledge of his worthlessness had raised."[77] In December 1861 Captain Nelson Chapin of the 85th New York Infantry vented his irritation about an inept outsider who had been installed as regimental quartermaster, an action apparently taken to fulfill some political favor. "I do not wish to complain," he told his wife from Washington, D.C., "but I think there has been some *red tape ism* or else there was some favoritism in the appointment of our quartermaster who should have been selected from the Lieutenants of the regiment." Chapin described how "for some cause somebody's friend from N. Y. City was foisted upon us and the result is we have not had hardly anything done in season or in order." Despite his irritation, the captain was confident that he would be able to put the incompetent new quartermaster in his place. "[B]ut we hope to *lick* the *cub* into *shape*," Chapin added, "and then things will run smoothly."[78]

Citizen-officers annoyed by the unfairness of promotions and appointments were occasionally quite vocal in their criticism, some even taking their grievances to the press. In an anonymous letter to the editors of the Washington, D.C., *National Republican* in March 1862, Lieutenant Henry Perkins Goddard expressed his utter disgust at the system of promotion through patronage he saw unfolding in Company G of his 14th Connecticut Infantry. "For instance: a second lieutenancy is vacant; next in rank stands an orderly sergeant, a man of sound discretion, fair education, correct habits, and, from eight months' instruction in camp duties, military discipline, and drill, well qualified to fill the place to which he is by law entitled, and to wear upon his shoulders the mark of an officer," he wrote. "But no; both his qualifications and just claims are ignored; merited promotion is refused him, and by the aid of the lever that moves the world, a pampered pet of wealth and fashion, in the shape of a pale-faced, beardless boy, or a drawing room fop, is raised from the lap of unmanly and enervating luxury, and presented to a company of camp-worn or battle-scarred soldiers as an officer to be by them 'respected and obeyed as such.'" Goddard's hypothetical dilettante officer possessed none of the qualities he believed essential to a good company-grade officer. "Ignorant of camp duty, military discipline and drill, he is not capable of imparting instruction to the men; and even if this disability were removed, his feeble arm cannot swing a sabre, or guide a war horse." Goddard imagined this effete son of privilege falling ill after a few weeks of the rigors of camp life, after which he would use his connections to obtain a sick furlough. While the foppish appointee was on sick leave, useless to his men or his country, Goddard bitterly mused, the "Government pays him an ample salary for parading the Avenue or lounging in graceful ease around the fashionable hotels, while the *soldier,* whose qualifications are in every respect superior to his own, and over whose head he was promoted, remains in camp, and does double duty, at fourteen dollars per month."[79]

"I will not, by any personal allusions, resurrect the bitter feelings of jealousy that existed for a time," Sergeant Major Stephen F. Fleharty said of the poisonous environment in the 102nd Illinois Infantry during the regiment's reorganization in 1862. "Suffice it to say that the extreme desire for official preferment had a very demoralizing tendency. Men of little or no capacity aspired to the highest positions in the regiment." Fleharty recalled an example of the "recklessly ambitious spirit" of aspiring junior officers while his regiment was stationed in Knoxville, Tennessee. "One of the newly promoted captains was but half satisfied with his responsible position," he remembered, "and learning that the Adjutancy was vacant, a bright idea struck him. Forthwith he went to wire-pulling, and approaching Lieut. ——, explained to him that he desired to be promoted to Adjutant of the regiment, and asked his support!"[80] Corporal Alonzo Brown of the 4th Minnesota Infantry recalled the bribery and lies of officer candidates seeking new recruits' support in 1861. "[T]he tricks, palaver and 'soft soap' of the political candidate, who asks the voter about the health of his family and distant relatives, were soon manifested, and the misrepresentations, lies and impositions that were practiced by some of those who were working for recruits, in order that they might become officers in some of the companies, would cause Ananias, the patron saint of liars, to blush for shame," the corporal fumed. In Brown's regiment candidates for commissions promised recruits that they would be appointed sergeant, musician, clerk, or some other choice position in return for their votes. "Half a dozen men, perhaps, would be promised the same office, and after they were sworn in and they discovered the impositions and chicanery that had been practiced upon them, it was fatal to the character of many of those officers for truth," he remembered. Once secure in their new commissions, these unscrupulous new officers "seemed to care nothing for that. They had got in; donned their shoulder straps, 'old cheese knives,' and were ready to be respected and obeyed accordingly."[81] Private Carlton McCarthy of the Richmond Howitzers bemoaned the gradual erosion of the election system through interference and direct appointment of new officers. As he put it, "Instead of the privilege and pleasure of picking out some good-hearted, brave comrade and making him captain, the lieutenant was promoted without the consent of the men, or, what was harder to bear, some officer hitherto unknown was sent to take command." In addition to introducing the taint of corruption to the process, favoritism cut at the most fundamental notion of the citizen-soldier ethos: that volunteers had the right to govern themselves and define the terms of their service by choosing their own leaders. "This was no doubt better for the service," McCarthy admitted, "but it had a serious effect on the minds of volunteer patriot soldiers, and looked to them too much like arbitrary power exercised over men who were fighting that very principle."[82]

Volunteers, and many citizen-officers, often disdained appointments for patronage because such acts assaulted their sense of fairness and because they saw it as symptomatic of the societal corruption that traditionally threatened republics. Republican governments, the theory went, became corrupted through greed, luxury, or exploitation; history was replete with examples of this pattern, from ancient Greece and Rome to Europe. The path to corruption wound its way through excesses of patronage and favoritism. When a republic became corrupted, an elite few could dominate the free majority for their own purposes and benefit. Political corruption led to moral decay, the death knell for the republican form of government; survival, then, depended upon a virtuous citizenry willing to sacrifice itself to combat moral decay and corruption.[83] Volunteers who discovered that the realities of Civil War service were often inconsistent with their democratic prerogatives sometimes faced severe disillusionment after witnessing displays of favoritism and corruption in the promotion process. As Union volunteer Alonzo Brown put it, "Our victims soon discovered that they were not, as soldiers, controlled by a republican form of government, but by martial law, and that little errors or indiscretions that would not be noticed in civil life were, according to military law, punished with the most severe penalties, and the code of punishment in the army regulations which prescribed among its penalties 'shall suffer death or such other punishment as shall be inflicted by the sentence of a court martial,' occurred with alarming frequency."[84]

Though corruption, patronage, and favoritism offended republican sensibilities on both sides, these seemingly arbitrary practices often represented the quickest path to an officer's commission. Political skill was an invaluable asset for volunteer junior officers negotiating the labyrinth of military advancement In practice, appointments to officer commissions usually came at the recommendation of regimental, brigade, or division commanders, with confirmation by state or national authorities usually a mere formality. Aspirants to higher rank within companies and regiments had to read the political and psychological landscape of those in power and make their bids for promotion or appointment with subtlety and skill. In 1862 Lieutenant Theophilus Perry of the 28th Texas Cavalry described the treacherous feelings within that regiment to his wife. "There is no doubt that Col. [Horace] Rand[a]l will be a Brigadier as soon as the President can send the commission. Col. [Eli H.] Baxter will take command of our Regiment. He will make Lieutenant [William Neal] Ramey of [Captain Patrick H.] Martins Company his Adjutant. It is a good appointment I think." Perry hoped to be appointed regimental quartermaster but was unsure that he possessed his commander's confidence and feared duplicity. "I do not think Col. Baxter will make me Quartermaster in case of a vacancy. I do not think he is a sincere friend of mine, though he always has treated me well. I have not asked him for the position, for if I was disposed to as I am not, I do not regard it as delicate to ask for a place before it is vacated." The Texan seemed to believe another candidate for the position would do a good job as quartermaster and apparently did not resent the possibility that he might be passed over for the appointment. "I have some intimation that he will probably appoint John Williams, but this is a secret," he confided to his wife. "Jno. [Williams] would fill the Position very well. Col. Baxter will make Mr. [Iverson]

Lane Commissary if it become[s] vacant: this too is a secret. I shall be glad of that. I desire to see Mr. Lane promoted. But every thing is uncertain." He believed that Baxter was making his decisions with an eye to his own postwar political fortunes rather than for the good of his regiment, and Perry's distaste for this behavior is subtly evident in his letter. "Col. B is anxious so to conduct as to make friends at home that would be useful in the future, for political supporters," he informed his wife. "All this I believe, but I keep my own thought, only sharing them somewhat with Major Lane who is my Friend." Perry then moved on to his opinion of the qualifications and moral character of various other candidates for commissions. "Col. Randol [sic] will make Adjutant Howard, Adjutant for him when he becomes General. I think a much better appointment could be made. I put Howard, Baxter, & Rene Fitzpatrick in the same category. They are inclined to dissipate, and the two latter, clearly in a manner dissipated to even speak a loud to ladies. I am disgusted with them." Perry loathed the favoritism and political wrangling in the elections almost as much as he disapproved of the character of some of the candidates. "Col. B. & Rene are as thick with each other as they can be, & are birds of a feather," he concluded. "They are not congenial companions for me, though I believe that Rene is a friend to me. But it is doubtful whether men of moral sensibilities like either of them have can be true friends to any body. Baxter has political aspiration, that he will seek to gratify at most any cost."[85]

Captain Nathaniel Lowe of the 5th New Hampshire Infantry stood as candidate for major in July 1863 and lost by a close vote despite making no real effort to lobby for the position. Curiously, the defeat seemed to bring him a sense of contentment rather than disappointment. "I got news from the Regt last night that the Officers had been voting for Major & that Capt Low[e] came within one of getting it. I was very much pleased with the vote as I had never told any of the line Officers I wanted it." Lowe disliked the "wire-pulling" necessary to win higher office and was gratified that his brother officers displayed such regard for him without the need for electioneering. Still, he could not help but detect a whiff of corruption in the process. "Capt Tilton the man that beat me voted for himself & got it or that is got the majority," wrote Lowe, but he was certain that his influence back home was greater than that of his opponent. "I got lots of letters from the Officers this morning, saying they wanted me to stick by the Regt & they would stick by me, so I suppose they will pour a flood of letters into New Hamp to the influential men." Lowe seemed to think of the process as a sort of game and found the esteem of his comrades flattering. "It will be some sport & besides nuts for me, as there are six Captains that outrank me & should be promoted before me, but most of them stand one side & go in for me." He also did not scruple to ask for patronage of his own. "I dont know how it will end. I wish you would ask Geo Pierce to speak to Gov Gilmore, tell George, Nat Head & Allen Tenny will pitch in if they have not already."[86]

Captain Lowe's example notwithstanding, corruption in the appointment and election process did much to undermine the egalitarian, merit-based spirit of the democratic prerogatives in Civil War armies. Union and Confederate volunteers alike loathed even the hint of aristocracy, particularly that of an incompetent or self-interested clique entrusted with the lives and destinies of themselves and their fellow citizens. Perceptions of corruption even led officers like Lieutenant Goddard to question the rightness of their cause and the righteousness of the republic for which they were fighting. "What wonder, then, that dissatisfaction exists in regiments where such injustice, such open transgressions of military law, are practiced and allowed," he protested, "and what conclusion is left for the soldier to form, but that, because he cannot command influence and wealth, the country for which he fights cares not for him, and will not protect him in his rights." Goddard decried "this unjust, this ungrateful system of appointments and promotions" perpetrated by "this hotbed culture of brigadiers, colonels, captains and lieutenants. Let the laurels a soldier has won rest upon his brow," he urged, "not to be torn away to decorate the head of a military ignoramus."[87]

Modest or principled candidates who preferred to rely on their own merit rather than on electioneering or political maneuvers could still win a commission, though the path was often a more difficult one. In the first weeks of the war, Josiah Favill expressed his confidence that he would rise from the ranks and earn an officer's commission through hard work and ability. "True, it is not much to be a private soldier, and I have always looked at war through the commissioned ranks, but in this particular case it will not make so much difference, as men in all conditions of life, rich men, scholars, professional men, and young fellows from college and school are all anxious to go as privates, so I shall trust to luck to gain promotion by attention to duty and by my knowledge of military affairs."[88] Charles Morfoot of the 101st Ohio Infantry eschewed recognition for his abilities by passing up an opportunity for easy advancement; this proved a wise strategy for his long-term ambitions to become an officer. When word came in early 1863 that his commanders intended to form a mounted infantry company "made up of such that have distinguished themselves for bravery and good sold[i]er[l]y conduct" and that he would be invited to join it, Morfoot sensed that his chances for an officer's commission would be greater if he remained with his regiment. "I dont expect I will leave the regiment for there are many hungry seargents electioneering I dont do[ubt] that my name is as high as theirs," he explained to his family. "[T]he officers asked me if I wanted my name on the roal of honor I told them do as they thought best if they thought I was worthy all right I would not electioneer so it seems they thought me worthy." The Ohioan remained with his regiment, and in 1864 his patience was rewarded with a lieutenant's commission.[89]

Ambitious enlisted Union volunteers could also obtain a commission beginning in 1863 by applying for company officer positions in one of the newly recruited United States Colored Troops (USCT) regiments. The colored regiments were to be staffed exclusively by white officers, most of whom would be drawn from the ranks of experienced enlisted men in white units. Many of these applicants tended to be motivated by ambition rather than zeal for racial equality. According to historian William A. Dobak, "contemporary public opinion about race guaranteed that opportunists would far outnumber abolitionists in the officer corps as a whole."[90] Even those applicants who successfully acquired USCT commissions could occasionally expect a certain stigma with the honor. "You have doubtless heard that the Governor is enlisting negroes and forming negro regiments," wrote Chauncey H. Cooke of the 25th Wisconsin Infantry in 1863. "They are officered by whites and there are a lot of candidates for positions in all the white regiments. Some 25 have applied for positions from our regiment. There is a lot of joking on the side about the fellows that want to officer the nigger regiments."[91] Ridicule aside, for candidates who could endure the bottleneck of bureaucracy and the inefficiency of the officer appointment and examination systems, a USCT commission proved tantalizing to those unwilling or unable to subject themselves to conventional paths to officership.

Whatever the means to a commission, aspirants to command in Civil War armies had to account for the demands and expectations inherent in the American citizen-soldier ethos. "It is precisely because democracy is an advanced stage in human society, that war, which belongs to a less advanced stage, is peculiarly inconsistent with its habits," Union colonel Higginson declared.[92] Higginson's assessment reflected the views of many Union and

Confederate leaders who saw the most salient elements of the citizen-soldier ethos as significant obstacles to the creation of an efficient, effective volunteer junior-officer corps. Citizen-officers themselves came to realize that the election system sometimes undermined their authority and, when abused or circumvented, could lead to inefficiency, indiscipline, and corruption among their volunteers. Nevertheless, the shared citizen-soldier ethos and the democratic prerogatives of the republican tradition continued to inform the creation of the volunteer officer corps in both the Union and Confederate armies during the first years of the war and remained a persistent consideration that leaders on both sides had to accommodate. While appointments and promotions through seniority were the predominant advancement paths for new officers after the 1862 reorganizations, the officer-election system would remain in effect in the Union army for the duration of the war. Only in February 1865 did the Confederate Congress finally gave in to pressure from army leaders and abolish its election system by granting the president the sole authority to appoint or promote officers. But by then it was too late to affect the nature of the Confederate junior-officer corps in any appreciable way.[93]

Both sides' conscription policies contained several clear concessions to the citizen-soldier ethos, particularly in the preservation of officer elections. Professional officers and civilian leaders on both sides were disturbed by the indiscipline that these elections seemed to encourage, and veterans of the Mexican War feared a repeat of the problems from that conflict. Citizen-officers themselves struggled with the problems inherent in the election system; those who learned to appreciate regular-army discipline or distrusted the raucous electioneering of their volunteers' democratic prerogatives came to abhor the wire-pulling necessary to win commissions. Officers and volunteers alike came to resent the corruptible process even as they fought to preserve their traditional right to elect junior commanders they deemed worthy of the honor. The election process itself was often compromised, and indignant volunteers could do little to remedy violations except to resist the authority of unwanted officers. The additional corruption and injustice of appointments through patronage could destroy unit morale, erode officers' authority, and interfere with their efforts to instill discipline and hierarchy in their volunteers. Sporadic institutional efforts to improve the quality of junior officers through boards of examination had a slow but significant effect after 1862. While officer elections, appointments, and patronage were unavoidable components of Civil

War volunteer armies, the system seems to have worked more or less as intended. Even so, the controversies over officer elections confirm how unsettled the democratic prerogatives of the republican tradition were in the antebellum period. Democracy was not something everyone agreed about, either in its definition or its procedures—it was an ideal to be revered and defended but to be watched over with a wary eye.[94] The Civil War armies' disquiet about officer elections and competence also reflects the ongoing debate on both sides of the Atlantic about whether the right to vote should be limited by capacity. Both proponents and opponents of the democratic election of junior officers expressed misgivings about the entire process, their uncertainty consistent with the larger discussion of how compatible republican and democratic ideals really were, particularly in times of crisis. Though the citizen-soldier ethos remained consistent for Civil War soldiers, these debates show the unsettled and contested nature of democracy in nineteenth-century America.[95]

Though elections fell into disuse by the middle of the war, the Union and Confederate officer-election systems permitted soldiers to shape their military service on their own terms by emphasizing the voluntary nature of their status. Officer elections also ensured a measure of mutual dependence between officers and volunteers essential to the citizen-soldier ethos, thus reinforcing the ties of loyalty necessary for competent and effective command. Volunteers' conceptions of their service and their right to choose their own officers would, over time, evolve under pressure and through necessity. But in the war's early years, the rather haphazard system for creating a volunteer junior-officer corps, a system born of compromise and of pragmatism, reflected the long antecedents of the citizen-soldier tradition. That venerable heritage left an indelible mark on the character and leadership of the Civil War volunteer armies for the entirety of the conflict.

3

The Challenges of Company Leadership

Armies often reflect the societies from which they are drawn. Nowhere is this more emphatically true than in the Union and Confederate citizen armies of the Civil War. While volunteer military service was the obligation of all citizens of a republic, the military profession itself was not considered a particularly reputable pursuit for self-respecting Americans concerned with liberty, individualism, and autonomy.[1] Untrained, inexperienced citizen-officers seeking to organize and command independent-minded citizen-soldiers constantly labored to legitimize their authority, and it was no easy task. Civil War volunteers constantly tested the notion that they had to be subject to army discipline and took every opportunity to remind their officers that they were not, nor would they ever be, intrinsically superior by virtue of their commissions. Commanding such men, their officers found, required special considerations. "The relation between officer and soldier is something so different in kind from anything which civil life has to offer, that it has proved almost impossible to transfer methods or maxims from the one to the other," Union colonel Thomas Higginson wrote in 1864.[2] All American volunteers were citizen-soldiers, but their military service was temporary, and they retained their civilian identities. This presented unique leadership difficulties for officers, who sought to exert their authority while also sharing these same characteristics and ideological expectations.

Civil War companies usually consisted of one hundred men or fewer, and company-grade officers often knew each volunteer in their unit personally; in fact, most shared mutual histories, community ties, or even blood relations with their soldiers. Company officers' decisions for good or ill also had a direct effect on whether or not their men lived or died. Union and Confederate citizen-officers were faced with an exceptionally difficult task, in that they called upon coequal citizens to forgo their survival instincts, their democratic prerogatives, and even their sense of individuality in ways that often seemed unnatural to them. The leadership challenges that these leaders faced, and the solutions they employed to meet these challenges, were unique to the Civil War experience. Camp life, drill, marching, and other duties occupied the majority of the daily routine of the volunteers' experiences. The leadership exhibited by officers in tiresome or mundane periods was critically important, for it shaped experiences, formed expectations, and dictated the actions, instincts, and training that the men all had to bring to bear in times of crisis. As Higginson explained: "Courage is cheap; the main duty of an officer is to take good care of his men, so that every one of them shall be ready, at a moment's notice, for any reasonable demand. A soldier's life usually implies weeks and months of waiting, and then one glorious hour; and if the interval of leisure has been wasted, there is nothing but a wasted heroism at the end, and perhaps not even that." Effective military leadership not only facilitated the preparation of troops for combat but also allowed citizen-officers to interpret and transmit values and meaning to the war and to establish their position in the hierarchy of army life. Failure to fulfill these basic obligations could have catastrophic results in a crisis. "The penalty for misused weeks, the reward for laborious months, may be determined within ten minutes," warned Higginson.[3]

The task of unraveling and interpreting Civil War citizen-officer leadership challenges is difficult, primarily because officers tended not to address these topics in great detail in their wartime correspondence and papers. The writings and professional literature of the regular-army officer corps of the antebellum period is mostly untroubled by deep contemplation of such matters, and this attitude seems to have carried over to the regulars' volunteer counterparts in both the Union and Confederate armies. Historian Samuel J. Watson notes that "[d]espite its high level of education, the [antebellum] army officer corps as a whole was remarkably unreflective, or at least inarticulate, about its tasks.... [A]ntebellum officers rarely analyzed or reported the details of military operations and drill in any depth outside of the official reports of senior commanders and *ad hoc* boards composed of a few specialists who were specifically charged with doing so."[4] This apparent lack of self-scrutiny on matters of leadership is all the more remarkable given the professionalizing impulse that seized the U.S. military during the years prior to the Civil War.[5] As for early war volunteer officers, the pace of their abrupt integration into army life, the scarcity of professional officers to serve as examples, and the lack of a formal training or acculturation apparatus all may have contributed to their lack of reflection. Simply put, novice citizen-officers were often too busy or too overwhelmed with the task of learning their jobs that they had little time or energy to ponder deeper questions of command, authority, or leadership.

In the absence of extensive institutional guidance, an officer's acquisition of command skills was highly informal and often haphazard. Neophyte officers with no formal training had to rely upon their natural abilities, their antebellum civilian experience, and their observations of effective or experienced regular-army officers for guidance in learning their craft. For many, particularly those serving in the early months of the Civil War, there were few professional examples to be found. Most citizen-officers had minimal practical military experience, and the hierarchical, formal, demanding culture of army life seemed alien and uncomfortable. "My post is no sinecure, be assured of it," noted one harried Confederate officer new to company command. "My hands are full—perfectly full. I have no hope of being a popular Capt. I am only trying to make a good one.... No one can imagine the amt. of work required of an officer as green as I am in Tactics."[6] Even worse, as historian Joseph T. Glatthaar finds of officers in the Army of Northern Virginia, many "entered military service with warped perceptions of officership. All they had to do, so they believed, was follow a simple formula for success: act courageously, with manhood and dignity, and men would follow them." For these untested officers, "Leadership and fighting were instinctual. Simply study the tactics manual, drill the soldiers, and they would succeed in combat. Yet they lacked executive ability and attention to detail—two qualities that prewar Southern society did not promote."[7] Union citizen-officers labored under the same misconceptions about the nature of command. Many of them faced resistance and even outright mockery from their volunteers when they failed to meet the men's expectations.[8] "Drill is aching funny," S. Millet Thompson of the 13th New Hampshire Infantry noted in his diary in 1862. "[Officers' m]istakes are corrected by making still worse mistakes." Thompson described the derisive reactions of his fellow soldiers to company officers' hapless attempts to master the art of drill. "The men in the ranks grin, giggle and snicker," he wrote, "and now and then break out into a coarse, country haw-haw."[9] As Pennsylvanian Levi Bird Duff observed in 1861: "Our company officers have frequently tried to learn us the skirmish drill but not knowing it themselves they were of course incompetent to teach it. Every time they attempted to teach us they were openly laughed at & finally the[y] relinquished the task. Thus we were left without the knowledge of that which it was most important for us to know."[10]

Adapting to the exactitudes of army life required citizen-officers and volunteers alike to suppress years of instinct and custom carried forward from their civilian lives. The officers, innocent of even the most rudimentary military training, had first to learn the duties of common soldiers before they could begin the process of mastering their own leadership role. They could overcome the handicap of inexperience with time, application, and the lessons learned by making mistakes; in fact, trial and error proved the most common, if not the most efficient, method for citizen-officers to educate themselves about their duties. As Colonel Higginson explained of this painful learning process, "any volunteer officer will admit, that, though the tactics were easily learned, yet, in dealing with all other practical details of army-life, he was obliged to gain his knowledge through many blunders."[11] The insubordinate and amateurish nature of early Civil War armies compounded these problems for inexperienced citizen-officers, and volunteers' preconceptions about military service conspired to complicate the already daunting challenges of command. Higginson conceded the difficulty of maintaining military discipline among irreverent volunteers, particularly considering the inexperience of most officers; he noted that European critics of the American volunteer tradition often snickered, with some merit, that "[American volunteer] soldiers are relatively superior to the officers, so that the officers lead, but do not command them." The reason for this arrangement, the colonel believed, was due to both the temporary nature of American volunteers' military service and to the long-held ideological traditions of egalitarianism, individualism, and consent-based service inherent in the citizen-soldier ethos. "Three years are not long enough to overcome the settled habits of twenty years," Higginson admitted.[12]

Further, volunteers' rebellious attitude toward authority, and the ideological tradition that inspired it, intensified the challenge of command. Volunteers naturally disdained demands for their submission to officers' authority, yet obedience was an essential aspect of military service. Union and Confederate citizen-officers were all products of this mindset, and the habit of command did not often come naturally to them; therein lay the crux of the difficulty facing citizen-officers on both sides. "The weak point of our service invariably lies here," Higginson lamented, "that the soldier, in nine cases out of ten, utterly detests being commanded, while the officer, in his turn, equally shrinks from commanding. War, to both, is an episode in life, not a profession, and therefore military subordination, which needs for its efficiency to be fixed and absolute, is, by common consent, reduced to a minimum."[13]

For citizen-officers new to command, these problems must have seemed overwhelming, but their plight was not a hopeless one. British, French, and Prussian armies of the Napoleonic era in some degree successfully reflected the citizen-soldier model, and decades of European warfare had informed the professionals in the U.S. Army. That professional example set forth in army regulations and exemplified by West Pointers in turn proved an effective guide for citizen-officers of the Confederate and Union armies.[14] Wise volunteer officers took notice, and professionals from the regular army provided invaluable examples for leaders like Lieutenant Samuel A. Craig of the 105th Pennsylvania Infantry. "When I got a chance I listened to regular officers," Craig wrote in early 1862, "and to volunteers where I could find any who seemed to have good style."[15] Colonel Higginson believed that the best solution for citizen-officers seeking to learn how to command was to master the army's system as set out in regulations. "The system," he believed, "is wonderfully complete for its own ends, and the more one studies it the less one sneers." Though many volunteers were averse to the perplexing labyrinth of army customs and rules, Higginson argued that regulations served a logical and essential purpose. "Many a form which at first seems to the volunteer officer merely cumbrous and trivial he learns to prize at last as almost essential to good discipline."[16]

Even so, adjusting to command could require a gargantuan effort. New officers attempting to command volunteers steeped in the citizen-soldier ethos had to alter or suspend a lifetime of accepted traditions, instincts, and peacetime prerogatives fundamental to their identities as free Americans.[17] There was no magic formula to determine whether citizen-officers would master the challenges of military leadership or develop the requisite mental habits for effective command, nor was there a simple or systematic way for senior commanders to identify and promote promising junior leaders. Theories on what made for good officer material abounded. Confederate lieutenant John M. Porter of the 9th Kentucky Cavalry, who served with the famous cavalryman John Hunt Morgan, believed that a combination of youth and merit made the officers of his unit special and that prudent generals who learned to recognize raw talent in their subordinates could build an effective corps of junior officers. "The entire command embraced the flower of the youth of Kentucky and Tennessee," Porter recalled, "as noble a body of men as ever marched to the sound of music. The officers were all young men; none of the field officers were scarcely more than thirty years old, and the line officers, in almost every instance, were still younger." The vigor of youth, as well as their natural abilities and instinct for the burdens of command, the lieutenant believed, made up for the lack of military experience among his fellow officers. Moreover, Morgan exploited his own authority to appoint officers to positions of responsibility with liberality, a practice that Porter, himself an appointee, heartily endorsed. "General Morgan exercised great care and judgment in the selecting of his officers," he recalled, "and though it was hardly possible to err materially when he had so fine a body from which to select, all being competent, or nearly all, still, it shows his fine judgment to see how finely his regiments were officered, nearly all being his appointees."[18]

    Though generals could rely upon their own instincts and experience to identify and place volunteers with command potential, newly minted junior officers still had to learn the army way of doing things. Company-grade citizen-officers were an amalgam; their many roles included those of caretakers, motivators, disciplinarians, and instructors. Officers had to know when and how to defuse problematic or emotional situations within their companies. They had to learn how to resolve conflicts and manage egos. These men were expected to oversee difficult, wearying, or dangerous tasks to completion, often without guidance from above. They had to familiarize themselves with voluminous regulations and vague or arcane rules and to interpret these to the greatest advantage of their volunteers. Citizen-officers had to lend assistance and guidance to their men when required and to respect them as equal citizens while still maintaining a detached, competent air of appropriate authority. In short, successful Civil War military leadership at the company level was usually a matter of improvisation, requiring creativity, thoughtfulness, and confidence. Citizen-officers mostly taught themselves these skills. There were almost no training regimen for company command in either the Union or Confederate armies. While some regiments attempted to implement volunteer-officer schools or to provide instruction by regular-army officers or military-academy cadets, most junior officers had to learn their new duties on their own.[19] This hands-off approach to training was in sharp contrast with regular-army methods. The regular officer corps was the model for military command, and the regulations were the only detailed guide; consequently, the numerous remaining gaps in citizen-officers' professional knowledge had to be filled through guesswork, experience, or creative solutions. As Higginson put it, "[t]here were a thousand points on which the light of Nature, even aided by 'Army Regulations,' did not instruct him; and his best hints were probably obtained by frankly consulting regular officers, even if inferior in rank."[20] While regulations and handbooks did provide guidance on matters such as setting up a military camp, conducting drill, and filling out reports, they did little or nothing to show novice officers the essential skills of managing interpersonal conflicts, properly exercising military authority, or gaining the confidence or respect of their volunteers to ensure obedience to orders.[21]

Despite these significant shortcomings, examination of Union and Confederate correspondence, memoirs, journals, and the nascent professional literature contemporary to the Civil War reveals certain patterns in both citizen-officers' leadership challenges and the solutions they employed. Most important, to be effective leaders, junior officers learned that they had to treat their volunteers with discretion and sensitivity. Above all, these men had to be attuned to the needs, desires, and welfare of the citizen-soldiers in their charge without allowing their own behavior to undermine their military authority as commanders. "The first essential for military authority lies in the power of command," Higginson explained, "a power which it is useless to analyze, for it is felt instinctively, and it is seen in its results. It is hardly too much to say, that, in military service, if one has this power, all else becomes secondary; and it is perfectly safe to say that without it all other gifts are useless."[22] Higginson, applying the leadership lessons he had learned from experience, argued that in order for their military authority to be convincing, citizen-officers had to integrate the power of command into their leadership style, so much so that it became a habit. All other consequences flowed from this first basic requirement. Officers who successfully established their military authority could become effective commanders, and the key to doing this was to assume the habit of command. Those who failed to learn this had little chance of being a successful military leader or securing the obedience and respect of skeptical volunteers. As Captain C. C. Andrews of the 3rd Minnesota Infantry put it: "In time of war especially, whatever is required to be done at all, is required to be well done. . . . The captain will instruct them that the great thing in this matter is habit. If they become slow, negligent, or tardy in such duties, they will be behindhand when needed to form a line of battle against the enemy."[23]

Company-grade leadership and command require some examination. A vibrant body of modern literature on the subjects of military leadership and the requirements of command exists in contemporary military theory and practice.[24] In the 1860s, however, inexperienced citizen-officers new to their companies had few such resources to draw upon for assistance and little time or opportunity to seek out such help while learning their duties. A number of military manuals, guides, references, and handbooks for officers emerged during the Civil War. This literature was mainly the product of professional officers of the regular army and intended for Union use, though Confederates produced their own literature and unabashedly referred to enemy reference materials for instruction. A smattering of works produced by volunteer junior officers also appeared but did not achieve wide circulation or adoption.[25] Officers on both sides mainly relied upon the regulations promulgated by their respective governments, the intermittent examples of West Pointers or professionals, their own antebellum militia service, and most of all, their intuition and natural abilities to adapt and learn how to command volunteers.

Officers seeking to master the art of company-grade command had to demonstrate effective military leadership, the external demonstration or manifestation of internal values, choices, training, instinct, and talents with the aim to motivate others into action on behalf of a greater goal. It is, in a sense, superficial and depends greatly on an officer's ability to externally project an image of authority that persuades or compels observers to obey. Military leadership is also a great challenge because officers must compel subordinates to engage in activities that they may find foreign, distasteful, uncomfortable, hazardous, or downright repellent. Ultimately, it requires people to take the lives of others and to risk their own welfare in that effort. Officers display their leadership by behaving as leaders should: that is, by exercising command in the ways their subordinates expect them to. Command is the official responsibility and authority exerted by military leaders over subordinates by virtue of rank and position. It is a component of leadership, which also includes the technical skills necessary in organizing and maintaining a military unit capable of carrying out orders and observing discipline.[26] As such, the responsibility of Civil War company command required effective leadership, and citizen-officers' ability to lead influenced virtually every aspect of volunteers' wartime experiences.

Effective company leadership also required citizen-officers to assume the habit of command and to display it through their words and deeds. This required more than merely aping regular-army officers' comportment or conforming to the standards and behaviors spelled out in regulations and field manuals. The habit of command required citizen-officers to negotiate and interpret the demands of volunteers, to maintain their preeminence in the hierarchy of the armies' military culture, and to both teach and demonstrate correct military behavior to citizen-soldiers who fundamentally disagreed with many of its premises, all while maintaining discipline among volunteers. Officers were expected to incorporate the habit of command into their leadership style until it became instinctual. It was absolutely necessary that they assume a guise of military authority and maintain it until it became part of their nature, an obligation that proved difficult for new officers with little or no military background. Antebellum civic life, which stressed individualism, equality, and the prerogatives of citizenship over relationships of power and authority, compounded this difficulty. "Now for the exercise of power there is no preparation like power," Higginson believed, "and nowhere is this preparation to be found, in this community, except in regular army-training." As such, regular officers had been trained to easily assume the habit of command; to give orders and to maintain authority was part of their instinct. Not so for the citizen-officer. "Nothing but great personal qualities can give a man by nature what is easily acquired by young men of very average ability who are systematically trained to command," Higginson explained.[27] Faced with the necessity of quickly assuming the habit of command, new citizen-officers had to acquire the ability to adapt, to learn on the fly, and to take on roles they sometimes found uncomfortable or unnatural.

Many Union and Confederate citizen-officers also had to compartmentalize their republican beliefs and instincts toward equality. They had to first internalize the power of their position and to accept their new status as an authority figure over their former peers. This also included comprehending their place in the larger military hierarchy, an authoritarian order quite alien to the values and traditions of republican civic life. Some citizen-officers assumed that their civilian leadership experience would provide them with the necessary skills for command, but this was not always so. Higginson, echoing a common sentiment of officers who admired the regular-army model, pointedly disagreed with the notion that a volunteer's natural talents or antebellum status could substitute for the benefits of military training. "[I]t was always easier for a man of brains to acquire technical skill than for a person of mere technicality to superadd brains," he maintained, "and that the antecedents of a frontier lieutenant were, on the whole, a poorer training for large responsibilities than those of many a civilian, who had lived in the midst of men, though out of uniform."[28] While citizen-officers with antebellum leadership experience could draw upon their talents and apply them to learning the art of command, Higginson believed that they would always lack the superiority that "professional earnestness" yielded in the regulars. The reason for this, he argued, was that "[t]o the volunteer, the service is still an episode; to the regular, a permanent career." That sense of permanence in a profession, Higginson believed, imparted a thoroughness and perfectionism in regular officers that was exceedingly rare in volunteers. "How often one hears the apology made by citizen-officers, even those of high rank—'Military life is not my profession; I entered the army from patriotism, willing to serve my country faithfully for three years, but of course not pretending to perfection in every trivial detail of a pursuit which I shall soon quit forever.'" Higginson flatly rejected such excuses. "But it is patriotism to think the details *not* trivial," he declared. "If one gives one's self to one's country, let the gift be total and noble."[29]

Historian Fred Albert Shannon, in his award-winning study on the organization and leadership of the Union army, relied heavily on Higginson's observations to argue that West Pointers were best suited for the burdens of high command or staff work and that professional officers were generally superior to citizen-officers because of their background and training.[30] Despite this critique, it is abundantly clear that many Union and Confederate citizen-officers fulfilled their duties with great distinction and effectiveness. Many thousands of junior officers with little or no antebellum command experience comprised the company-grade leadership of both armies; they formed the sinews and tendons that held the armies together and provided the emotional spark necessary for their respective armies to endure the ordeal of the Civil War. Drawn from the communities of volunteers they led into battle, citizen-officers brought deep and abiding connections with their men, connections whose value is difficult to overestimate. Moreover, a number of citizen-officers with little or no professional military training became generals during the Civil War and achieved great distinction in their respective commands.

The challenges and difficulties facing citizen-officers in assuming the habit of command could be alleviated by the unique characteristics of the volunteers in their charge. In 1861 Lieutenant A. R. H. Ranson of the 2nd Virginia Infantry enthused about the virtues and self-regulating traits of his Confederate volunteers. "The men in the Ranks here are not soldiers such as are seen in ordinary Wars," he wrote. "You will find a Father and all his sons and sons in law and Grandsons in one Company. This is illustrated in a Co which came into camp to-day. No stringent rules are required to regulate our Army." The selfless virtue and personal responsibility of these volunteers, Ranson believed, made his duties as their commander much easier. Honorable character did much to ensure the fighting quality of a company, and Ranson felt that his volunteers' attitudes served as a stark contrast to the incompetence and lack of character he was certain must exist in the Union ranks. "Most of them are the best Gentlemen in the land," he declared proudly. "With such men, animated by such motion, where is the power to subdue them. No we will drive back this miserable hord of blunderers as sure as there is a God in Heaven."[31]

The volunteers in Lieutenant Ranson's company were exceptional, for most officers struggled to overcome their citizen-soldiers' resistance to military hierarchy. The nature and contours of Civil War citizen-officers' military authority were subjected to constant pressure from their volunteers, and that authority remained malleable throughout the war. While both the U.S. Army and the Provisional Army of the Confederacy relied on codes, laws, and regulations to govern the relationships between officers and men, in reality this relationship often had to be mapped without the benefit of systems or procedures. Captain John Alexander Dale, commander of an independent Confederate company later incorporated into the 3rd North Carolina Cavalry, described the ambiguous nature of his leadership situation in October 1862. "We are here now by ourselves and do pretty near as we please," he wrote. "I am commander in chief in this place but have nobody to command but my own men I have been wanting to get into a regiment ever since I was elected. [N]ow we have the name of being in one but I do not know who our field officers are and the companies are scatered from the Cape Fear to Virginia and I dont know when we will be called together."[32]

Company-grade citizen-officers like Captain Dale also had all the responsibilities of a volunteer soldier; that is, to follow orders, to maintain their equipment and uniform, to march, to drill, to stand picket duty, and to fight the enemy when called upon. Yet the range of officers' obligations were much more extensive than that of enlisted volunteers, and their responsibilities extended far beyond themselves or their immediate comrades. Citizen-officers had to ensure that not only were they personally competent and capable of executing orders but also that the volunteers under their charge were prepared to comply with those orders. They had to assume personal responsibility for their men's well-being; to see that they had sufficient food and clothing, shelter, firewood, and water; and see to it that they had clean and secure sleeping quarters. Volunteers required ammunition and muskets in good working order, canteens, knapsacks, shoes, tents, medicine, and innumerable other supplies, and every matter of company business seemed to require forms, often called "blanks," which company officers had to fill out and submit to headquarters every day.[33] Many of these tasks seemed distasteful to men unaccustomed to military bureaucracy and institutional hierarchy. Company officers' duties were often boring, tedious, and thankless, and while essential to the existence of their companies, such tasks usually went unnoticed or, worse, rankled the volunteers they were intended to benefit. "This is sunday but I dont hear an[y] church Bells nor See any sabbath School children going to sabbath School," Indianan William Bluffton Miller recorded in his diary in 1863. Instead, he complained, "the Drum and Bugle call are the substitute for the Bells. The company inspection was all the parade we had. That is done to let the officers see if we know how to keep our guns in order and our clothes clean." Miller, ever the stubborn citizen-soldier, found his officers' insistence on adhering to the routine of cleanliness and inspection condescending. "If we did not have them to tell us we would not know when Sunday come," he complained. "A private is not supposed to know anything."[34] Citizen-officers who received unwelcome orders from their superiors had to trust that these would not meet with significant resistance from volunteers like Sergeant Miller. Only effective military authority ensured obedience to such orders. At times this required officers to redirect the ire of their volunteers elsewhere. Company officers could tell grumblers that unpleasant orders came from above and there was no choice but to carry them out, thus reinforcing the hierarchy of military authority as well as emphasizing junior officers' and citizen-soldiers' place in the armies' pecking order.[35]

Military hierarchy emphasized how citizen-officers were set apart from the volunteers they led; the degree of this distinctiveness and separation varied but increased with every step up the ladder of command. Even the least experienced volunteer lieutenant in a Civil War company possessed, through his commission and the authority that went with it, a status apart from the most grizzled and veteran enlisted men. Whether officers rose, fell, or remained in place—and sometimes whether they and their volunteers lived or died—depended on their leadership abilities. Junior-officer leadership meant more than simply commanding volunteers in combat; most of an officer's time was spent in camp or on the march, dealing with discipline, administrative details, drill and training, and seeing to his company's well-being. Junior staff officers led in different ways, supervising a headquarters or unit, seeing to the details of a department, carrying messages and conveying orders, inspecting and reporting, or looking after the needs of senior officers. Whatever their assignment, company-grade officers were directly responsible for discharging their duties and executing orders, and failure to meet these obligations could result in serious consequences. Those who did not meet the expectations of their commanders could not expect to receive preferential treatment simply by virtue of their rank and status. Lieutenant Hannibal Paine of the 26th Tennessee Infantry noted in early 1863 that General Braxton Bragg occasionally had officers and volunteers alike shot to "break the tedious monotony of a dull camp life" in winter quarters near Tullahoma, Tennessee. Paine's morbid declaration may have been intended for shock value, but nevertheless he insisted that "[t]here have been several shot since we have been at this place both officers and privates. It was mostly for misbehavior or cowardice before the enemy in the late battle before Murfreesboro." He admitted, however, that no men in his brigade had been shot and that he chose not to attend any executions personally.[36]

Officers could also be held personally accountable for the failures of their men, some learning that failure to properly supervise their volunteers led to dire personal consequences. Lieutenant John Quincy Adams Campbell of the 5th Iowa Infantry complained that "one of the boys in the company fired a charge of damp powder out of his gun, for which he was arrested by the Colonel and I was arrested by the same *power* because I did not arrest the man who fired the gun. Not being in command of the company, I didn't consider it my business."[37] While campaigning in Virginia, Captain Henry Newton Comey of the 2nd Massachusetts Infantry wrote in his diary, "Secrecy was ordered and enforced to the extent that the Commander of Company D, Capt. Daniel Oakey, was placed under arrest because one of his men lighted a fire."[38] The burden of such personal responsibility, while sometimes harsh, served an essential purpose for junior officers. These men were expected to get results from their volunteers. This expectation could be antithetical to volunteers' basic instincts for survival and self-preservation, to their conceptions of themselves as coequal citizens, and in contravention of their personal or moral reservations about killing. Citizen-officers who lacked the will to compel or persuade their troops to achieve these results were of little military value. When these officers were made personally liable for the shortcomings of their volunteers, they became fully invested in securing obedience.

How, then, did citizen-officers ensure that their orders were obeyed? The most rudimentary method for securing obedience from volunteers was through coercion. The compulsion through external pressure brought to bear by the threat of punishment or consequence, coercion is a necessary element of military authority. Explicit and direct commands, which pressured subordinate troops to complete a task or execute an order, were crucial to achieving a military objective. In principle, however, coercion as an instrument of securing obedience was at odds with the citizen-soldier ethos of the American volunteer. External control by threat of punishment or force was necessary in some cases, but obedience compelled by force was impractical for achieving long-term, large-scale motivation and impossible in armies of independent-minded volunteers led by citizen-officers with little or no military training. Failure to comply with an officer's commands would, theoretically, lead to negative consequences in the form of discipline or punishment. More often than not, however, the dangerous consequence of compulsion was resentment and resistance, and those who chose to command through intimidation or fear could expect little loyalty from their men.[39] "Some officers think a private is a mere dog and are here only for them to domineer over and that accounts in a great measure for the feeling existing between the Rank and File," Sergeant Miller declared in 1863. "The private solder does his duty many times because he is compelled to. Not with the free good will that he would if treated as a white man should be."[40]

Still, coercion was a necessary component of company-grade command in many cases. Coercion is a form of external control central to armies throughout history—command and obedience are the keystones of any military organization, from the smallest squad to the largest army. While simple on its face, the explicit or implicit threat of punishment was not often effective, particularly when dealing with the citizen-soldiers of Civil War armies. Officers who issued their orders in demanding, severe, or disrespectful ways could foster bitterness among their men and consequently gain a reputation as a martinet or a tyrant. Those perceived as abusing their power to punish out of sadism, unfairness, or incompetence would lose the respect of their men, thus imperiling not only that officer's military authority but also possibly the well-being of his company. If a tyrannical officer pushed his volunteers' patience beyond the breaking point, he had few options left except the humiliation of resignation. Confederate volunteer Val C. Giles of the 4th Texas Infantry recalled the embarrassing departure of an especially demanding officer who, after enduring as much of his volunteers' abuse as he could stomach, "said when he left them that if he had to associate with devils he would wait till he went to hell, where he could select his own company."[41]

Once an officer gained a reputation as an authoritarian with his men, it could be exceedingly difficult to shake, and future demands that volunteers obey orders could trigger their immediate and instinctual resistance. Sergeant Miller of the 57th Indiana Infantry vented his anger at the heavy-handed punishment meted out by the officers in his regiment. "After Breakfast I was put on extra police duty for being absent at Roll Call last night. That is military and a man never gets any credit for doeing duty and if he happens to commit a little misdemeanor he is put on extra duty or punished for it. I find the American Soldier can be pursuaded better than driven and Some of our Officers who couldent hire a darky at five cents a day at home like to Show their Authority here." Miller's outrage resulted not from the fact that he had been punished for an infraction, but rather from what he saw as the disproportional severity of the sanctions. "They are the most tyranicle and over-bearing and have few if any friends among their men," he grumbled. "But others who indulge their men a little have good discipline and plenty of the best of friends. Our Officers have to drive their men and are fussing and fumeing about Something all the time." Miller, like many citizen-soldiers, believed he was honor bound to resist this sort of tyranny. "I would not give a cent for a Soldier that will not stand up for his rights," he declared. "He never ought to enlist."[42]

Volunteers like Giles and Miller had a keen sense of citizen-officers' motives behind their demands. Union and Confederate volunteers alike were usually willing to obey their officers' orders, even the most dangerous, demeaning, or apparently foolhardy ones, when they believed they were being asked to do these things for the correct reasons. On the other hand, when they suspected an officer's demands were dishonorable, unrelated to military necessity, or designed to curry favor with superiors, they resisted or refused to comply. Citizen-soldiers loathed officers they believed to be profligate with the lives of their own men, particularly when it was meant to achieve personal glory or promotion. Few things were more destructive to the morale of a company than an officer who did not care about their lives and well-being. Volunteers accepted the fact that their leaders had to exert a certain amount of pressure to motivate them to obey difficult orders, but citizen-officers had to walk a fine line in placing exceptionally burdensome demands upon their men. Not only did officers have to seem rational in their demands but they also could not ask too much of the men or expect them to obey orders for the wrong reasons.

When officers and volunteers inevitably disagreed about the constraints of their command relationship, coercion could be a particularly effective way to resolve an impasse. Lieutenant Willoughby Babcock of the 75th New York Infantry wrote of an extreme example when volunteers in his unit threatened to mutiny over the terms of their reenlistment. When only four volunteers obeyed an order to report for roll call, the captain of Babcock's company drew his pistol, aimed it at the mutineers, and demanded that they all fall in. "Some of our men grumbled very much to have a loaded pistol presented at their heads," Babcock wryly wrote, "but I think the spectacle will not harm them. There are no signs of insubordination now."[43] Coercion was sometimes necessary, but wise officers used it sparingly, for such measures could have an immensely destructive effect on volunteers' morale. "I had about as lief go to jail as undertake the command of any company in this regiment, so utterly demoralized are the men," Babcock later wrote of his unit. "It looks as though [our officers] proposed to make Pack Mules of us in addition to what we may have to do besides," complained Sergeant Miller of Indiana. "[B]ut a private has no soul in the eyes of Some Officers."[44]

Some volunteers, particularly Confederates, balked at what they saw as unreasonable encroachments by their officers on their very identities, bitterly resenting being treated, as they reasoned, like black slaves. Not only did citizen-officers' arbitrary military authority impinge upon their rights as citizens and volunteers, they felt, but it also called into question their status as free white men. As Thomas Reese Lightfoot of the 6th Alabama Infantry complained in 1861: "A soldier is worse than any negro on [the] Chatahooche river. He has no privileges whatever. He is under worse task-masters than any negro. He is not treated with any respect whatever. His officers may insult him and he has no right to open his mouth and dare not do it." Lightfoot added, however, that "[m]y officers have always treated me with the utmost courtesy, and I expect will always treat me so for I am going to obey orders."[45]

The element of persuasion was far more effective and essential to citizen-officer leadership than coercion. Historian Gerald F. Linderman identifies the prescription for the exercise of command in a Civil War unit as a fusion of authority and empathy, leniency and consistency, and above all persuasion. Volunteers desired that their officers share in their hardships and required that their leaders express sympathy and understanding for their problems. When the men inevitably erred or fell short of the army's standards, they anticipated that their officers would exercise good judgment and not punish them too harshly. They required, as equal citizens, to be treated fairly and justly by their officers and expected commanders to be sensitive enough to lead them through persuasion without abusing their authority.[46] Historian Lorien Foote also describes the efficacy of persuasion over coercion in maintaining order in the Union army. "Rather than organizational and institutional discipline, the Union army relied on pervasive cultural ideals of duty, self-control and self-discipline to keep the volunteers in line and fighting. Officers had to earn obedience rather than compel it."[47]

Citizen-officers and their enlisted volunteers also needed to place their trust in one another: volunteers had to trust their officers' abilities and their interest in their subordinates' well-being, and officers had to trust their volunteers' consent to obedience and dedication to their duties. Moreover, citizen-soldiers had to shed their instinct that they had a natural right to participate in the decision-making process. War was not, nor could it ever be, an exercise in democracy. Though they could choose their officers through election, afterward volunteers were required to obey them without question. Nevertheless, obedience was not a foregone conclusion. Colonel Higginson observed that "[*i*]*mplicit* obedience must be admitted still to be a rare quality in our army; nor can we wonder at it. In many cases there is really no more difference between officers and men, in education and breeding, than if the one class were chosen by lot from the other; all are from the same neighborhood, all will return to the same pursuits side by side." Consequently, "every officer knows that in a little while each soldier will again become his client or his customer, his constituent or his rival. Shall he risk offending him for life in order to carry out some hobby of stricter discipline?"[48] Rice C. Bull, a volunteer serving in the 123rd New York Infantry, explained that his regiment "was made up entirely of men from Washington County and each Company of men from the same or adjacent townships; their officers were older men, the friends of their fathers and mothers."[49] As historian Charles E. Brooks writes, Civil War officers had to "persuade and cajole" their men, who demanded that orders given to them be "reasonable and necessary" or else answer to them, to their families, and to the community once the war was over.[50]

The single most important way in which junior officers could secure the obedience and confidence of their volunteers was by demonstrating competence. For many, particularly those serving during the early months of the war, this required more than a little bluffing or playacting on their part. The learning curve for a Civil War company officer was steep, particularly for the many who lacked significant training. Volunteers, themselves uncertain of their own abilities, naturally looked to their officers to provide guidance, emotional stability, and reassurance in moments of doubt. Sometimes the mere appearance of competence in an officer, if convincing, was sufficient to persuade volunteers of his value as a commander. Stephen F. Fleharty of the 102nd Illinois Infantry was amazed at the impression that citizen-officers made upon his comrades because of their confidence and the competent way that they instructed the companies on the basics of drill. "[T]he embryo officers prosecuted the work of drilling and instructing the men with the energy of those who believed the perpetuity of the Government depended upon their individual exertions," Fleharty recalled. If an officer happened to bring a modicum of military experience with him, so much the better, while those who chanced to have combat experience were deemed experts in military matters by raw volunteers. "And with what supreme awe we looked upon a veteran officer—and there were several of this class in camp; perchance the heroes of one battle, and a three month's term of service. *Their* word was law. Who then would have dared to question their decision of any mooted point in tactics?"[51] Lieutenant Albert Livingston of the 3rd Florida Infantry succinctly told his parents in 1864, "Our authorities know what they are about & as long as this is the case the citizen & soldier should be content."[52]

Naturally, volunteers' sense of awe brought on by inexperience diminished as they gained their own experience; nevertheless, displays of competence were indispensable to building the trust relationship between citizen-officers and their men throughout the war. In an 1863 reorganization of Company F of the elite 1st U.S. Sharpshooters, for instance, company officers were chosen largely based on their combat experience and record. "The new officers had been connected with the company from its organization," records the official company history. "[T]hey were all roll of honor men, straight up from the ranks, and were men of distinguished courage and skill, as they had demonstrated already on at least fifteen occasions upon which the Army of the Potomac had been engaged in pitched battles with the enemy."[53] Volunteers' absolute requirement that their officers display competence could manifest itself in unusual ways. Soldier Albert O. Marshall described an 1862 election in Company A, 33rd Illinois Infantry, in which the men's sense of self-preservation overrode their deep esteem for their captain and delayed his deserved promotion. Captain Leander H. Potter, according to Marshall, was a capable and highly regarded company commander who was a candidate for lieutenant colonel of his regiment during its reenlistment elections. Yet the popular Potter received only six votes of the seventy cast. This, wrote Marshall, was "one of the strangest votes.... And stranger still, the six votes [in favor of Potter] were cast by the six men in the company the least friendly to him. The majority voted against him because they wanted him to remain in command of their own company." Rather than trust their welfare to a strange new captain, the volunteers of Company A preferred to keep their talented commander; they understood the value of an officer who knew his duties and placed the welfare and survival of his men first.[54]

Competence was crucial, and citizen-officers' incompetence could have corrosive effects on morale and the command relationships within companies. In February 1862 Sergeant James M. Williams of the 21st Alabama Infantry described how he undercut a company officer and friend because of that man's inept performance. "I have often spoken of the incompetence of Lieut. [Nathaniel] Whiting as an officer," wrote Williams. "You will not be surprised that there has been an explosion in the company on his account—Day before yesterday a very severe note was circulated, and signed by nearly everybody that was present in camp, reflecting upon him as an officer, and calling upon him to resign his office—I was among the signers of course." Williams expressed little regret about his destabilizing actions. "Nat. will never forgive me; he seems to look upon me as the Brutus whose friendly hand struck the unkindest cut of all—he says he will resign—but, somehow, I don't believe he will."[55] Lieutenant Whiting submitted his resignation in March, and the ambitious sergeant began angling for the post. For the next several weeks, Williams continually updated his wife on Whiting's status and worried that his opportunity for a commission would be foiled by red tape and incompetence. "The two resignations [including Whiting's] have not been heard from—I think that with their accustomed stupidity our officers have made a blunder and forwarded them without being properly endorsed here, in which case no notice will be taken of them," Williams told her. "Old Nat, is very sick of the soldiering that we have up here," he added, "and would give anything to be out of the scrape." Within days Williams got his desired promotion and took Whiting's place as a lieutenant in the company.[56]

Sergeant Major John Mark Smither of the 5th Texas Infantry likewise complained about the ineptitude of his officers and the favoritism that permitted them to rise over more suitable candidates—namely, himself. "Now I am not by any means ambitious, at least not too much so," he explained to his uncle from Petersburg's trenches in 1864, "but I am tired of being ordered around by every little squirt of a 2nd Lt. who can work around and get himself elected by a company of backwoods soldiers when I feel and know myself superior to the majority of them in point of qualifications requisite to the making of a good officer." Smither's resentment of such partiality ran deep and extended beyond his own unit. "There are plenty of officers in our Brigade and Army who are perfect numskulls," he complained. "It has not been from any fault of mine that I have not been promoted long ago." Though Smither was favored for a commission by a particular officer, his ambition been foiled by the death of that man and the subsequent reorganization of the unit he hoped to join. An opportunity to fill a vacant adjutancy vanished after his regimental commander was wounded and captured. The new colonel "recommended a favorite of his and obtained for him the Adjuntancy of the r and I have to do nearly all of his duties with my own. He is a clean young gentleman but rather a weak stick for an officer."[57] Smither never received the desired commission, ending the war as an enlisted man.[58]

Few errors could undermine or even destroy a citizen-officer's attempts to establish his military authority more quickly than obvious displays of incompetence or hypocrisy. Officers, like volunteers, possessed different degrees of ability, and soldiers could be exceptionally forgiving of an inexperienced leader's honest mistakes. But a lazy or inept officer could irreparably damage his standing with his volunteers or his fellow officers in a few moments. In 1861 Lieutenant Martin V. B. Richardson of the 4th New Hampshire Infantry described to his sister the downfall of two incompetent officers in his regiment. "There is a Capt who has shaken down the Government by making out False Pay Roles," he reported. "Col [Thomas J.] Whipple is under arrest for getting drunk and insulting Officers of equal Rank in other Regiments. He has been drunk most of the time since we landed, and it is no use to try to hide the matter any longer." Richardson feared for the well-being of his unit should the colonel retain his command. "If he remanes with the Regt He will have to alter his course or the Regiment will go to the d——l," he predicted. Not even the chaplain's intervention could redeem Whipple: "I am sorry that it has come to this pass. Mr [Martin] Willis carried the Pledge to him and he signed it, not to drink any more ardent spirits. But it will be impossible for Col Tom to let rum alone. He has steeped himself too long already—Poor fool, when he is so smart and when he has had such a good chance to be somebody." Richardson, dreading retribution for his incautious words about his commanding officer, begged his sister not to discuss the situation at home. "Don't tell any body how you get this new's [sic] about Whipple for should he remain, some of his friend at home might report me."[59]

Effective leadership by example had to be convincing, consistent, and constant. Moreover, volunteers believed that they were entitled to an explanation when their officers' demands struck them as unjust or unreasonable, or when officers did not live up to the expectations they maintained for the men. Philip Daingerfield Stephenson of the 13th Arkansas Infantry recalled his officers' unseemly behavior on one memorable Christmas and the loss of respect for them that resulted. "On that occasion, everyone got beastly drunk—officers and men, the whole army indeed, as far as I can remember! The preparations for it were deliberate. The carousing place of our regimental officers was our Captain's tent (Capt. George B. Hunt.) . . . Egg-nog was the liquor used, and by morning nearly every officer in the regiment was 'under the table.'" Stephenson primly noted, "My brother and myself were about the only sober men in the regiment and spent our time carrying men to their tents."[60] Lieutenant Babcock of New York likewise lamented his company commander's apparent laziness about mastering the intricacies of his duties and found the officer's irresponsible and hypocritical approach to command irritating. "Our Capt. don't know anything and won't learn nor try seriously to learn. He keeps out of the way and leaves me to attend to all the details of business. We came here 24 hours ago and have paid no attention yet to the orders in relation to roll-calls, parades, or anything of the sort. I suppose this p.m. I shall muster the company and command them at 'full dress parade' as it is called."[61] Babcock later worried that "Capt. [Isaac S.] Catlin is not doing much in the way of posting himself in military tactics. He conducts the men to and from dinner or supper with some grace and propriety, but so far as drilling is concerned, he does nothing. I am working at it some and learning a little."[62] Union volunteer and future officer Levi Duff worried about the welfare of his company when left in the hands of incompetent lieutenants. "Our captain has been sick ever since we arrived in Washington," Duff wrote to his wife in August 1861. "He went home yesterday but expects to return again in about ten days. We will be in a bad fix if we should happen to loose him," he added. "Our Lieutenants are of no account at all. Instead of improving as men would ordinarily under such circumstances, they are getting worse every day, at least it seems so. They have lost the confidence of every member in the company." Duff at least tried to keep his misgivings about the lieutenants to himself, unlike several of his comrades. "Some of the men talk very freely & loud about them, but I take care to keep my mouth closed, well knowing that talk will not better the matter, but on the other hand increase the discontent in the company[.]"[63]

Effective citizen-officers not only had to demonstrate competence and consistency but also had to display confidence in their own abilities and in the capabilities of their volunteers. Soldiers trusted commanders who were confident and at ease with their roles as officers and were less likely to question or resist their military authority. Confidence and cockiness were by no means equivalent; a cocky citizen-officer would likely merit the scorn of his men, while a confident officer often inspired affection and obedience. Confident officers possessed the knowledge and wherewithal to face challenges, solve problems, comply with orders, and display optimism in the face of adversity. Lieutenant Francis M. Guernsey of the 32nd Wisconsin Infantry was one such leader; he was practically sunny when wrote to his wife in January 1863 about the tribulations of war. "A soldiers life in view of all the hardships and dangers he has to endure has many attractions," Guernsey told her. "[Y]ou may laugh, Fanny at the idea and wonder what attractions there can be in forced marches, raw pork & hard crackers, and a bed on mother earth with a broad blue sky for a shelter I suppose it is the free and easy way we live constantly exposed to danger, ever on the watch, and always in a state of excitement."[64] Captain Robert E. Park of the 12th Alabama

Infantry likewise labored to display optimism and good cheer, even in the direst of circumstances. At the Battle of Gettysburg, Park's company took a severe mauling. Afterward, he recalled a particularly horrifying scene. "We continued to advance and soon made a charge upon the enemy not far from the Seminary. We ran them some distance and halted. There Lieutenant Wright was wounded in the head, by my side." The captain soon realized the seriousness of his subordinate's condition. "I spoke to him and he calmly asked me to examine his wound, and tell him frankly whether I thought it would prove fatal," remembered Park. "I looked at his bloody head, lifted the hair from over the wound and found his brain exposed, the bone on top of his head having been carried away. I answered him cheerfully and reassuringly, bidding him lie close to the ground until he could be removed." Knowing the rest of his company was watching him, Park gave Wright a drink from his canteen, ensured that the wounded lieutenant would be carried safely from the field, and returned to the fight.[65]

Along with confidence and optimism, officers had to establish and project a convincing command presence to be effective leaders. Command bred authority, and authority ensured obedience. While essential to establishing a volunteer junior officer's military authority, a command presence took time to establish. Meanwhile, citizen-officers seeking to reinforce their military standing over their citizen-soldiers could depend on the more immediate effects of external leadership cues. The trappings of office, the presentation of officerlike comportment, and above all the projection of the habit of command helped create legitimacy and bolstered their efforts to persuade the men of their fitness to lead. Historian John Keegan characterizes command as a mask, a role to be assumed at need to achieve the necessary effects for establishing and maintaining the authority necessary to accomplish the ends of leadership. In Civil War companies the persona of command heavily depended on intangible factors like a citizen-officer's presence, charisma, and personal magnetism. So much of a military leader's ability to convince his troops to submit to his authority depends on what Keegan calls "mystification," the "medium through which love and fear, neither ever precisely defined, cajole the subordinate to follow, often to anticipate, the commander's will."[66]

Citizen-officers' effective displays of presence created a strong impression in volunteers, helping them form a basis for persuading the men to consent to their authority. Some novice officers found it useful to practice their command presence and perfect the persona of the authoritative leader.

Pennsylvanian Samuel Craig, for instance, noted the difficulty of projecting a convincing command presence in drill and described his improvised solution to the problem. "Have found since taking hold as an officer that my duties differ vastly from those before as a private soldier in the ranks," the lieutenant wrote in his diary in 1862. "Until now I had never uttered a command to another soldier as a soldier. So during the first weeks I would slip away to some distant secluded spot, and there by myself practice my voice in giving commands in the manual of arms, marches and usual maneuvers of drill to the surrounding stumps and trees." Presenting a confident command presence was a key leadership technique. Moreover, volunteers expected their officers to know the solutions to problems and to display the temperament necessary to overcome obstacles while under pressure. Craig discovered that competence alone was not enough to ensure his military authority; to be an effective commander, he had to convince his volunteers that he was a leader. "I *knew* the commands, yes, had been myself drilled with them, and had studied them in books of tactics, but to give commands in proper voice, inflections, tones and accent, and in good style, as these older officers have learned somehow, is not at first just so very easy."[67]

Effective citizen-officers also had to lead their volunteers with clarity and decisiveness, even when circumstances were confusing, unnerving, or detrimental due to errors. Officers were reluctant at times to issue orders that they knew would be contentious or unpopular because they dreaded open disobedience and the undermining of their authority. Guard duty, an especially onerous burden for men who preferred a full night of sleep instead, was a particular troublesome spot for some officers; many simply declined to order their volunteers to do it. "I don't believe there are 20 regiments in the Army of the Potomac in which Guard-duty is properly done," complained Captain Robert Gould Shaw of the 2nd Massachusetts Infantry. "A great many of the officers are worthless & are therefore very angry when anyone tries to oblige them to do their duty."[68]

Other officers had to contend with the ingenuity of their own disobedient volunteers who worked tirelessly to circumvent orders. In 1863 Iowa volunteer Charles O. Musser described this insubordinate behavior on campaign in western Arkansas: "[W]hen we Stop at a plantation, the poultry, pigs, and beef has to Suffer. Some of our boys just now passed here, driveing a fat Steer. [T]hey are taking him out of Sight of the officers to kill him." Musser bragged that his regiment's officers were powerless to stop their volunteers' pillaging. "We play some Sharp games on our officers. What an old soldier can't think of is not worth thinking of in the way of forageing or any thing connected with the life of a Soldier. [W]hen there is orders not to Shoot, we bayonette the hogs and beef [instead]."[69]

Volunteers were less likely to engage in this sort of insubordination if they trusted their officers. Trust between volunteers and their officers, a fragile sentiment at best, was essential to establishing an officer's military authority. The cultivation of personal relationships and the feelings of common cause, kinship, and trust that resulted from these bonds greatly assisted citizen-officers in their efforts to persuade their men that they were commanders worthy of loyalty and obedience. Trust, perhaps more than any other aspect of the military relationship, depended on the establishment of a personal connection between officers and their men. On the one hand, citizen-soldiers had to trust that their officers would not abuse their temporary surrender of personal liberty by leading imprudently. On the other hand, citizen-officers had to trust volunteers that, despite their status as equals in the Republic, they would obey and conform to the indignities and discipline of military life. There was no greater sacrifice for a citizen than to surrender his most fundamental privileges: his life and liberty. For the antebellum citizen-soldier, then, to give up freedom and reduce himself to subservience and almost total dependence on another was offensive to his nature. But everything depended on this tenuous and, to their mind, unnatural arrangement—the lives of individuals, of units, of armies, and ultimately of nations were at stake.[70]

Direct appeals to loyalty or to emotional bonds between citizen-officers and volunteers had to be highly individualized. The success of such measures depended largely upon connections of camaraderie, loyalty, and common cause that wise commanders labored diligently to cultivate. Company officers who could build a rapport with their volunteers were able to translate that connection into a relationship of mutual trust, essential to ensuring that their orders would be carried out. Those who failed in this did so at their own peril. Brothers Walter and Robert Carter of the 22nd Massachusetts Infantry described their company commander's disconnected manner in unforgiving terms. "Captain [John J.] Thompson is one of the kind of men not at all genial or easy to get acquainted with," they wrote in 1862. "[H]e is not in the least *upper crust,* for he messes with his men, and hates salutations and red tape, but he is a stern man, hard to get on the right side of, and difficult to understand; and now, while sick, is grouty and cross." The Carter brothers summed up their captain's leadership style on a spiritless note. "He is a brave man, and a good officer, I guess, but, as a man, with all the feeling natural to us, I don't think much of him." Thompson would later be cashiered from the service after going absent while on sick leave.[71]

Citizen-officers were unlikely to be successful if they could not earn the respect of the men, and the best of them made a conscious effort to maintain personal connections with their troops. Confederate volunteer Lorenzo Miears of the 3rd Arkansas Infantry remembered that a favored company officer "would come around of night & chat with his men. He called me his Little Sargent." Another of Miears's favorite officers "was little in stature but big in gas, a great talker & a good officer & man in every way."[72] Many volunteers came to see their officers in familial terms, as fathers, uncles, or older brothers whose courage under fire and willingness to share their hardships defined their worth as commanders.[73] Captain Andrews of the 3rd Minnesota Infantry urged his fellow officers to cultivate these connections with their volunteers and emphasized their familial nature. "In his private intercourse, the captain should be kind and affable toward his men," he explained. "In some sense, he stands *in loco parentis* to them." These connections were essential to maintaining the trust necessary to preserve citizen-officers' military authority. Andrews believed that, ideally, "[t]here should be free opportunity for the interchange of views and sympathies" between officers and men, that an officer "should always be accessible to his men."[74] Occasionally, this meant relaxing discipline and overlooking minor infractions of the rules in the interests of cementing the bonds between leaders and subordinates. Captain William Harrison Martin, a company commander in the 4th Texas Infantry of the famous Texas Brigade, perfectly embodied this easygoing command style. Martin earned the nickname "Old Howdy" from his volunteers because he "always tipped his fingers to his hat brim and said 'howdy' rather than saluting." Apparently, though a brave officer, Martin was passed over for promotion until late in the war because his superiors believed that "he cared too much for his men to be a good military leader" and would allow them to drink and carouse while responding with merely a "stiff warning."[75] Whether strict disciplinarians or easygoing father figures, citizen-officers usually possessed an advantage over their regular-army counterparts because they shared common origins and civilian backgrounds with the volunteers they led. These officers were not merely military authority figures; most had shared pasts and long-term associations with the men in their companies and with the neighborhoods and communities from which they came. Officers had to balance the demands of their duties and the requirements of their orders not only with the emotional attachments that they brought with them to the field but also with the knowledge that they would one day return to civilian life alongside the very men they had led into battle.

Familiarity and active involvement were indispensable components of the relationship between citizen-officers and volunteers. Union volunteer William Henry Harrison Clayton believed that troops from the western states had an advantage over their eastern comrades in that regard, contrasting the perceived priggishness and detachment of eastern citizen-officers with the easy familiarity of their western counterparts in his own 19th Iowa Infantry. "I had heard a great deal said about the superiority of western troops over eastern troops, but was inclined to disbelieve it, but I think that there is in fact a great difference," he wrote to his brother in 1864. "For this there is several reasons one great reason is that the men do not have confidence in their officers. Their officers do not associate with the men as ours do, and will not let any one go to their *tent* unless he has special business there." Clayton, like many other citizen-soldiers, was immediately suspicious of aloof or pretentious officers unwilling to foster what he saw as a healthy degree of familiarity and respect with their volunteers. "They are also much more strict," he added, "and put on a great deal of *style*."[76] Charles Musser's grievances toward the officers in his regiment echoed those of his fellow Iowan. "[I]f we had officers that were officers, we would be better off," groused Musser from his camp near Helena, Arkansas, in the summer of 1863. "[The commander] has not been with the regiment Since we left St Louis. [W]e do not know where he is now." The officer's absence left the unit bereft of leadership and useless for its military purpose. "[W]e are like a flock of sheep without a leader," Musser complained.[77]

When the delicate balance of familiarity between officers and their men was upset, the consequences for a unit's morale could be toxic. In April 1863 Peter Welsh, a volunteer serving in the Irish Brigade's 28th Massachusetts Infantry, complained bitterly when the regiment's commander, Colonel Richard Byrnes, a regular-army officer prior to the war, brought in several new lieutenants as replacement company officers. "[The colonel] is not proving to be so good an officer for the regiment as he appeard to be at first," Welsh wrote to his wife. "[H]e has done a very mean action of late which has caused a great deal of trouble among the officers and will cause a goodeal more," he told her. "[I]nstead of promoting men of his own regiment to be leutenents to fill vacancies he has got sergants and privates out of other Mass regiments and brought them into this regiment[.]" Welsh suspected that Byrnes was acting mainly out of self-interest, filling up depleted companies with strangers in order to preserve his own command of the regiment.[78] "[T]his is the meanest act i have heard of any comanding officer doing in this army and especialy as his motives are purely selfish," the soldier groused. If the 28th Massachusetts fell below the troop strength proscribed by recent rules, the "Colonel would lose comand of it as the law provides that such batallions shall be comanded by no higher officer then a major[.] [S]o in order to keep his own fat birth he has done a great injustice to the men a great many of whom are much more competent to hold comisions then the strangers he brought in," Welsh fumed. The old company officers of 28th Massachusetts collectively protested Byrnes's actions, which led him to place at least two captains under arrest. "[O]ne of them is our captain," explained Welsh, "who is a gentleman in every way and a brave soldier those two [officers] were the leaders of the oppisition to his scheme so he tried to wreak his wrath on them he had them court marshaled but made nothing of it[.]" The regiment was under orders to move out, however, so Colonel Byrnes had no choice but to turn the offending officers loose. "[He] released them from arest to take comand of their companies and when they came to take comand we gave them three rousing cheers," Welsh gloated, "and that mad[e] him so mad that he ordered them under arest again and they have not been released yet[.]" Though Byrnes went on to compile a distinguished combat record before his death at Cold Harbor in 1864, Welsh and others apparently never forgave the colonel for his behavior.[79] "[There] is a good many of our officers resighning and i think the most of the old officers will resighn if the Colonel remains in comand," he grumbled.[80] In fact, by the fall of 1863 Welsh's prediction came true: his captain resigned after the incident, and "our company was left then without any officer but a young fellow who was not long promoted a second Leutenant[.]"[81] As late as 1864 Welsh continued to suspect Byrnes of corruption in his selection of company-grade officers. "That mean scoundrel of a Colonel of ours is sending out a lot more strange officers to the regiment," Welsh seethed that year. "[I]t is generly believed here that he has been selling comissions in Boston some of them are men who were dismissed from the service in other regiments[.]"[82] Suspicions about the quality of these new additions may have been justified; of the four new lieutenants who joined the regiment in the spring of 1864, one had his commission canceled, a second was court-martialed and reduced to the ranks, and a third resigned his post within a few weeks.[83]

For outside officers assigned to unfamiliar volunteer units, many had to contend with an immediate disadvantage in establishing personal connections with their men. New officers had to resort to a variety of techniques to cultivate rapport and trust and establish their essential authority. Lieutenant Edward Lee, newly transferred to Company D of the 27th Massachusetts Infantry in March 1862, wrote to his mother of the problems he faced upon taking charge of volunteers unknown to him. Lee's captain had gone on leave, "thus leaving me in command of a company not a single man of whom I knew, & not knowing what had been his course of treatment, a rather delicate position, as a new man in carrying out his own ideas of discipline might cut across his commander's peculiar hobby. We all have one you know." Lacking the essential personal connections with his new command, he was fortunate that the men were a well-behaved group. Soon they accepted the lieutenant's military authority, much to his relief. "I presume I shall experience no particular vexation, the men being a very good group of men & quiet & well disposed," Lee assured his mother. "I was introduced to them just before going out to Dress Parade on Monday. Was rec'd with immense applause!" Lee could rightfully boast of this unusually warm reception. Lacking a shared past with his men, the young officer decided to appeal to his volunteers' emotions to establish his military authority. "Called upon to respond in a few *feeble remarks,* touching in a few *eloquent* words upon the topics of patriotism, duty to our *'bleeding'* country, the *necessity of obedience to orders* (that I brought in *heavy*) winding up with a tribute of admiration of all soldiers wearing the blue uniform, the 27th reg't especially & Company D. in particular (renewed applause), taken altogether a very *touching* scene." Lee wryly concluded that his speech would "appear in the next issue of Frank Leslie from sketches by our own artist taken on the spot—there now, if that isn't sensation for you, what is?!!!"[84] Self-deprecation aside, through intuition and experience, and to his good fortune, Lee was able to achieve one of the subtlest and most difficult tasks facing military leaders new to company command—namely, securing the loyalty and submission of an unfamiliar company of volunteers. Had he not been able to persuade them that he was an officer worth following, the lieutenant's tenure as commander would have been far more difficult, if not impossible.

Effective officers like Edward Lee also appealed to the nationalism and patriotism of their volunteers to motivate them or inspire them to endure hardship. "It requires a pure article of patriotism, and a large quantity of it," mused John Beatty, commanding officer of the 3rd Ohio Infantry, "to make one oblivious for months at a time of all the comforts of civil life."[85] Beatty, whose regiment saw hard service in Virginia, was amazed by the patriotic fervor of his men in the face of adversity. After a six-hour march in a constant downpour, the Ohioans camped, lit their fires, and began a rousing chorus of "The Star Spangled Banner" to keep their spirits up. "A hundred voices join in," Beatty recounted in his diary, "and the very mountains, which loom up in the fire-light like great walls, whose tops are lost in the darkness, resound with a rude melody befiting so wild a night and so wild a scene."[86] But there were limits to the efficacy of patriotic fervor as a motivating instrument in an officer's arsenal. William Wilson, who commanded the 6th New York Infantry, scoffed at the sentimental image of the "heroic volunteer bidding good-bye to wife and children, and rushing to the field with 'patriotism, glory or death' as his watch-words." He thought differently: "This view of the case is absolutely absurd. The American volunteer was a high-class man for the position of a private soldier. In fact he represented the brain, muscle, and will, of the nation embattled. At the same time he was by no manner of means a fool, and of all other created beings he had the least possible romance about him." Wilson was pragmatic about of the uses and limits of patriotism, putting far more stock in the mutual understanding hewn out of the command relationships officers established with their volunteers than in the sentiments of nationalism or ardor. The typical Civil War volunteer was, to Wilson, "in fact, a strong, cool man, brave by heredity . . . clever enough to recognize the fact that to carry out his contract of service obedience and discipline were essential, but not in any shape a 'gusher.'"[87] Nevertheless, patriotic zeal could prove a powerful sustaining force in dark times. Anticipating deadly fighting in Tennessee in the summer of 1863, the Indianan William Miller declared: "Let it come but I wonder who or how many of us will be left to tell about it in years to come and think with pride when they Soldiered for the Union. Their names will pass to generations unborne and be blessed by them for protecting the Union."[88]

While shared pasts and mutual respect helped citizen-officers establish and maintain personal connections with their men, a lack of familiarity could also be exploited to advantage by unscrupulous volunteers who constantly and persistently tested the boundaries of an officer's authority. Lieutenant Samuel Storrow of the 2nd Massachusetts Infantry recorded an incident in his diary when his men tested the limits as soon as he arrived in his new company. "Entered duty today," Storrow wrote during the Atlanta Campaign. "Was assigned last night at parade to Co. D. Capt. Oakey is north on leave of absence & I am in command of the Company. Corps. Bruce, Tooms, & [?] were absent from tatto[o] roll call last night. They reported that they had been down town to buy tobacco. Had them up this morning & on Capt. Gr[afton's] (Off. of the day) recommendation let them off, telling them that if they did well they would hear nothing more about it."[89] Storrow's leniency may have won him some temporary favor among the volunteers, but he struggled to maintain discipline among them for the rest of his time in the company. Later, while messing with his fellow officers, the lieutenant noted, "At dinner the subject of familiarity between officers & men was brought up, remarks being made in animated version upon the conduct of some of our line officers." Storrow learned his lesson about maintaining appropriate formality with the men after the tobacco incident, deciding to change his approach and establish his military authority through the stern application of discipline. Five days later he punished the greater part of his company, including a number of sergeants, upon discovering "almost universal" drunkenness and gambling after the theft of two barrels of whiskey from the company commissary. Storrow wrote that the "guard-house was full, & the Officer's own room was crowded with men bucked & gagged, being obstreperous cases. . . . It was the biggest drunk ever known in the annals of the 2nd. But it only served to show the strict discipline[,] for retribution followed, severe and speedy." The offenders were arrested, those with noncommissioned rank had it stripped, and the rest were trussed up as punishment, or as Storrow phrased it, "graced the trees around camp."[90]

Stern discipline, while essential for rebellious volunteers, was still a poor substitute for personal connections in building loyalty. These ties occasionally evolved beyond loyalty, however, into a sense of paternalism. Citizen-officers sometimes imagined their roles as elder brothers or fathers to their men. Historian Peter S. Carmichael believes that this relationship was especially pronounced among Confederate officers of privileged backgrounds, who developed an elitist view toward the rank and file in their charge. Southern junior officers, particularly those from aristocratic or slaveholding classes, often saw themselves as socially and morally superior to the common men they led, thus a sense of paternalism came naturally. Many of these elite young men had been conditioned to exercise authority in a hierarchical society, and even upper-class Southerners without formal military training could rather naturally adopt the habit of command more easily than officers without this upbringing and outlook.[91]

Some elite officers were willing to endure a bit of teasing to reinforce their image as benevolent fathers or indulgent older brothers to their irreverent, if affectionate, volunteers. Captain Richard W. Corbin, a young staff officer from an elite Virginia family, described the ribbing he took from the rank and file about his immaculate appearance while serving in the trenches near Petersburg in 1864. "My saddle, that masterpiece of English saddlery, and my boots, those masterpieces of French cordwainers, are the objects of never-ending admiration on the part of the officers of this army," Corbin wrote to his mother, "but the men, who must be excused for not being so appreciative (poor souls) are disposed to be a little sarcastic at my expense. When they are marching by they will sometimes say jocularly 'Come out of them boots, I say, Mister; I see your head a-peeping out,' or else 'Get a corkscrew for the gentleman, he wants to get out of his boots.'"[92]

While this leadership style came naturally to certain Confederate officers, paternalism was by no means limited to Southerners. Many Union citizen-officers, particularly those from privileged social backgrounds, maintained elitist attitudes toward common soldiers and tended to view their role as being moral and social superiors with a duty to improve their men's condition. These elite officers, many of whom originated in the metropolitan Northeast, often possessed a strong impulse for reform and saw themselves not only as military leaders but also as agents for social change. As historian Lorien Foote has found, some tended to view their roles "as shepherds to sheep," whose purpose was to "direct and uplift the masses through educational and philanthropic efforts, and maintain control and order over the masses, who lacked the capacity to govern themselves."[93]

Though condescending, this leadership style could be effective, and volunteers usually accepted their officers' paternalistic overtures. But Union and Confederate volunteers alike deeply resented displays of arrogance or tyranny in their commanders, and when officers crossed the invisible line between condescension and authoritarianism, the men reacted strongly. For example, Confederate soldier A. L. Harrington described his response to a particularly tyrannical officer in vivid terms. "He put ... [me] in the gard house one time & he got drunk agoin from Wilmington to Gol[d]sboro on the train & we put him in the Sh——t House So we are even."[94] Domineering or aristocratic officers were kept in check by such acts of resistance, a practice encouraged by the citizen-soldier ethos and, until the system was largely abandoned, through officer elections. Nevertheless, volunteers on both sides valued their status as equal citizens far more than the attentions of paternalistic or condescending commanders, however well-meaning they may have been, and continually reminded officers of this. While paternalism could serve as an effective leadership technique, such a caretaking role could frustrate citizen-officers who preferred that their volunteers behave in a soldierly fashion. In May 1862 Captain Robert Dickinson of the 21st South Carolina Infantry was annoyed by the sense of entitlement some of his soldiers demonstrated. Dickinson lamented that "being Capt of a Company of men who have been previously spoiled is not what it is cracked up to be for I have a great deal of trouble with some of them especially with these two Brown Boys who are always sick and not sick neither and nothing can satisfy them but to go home and stay and hold an office and get paid for their services." Dickinson believed that the troublemakers "would not be satisfied in any Company unless the Capt lets them do that and if not they are always sick, and become perfect nuisances in the Company." He sternly established his authority despite the knowledge that doing so risked the ire of the boys' family at home. "I have put a stop to all such pretentions and perhaps they will write dreadful things about me to their parents. [I]f they do I have the assurance that I have done my duty." The captain sensed the caustic effect that could occur among his volunteers if the situation persisted and wisely acted to put the grumblers in their place. "[T]he Company are all down upon them for their lasiness. [T]hey are not positively worth to the government the powder and shot to blow their brains out."[95] Though disgusted by these shirkers, Dickinson acted swiftly to assert his position as both authority figure and arbiter of the rules, thus saving himself and his company significant trouble down the line.

Developing antebellum military professionalization, with its formality, strict adherence to discipline, and career-oriented terms of extended service, presented a significant challenge to the citizen-soldier ethos. Civil War citizen-officers emulated the professional-officer model out of necessity to cope with the challenges of war and military life. In fact, many disdained elections and openly admired the regular army's discipline. Confederate lieutenant George Anderson Mercer, for instance, noted a particularly well-regarded unit of sharpshooters while stationed in Savannah in 1862 and remarked that these soldiers "attracted particular attention; their superiority is easily explained—their officers were appointed and not elected."[96] Further, some coveted the regulars' authority and pushed their men to discard their amateurishness and inefficiency. After refitting his regiment following its severe mauling at the First Battle of Bull Run in July 1861, Lieutenant Josiah Marshall Favill of the 71st New York Infantry described his transition from the volunteer's inexperienced and ineffective mentality to a more disciplined, professional model. "I felt very different to what I did in April," he explained. "The regiment looked well, was fully armed, clothed and equipped, and officered, for the most part, by as fine a body of gentlemen as ever exchanged a civil for a military life. We were especially fortunate in having many officers thoroughly well up in tactics, and having in the ranks over a hundred old soldiers, who had served in the regular army of either the United States or Great Britain." Favill believed that the benefits of this change not only in his own but also in his regiment's leadership culture were self-evident. "All who know anything of the service will appreciate the advantage of having these old soldiers to instruct the recruits in the many details that can never be learned theoretically."[97]

Robert Gould Shaw likewise decried the unsoldierly conduct of his enlisted volunteers. The lieutenant complained to his mother in a Christmas 1861 letter of the sense of privilege and entitlement rife among his Massachusetts company. Upon receiving a number of mittens knitted for his soldiers, Shaw wrote: "The men were all glad to get them, though, as usual, they didn't express their thanks. They get so many things that they are spoilt, and think they have a right to all these extras. Thirteen dollars per month, with board, lodging, and clothes, is more than nine men out of ten could make at home. Poor soldiers! Poor *drumsticks!*" Shaw thought better of his expressions of contempt, however, and reminded his mother of his role as a surrogate parent to the volunteers of his company. "But this is not the sort of language for me to use," he added, "who am supposed to stand in the light of half mother to the men of my company."[98] Officers on both sides often lamented the indiscipline and unsoldierly bearing of their volunteers, but they could do little to force them to shed the habits and attitudes of civilian life. Civil War volunteers naturally distrusted authority, particularly when it carried a whiff of inherent, unearned superiority or a refusal to share in hardships. To counter this natural distrust, citizen-officers took the idea of shared sacrifice quite seriously, and their examples of selflessness and attentiveness could make lifelong impressions on the men they led. One Massachusetts private, for instance, described the scrupulous care exercised by his company commander for his men and the importance of that in maintaining a personal connection with them. "Captain commenced immediately to arrange the affairs of the company and see what we required and tryed to provide us with what was needed," he wrote to his sister in 1862. "The company like him more than we do any other officer we ever had when he returned to us he came directly to our tents passed in to them all shook [hands] with every man spoke a kind work to each one and all this before he saw the officer of the regiment as the company from which he was promoted[.]" The captain's leadership paid dividends, forging bonds of loyalty between himself and his men and serving as a stark contrast with other, more aloof officers in the regiment. "The boys were pleased to see him and he appeared really pleased to see us I do not remember of any other man doing that. They'll come and stick their heads in to the tent and that is about all."[99]

There were ample opportunities for citizen-officers to demonstrate their leadership through personal connections, concern, and shared sacrifice while in camp or on the march. When evaluating an officer's worth, volunteers placed heavy demands upon them. They could quickly gain the trust of their soldiers by displaying a personal interest in their well-being and comfort. At times, this required officers to serve as an advocate on their behalf, particularly when the demands placed upon them by commanders caused undue stress. Lieutenant James Newell Lightfoot of the 6th Alabama Infantry described his captain's efforts to shield subordinates from a particularly detested authoritarian colonel. "Our Col. is coming down upon our Regiment now pretty tight," Lightfoot wrote, "getting us under verry strict discipline our men would be a little despaired if it was not for our Captain. But as you know he is one of the best men in the world to his men."[100] Iowa private William Clayton also noted an admired officer's example of shared sacrifice in 1862, telling his brother, "While on the march he will walk half the time and let boys who are unwell or tired ride his horse."[101]

As citizen-soldiers, volunteers expected their officers to not only share in their hardships but also to serve in a common cause. For volunteers, shared hardship could serve as evidence of an officer's commitment to that common cause; failure to share their volunteers' discomfort, however, would often be construed as precisely the opposite. For instance, Pennsylvanian Levi Duff recounted the poor example of a regimental commander who lost the confidence of his men because of a raincoat. "We have just come in from regimental drill of one hour in the rain," he informed his fiancée in 1861. "The boys are all complaining of the colonel—not because he drilled us in the rain but because he had the impudence to wear an India rubber coat when he well knew that the privates could not afford such a covering. He is fast getting the ill-will of all the men in the regiment, & judging from the progress of this feeling within the last few days, in a week he will be as little respected as Col. [Irvin] McDowell." The offending officer, Duff reasoned, could have easily won over his soldiers simply by sharing in their discomfort; his insensitivity or unwillingness to do so thoroughly discredited him in their eyes. "It may be truthfully affirmed that [he] cares nothing about his men—at least he never looks to their comfort in any respect. We might starve, drown or die by any other mode & he would never know it, until on going into the field for regimental drill, he would not find his regiment." Duff believed that this attitude had had a fatal effect on the regiment's morale. "These things have already had their legitimate effect upon the men. Some days when we go out on regimental drill the men do just as they please. This annoys him so much that he can scarcely sit on his horse, & he never ceases to sweat while he is on the field, which conclusively proves to all men that he is unfit for the position he holds. A man who cannot govern his own temper, cannot govern a regiment of a thousand men." The Pennsylvanian had little faith that the authorities would intervene and remove the unfit colonel; moreover, he predicted that, given the opportunity, the men in the regiment might take matters into their own hands. "If the committee which was authorized by Congress to inquire into the qualifications of the volunteer officers, is ever appointed & does its work thoroughly, we may have some hope of losing him soon," Duff concluded, "otherwise we will be bothered with him until we go into battle some time, when I have no doubt he will be summarily disposed of."[102] Fortunately for this commanding officer, he eventually learned to control his temper when drilling his troops. A week later Duff reported that "[o]ur col. for the last two or three days has been more respectful to his men when on the field than usual. We got along very smoothly this morning; & if he would only keep cool & not open his mouth except in giving commands we would never have any trouble."[103]

The citizen-soldier ethos dictated equality, while military necessity, regulations, and the example of the regular army demanded a strict hierarchy of authority. Despite this tension, Civil War volunteers were far more inclined to follow officers who did not hold themselves out as better than their men. One way to accomplish this was for officers to accept with grace a certain amount of irreverence from volunteers. Captain Corbin described this delicate arrangement to his mother in 1864. "In the Confederate army officers of all ranks, whose faces are not known by the men, are equally exposed to a volley of chaff, for the Southern soldier is an inveterate joker he even chaffed his idol, Stonewall Jackson, for his ungainly seat on horseback," the Virginian observed. "And yet if you speak to them [Confederate soldiers] civilly they will always give you an intelligent and ready reply. Provided you are not arrogant or overbearing they will invariably try to oblige you with alacrity." Corbin provided an example of this irreverence in a humorous anecdote. "As I was riding along the lines with the chief engineer of the army, General Smith, a very smart and stylish fellow, rather rigid in his attitude and carriage, we came to a Mississippi regiment, and I distinctly heard one of the privates remark to a comrade: 'I say, Bill, look at that there officer; he's rather stiff and stuck up, ain't he?' 'Yes,' answered the other, with that drawl peculiar to some southerners, 'I reckon he had ramrod tea for breakfast.'"[104] Volunteers like that anonymous Mississippi private used humor not only to bring levity to but also to reinforce their status as coequal citizens. No citizen-officer, no matter how exalted, was above the irreverence of a volunteer. Officers had to possess enough humility and self-control to learn from their mistakes and endure their volunteers' teasing; this in itself could be a challenge for the thin skinned or humorless among them. Wise leaders also had to strike a difficult balance between authority and connection. They had to maintain a command presence and yet could not afford to be too lofty, detached, or arrogant.

Volunteers also expected that orders given by their leaders to be logical. Because of these expectations, citizen-officers could not rely solely on the power of their position nor on the strength of their personal qualities or emotional connection to their volunteers. They also had to be prepared to reason with their men, in varying degrees, when they gave orders or made requests. "The white American soldier," wrote Colonel Higginson, "being, doubtless, the most intelligent in the world, is more ready than any other to comply with a reasonable order, but he does it because it is reasonable, not because it is an order." Higginson believed that American volunteers obeyed not because they were led, but because they reasonably consented to obedience. "With advancing experience his compliance increases," he wrote, "but it is still because he better and better comprehends the reason. Give him an order that looks utterly unreasonable,—and this is sometimes necessary,—or give him one which looks trifling, under which head all sanitary precautions are yet too apt to rank, and you may, perhaps, find that you still have a free and independent citizen to deal with, not a soldier."[105] The reasonableness of an order could become a matter for dispute, and volunteers' instinct for skeptical compliance with authority no doubt undermined the military authority of officers unwilling or unable to reason with them.

The heavy expectations that volunteers placed upon their officers helped ensure that officers did not place greater demands upon them than they were able to bear. It also reinforced the concept that citizen-soldiers, despite their subordinate military status, were still equal citizens to be treated with respect. Volunteers retained an element of consent as a condition of their service, and they required their officers to explain how orders, particularly incomprehensible ones, would serve the military goal at hand. Sergeant Miller, an Indianan who seems to have regarded officers as a perpetual nuisance, wrote about a captain's refusal to explain orders in one 1863 diary entry that practically drips with sarcasm. After marching his men out some distance from the company's camp to drill, the captain halted them and asked whether they had brought their cartridge boxes. Apparently, it was common practice among the volunteers in the company to leave cartridge boxes behind in such instances as they were "havey and cumbersom and of no use in drilling[.]" The captain used the opportunity to berate his men, along with Sergeant Miller, and ordered them to double quick back to the camp to retrieve their ammunition. "This Shows up the character of the man," Miller groused. "If he had told us before we were doeing wrong we would not repeated it. But he was showing his authority and teaching us poor ignorant privates what it was to have such an intelligent and honorable gentleman for a captain. And then it demonstrated to us that he was such a 'brave man' and one who it would not do to set his authority at defiance," the sergeant seethed. "Then it taught all of us [to] love him for the lesson."[106]

Officers who possessed the ability to interpret and explain their demands to their volunteers rather than merely coerce or manipulate them stood a much greater chance of winning the confidence of their troops; those who struggled to master this skill likewise struggled to win over their men. The volunteers of the Civil War era were simultaneously both citizen and soldier but understood that war was a practice alien to that of the typical citizen and adopted the conflict as uniquely theirs. For these citizen-soldiers, then, war was an abnormal state that demanded ideological flexibility. The rigors of army discipline, the stress of separation and dislocation from their civilian identities, and the physical and psychological hardships of war all created significant leadership challenges for citizen-officers attempting to exercise command. Whether real or simply imagined, war set fighting men apart from civilians in their own minds; they believed that it required more of them than it did of ordinary citizens. The Civil War demanded much of the civic prerogatives that these citizen-soldiers carried with them, and so they modified their expectations and adapted their values while clinging to those most important to them. As Higginson concluded, "If a regiment is merely a caucus, and the colonel the chairman,—or merely a fire-company, and the colonel the foreman,—or merely a prayer-meeting, and the colonel the moderator,—or merely a bar-room, and the colonel the landlord,—then the failure of the whole thing is a foregone conclusion."[107]

No matter which leadership techniques company officers chose to rely upon, the citizen-soldier ethos and the democratic prerogatives of the republican tradition demanded that they act with fairness, justice, and consistency in their dealings with volunteers. Weaned on egalitarianism and keenly aware of their voluntary status, the soldier's sense of justice and fairness demanded much from junior officers. Consequently, these men had to learn leadership skills in complex and nuanced ways, with little professional guidance or institutional support. Perhaps more than any other military relationship during the Civil War, the command relationship between junior officers and their volunteers required personal commitments founded on faith and trust. The citizen-soldier ethos compelled free citizens to place their freedom and their lives in the hands of fellow citizens in times of war; they surrendered their natural rights for a temporary period, faithfully trusting that this voluntary act of selflessness would be repaid with care, respect, and competent leadership in the service of cause and country.

While company officers in both armies looked to regular officers and regulations for guidance on the art of command, they had to learn how to manage this delicate relationship through instinct, common sense, and experience. Officers became convincing authority figures through displays of competence, courage, and respect; those who succeeded in their efforts secured the loyalty and obedience of their volunteers, while those who failed could expect derision, disobedience, or outright defiance. The command relationship between citizen-officers and volunteers was hardly the ideal sought by regulars, but somehow it seemed to work. Inexperienced volunteers led by equally untried citizen-officers managed to adjust to the unfamiliar demands of army life, sensibly charting the unfamiliar boundaries of military authority and discipline, discarding the extraneous or the impractical, and mutually shaping the relationship between them to conform to their understanding of military service. Although the discipline of Union and Confederate volunteers never compared favorably to that of the regular army, over time citizen-officers and volunteers on both sides managed to strike a balance between obedience and respect that they felt was acceptably consistent with their cherished ideals.

4

Citizen-Officer Culture

Days after the death of his company commander at the Battle of Antietam and the promotion of his company's first and second lieutenants, Sergeant Major Henry Perkins Goddard of the 14th Connecticut Infantry found himself an acting officer with the promise of a commission from his state's governor. "I have just been appointed Acting 2nd Lieutenant of Co. G of this regiment, with the understanding that my name will be nominated to Gov. Buckingham for the position," he wrote to his mother with pride. "Send me one pair of Infantry 2nd Lieut. Straps," Goddard requested, along with a sword, a sash, and other furnishings required for his new position. "Truly God is good to your boy," the new citizen-officer proclaimed, signing his letter, "For the last time S'gt Major 14th C.V."[1] Less jubilant than Goddard, but no less pleased with his promotion, Confederate artillerist William R. J. Pegram likewise found himself unexpectedly elevated to junior command in March 1862. After taking charge of the Purcell Battery in the Army of Northern Virginia, Captain Pegram was rather sheepish about his new status. "I don't think I will ever get use to the title of Captain," he admitted to his sister soon after his promotion. "When I hear myself called Captain, I generally look around to see if Capt. Walker is present." Nevertheless, added Pegram, "I don't intend to allow any thing except my duties to God, to interfere with my duty to my country."[2] When they received their commissions as citizen-officers, junior commanders like Lieutenant Goddard and Captain Pegram entered an exclusive fraternity fraught with challenges, difficulties, and opportunities of all kinds. Civil War citizen-officers developed a unique interior culture during the four years of conflict, a culture informed, in part, by the example of the regular-army officer corps and shaped by the powerful, sometimes paradoxical influence of the American citizen-soldier ethos.

West Point-trained regular officers and the professional military culture they embodied were essential to the creation of a distinctive volunteer officer culture in the Union and Confederate armies. The antebellum U.S. Military Academy at West Point, under the guidance of Superintendent Sylvanus Thayer and instructors like Dennis Hart Mahan, produced generations of professional officers schooled in engineering, science, and the military arts. Thayer, Mahan, and Major General Winfield Scott advocated professionalism; a rigorous, scientific curriculum for officers; extended terms of service; and esprit de corps. Even for those who chose not to pursue a permanent career in the army, a West Point education was an attractive offering for young men of ambition and ability; the engineering component of the academy's curriculum alone was one of the finest in the world.[3] At the outset of the Civil War, Union and Confederate citizen-officers relied heavily on regular-army officers' professional examples to guide their self-education. Northerners and Southerners shared a common understanding of the proper behavior of an officer because many of the senior commanders in the new volunteer armies were West Pointers. Consequently, their vision of what an officer should be was based principally on the professional culture of West Point and disseminated through the regulations, policies, doctrine, and traditions of the antebellum U.S. Army.[4]

As they gained experience with their commands and discovered the challenges of leadership, many citizen-officers came to appreciate the precision, formality, and professionalism of regular-army officers. Some, like Captain Oliver Wendell Holmes Jr. of the 20th Massachusetts Infantry, took great pride when observers compared their volunteers and to the regulars. In 1863, while sharing with his father the braggadocio of a certain volunteer officer, Holmes complained about the unprofessionalism of this man's demeanor. "What a joy it is to have a man thoroughly educated in his biz. wellbred, knowing what's what & imparting his knowledge," Holmes declared, "in place of one who tells you his Regt (not such a remarkable one except for a Penn Regt) has been in 42 battles & other unending blowing about himself." He thought such vanity was unseemly, comparing the volunteer officer's "blowing" unfavorably to the regular officers he had seen. "I was talking to Hall about this *blowing* being something I didn't much like or understand & he said 'Yes your Regt is more like old times' (meaning thereby the old Regular Army where Officers *were* gentlemen) 'than anything I have seen in the Army.'" Holmes was thrilled at the favorable comparison to regulars. "[I]n connection with other remarks about the perfection of their present condition and their behavior in the Field rather pleased me," he enthused. "I really very much doubt whether there is any Regt wh. can compare with ours in the Army of the Potomac. Everyone says this, perhaps, who belongs to a good Regt but still I fancy I am right from the evidence of many things."[5]

Union volunteer Abner R. Small noticed an increasing aloofness in the way his company's leaders related to their citizen-soldiers early in the war. The officers in Small's 16th Maine Infantry began to adopt aspects of the professional-officer model and to impose standards akin to the regulars, altering the entire atmosphere within his regiment. "We were in camp, and drill and discipline became our only portion," he recalled. "We began to be conscious of the immensity of icy space between the officers and the rank and file. Friendly neighbors in civilian life, one spreading manure and the other cleaning fish, were now immeasurably apart." These citizen-officers' chilly new professionalism, he found, seeped into the noncommissioned officers of his regiment as well. "The fourth corporal of Company G was deep down in the glacial crevasse," Small remarked. "He was occasionally corporal of the guard. This tended to increase his chest measure and conceit, but it failed to raise his perpendicular and official consequence above the lowest notch in the ice."[6] William Pegram spoke approvingly of a similar change in the quality and military culture among the citizen-officers of the Army of Northern Virginia in 1862. "General Lee is getting rid of all incompetent officers and cowards, by a simple order relieving them from duty, without any Court. The result of it is, that the whole army is in a much better state of discipline than heretofore," the captain wrote to his sister.[7] Regular officers on both sides educated their volunteer counterparts when possible, or alternatively, shamed them. After a display of lax march discipline by company officers, for instance, Union volunteer Levi Bird Duff recalled the scornful words of Brigadier General Edward Ord, a tough-talking West Pointer, to the green troops under his command. "No sooner had we halted than the men began to open their haversacks preparatory to eating," wrote Duff to his fiancée. "Gen. Ord turning to his aid indignantly remarked, 'That's the *hell* with them volunteers they never halt but they eat.' He told them to put up their haversacks & shoulder their arms & march forward, which was done," doubtless with a certain amount of embarrassment among the more easygoing volunteer officers in the brigade.[8] Given these pressures to conform to regular-army discipline, over time both Union and Confederate citizen-soldiers and their leaders saw a gradual but unmistakable cultural change take place within the junior-officer corps. "Soldiering was no longer an enthusiasm, nor a consciously difficult endurance, it had become ordinary every-day life," noted a soldier of the 35th Massachusetts Infantry, measuring the changes in discipline and regularization within his regiment from 1862 to early 1864. "[T]he men went about every duty quietly, but with assured confidence. We remarked among the new troops a harsher discipline than prevailed in the army of 1862."[9]

Military acculturation among citizen-officers is perhaps best understood not as professionalization, but rather as a form of regularization—that is, a conscious adherence to many of the professional standards, regulations, customs, and systems of the regular army, but with certain modifications and concessions to the persistent citizen-soldier ethos of the republican tradition. Citizen-officers were therefore an amalgam: part volunteer, with many of the ideological accoutrements and demands of the citizen-soldier ethos, and part military professional, learning their new vocation, innovating and adapting their command methods, coping with the challenges of a vast military bureaucracy, and instilling discipline, system, and efficiency in the volunteers they led.[10] The senior leadership on both sides hoped their junior officers would mature and pressed for a more professional model among their officers into 1863 and 1864. In 1863, for example, the Confederate War Department decried the persistence of officer elections, "since inseparable from it [arise] an undue regard to popularity... and a spirit of electioneering subversive of subordination and discipline."[11] The Federal War Department had similar concerns, mandating additional competency examinations for certain officers.[12] Citizen-officers were not always successful in their efforts to evolve from untrained amateurs to competent military leaders with the essential characteristics of professionals. As historian Andrew Haughton observes of the Army of Tennessee's officer corps, "few volunteer soldiers would ever feel confident enough to propose any modification [to doctrine or tactics]. The lower ranks of its officer corps were, consequently, largely barren of... [the] innovative officers" necessary to effect significant improvements in training, leadership, or doctrine, resulting in intellectual stagnation and tactical inflexibility among that army's leaders.[13]

While regularization was a powerful process that altered the citizen-officer cultures of Union and Confederate armies, volunteer officers did not set aside their ingrained ideological expectations entirely in favor of regular-army professionalism. Citizen-officers and volunteers who admired the regulars' model did not necessarily adopt a spit-and-polish approach to their duties. They still retained many of the customs of civilian life, and the deference and formality of regular-army military culture did not always penetrate the citizen-soldier ethos. In May 1862 Captain John William De Forest of the 12th Connecticut Infantry spoke of the favorable appraisal his evolving volunteer regiment received from a regular officer with a reputation as a disciplinarian. "The Twelfth has lately had a compliment from the grizzled martinet," De Forest wrote to his wife. "[H]e told the lieutenant colonel that our dress parade of the day before yesterday was the finest he had ever seen. This from a veteran regular officer is great praise, and flatters us more than you can probably imagine. He is rarely so gracious; he says that we are as lacking in discipline as we are praiseworthy for drill; and alas! He is right."[14] Captain De Forest's description of his regiment's dual character perfectly illustrates the paradox of citizen-officer leadership and the regularizing impulse among Civil War volunteer troops. Despite their improvements in drill, parade, and the technical aspects of soldiering, volunteers often retained their civilian indifference to military formality and their militia disdain for army pomposity. "Not that our men are mutinous or disorderly," De Forest explained. "[O]n the contrary they are as obedient and quiet as sheep. But they don't touch their caps when they meet an officer; they don't salute promptly and stylishly when on guard; in short, they are deficient in soldierly etiquette." In 1863 Union volunteer William Bluffton Miller begrudgingly acknowledged the military necessity of respect for authority in recounting the punishment assessed toward an insubordinate sergeant in his regiment. "While on Dress Parade Serg. Sweany of 'Co A' was brought out and the Stripes cut off his arm and reduced to ranks for curseing Lieut [Harrison H.] Wheeler of [the] Same Company," Miller chronicled in his diary. "I guess Sweany was not much to blame but it would not be 'Military' to let him escape," he admitted. "The private Soldier has to account for his own Sins and the officers too. That is according to 'Red Tape.'"[15] The double nature of the citizen-soldier extended to citizen-officers as well. De Forest recounted the story of a young lieutenant in his regiment, newly promoted from sergeant, who made the error of saluting a general with an apple core in his hand and while out of proper uniform.

The lieutenant received a severe reprimand from the general, much to De Forest's amusement.[16]

Union officer August V. Kautz, distilling his experiences at West Point, on the frontier with the antebellum regulars, and as a general of volunteer troops during the Civil War, spoke of the difficulties young officers in the regular and volunteer services alike would face in growing accustomed to military life. In 1865 he advised novice lieutenants to exercise discretion and sensitivity in taking on new assignments. "It is a trying time to a young officer when he first joins his Regiment; he enters upon a new scene in his life, and is thrown with companions who will try all his qualities, and he will not be fairly domesticated in his Regiment until he has found his level." Kautz warned that, to integrate themselves into the hierarchy of army life, new officers must first accept their lowly place in their unit's pecking order. "As a rule he must begin at the foot of the ladder, and work his way up," he wrote. "He may be young, and therefore inexperienced; he may have no fondness for books, and therefore not learned," Kautz added, but these deficiencies could be overcome with time and diligence.[17]

Most Union and Confederate captains and lieutenants served in infantry or cavalry companies, in artillery batteries, or in staff or administrative capacities; both armies depended heavily on volunteer officers to manage the most junior levels of command. It is difficult to overstate the magnitude of expansion in these armies and the consequent demands placed upon citizen-officers to lead new troops. Between April and July 1861, the Union army grew to twenty-seven times its prewar levels, and by 1865 its strength levels reached more than one million men, with the then-unprecedented expenditures of more than $1 billion per year. The Confederate army, which did not exist prior to 1861, grew at a similarly rapid rate with a massive influx of volunteers; during the course of the war, at least one million men fought for the Southern cause. In composition, both the Union and Confederate armies were essentially vast volunteer forces with a leavening of regulars, and both would remain so throughout the war.[18]

The overwhelming majority of new recruits were volunteers. Regular-army officers educated at West Point were precious commodities in both the Union and Confederate armies, and most ascended beyond the company level rather quickly, taking commissions as colonels of volunteer regiments or rising to senior command after a relatively short period of time.[19] Consequently, volunteer officers at company grade were quite often extremely inexperienced when they assumed their posts and thus had to learn their military responsibilities in a hurry. The senior leadership expected all officers, no matter what their background or military training, to conform to the intricate and sometimes byzantine administrative standards of their respective war departments. This created a rather steep learning curve for novice citizen-officers in the first years of the war; the Union and Confederate staff departments both required a substantial level of technical knowledge and bureaucratic acumen to learn the procedures, paperwork, and customs of service that regular officers had already mastered as part of their professional training and experience.[20]

Despite these initial difficulties, citizen-officers gradually adapted to the challenges posed by commanding a company of volunteers. Company commanders on both sides followed many of the same antebellum U.S. Army practices and procedures, and Union and Confederate volunteer officers defined their formal military responsibilities in similar ways. The guidelines, rules, and traditions governing their roles and duties were quite similar in both armies, adapted as they were from a long lineage of formal regulations, manuals, and customs stretching back to the War of 1812.[21] By 1861 both sides widely followed the drills, procedures, and tactics in William J. Hardee's *Tactics* and later in Silas Casey's *Infantry Tactics,* John Gibbon's *The Artillerist's Manual,* and others. (Hardee would go on to serve as a corps commander in the Confederate Army of Tennessee, while Casey and Gibbon became generals in the Union army).[22]

Captains typically led single companies, with a first lieutenant and a second lieutenant, sometimes called subalterns, to assist them. Actual numbers in infantry and cavalry companies varied greatly; the nominal strength of an infantry company was around one hundred men, including the three commissioned officers. A more realistic approximation of a representative Union or Confederate volunteer infantry or cavalry company's strength often fell between fifty and seventy-five men, with extreme variations in these numbers. Union and Confederate artillery batteries usually consisted of four to six guns, each served by around twelve men, though also with wide variations.[23] A company or battery commander was the ultimate authority within his unit and bore the responsibility for the discipline, military effectiveness, and personal well-being of his volunteers. August Kautz described a Civil War company commander as "a small sovereign, powerful and great within his little domain, but no imbecile monarch ever suffered more from intrigues, factions, and encroachments, than an incapable Company Commander; no tyrant King must contend more with rebellions, insurrections, and defections, than an arbitrary and unjust Captain."[24] He exhorted junior officers to pursue professional excellence in anticipation of commanding a company "so that when the responsibility falls upon him, he may be prepared for it."[25] Citizen-officers in both armies were expected to follow the regular-army practices of professional improvement and self-preparation for the duties of command. Major General Daniel Butterfield, whose 1862 *Camp and Outpost Duty for Infantry* provided junior officers with a detailed handbook on duties in the field, urged young officers "unexpectedly taking up the profession of arms without previous experience or study" to apply the "*same vigilance, energy, and constant attention that gives success in any pursuit in life*" to their military obligations. Regimental and company officers alike, he cautioned, "can not know too much" of the requirements of command, "and they may know too little of it."[26]

A volunteer captain's formal responsibilities while serving in a Civil War line company required mastery of all of the duties expected of his subordinate lieutenants as well as the additional obligations of commanding his company, seeing to its training, fighting effectiveness, and overall well-being, and periodically serving as officer of the day for the regimental camp. These duties can perhaps be best understood through the framework Kautz applied in his *Customs of Service*. Formal command, or as Kautz called it, "government," included training and drill, discipline, and "a cultivation of a military spirit and pride in the profession among the men." The administrative side of command included filling out the orders, reports, returns, descriptive lists, and other minutiae of recordkeeping, the seemingly endless paperwork that afflicts most bureaucratic organizations. For a company commander to successfully govern his unit, Kautz maintained, he must demonstrate a "strict attention to duty, an honest regard for the men, and a constant self-respect, guided by equal and exact justice to all . . . , provided it is accompanied by sufficient knowledge of the duties of the position. Ignorance in this respect cannot be compensated for by any talent for other things, however capable."[27]

Company commanders were responsible for settling disputes between the men under their command, for rewarding good behavior and merit, and for punishing offenders. Kautz warned, "punishment should not be debasing in its nature, unless the offence has a similar character, and the penalty should be proportionate to the violation." Above all, junior commanders were to maintain a demeanor of calmness and composure, particularly when handling disciplinary matters. "Whatever course is pursued, it must be free from passion, and in accordance with justice," he counseled. "If the Captain permits his feelings to manifest themselves, the moral effect of his treatment will be lost upon the men, whether it be for or against the offender."[28] As Captain C. C. Andrews of the 3rd Minnesota Infantry explained: "The captain is required to exercise authority with strictness, yet with justice and kindness; and to secure prompt and faithful obedience. His commands should be plain and positive." Moreover, added Andrews, an effective company officer had to maintain control over his own emotions in disciplining his men. "He should be careful that [his orders] are within the scope of his proper authority—that they are uttered with spirit, but without passion. It is easier for him to transgress authority than for his men; but he has no more right to do so. He has no right to insult them by rude or profane language; nor to resort to such degrading punishments as tend to cast a reproach upon the corps."[29]

Kautz urged company commanders to adhere to a set routine while in camp or garrison to encourage discipline within their units. According to regulations, days were to begin at sunrise with reveille and a roll call; inspection; police or stable call, in which the company's horses and the grounds around the camp were put in good order; surgeon's or sick call; and the call to breakfast. Once the men had eaten, guard mounting took place under the supervision of senior noncommissioned officers or lieutenants. First sergeants' call occurred sometime in the middle of the day, where first sergeants of each company reported to the regimental adjutant's tent to turn in company reports and receive instructions for the captain. The rest of the day was usually occupied with drill, paperwork, guard duty, dress parades, dinner call, a retreat roll call with another inspection, and taps around 9:00 or 9:30 P.M., at which time the men were required to extinguish their lights and maintain quiet in camp. While on campaign, the company routine was largely occupied by marching and fighting, but much of the same routine was preserved.[30] As the officer of the day, company officers were charged with ensuring the cleanliness, order, and security of the regimental camp on a rotating basis. Union officers of the day were required to wear their officer's silken sash "across the body, scarf fashion, from the right shoulder to the left side, instead of around the waist, tying behind the left hip as prescribed."[31] Captains were also occasionally sent on detached service to oversee recruiting efforts at home.

First and second lieutenants had simpler responsibilities than company commanders, though in some sense their formal duties were more nebulous. They were expected to assist their captain in his duties, and these could vary considerably depending on the command style, personality, preferences, and abilities of that officer. Both Union and Confederate regulations charged lieutenants with overseeing a squad within the company and seeing to "the supervision of its order and cleanliness; . . . captains will require their lieutenants to assist them in the performance of all company duties."[32] Lieutenants monitored the condition of the company, seeing to weapons and equipment, and commanding the company in the captain's absence. They were also responsible for assisting with the company books, the company fund and paperwork, and carrying out inspections, drill, and company discipline. Lieutenants also served as officers of the guard, commanding guard details and ensuring that the regimental camp was secure. Guard mounting, a somewhat intricate ritual requiring practice and precision, sometimes proved a challenge for lieutenants and privates alike.[33] Private Wilbur Fisk of the 2nd Vermont Infantry was offhanded about the procedure. "Guard-mounting isn't a very important, or a very imposing affair, but I suppose it is one of those little things that are necessary to keep up a wholesome state of discipline among the troops. . . . All the officers of the day from each regiment, brigade, and the field, in the Division, were arranged in line in front of the pickets, at a distance varying according to rank." Fisk was acerbic about the flashy martial spectacle the officers attempted to present. "Quite a splendid line of them were there, with their red sashes on, and their dainty little swords hanging by their sides."[34]

The technical and administrative aspects of officer life required practice and experience to master, but the military culture of citizen-officers involved much more than merely learning regulations and imitating regular officers' examples. For volunteer officers, regularization and gentlemanliness went hand in hand; this was the essence of officerlike behavior. The ideal citizen-officer, they believed, should embody the values of self-restraint, self-reliance, Christian virtue, courtesy, loyalty, ambition, and particularly among Southerners, chivalry.[35] While antebellum occupations and classes may have set the expectations for their gentlemanly manner, they did not exclusively dictate the terms of officer behavior. These men relied on the example of the regulars to set the tone for their own military comportment. To James B. Griffin, a South Carolina officer and elite antebellum planter serving in the Hampton Legion, the gentlemanly qualities of his fellow citizen-officers and the professional example set for them by those with regular-army experience were an ideal representation of his aspirations as a new officer. "There is a regular Cavalry Camp here, no infantry," Griffin wrote to his wife from Ashland, Virginia, in 1861, "under the direction of army Officers. Every thing is conducted here strictly according to army regulations. I am very well pleased with the place and am delighted with the Officers." Griffin also lauded the gentlemanly professionalism of his West Point–educated colonel, Kentuckian Charles W. Field. "Col Field who is in command here, is one of the finest gentlemen I ever had the good fortune to meet. He is courteous and affable to every one. But a strict disciplinarian. I expect he will not be so popular with some of our Boys, who do not like to come down, square to the rules." Griffin was eager to learn from the professional, gentlemanly example set by Field and the other regulars in his camp. "My men are very comfortably quartered," he reported to his wife. "And I have a very nice room in the house used by the Col and other Officers, situated right in the midst of the camp. I am very comfortably situated, and think it will be a real good schooling for me as well as my men."[36]

Moral suasion was more subtle than displays of gentlemanliness or professional acumen, but perhaps it was even more essential to officer culture. Citizen-officers were expected to set an example through their personal moral character, particularly through their representation of Christian virtue. Not all citizen-officers were Christians, nor were they all virtuous or moral, but moral suasion by means of a virtuous example could be an extremely powerful instrument in securing the loyalty and compliance of volunteers as well as ensuring the affinity and approval of fellow officers. Lieutenant Robert Augustus Stiles of the 1st Virginia Howitzers remembered Captain Pegram as a paragon of Christian virtue and personal character. "[Pegram] had always been such a modest, self-contained and almost shrinking youth that his most intimate friends were astonished at his rapid development and promotion; but it was one of those strongly marked cases where war seemed to be the needed and almost the native air of a young man." To the lieutenant, Pegram embodied all the best aspects of the Christian gentleman and the virtuous warrior. "He was in some respects of the type of Stonewall Jackson, and like him combined the strongest Christian faith and the deepest spirituality with the most intense spirit of fight," Stiles recalled after the war.[37]

Citizen-officers who infused a culture of moral excellence into their companies could be a powerful force for securing the commitment of volunteers to their cause. When soldiers perceived their officers to be virtuous men of conviction and character, they were more willing to give them their admiration and their allegiance, often to extreme degrees. Moreover, when citizen-officers embodied the image of the virtuous leader, they played a critical function in preserving the emotional and ideological integrity of their unit, often representing a moral center of gravity through their virtuous example and helping provide meaning and order to the unnerving experience of war. Sergeant William McKnight of the 7th Ohio Cavalry described the profound personal attachment he formed with his company commander in an 1863 letter to his wife. "He and I are like true Brothers. He sticks to me all the time. He says he Could not get along without me. I got the Praise of being the Best looking and soldier like Orderly in the whole Battalion you know that is not so." McKnight later earned a lieutenant's commission and saw this officer as an example of how to be a good commander. "Captain is one of the Best men moraly as wel as intelectualy that ever I met with," he wrote. "If he was to leave the Company I would be lost for he has been a Father to me ever since I Came into the Company."[38]

As officers and gentlemen, company leaders were held to a higher standard of personal conduct, integrity, and behavior than were their enlisted citizen-soldiers. Gentlemanly or officerlike behavior helped create a culture separate and distinct from the wickedness and coarseness of some of the men in the ranks. "I injoy Myself among the Officers they make the world of me," wrote newly promoted Lieutenant George W. Browning of the 54th Ohio Infantry. "[I]t is much pleasanter to be among Gentleman than among a lot of boys as some are in Brooklyn But I dont ask any odds I no my Buis and will attend to it," he declared to his wife.[39] Lieutenant Alfred E. Doby of the 2nd South Carolina Infantry lamented the corrupting effect of military life upon his own gentility and virtue. "The constant association with all the coarse elements of humanity, with the boundless profusion of bloodshed that is constantly before our eyes, & all the abominable vices, untempered by the sweet & angelic influence of woman's society, is enough to upset what virtues may be possessed of at home," he wrote to his wife in 1863. "But we will throw off our rough & coarse habiliments of war when we get home & learn to resume the more refined elements of nature." Doby believed that his soiled virtue could be rejuvenated by spending time in the company of his wife and daughter, and his gentility restored. "With you & Elise to care for, Darling, & to love me in all the trials & vicissitudes of life, I have no fears of being recusant or worthless in preforming the duties of life. Your love will ever be a stimulant & an incentive to be virtuous & pure, & always careful to promote your happiness & cultivate your affection."[40] Other citizen-officers felt pride in the quality and gentility of their fellows and took pains to point out the virtuous nature of their comrades and brother officers. Lieutenant S. Millet Thompson of the 13th New Hampshire Infantry described the high moral character of two of his companions to a female cousin. "Kittredge, Ames and myself make an amiable trio. They are the only two young men whom I have made much acquaintance with, who neither drink, smoke, chew nor swear—so we match exactly. 'Good company or none,' is my motto."[41]

Occasionally, citizen-officers like Browning, Doby, and Thompson, inclined to the pursuit of Christian virtue, did not just limit their moral enterprises to improving themselves. Captain Stephen David Clements of the 41st Georgia Infantry, for example, informed a female correspondent of his intention to implement a Sunday school for the volunteers of his company, much to the delight of the lady. "I approve of your plan of filling up your leisure hours in trying to improve the minds of your men," the lady wrote to Clements, "& the sabeth school teachings will be long remembered by them, and may it be a means of bring[ing] them to his mercy seat in these responsible & thrilling times, & may they obtain that grace which will make them equal to the emergency, and may all of the soldiers in every regiment listen to the Gospel of Christ and yield to him their hearts & their lives." Clements's correspondent echoed the sentiments of many of her fellow Southerners, who believed that by demonstrating virtue and spiritual devotion, the Confederacy could achieve victory against all odds. "[M]ay these Confederate States have the honour of being the first nation that ever gave itself fully to the Lord, is the prayer of one who feels so deeply for the deranged condition of our country," she declared.[42]

Lieutenant George M. Lalane of the 2nd South Carolina Infantry was tormented by self-doubt, anxious that he would not present a virtuous example to others, particularly to his brother Paul. In his diary Lalane poured out his fears with harrowing candor. "Sunday. A sermon from Mr Dickson's brother. I feel distressed about myself—the vile nature that I have, a mind full of uncharitableness, carnal thoughts and a soul with the world's impress not entirely effaced. My God purify my thoughts and sanctify my wishes, particularly—O that I had Wisdom that I might impart it to Paul, my dear brother. That I might not only teach him to be just and honorable and gentlemanly but that I might guide his feet in the straight and narrow way that leadeth to eternal life!" Lalane outlined his sins and shortcomings, confessing them one after another in his diary. "I have too much Vanity—I do not govern my tongue enough neither do I my thoughts," he wrote. "I must have more strength of mind—less regard for the world."[43] Later Lalane extolled the Christian virtue of two fellow officers in his diary, admiring their example to him and to others. "Capt. Johnson is an engineer indeed. I have seldom seen a man so brave, so consciencious, so full of determination and energy. Always at work—never tiring. He before the war studied for the ministry. Col. Elliott is also a Christian by profession. O! that all of our officers were like these!"[44]

Even in death, citizen-officers were careful to preserve the virtuous reputations of themselves and of their fellows. Survivors who wrote to dead officers' families meticulously extolled the personal qualities and Christian virtue of the departed in extravagant, sometimes cloying terms. Captain Samuel Thompson Buchanan of the 48th Virginia Infantry, captured at the Battle of Spotsylvania Court House and imprisoned at Point Lookout, Maryland, died while incarcerated in 1864. Writing to Buchanan's father, the captain's commanding officer, Colonel Robert H. Dungan, recounted his friendship with Captain Buchanan and affirmed the son's personal character and Christian virtue. The colonel's letter illustrates the moral characteristics many citizen-officers expected of themselves and of each other. "Prior to the war, he was my friend and schoolmate, messmate and fellow officer in arms," wrote Dungan. "And in every relation we ever sustained I always found him my courteous, sober, and faithful friend. He was remarkably good humored. I never saw him mad in my life. His morals were unimpeachable and even the corrupting influence of the army failed to impair them in a single respect." Buchanan's inner character, Dungan continued, translated into admiration from his volunteers and his fellow officers. "He was respected by all who knew him, admired and beloved by his intimate friends." The captain was, in Dungan's estimation, a conscientious and honorable young man who fulfilled all the essential criteria of a Christian gentleman. "He was a frequent payer of his bills, a close attendant at (divine) services while in the army and always gentle and kind to his fellow soldiers."[45]

Citizen-officers who failed to live up to their volunteers' standards of morality and Christian virtue could face damaging personal and professional consequences. Just as virtuous citizen-officers could serve as a powerful example to the men they led, those with a less virtuous reputation could stain their entire regiment's honor through their behavior. "Col. Wormer offered me a captaincy again this morning, but I did not answer definitely," Lieutenant Watson B. Smith of the 8th Michigan Cavalry wrote to his father in 1863. "The fact is I think the 8th a very poor regt. as far as its officers are concerned. 4 Capt's. & 2 Lieuts. have been dismissed [from] the service in disgrace & I am inclined to think I had better remain where I am & perhaps something may turn up promoting me out of the regiment."[46] August Kautz warned young lieutenants to avoid vice to preserve not only their personal reputations but also their professional prospects and military authority. "As a rule [a young officer] cannot claim the privilege of indulging in the vices which the older officers too often consider themselves entitled to, without prejudice to his reputation," he cautioned. "[H]e must first lay in a stock of virtues, and secure a capital, before he can run any risks with his military fortune." Intemperance and profligacy could have particularly disastrous effects upon them, Kautz believed. "Drinking and gambling are the great vices that every young officer should avoid; even a moderate indulgence will keep his finances always in a state of pressure."[47]

Company officers faced challenges and dangers of all kinds in their duties; human weakness and occasional mistakes were inevitable on their part—and expected. Citizen-officers with a habit for drunkenness, however, could expect little leeway in either army. Any who allowed intoxication to interfere with his judgment and command responsibilities abdicated the sacred trust between himself and the volunteers who depended upon him for their safety and well-being. Even so, alcohol was a common temptation. Despite warnings to the contrary, citizen-officers indulged in drinking from time to time, which presented problems for the officer corps of the Union and Confederate armies alike. "Without a doubt," historian Joseph T. Glatthaar asserts of the Army of Northern Virginia, "alcohol abuse emerged as one of the greatest problems among the officer corps."[48] Historian Steven Ramold likewise finds,"[a]side from their adherence to the ethos of the citizen-soldier, Union troops took no stronger perception of themselves into the army than their right to drink."[49] Levi Duff's complaint about his company officers was all too common: "To say the truth, our officers (with the exception of 2nd Lieut. Howard who has not yet learned to get drunk) are drunk half the time. Some times we do not see them for several days & when they are present they never look after the interest or the comfort of the men."[50] Despite these troubles, alcohol sometimes provided citizen-officers with unique opportunities to bond with one another and with their superiors. Major Sandie Pendleton of Stonewall Jackson's staff described the felicitous effects of one such event in April 1863, shortly before the famous general's mortal wounding at the Battle of Chancellorsville.

"Yesterday afternoon a wagon came with a present of a box of wine for the General. It was just after dark . . . when a message came round inviting the gentlemen of the Staff to come & drink wine with the General in his tent." Pendleton credited the wine with improving the quality of conversation in the impromptu gathering. "In such a cortêge there could scarce have failed to be congeniality & pleasantry, and as the wine circulated, & warmed the blood & quickened the intellect & fired the imagination, there was sprightly conversation & playful jest, grave argument & mirthful anecdote, badinage & seriousness, in which the hours passed rapidly." Soon enough, Pendleton and the other staff officers had imbibed sufficiently to put themselves at ease around their imposing commander, "and we forgot that we were in the presence of the one who sealed the destinies of this nation & at whose beck thousands stood ready to rush to the deadly combat."[51]

Even citizen-officers who attempted to set a virtuous example by exercising moral restraint could find themselves hindered by the immodest behavior of their fellow officers. Lieutenant Samuel Storrow of the 2nd Massachusetts Infantry described an awkward evening when his commander and several company officers got drunk during the March to the Sea in 1864. "After supper a lot of us [officers] circulated the apple jack around a big rail fire & thought what they were doing & saying at home about this time," he wrote in his diary. "Then the Colonel got a lot of darkies up in front of his tent & made them dance for our amusement, & the brigade band serenaded us & we had a jolly time all around." The canteens of hard cider went from "mouth to mouth with inconceivable rapidity," an appalled Storrow wrote. Military etiquette prohibited any of the junior officers from leaving the gathering until the colonel had dismissed them, and so the lieutenant had to prolong his participation in the grotesque spectacle. "The upshot was that the Colonel got as screwed as a boiled owl," he smugly added. One of Storrow's fellow company officers was clever enough to excuse himself from the gathering, but "the rest of us were nailed & had to see it out." Storrow, fed up with his unit and its officers after this incident, managed to secure a transfer out of the regiment.[52]

Conflicts between officers were an unfortunate but inevitable facet of their experience. Their responsibilities in a Civil War company required these men to perform demanding duties while working in close quarters with a diverse array of personalities, often while in significant distress. Though officially prohibited by the Articles of War, some Union and Confederate officers even took the extreme course of challenging a fellow officer to a duel of honor over perceived slights or festering grudges.[53] Violent confrontations between feuding citizen-officers sometimes occurred, but simple personality clashes within companies or regiments were a far more common problem. Willoughby Babcock of the 75th New York Infantry wrote, "[i]n the formation of volunteer regiments, all sorts and conditions of men were thrown together through the arbitrary assignment to the regiment, of companies coming from different parts of the State." He believed that the potential for personal conflict was greater among officers than enlisted volunteers due to the nature of their responsibilities. "The officers naturally came in closer contact with one another [than] did the men of the regiment, since there were only three commissioned officers to each company of a hundred men. Special drills and officers' schools brought them together constantly for a common purpose. Thus it was important that there should be the least possible friction among those who would have to cooperate in making an efficient regiment."[54]

August Kautz counseled young officers to handle personal conflicts carefully, keeping the well-being of the company at the forefront of their words and actions. "It will be an unfortunate thing if there is found to be an incompatibility among the officers of the same company, for the more they harmonize and agree the better it will be for all parties," he advised. For Kautz, such harmony had both personal and military benefits for the officers and their soldiers alike. "[O]n the contrary, if they should be antagonistic to each other, they will themselves be greatly inconvenienced, the company will suffer in many respects, both in discipline and comfort." In cases when differences could not be satisfactorily resolved, Kautz advised patience or, alternatively, acceptance. "There is no easy remedy for such a condition of things, transfers are not easily arranged, and a detail for detached service cannot always be obtained, and they must often be borne with until promotion or some other chance effects a change."[55]

In some cases the bonds of fraternity between officers were quite fragile, and rifts over personal disagreements or slights of honor could splinter a unit's command structure. In 1861 Lieutenant James P. Douglas of the Good-Douglas Battery wrote to his sweetheart in Texas of the bitter feelings he harbored for his commanding officer, Captain John J. Good. "I am at present in some doubts what course I shall pursue, whether I will remain in this service or resign," he fumed from winter quarters in Arkansas. His spat with Good had colored his entire attitude toward military service, at least any under the authority of the captain. "There is little inducement to remain here during the winter as our camps will be quite dreary and uninteresting. Sometimes I think I will ask for a furlough this winter," Douglas mused, "again I think I will resign and either go directly to Texas, or by way of Kentucky as there is some prospect of a fight there soon." Douglas was vague about the reasons for his enmity but adamant that the situation could not be amicably resolved. "I have sufficient reason for resigning as Capt. Good has not acted toward me as a brother officer should. He is not the man I once thought him, and I would be altogether justifiable in resigning my office as I cannot agree with my commanding officer." Good later transferred to serve on a military court, and Douglas, who did not resign as he claimed he would, was eventually promoted to captain and given command of the battery.[56]

"I don't Like that Large gentleman as well as I wish I did," Lieutenant Browning of the 54th Ohio Infantry wrote of a feud between himself and an unnamed fellow officer in 1863. "But We agree much Beter than a good many doe," he continued, adding, "Some of the officers are at Swords Point." Browning's opponent, he bragged to his wife, ceased to give him trouble after a sharp confrontation between the two settled their differences: "he has ben as good as a whiped Puppy Since I gave him hell friday night." He took solace in the fact that his antagonist would be leaving the officers' mess soon. "But his dear wife is comeing and then they will Board I supose and I shall have nothing to do with him," Browning declared.[57]

Occasionally, enlisted men were dragged into these petty feuds, with predictably destructive consequences for their unit's morale. Sergeant Charles G. Blake of the 34th Massachusetts Infantry, an enlisted man who would eventually earn a commission as a lieutenant, complained to his wife about a particularly quarrelsome commander in 1863. "[T]he Lieutenant Colonel [William S. Lincoln] of this regiment is a cross double faced ignorant old granny," he wrote. "There is scarcely a private in this regiment but can learn him to drill and as a man there is not a spark of manhood about him. . . . When I have any business at head quarters I always make up my mind to have a row." Blake described an incident where Lincoln dressed him down for turning in a company report that omitted the signature of Captain Charles L. Chandler, his company commander. "[T]he old H——lpestle pitched into me rough about it," Blake griped. "If the Captain's name had been signed to it then of course I was not responsible for it and in either case he had no right to say a word to me about it but *should* have sent to the commander of the Company for corrections. Any one who has a grain of military knowledge or common sense knows this." Even worse, Lincoln's unjust rebuke offended the sergeant's sense of manhood and honor, and he responded with a display of gross insubordination. "Well as I never yet stood a damning from any man whether high or low without a cause," Blake told his wife, "I did not take it very kindly but gave it back as good as received. I got mad and so did the Colonel and he ordered me to my quarters under arrest."⁵⁸

When Captain Chandler learned of the incident, he attempted to have Sergeant Blake released but Lieutenant Colonel Lincoln refused to comply. Then, according to Blake, "the Captain got mad and gave him [the lieutenant colonel] h——l. He told the Colonel that the affair proved just what he was viz. a man unfit for his position and without a spark of military knowledge. [A]nd came off and left him to his reflections." The captain's tirade apparently achieved its desired effect, for about half an hour later, the sergeant was released from custody. The damage, however, had been done. Blake told his wife: "As it is the affair is not yet over with as Col Lincoln will find out. I can *prove* things against him which would dismiss him from the Service if he was tried." Blake believed that he had evidence of Lincoln's misconduct, complete with a witness to corroborate his charges. "One time when we were in Washington I was in his room Lieut Ripley being also there and one remark he then made shows what kind of a man he is. He said that My Captain was a "*d——n mean, stubborn, conceited, Cuss.* Is that proper language for a Lieut Col. to use in presence of a non-commissioned officer of the Company? It is in *direct* violation of the Articles of War." Blake's misfortune at being caught up in the ongoing feud between the lieutenant colonel and the captain undermined any remaining respect he might have had for Lincoln. "Thank God I am not afraid of him," he wrote, "and his fretting and fuming rather excites division than any fear to say nothing of respect."⁵⁹

As divisive as such feuds could be to the leadership of Civil War companies, the fraternal bonds between fellow citizen-officers could have an equally potent restorative effect on the harmony and morale of volunteers. In 1862 Confederate lieutenant John Hampden Chamberlayne described the respite that he found in his friendship with a literate and well-spoken fellow volunteer officer. "Conway Howard shares my quarters and helps greatly to halve the tedium," Chamberlayne wrote to a friend, Sally Grattan, in the summer of 1862. "[H]e is a surpassingly good companion, and knows much, both of things & men & books. It is a great thing to have almost all the times some person near one whom one has known before, especially at such periods as this when the present is often not pleasant & the future so clouded as to preclude even the often false & vain hopes which we indulge in time of peace." Chamberlayne valued his irenic conversations with Howard because they gave him an opportunity to reconnect with his peacetime self. These pleasant conversations permitted both men to lay aside the duties and burdens of their positions and, for a time, to remember what it was like to be a civilian. "Conway & I sometimes sit and talk of things & people so entirely on a peace establishment that we almost forget the miserable war with all its death & discomfort, separation, hope deferred, suffering, want, and ruin."[60]

In an 1862 letter to his mother, Lieutenant Chamberlayne attempted to explain the intimate, almost filial connections he formed with the other officers in A. P. Hill's Division of the Army of Northern Virginia. "You must pardon the egotism, but I must tell you all, & am proud of it, that when the news first came that the Col. [R. Lindsay Walker] would be transferred & I wd be ordered to follow him, the officers of the artillery every one of them told me how sorry they were, praised & complimented me in terms that I could hardly tell you, and so moved me by their expression of esteem & regard that I was indeed loath to leave so many whom I found strangers & have made friends & well wishers." Chamberlayne was overwhelmed by the intensity of these displays of friendship from his fellow citizen-officers. "Many other officers, of Infantry & Staff, including Gen. Hill, were also or seemed flatteringly reluctant to have me go," he added, "& altogether I have seldom been more gratified by evidence of friendship."[61]

Commissioned officers are, in the most basic sense, military leaders upon whom a state or other body has bestowed the necessary authority to command subordinates. They have no intrinsic or personal power. While loyalty, charisma, kinship, and the like can play important roles in the military relationship between officers and soldiers, a commissioned officer's actual authority is drawn directly from a sovereign power. This authority, vested in the nation, is limited to executing the responsibilities of a finite assignment, duty, or position. In the case of Civil War citizen-officers, this took the form of a commission, a tangible document entrusting them with the authority of their position and requiring them to discharge their duties. Citizen-soldiers were aware of the gravity of this document; many sent their commissions home to their families for safekeeping. "Enclosed I send you my Commission take good care of it," Lieutenant Courtland G. Stanton of the 21st Connecticut Infantry wrote to his wife. "You can have it framed if you like," he added.[62] Furthermore, commissioned officers had the option to tender their resignation, though officials were not required to accept it. "One good thing in haveing a commission is if a fellow gets sick or tired of sogering he can resign and go home to his Mamy," Lieutenant George Washington Whitman noted.[63]

A commission could bring significant material benefits for a citizen-officer. "There is a great difference between the life of a private and that of an officer, I find," wrote Lieutenant Robert Gould Shaw of the 2nd Massachusetts Infantry in 1861. "We have cots to sleep on, much better fare, and servants in abundance from among the men. When we get our company full, I shall have more liberty, for then the other officers will be at the camp."[64] Besides the obvious advantages in status and prestige, many citizen-officers could expect significant improvements in comfort, pay, and overall quality of living over the average enlisted man. A Massachusetts soldier wrote with pride of his brother's promotion to lieutenant, describing the benefits that such a change in status would bring. "George looks grand in his new uniform. I am glad of his promotion. It is easier for him, he can get better food to eat. Commissioned officers can buy anything in the rations at the commissaries, jet tea, sugar, fresh meat, potatoes & just at cost prices to Uncle Samuel," he wrote.[65]

"I wrote you a letter a couple of weeks since (which I suppose you received) telling you of my appointment to a second Lieutenancy in Co D," George Whitman of the 51st New York Infantry reported to his mother in 1862. "I like the position first rate and am getting along very well indeed, and as the pay is *good,* I am glad both on my account and yours, *Mamy.*"[66] Union captains received $115.50 per month, first and second lieutenants received $105.50, and staff officers usually received an additional allowance of $15 per month for expenses. Confederate captains and lieutenants typically received a few dollars less than Union officers, and their pay was further diminished by the severe inflation of the Confederacy's currency. Even so, company-grade officers received nearly ten times more per month than a typical private. Union privates, for example, earned $13 per month until June 1864, when their pay was increased to $16. Shamefully, black enlisted troops of all ranks in the Union army were paid just $10 per month, of which $3 was deducted for clothing. This amounted to the same pay as black laborers employed by the U.S. government. Confederate privates were paid at the antebellum U.S. Army rate of $11 per month, which was raised to $18 per month in 1864, though naturally in devalued currency.[67]

Given the relatively extravagant difference in pay between officers and enlisted men, along with the freedom and added independence of their position, some citizen-officers seized any opportunity to see to their own personal comfort. Though there were exceptions, most citizen-officers of company grade shared the same hardships and dangers as their enlisted volunteers; they slept in tents or under the open sky, marched in the heat and mud and rain, ate what rations were available, and attempted to share in their volunteers' sacrifices. Lieutenant Joseph J. Hoyle of the 55th North Carolina Infantry, for example, described the spartan living conditions of the officers in his company in April 1863. "We are down here with out anything except a blanket," Hoyle wrote of his regiment's camp near Suffolk, Virginia. "I and Capt have two blankets a piece. We are faring *like soldiers now,* you may be sure. Yet our men are all cheerful and in good spirits."[68]

Resourceful or clever citizen-officers learned how to avail themselves of the privileges of rank without being too ostentatious about it. Given such opportunities, many could not resist securing comfortable quarters, fine food, and strong drink when possible, thus placing the well-being of their men before their own proved a difficult lesson for some citizen-officers to learn. Captain E. L. Coleman of the 4th Louisiana Infantry Battalion described the opulence of the officers' winter quarters near Blackburn's Ford, Virginia, in vivid detail. "The officers have a double house, that is two rooms for 4 officers. My mess is a very nice one, we have one room for a bed room and the other for a mess room or parlour," Coleman wrote. "Our furniture has all been made to order and consists of a cubbord a table and some benches and a few camp stools. We also have two magnificent mantlepieces. The whole are made of imported (rosewood) in imitation . . . and if you *were not a judge* you would take it for /Rosewood/. I tell you that we are living in style," Coleman exulted. By contrast, enlisted men in his company were quartered "so that from seven to ten are in one house." The captain also could not resist boasting about the richness and variety of the officers' rations in his company. "[W]e have fresh oysters here when ever we feel like eating them, we have them in all styles, fired, stewed, and raw. We have turkeys once and awhile and other little delicacies of the season, such as olives, pickles, and every morning we have a champagne cocktail before breakfast. What do you think of that?" Coleman, perhaps abashed at the overweening tone of his description, attempted to inject a touch of modesty. "You will see by this letter that although I am away from home, still I am not so bad off as some poor devils are at home, and all I wish is that all my friends at home, may get along as well as I do."[69]

An officer could quickly earn his volunteers' contempt by perceptions that he lived easily, used his rank and position for advantage, or other such hints of corruption anathema to the republican tradition. One of the quickest ways for him to alienate his men was to violate the egalitarian notions of citizen-soldiers by abusing his power. This was easily accomplished by displays of extravagance, laziness, or greed normally denied to enlisted men. From his camp in Rolla, Missouri, in 1862, Theodore Preston Kellogg of the 13th Illinois Infantry described the resentment he and his fellow volunteers felt toward greedy officers in his regiment. "[T]he officers as a general thing I do not like they think too much of the almighty dollar & too little of their country," he complained to his wife. "[T]hey are making more money now than ever before & are not very anxious to close the war. [B]ut there are exceptions some of our officers are real good honest men who came from pure patriotism but they are few & far between but enough of them." For Kellogg, his officers' rapacious behavior reflected corruption as well as tyranny. "[T]hey are over us and if they are tyrants all we have to do is to grin & bear it. Do the best we can & hope for the end of the war."[70]

Moreover, volunteers were unreservedly scornful of officers who appeared to abuse the privileges of rank. Massachusetts private Warren Lee Goss recalled a particular officer's tendency to excuse himself from dangerous duties due to illness. The man "had not shown a disposition, proportionate to his rank, to face the enemy, [and] hired two men to carry him on a stretcher to the hospital boat; and this valiant officer was absent from the army nearly a whole year." Goss blamed this kind of behavior on a combination of cowardice, greed, and corruption. "We believed at that time that some of the hospitals at the North, for the sake of the money made on each ration, sheltered and retained skulkers," he complained.[71]

John De Forest found irritating the luxurious accommodations he discovered a pair of junior officers enjoying in occupied New Orleans in 1862. The captain was even more offended that these two were not generals or colonels but merely a lowly adjutant and an even lowlier lieutenant of the line. "Of course I was not indignantly surprised to find the field officer grandly lodged and abounding in foraged claret," he informed his wife of his visit to the lieutenants' apartment. "But I really was disgusted at receiving an even more luxurious hospitality from a mere lieutenant." De Forest described the quarters as a "treasure box" full of "Parisian furniture" and other trinkets worth thousands of dollars. The commandeered house had been built by a rich New Orleanian for his French mistress before the Civil War; the owner had departed the city to take up a commission as a captain in the Confederate army, and Union occupiers evicted his mistress from her gaudy lodgings. "The bedsteads are lofty four-posters, elaborately carved and of solid mahogany," De Forest grumbled, and the bedroom contained "a small bureau encrusted with patterns of gilt enamel set in tortoise shell." The quarters also contained a smoking room, a "Moriscan" courtyard, "Swiss boxes, delicate wood carvings, amber-mouthed Turkish pipes, volumes of engravings, dress swords, old Toledo blades and inlaid pistols," along with an elaborate kitchen managed by "a noted *artiste,* a handsome quadroon named Alick, formerly chief at one of the best restaurants here." The officers' apartment was littered with a variety of silks, satins, jewelry, and expensive civilian clothing, including a "superb crimson scarf, such as is worn by officers" discarded on "a pile of soiled linen." De Forest groused that the "adjutant and the lieutenant who lodges with him are making themselves at home; for instance, I heard the latter say, 'I think I shall send this thing to my wife.' He held in his hand a large tortoise-shell fan which I judged must have cost fully one hundred dollars." The captain suspected the ignorant lieutenant "had no idea of its value and had never heard of fans worth more than a dollar or two." These young men also enjoyed a fully stocked wine cellar full of madeira, vintage burgundy, and iced sauterne. The lieutenant boasted to De Forest "that in one day he and his friends drank forty-six bottles," though the captain found the appropriated burgundy "soured and corky, although he did not know it, the barbarian."[72] High-living officers like these were the bane of volunteers; while some degree of difference in lifestyle and quality of living between officers and enlisted men was expected in both armies, as well as between officers who served in garrison and those who served in the field, if too great they could foster deep discontent and resentment.

Along with the prospect of more-comfortable living arrangements and fare, some citizen-officers enjoyed the luxury of body servants, waiters, or valets to see to their everyday needs in camp or on campaign.[73] Confederate officers occasionally brought family slaves to camp with them, though this practice appears to have declined over time. Sandie Pendleton wrote home in 1863 to inquire about the health of Buck, a favorite family slave, and to describe his own difficulties in securing a reliable body servant while on campaign with the Army of Northern Virginia. "Send & ask particularly about him for me & let me hear how he is in every letter," Pendleton wrote, "for you can't tell how much I miss him. It is utterly impossible to get another boy here, and it is right hard to manage without one."[74] Lieutenant William H. S. Burgwyn of the 35th North Carolina Infantry often referred to his slave and body servant as "my boy Pompey," whom he described as "my valet de chambres and man of all work and deeds" in letters to his family.[75] Other slaveholding Southern officers who might not necessarily maintain "body servants" on campaign still expressed keen interest in exerting their authority as masters over their slaves at home. Captain Ujanirtus Allen of the 21st Georgia Infantry, for instance, instructed his wife to have a family friend whip a rebellious slave "from head to foot, not less than two or three hundred.... If he is not whipped you might as well set them all free."[76] Allen, like other slaveholders, also wished to remind their slaves of their master's benevolence even when off at war. "Remember me to the negroes;" he told his wife, "tell them that I always like to hear of their doing well, and being faithful to their business and hope they will give a good account of themselves."[77]

Union and Confederate regulations permitted company officers to detail one soldier as a waiter, provided that the man consented to the assignment. Noncommissioned officers were forbidden to perform this duty, and private soldiers were prohibited from being "employed in any menial office, or made to perform any service not military, for the private benefit of any officer or mess of officers."[78] Other citizen-officers benefited from personal or family wealth, which eased their burden of military service considerably. George Whitman wrote of the luxury of sharing a mess with his affluent company commander with black body servants to wait upon them. "Our Captain is a young man from Buffalo N.Y. named Hazard whose father is very rich and we live in fine style I tell you," the New York lieutenant boasted from New Bern, North Carolina, in 1862. "Cap has bread made in the Citty and buys lots of eggs, fish Oysters chickens, milk and everything else he can see. We have three nigger boys to cook and wait on us, but Cap can afford it so I dont care."[79]

Rank had its privileges, and some citizen-officers adopted an elitist attitude toward enlisted men outside their fraternity. Occasionally, they went to great lengths to maintain the exclusivity of their caste, even so far as to circumvent the military hierarchy they had agreed to be a part of. In July 1862 Colonel William Lord DeRosset of the 3rd North Carolina Infantry recommended that Private Cicero Craig be promoted to lieutenant in the regiment's Company I for "conspicuous gallantry" during the Seven Days' Campaign. Brigade headquarters quickly confirmed the promotion. DeRosset then personally asked Governor Henry Toole Clark to approve it, and "the Governor promised to have the commission for Lieutenant Craig mailed to him without delay." Meanwhile, the new lieutenant took up his post in Company I, much to the disgust of a particularly elitist pair of company officers. These two aggrieved men went behind Colonel DeRosset's back, approaching the governor directly and warning him "that if Craig was made lieutenant of the company the men would resist and disband." Clark took these officers at their word, and without consulting the colonel, he revoked Craig's new commission and ordered Company I to fill the vacancy by election. The regiment's reaction to all this meddling was predictable. As DeRosset recalled, "the officers of the Third held to the original understanding with the Governor that all promotions and appointments should be made by or upon the recommendation of the commanding officer of the regiment," and the colonel refused to hold the election. DeRosset went further, telling Governor Clark "should he insist upon it, that he could consider his resignation as being before him." DeRosset explained "that the discipline of the men in his regiment was his responsibility as much as that of the company officers, and he would be responsible for results." As for the two conniving officers who tried to sabotage Craig's promotion, the colonel dryly remarked that "[a]s a finale, both officers referred to very soon ceased to hold their positions, and, for some forgotten reasons, were allowed to go home."[80]

For all the advantages and benefits, some citizen-officers struggled to determine whether the loyalty and regard of their comrades and subordinates was genuine. "I cant tell whether the men like me or not," worried Confederate officer James Griffin in 1862. "[T]hey are very respectful to me, but that they are obliged to be—Military authority is the most powerful known to man. But doesnt do harm unless abused—I think the officers generally like me and most of the men two [sic] but some of them I reckon do not." Griffin, an aristocratic planter from South Carolina, illustrated the insecurity many citizen-officers felt. Such apprehensive officers were often preoccupied with their status, reputation, and personal honor to the exclusion of all else. Even so, Griffin knew that as a commander, he could not expect to please everyone. "An Officer," he ruefully concluded, "as a general rule, who does his duty is apt to make some Enemies."[81] Sometimes feelings of insecurity prompted citizen-officers to ease their anxieties by adopting an exaggerated military manner; rather than simply presenting a confident command presence, they instead made themselves into overbearing, pompous caricatures. More often than not, these efforts failed, eliciting the contempt of volunteers and fellow officers alike. "There are a great many officers in the Service that go home and it would be just as well if a great many more would go and stay there for all the advantage they are to the Army," Lieutenant James H. Gillam of the 123rd Ohio Infantry wrote to his wife in 1862. "[F]or there are some that know that they are officers and that is all they do know, for I find with all the diligence and study that I can give the matters that I do not know the half that should." Gillam could sense insincerity, and like most citizen-soldiers, he abhorred such playacting. "This thing of playing Soldier and putting on stile will have to be dispensed with if everything Rebelious is put down," he declared.[82]

Just as a convincing command presence was indispensable to an officer's effective leadership, it was also a critical component of citizen-officer culture in both the Union and Confederate armies. Uniforms, insignia, and other symbols of rank were obvious and essential aspects of any officer's command presence. Swords, braid, shoulder straps, and the like were important external cues for reinforcing their military authority and for maintaining discipline among their volunteers.[83] Yet another, more subtle function of the regalia of command was to remind citizen-officers themselves that they were a part of the same distinctive fraternity as the regulars; perhaps not equivalent in experience, training, or even ability, but nonetheless due the same respect from subordinates and held to the same expectations as professional officers. Many junior-level officers took great pride in the acquisition and display of emblems of rank, and no military symbol had more power than the sword. In both the Confederate and Union armies, only commissioned officers, senior sergeants, and cavalrymen were permitted to carry swords. Regulations required officers to wear the proper uniform, and Union officers were required to carry a sword at all times while on duty.[84] Officers in either army who were placed under arrest for any offense were required to surrender their sword as the symbol of their official authority.[85]

For all their commitment to the egalitarianism and democratic prerogatives of the citizen-soldier ethos, many Civil War citizen-officers could not help but be drawn in by the symbolic power of the sword. As historian John Keegan writes: "Europe, almost until the end of the *ancien régime,* remained a society in which the ruling class was also a military class. The sword, accoutrement *de rigeur* of anyone pretending to the title of gentleman, was the outward symbol of that identification." An officer's sword served as a link to the power and gentility of aristocracy as well as to the traditions of the elite military class represented by the regular officers of the U.S. Army. It also represented a connection with the virtuous, the romantic, and the sentimental. Cincinnatus and his Roman tribunes wore swords, as did the cavaliers of Lord Tennyson and Sir Walter Scott; even George Washington and the heroes of the American Revolution carried swords into battle. The weapon's significance, like the military profession itself, evolved to reflect the society it served. As Keegan writes, "The old swordbearing class, which had justified its social primacy by its availability to lead in battle, gave up its monopoly of military leadership to a new class, drawn partly but not exclusively from it, whose sole purpose was officership."[86]

An officer who surrendered his sword in battle yielded up his authority and placed his personal honor at the mercy of the victorious enemy. Thomas Blackburn Rodgers of the 140th Pennsylvania Infantry described his capture in the Wheatfield during the Battle of Gettysburg and the subsequent humiliation of surrendering his sword to his captors. "When we came out of the woods three Confederate battle flags flashed by us, and we were in the hands of the enemy," he wrote after the battle. "The guard who escorted us to the rear was in charge of a sergeant, a good-natured fellow, for when he demanded my sword I declined, saying that I would deliver it only to an officer. It was evident that neither of us understood the ethics pertaining to prisoners of war." The Confederate sergeant did not like the idea of keeping an armed enemy officer in his custody and insisted that the major surrender his weapon. After a few minutes of heated negotiations with his indignant prisoner, the sergeant relented. "He argued with me for some time, but finally concluded that I was right in my contention, and I kept the sword," Rodgers remembered. But he would not be permitted to keep his sword for long. "After going about half a mile to the rear a handsome young officer of Longstreet's staff rode up and said, 'Sergeant, what is that officer doing with is sword on?'" Rodgers recalled. "The sergeant explained that he wanted me to give it up, but I had declined to surrender it to any one but an officer. 'Very well,' he said, 'I am an officer and he can give it to me.' which, of course, I did, glad to be rid of it, as I knew I could not keep it." Despite his dire circumstances, Rodgers could not help but be amused by the peculiar debate. "He must have smiled at the absurdity of the thing," the Pennsylvanian said of the nameless staff officer. "Later that evening we were halted at a farmhouse to get water, where Gen. Longstreet had his headquarters," Rodgers wrote. "I saw the young officer exhibit my handsome sword with the remark that he had captured it from a Yankee officer. Of course, I remained discreetly silent."[87]

Some enlisted volunteers were bemused by the mystical symbolic power that their citizen-officers invested in their swords. Private Fisk of the 2nd Vermont Infantry, for example, was scornful about the immoderate admiration officers and civilians, especially ladies, exhibited for the weapons. "Speaking of swords," wrote Fisk. "I cannot refrain from wondering at the magic charms it always seems to have for the wearer. All of the virtues imanagable [sic] seem to be concentrated in this little, useless weapon of war," he grumbled. "All of the soldiers are half mad with eagerness to wear one, all I mean except myself." He readily conceded the mysterious advantages that the ostentatious display of an officer's sword conveyed upon its owner, and his sardonic assessment drips with satire. "It is always a sure passport to the most select society, and we privates esteem it our highest delight to render homage to the wearer, no matter who he is, or what are his antecedents." Fisk turned his sarcasm into an egalitarian critique of the citizen-officer corps as a body. "Why, I have seen men of no sort of consequence above the average of soldiers generally," he proclaimed, "suddenly raised to vast importance in this little world of ours, upon getting the privilege of buckling one of these swords around their waists, and dragging it dingling along after their feet."[88]

Moreover, Private Fisk continued, every common soldier would be wise to aspire to the wearing of an officer's sword, and the "sword mania" so prevalent among volunteers was thus a thing to be encouraged. "Doesn't a soldier know that with a sword by his side, he is free from a thousand vexations that a soldier with a musket is subject to? That it gives him a thousand privileges from which a private is disbarred? Don't they know that newspapers will speak of their services in longer paragraphs if they live, and give them a longer obituary if they die? Don't they know, too, that the ladies will smile upon them more sweetly, and welcome them more cordially if they wear a sword, than if they carry a gun?" Fisk placed much of the blame for "sword mania" upon the ladies at home, who emphasized their sweethearts' rank and status over their actual abilities. He pointed out that officer swords were a "child's plaything" compared to the heavy muskets of humble citizen-soldiers like himself, and they were "of no consequence whatever in the bloody earnest work of fighting this rebellion." Fisk could not resist a final sarcastic parting shot at pompous officers and their useless "toad-stabbers," as his comrades called the blades. "That dashing officer—that captain or lieutenant that you think so well of, never hurt one of them [Confederates] with his weapon," Fisk avowed. "His courage was good enough, but the simple reason was, poor fellow, he had nothing to hurt them with."[89]

Despite the ridicule soldiers heaped upon such prideful displays, most citizen-officers relished the prospect of owning and wearing the accoutrements of their office. Outfitting themselves with the required uniforms and equipment, however, could prove an expensive proposition for those of limited means. Captain John W. Harris, a brigade staff officer in Cheatham's Division of the Army of Tennessee, implored his mother to help him obtain suitable pieces of his uniform in 1863. "Please get someone to go to Waggener the tailor," Harris begged his mother, "and tell him to make me a pair of navy blue pants with lace stripes and if possible have them sent out to me, a uniform now out here costs three hundred & fifty dollars, and it is an impossibility almost to get a good one at that."[90] New lieutenant Henry Clay Matrau of the 6th Wisconsin Infantry also sought financial help from his family to fit himself out in the proper attire. "I need some more money to enable me to get a respectable outfit," Matrau wrote to his parents, "such as a sword and belt, Officers uniform, &c, &c. I wish to make as respectable appearance as possible and my clothes are rather seedy now."[91]

Harris and Matrau, like all Union and Confederate citizen-officers, were responsible for outfitting themselves with the required accoutrements of their position.[92] In theory, at least, enlisted volunteers relied upon their respective governments to provide them with basic items of clothing and equipment. Citizen-officers did not share the same privilege. Since they were expected to conform to uniform regulations regardless of their personal finances and were expected to comport themselves in a gentlemanly and officerlike fashion, these expectations occasionally created temporary financial hardships for citizen-officers on campaign and for the families at home who supported them. "I should send for some things if I had the money but will get along," newly promoted lieutenant George Washington Weston of the 26th Iowa Infantry wrote to his wife during the Siege of Vicksburg in 1863. "I bought a coat of Capt Johnson. [H]e let me have it cheap and it is nice, all I nead now is a sword cap boots and vest and I shall manage to get them." Weston tried to reassure his wife that all of these expenses were entirely necessary for his new position. "I shall be just as prudent and saveing as I possibley can be," he promised, "but an officer must dress differant from the privates or he *cannot* get along." Weston hoped that she would be able to solicit help from their friends and neighbors to see him properly attired. "Ask Mr C if he dont think my friends can aford to present me with a sword to fight for freedom, but you need not tell him that I told you to. I realy wish they would not that I care so much for the cost of it but it would please me for many reasons."[93] Confederate citizen-officers faced similar financial travails, though with the added difficulties of national material shortages and the extreme inflation of their currency. A financial scandal in 1863 and 1864 added to their difficulties in procuring uniforms when a large amount of cloth intended for military use was unaccountably diverted to rear-echelon officers. The scandal and its resulting shortfalls in cloth created significant material shortages for officers serving in the field. By the end of the war, many Confederate citizen-officers relied almost exclusively on their beleaguered families to provide them with homespun butternut cloth or gray-jean wool for their makeshift coats and trousers.[94]

Civil War volunteers eagerly anticipating promotion were sometimes premature in their haste to acquire an officer's regalia. Courtland Stanton of the 21st Connecticut Infantry ordered his lieutenant's sword and uniform before his promotion was even official and hoped that he had not erred by acting quickly. "I think I shall find it pleasant to stay here notwithstanding the little difficulties. I now have all the priveledges of an officer—which are many," he wrote to his wife in 1864. "I expect that I shall get the *Shoulder Straps* soon. . . . This thing has been in the wind for some time allthough I did not write you any thing about it for I intended it as a suprise but I had not reckoned on this Acting business." Stanton, like many citizen-officers of modest means, expended a great deal of energy worrying about how to pay for the exorbitant costs of outfitting himself as a proper company-grade officer. "I think I will write Ben now that he can send along that *Sword* he proposed my friends should give me. I have got an old one which with the Reb Belt is my present fit out. It will cost me considerable to[o] If I get promoted Clothes are so high."[95] Once correctly outfitted, however, citizen-officers were usually quite proud of the dashing figure they believed that they cut. Captain Charles J. Mills, a staff officer, took great satisfaction in his gallant military appearance during a visit to Boston in 1864. "The next morning I rode in from Camp, creating rather a sensation along the way by my full uniform, sash, gauntlets, boots, spurs, and sabre," Mills gloated. "It was the proudest day of my life."[96]

Occasionally, citizen-soldiers or civilians demonstrated their admiration for beloved officers by gifting them with the symbols of their position. George Whitman experienced such an event in 1862, which understandably filled the young lieutenant with pride. "The boys in our company gave me quite a surprise yesterday. I was in my tent, washing and getting ready to go on parade, when our Orderly Sergeant came to my tent and said some of the men wanted to see me out at their quarters," he told his mother. "I suposed there was some little difficulty they wanted me to settle but when I got there I found the Company all formed in line and all hands seemed in might good humor by the way they grined, and one of them went into his tent and brought out a splendid sword and sash, sword belt, shoulder knots, sword knot, and everything complete, and gave them to me, in behalf of the company." Whitman was moved by the gesture. "I was quite taken aback I tell you," he confessed, "as it was done so quietly that I was taken by surprise and my being in the company such a short time, that it was the last thing that I expected."[97] Lieutenant Arthur L. Conger of the 115th Ohio Infantry positively radiated gratitude and patriotic ardor as he thanked a lady who had presented him with a sword. "Miss Edgerly: To you and to those whom you represent I tender my most sincere and heartfelt thanks for this token of your respect & Esteem," wrote Conger, "and the only assurance I can give you that it shal[l] not be dishonored while in my keeping is that it is my most earnest prayer that should my hand draw this sword in defence of any cause other than that of right and justice may it be wrenched from that hand and used as a weapon which shal[l] take my own heart's blood."[98] Citizen-officers cherished such displays of affection and loyalty; gifts of swords or rank insignia reinforced their military authority, reassured them of their distinctive status as commanders, and affirmed them as friends, fellow citizens, and gentlemen worthy of honor and respect.

Swords, shoulder straps, and the gilded sleeve braids that wisecracking volunteers sometimes called "chicken guts" were more than just insignia of rank or tokens of martial vanity. This regalia had significant emotional and symbolic meaning for the men who wore them into battle.[99] The trappings of authority were especially important to citizen-officers because they represented a tangible manifestation of the honorable burden of command. Moreover, they symbolized admission into the exclusive club of officers and gentlemen and served a practical purpose in camp and on the battlefield. Though membership in the fraternity of officers included significant benefits, theirs was also an arduous calling. Citizen-officers had to maintain a delicate equilibrium in commanding their volunteers while learning a dangerous and difficult profession quickly, under intense pressure, and in the face of widespread resistance to regularization and military discipline. Combat was the ultimate ordeal for Union and Confederate citizen-officers, however, putting their hard-won lessons in leadership, professional competence, and courage to the supreme test.

Oliver Wendell Holmes Jr., who would later become an associate justice of the U.S. Supreme Court, served as a company officer in the 20th Massachusetts Infantry, the "Harvard Regiment." Wounded multiple times and promoted for bravery and leadership, 23-year-old Holmes left the army in 1864, physically and emotionally broken by his experiences.

Historical & Special Collections, Harvard Law School Library

Henry Livermore Abbott was widely admired for his steady leadership and gallantry under fire. Eventually promoted to major, Abbott was killed leading the 20th Massachusetts Infantry at the Battle of the Wilderness in 1864. He was just 22 years old at his death.
Historical & Special Collections, Harvard Law School Library

John Pelham in the uniform of a West Point cadet. Though shaken by his first exposure to combat at the First Battle of Bull Run, Pelham quickly established a reputation as one of the Confederacy's most daring and capable young combat leaders. In March 1863, Pelham was killed in action in Virginia while leading a cavalry charge.

Alabama Department of Archives and History, Montgomery, Alabama

Reunion of 20th Massachusetts Infantry officers at Harvard University, 1869. Among the officers pictured is a frail-looking Oliver Wendell Holmes, Jr., seated second from left. Attrition rates among junior officers were extreme on both sides of the conflict, and the unique challenges and shared peril of command often strengthened the emotional bonds between them.

Historical & Special Collections, Harvard Law School Library

Ephraim Cutler Dawes in a major's uniform. At the Battle of Shiloh in 1862, Dawes witnessed the near-disintegration of his inexperienced 53rd Ohio Infantry after the emotional collapse of his commanding officer. Dawes and other company officers rallied their regiment, narrowly averting disaster.

Dawes Arboretum Collection on Ohio Memory, call. no. Om772-897058-001

Officers of the 114th Pennsylvania Infantry and black attendants near Petersburg, Virginia, 1864. The labor of body servants, valets, orderlies, and slaves eased the burden of service for some junior officers and demonstrated the intrinsic privileges of an officer's commission.

Library of Congress Prints and Photographs Division

Two unidentified officers in Union captain's and lieutenant's uniforms, displaying the regalia of command. Swords, sashes, shoulder boards, and sleeve braid all served as essential reminders of an officer's authority.
Liljenquist Family Collection of Civil War Photographs, Library of Congress

Junior officers with subdued rank insignia, Army of the Potomac, Culpeper, Virginia, September 1863. Late-war regulations permitted subdued insignia to help make officers less conspicuous to enemy sharpshooters.
Library of Congress Prints and Photographs Division

General August V. Kautz, author of the manual *The 1865 Customs of Service for Officers of the Army* for company commanders. Officers on both sides of the conflict relied on military manuals to learn the intricacies of their duties.

National Archives, 111-B-1916

Staff officer Captain David Power Conyngham of the Irish Brigade, Bealeton, Virginia, 1863. Unlike their counterparts in line regiments, staff officers often owed their positions to appointment or patronage rather than to election.
Library of Congress Prints and Photographs Division

5

The Early War Combat Experience

"I have seen what Romancers call glorious war," Confederate artillery officer John Pelham wrote to his father a few days after the First Battle of Bull Run in July 1861. "I have seen it in all its phases. I have heard the booming of cannon, and the more deadly rattle of musketry at a distance—I have heard it all nearby and have been under its destructive showers; I have seen men and horses fall thick and fast around me." The young lieutenant struggled to articulate the shattering emotional consequences of his first combat experience. In battle he had seen the best and worst of human nature, and combat was not what he had expected it to be. "I have seen our own men bloody and frightened flying before the enemy—I have seen them bravely charge the enemy's lines and heard the shout of triumph as they carried the position," he told his father. "I have heard the agonizing shrieks of the wounded and dying—I have passed over the battle field and seen the mangled forms of men and horses in frightful abundance—men without heads, without arms, and others without legs." Pelham's youthful illusions about the glory of war were swept away in a single day, leaving him and many others full of uncertainty about the nature and meaning of the war that had yet to be decided. "All this I have witnessed and more, till my heart sickens; and war is not glorious as novelists would have us believe." Moreover, Pelham was appalled by the strange sense of exhilaration he felt in combat, given its terrible consequences and the human suffering it caused. "It is only when we are in the heat and flush of battle that it is fascinating and interesting. It is only then that we enjoy it. When we forget ourselves and revel in the destruction we are dealing around us. I am now ashamed of the feelings I had in those hours of danger."[1]

Bull Run was the first major combat experience for most Civil War citizen-officers and volunteers and their first true exposure to the realities of fighting. The unexpected slaughter of this initial battle stunned many who participated in it. Confederate captain Thomas J. Goree of Brigadier General James Longstreet's staff described the astounding intensity of fire in the battle and lamented how inexperienced citizen-officers ran away at their first taste of combat. "All the time we were exposed to a heavy firing from the batteries on the hill (and I am sorry to say that a portion of the 5th North Carolina Regiment in our Brigade made a pretty fast retrograde movement, but the most of them soon rallied and returned. 2 captains, however, declared that they couldn't stand it and left the field.)"[2] Lieutenant J. A. McPherson of the 6th North Carolina Infantry stood firm under fire at First Bull Run; nevertheless, he marveled that he was not struck down and wondered how anyone could have survived the experience. "I never thought I could stand the fire of bullets as I did that day; and how I escaped being killed I do not know," McPherson wrote a few days after the battle. "[I]t was just an act of providence that we were not killed by hundreds. About 100 of our regiment were killed and wounded—17 killed and some mortally wounded."[3] Pelham was also amazed that he had escaped death, given the sheer magnitude of the enemy's fire. "You may want to know my feelings," the lieutenant wrote to his father. "I felt as cool and deliberate under the shower of lead and iron as if I had been at home by our fireside—I did not feel fear at any moment; I can't see how I escaped—a merciful Providence must have been watching over us and our cause."[4]

Many fresh citizen-officers taken aback at the savagery of First Bull Run fretted over the consequent difficulties it created in their efforts to lead their companies. Lieutenant George Baylor of the 12th Virginia Cavalry described his inexperienced unit's immense problems in withdrawing while under fire. "Companies C and G, though suffering heavily, were unflinching and holding their own against largely superior numbers, when the order was given to fall back and form a new line," Baylor remembered. "This was done, no doubt, to present a front to the foe now outflanking us. It was, however, an unfortunate move. Few men can retire calmly under a galling fire, and the execution of this order resulted in stampeding some good soldiers, but the large majority re-formed and again advanced, and our right at the same time moving forward, the enemy was pressed back and soon in flight."[5] A number of Confederate volunteers, awed by the destruction they had witnessed, assumed that the battle had been lost. Some of them ran for cover, others wandered off into the woods and fields, and a few simply sat down in place and ignored their officers' frantic entreaties to rally.[6]

Inexperienced officers' uncertainties about their own competence compounded their fearfulness in battle, as Captain Newton Martin Curtis of the 16th New York Infantry described of his first independent command experience at Bull Run. When the brigade commander ordered his regiment to send a detachment of four companies forward to test the Confederates' strength, he called for the maneuver to be led by an experienced officer; Curtis recalled that the order particularly emphasized the words "an experienced officer." Unfortunately, there were no officers in the regiment with any real military experience save one, Captain Frederick Tapley of Company B. Tapley had done some Indian fighting as a noncommissioned officer in the regular army before the war, but as the most junior captain in the 16th New York Infantry, he did not have sufficient seniority to lead the detachment. Curtis, though completely new to military life, was the senior captain and therefore took command of the four companies sent forward. After a brief skirmish, Curtis recalled, "Captain Tapley came hurriedly from the right of the line, calling out, 'Captain Curtis, why don't you obey the order to retreat?'" He was baffled and replied that he had had received no such order. Tapley explained to him that a bugle call had sounded, which was, in fact, the order to retreat. The embarrassed officer withdrew his men from the woods and returned to the Union line, none the worse for the experience.[7]

Not all units shared this good fortune. Union officer John S. Ellis, a Californian temporarily attached to the 71st New York Infantry, saw firsthand the widespread shortcomings of green volunteers led by well-meaning but inexperienced citizen-officers. "I cannot here relate all the scenes I saw, the horrible wounds inflicted, and all the incidents of this most shameful and unnecessary battle," Ellis wrote after the battle, "for which the troops feel they were sacrificed by the stupidity of their generals. Suffice it to say our men fought bravely; and I can only account for the panic with which they were seized by the facts that the teamsters took fright and drove their wagons pell mell through them, and that many of the regiments had totally incompetent field and company officers—many of whom acted cowardly—and the most of whom didn't know what to do."[8] Inexperienced citizen-officers were nearly as dangerous to their own side as they were to the enemy in early war engagements. Captain Goree described General Longstreet's perilous efforts to instill order among his green troops amid the fear and excitement of their initial encounter with the enemy at First Bull Run. "At one time Genl L[ongstreet] was himself exposed to fire from both the enemy and our own troops," Goree wrote soon after the battle. "He had ordered up his reserve, the 7th Va. Regt. (and fearing that they in their excitement might fire before he was ready for them) he placed himself immediately in front of them." According to Goree, this decision nearly proved fatal. "No sooner than they were in position and while the Genl was before them," the captain said of the trigger-happy Virginians, "they commenced firing and the Genl only saved himself by throwing himself off his horse and lying flat on the ground."[9]

Regular-army officers who participated in the battle were dismayed by the mediocre performances of volunteers. Lieutenant Eugene Carter, a West Pointer and a company officer in the 8th U.S. Infantry, admitted that the Union army had been "whipped, and it ended in a total rout" at First Bull Run, in no small part because of citizen-officers' ineptitude. Carter took command of his company when the acting commander was wounded in the leg, and his regulars lost heavily in the battle. He admitted that while his men "could only be kept together by the most superhuman efforts of our officers," the undisciplined volunteers facing their first combat were almost worthless under fire. "You will hear great stories about the bravery of this and that regiment of volunteers," Carter wrote to his father soon afterward, "but believe me, most of them acted like cowards in my division. I was on the hill and saw them, and had it not been for our regular batteries, the whole army would have been taken prisoners and killed."[10]

Nevertheless, novice citizen-officers' combat experiences at First Bull Run provided them with valuable initiations into the terror and confusion of battle, forcing them to learn the indispensable survival skills mandatory for successful combat command. While these lessons were often emotionally and physically painful, they were also valuable, and the suffering that citizen-officers experienced in their first engagements imparted essential experience for the future. "It is probable that in no battle of modern times, in which thirty-five thousand men were engaged," Newton Curtis reflected, "was there so small a number of officers educated in the science and art of war; nor was there a battle which was the nursery of so many who came to great prominence in the profession of arms, as those who rose from the mob-like forces which contended at Manassas." Captain Curtis knew that these first tentative steps would produce invaluable combat leaders for vastly inexperienced volunteers, company leaders who adapted their skills and habits to maximize their effectiveness as combat commanders at higher grades. "Those who became the most prominent were of the field or line, and generally the junior in years, as well as in rank, of those holding higher commands; the men who attained the greatest success were, chiefly, graduates of the Military Academy," he observed. "A number of captains and lieutenants rose to the command of corps, divisions, and brigades."[11]

The Battle of Shiloh, fought nearly a year later on April 6 and 7, 1862, was the first major combat experience for most western citizen-officers and volunteers. Shiloh was a battle of unprecedented deadliness, and the two-day bloodbath swept away any remaining hopes that the war could be brought to a swift and decisive conclusion. The butchery there also stunned its participants, winnowing unfit, cowardly, or incompetent citizen-officers from the armies and providing those who survived a sobering preview of what lay ahead for them.[12] Like First Bull Run in the East, Shiloh was a brutal learning experience for inexperienced citizen-soldiers serving in the West. For twenty-two-year-old lieutenant Ephraim Cutler Dawes of the 53rd Ohio Infantry, Shiloh represented a turning point in his education as a volunteer junior officer. On the night of April 5, with the war not quite a year old, Dawes and his regiment found themselves in a remote and unexpected place. The 53rd Ohio, part of Colonel Jesse Hildebrand's brigade in Brigadier General William Tecumseh Sherman's division of Major General Ulysses S. Grant's Army of the Tennessee, was bivouacked in the forests and fields alongside the Tennessee River not far from a strategically important bend called Pittsburg Landing. Dawes, who was a recent graduate of Marietta College in Marietta, Ohio, had joined the regiment the previous fall as adjutant. The position required him to serve directly under the regiment's commanding officer, Colonel Jesse J. Appler, who had been instrumental in organizing and recruiting the 53rd Ohio. Furthermore, the colonel had some antebellum militia experience, while most of his volunteers and officers, including Dawes, had none whatsoever.[13]

Unfortunately, Appler was a nervous man, and his disposition on the night of April 5 did nothing to inspire confidence in his inexperienced volunteers. The colonel had been awake for most of the night, pacing through his regiment's camp and fretting over rumors of rebel cavalry in the dark woods beyond the firelight. He had sufficient reasons to be concerned. The 53rd Ohio Infantry, like most other units in the Army of the Tennessee, was a new regiment full of green recruits. The Ohioans had received their muskets in Paducah, Kentucky, only a few weeks prior to their arrival in Tennessee. Most of the volunteers had never once fired their weapons, nor had they been drilled in their use by their novice officers. Even worse, by the time the 53rd Ohio arrived at their camp near Pittsburg Landing, about two-thirds of the men were incapacitated by illness and were unfit for duty.[14]

Earlier in the afternoon of April 5, Lieutenant Dawes watched an increasingly anxious Colonel Appler send out patrols, dash off worried reports to an irritated General Sherman, and worriedly speculate about the popping of gunfire in the deep woods. His compulsive nervousness grated on his officers and men alike, but Dawes and his comrades felt powerless to alter their circumstances. Apparently, even Sherman began to find Appler irritating. After receiving one too many panicky messages, the prickly general finally erupted. Through a staff officer, Sherman reportedly told the colonel to "take your d——d regiment back to Ohio. There is no enemy nearer than Corinth." To make matters worse, Dawes recalled, the general delivered the salty rebuke within earshot of several of Appler's enlisted volunteers, who apparently had a good laugh at their fretful commander's expense.[15] If the raw Ohioans had known what was about to happen to them, they probably would not have been so amused. At about four o'clock in the morning on Sunday, April 6, a frantic Appler roused Dawes from his tent, shouting that the long-dreaded Confederate attack on the Union camp was underway. The lieutenant scrambled from his cot in time to see the agitated colonel issue a flurry of conflicting and nonsensical orders to his scattered company officers. Appler then dispatched a courier to division headquarters warning that the enemy was attacking in force and begging the general for instructions. Sherman, still skeptical, supposedly replied, "You must be badly scared over there." Soon, though, it was obvious that Appler had not been crying wolf and that a heavy attack from elements of Major General William J. Hardee's Third Corps of the Army of Mississippi was underway.

As Colonel Appler hastily attempted to form the 53rd Ohio Infantry into a makeshift line of battle, Dawes recalled half-dressed company officers stumbling from their tents in confusion and shouting orders at their bewildered and frightened volunteers. The crackle of Confederate gunfire intensified in the early morning gloom, and as gray columns began to appear in the woods, Appler ordered Dawes to take the regiment out toward the approaching enemy. The lieutenant rushed to obey; then, apparently confused, the colonel changed his mind and ordered Dawes to countermarch the regiment back through its camp instead. As the baffled Ohioans tried to figure out what their commander wanted from them, hundreds of frantic teamsters, orderlies, servants, sutlers, and stragglers streamed out of the Union camp and pelted for the army's rear. After disentangling themselves from the mess, the 53rd Ohio finally managed to form a firing line with the rest of Hildebrand's and Col. Ralph Buckland's brigades. Nervous volunteers loaded their unfamiliar muskets and waited for the Confederates to come into range.

The 53rd Ohio fired its first shots of the Battle of Shiloh at around 7:00 A.M., Lieutenant Dawes recalled. The attackers faltered at the volley, reformed, and paused again under the Union troops' heavy fire. Then, just as it appeared the enemy assault would peter out, disaster struck the regiment. The jittery Appler, out of position behind his regiment's left wing, apparently lost his nerve and began crying out, "Retreat, and save yourselves!" at the top of his lungs. The companies directly in front of the colonel tried to obey and began falling back before the enemy. But Companies A and F, on the far right of the regiment's line, could not hear Appler's orders over the roar of gunfire and remained anchored in place. The 53rd Ohio split in half at the worst possible moment, with Appler racing over to the stalled companies on the right side of the line, and Dawes swept along with the retreating companies on the left. As the regiment collapsed on itself, the other units on the line also began to waver. It was all too much for Appler to handle. According to Dawes, the terrified colonel dashed off the firing line and flung himself to the ground behind a tree, even as his outnumbered and inexperienced company commanders attempted to hold their places in the disintegrating Union line. Dawes claimed that Appler "looked up; his face was like ashes; the awful fear of death was on it; he pointed over his shoulder with his thumb in an indefinite direction, and squeaked out in a trembling voice, 'No; form the men back here.'" In that instant Dawes realized the true peril of the situation. "We were in the front of a great battle. Our regiment never had a battalion drill. *Some men in it had never fired a gun.* Our lieutenant-colonel had become lost in the confusion of the first retreat, the major was in the hospital, and our colonel was a coward!" The lieutenant knew that something had to be done, and quickly, but that his colonel was in no fit state to salvage the deteriorating situation. The young adjutant replied "with an adjective not necessary to repeat, 'Colonel, I will not do it!'" After this act of defiance, Appler decided he had had enough. The colonel, Dawes recalled, "jumped to his feet, and literally ran away," with a large number of his frightened volunteers hard on his heels.[16]

To his credit, the young lieutenant refused to panic. Turning to the regiment's sergeant major, a friend from his Marietta College days named William Blackford Stephenson, Dawes passed on orders to the company commanders to close the gaps in the regiment's ragged line. He then went to a levelheaded line officer, Captain Wells S. Jones of Company A, explained that Colonel Appler had fled, and that he, Jones, was now the senior officer on the field and in command of the 53rd Ohio. Jones took the news in stride and calmly replied, "All right, get the men together; tell every company commander my order is to stay at the front, and come back as quick as you can." As Dawes jogged down the line to relay Jones's orders, he passed Company F. Its commander, Captain James R. Percy, brandished his sword as the adjutant ran by, calling: "Tell Captain Jones I am with him. Let us charge!"

Dawes finished relaying Jones's orders and returned to Sergeant Major Stephenson. By then another crisis had arisen. At least half of what was left of the regiment had fallen out of line and simply melted into the woods while Dawes was away. In his absence the 53rd Ohio's brigade commander, Colonel Hildebrand, had ridden up and ordered his regiments to fall back to "the road" and rally. Unfortunately, Hildebrand had not bothered to tell anyone precisely which road he meant before galloping off again. An exasperated Dawes ran back to Captain Jones, who was occupied with directing Companies A and F under increasingly heavy fire, and informed him of the new problem. There was nothing to be done about it, though, and Jones's companies simply stood their ground and kept blasting away at the approaching enemy columns.

Soon a number of retreating Union regiments streamed past in disorder. Among them Dawes recognized an enlisted volunteer from an Illinois regiment and called him over. The man, Corporal William M. Voris of the 17th Illinois Infantry, was a veteran of the earlier fight at Fort Donelson and a man whom Dawes knew to be a steady soldier.[17] Voris's calming presence proved a welcome boon for the anxious Ohio troops. After helping the Ohioans scavenge extra ammunition, recalled Dawes, Voris "went along the line, telling the men he had seen the elephant before, and had learned that the way to meet him was to keep cool, shoot slow, and aim low. He said, 'Why its just like shooting squirrels, only these squirrels have guns, that's all.'" As the 17th Illinois Infantry rallied and moved out, the amiable corporal departed with a friendly wave and a "Good-bye," leaving Dawes and the remnants of the 53rd Ohio in much better spirits.[18]

The regiment's surviving officers eventually saw the folly of trying to hold their ground and ordered their shattered companies back toward Shiloh Church, where they hoped to find the rest of their brigade. Of the seventy men of Companies A and F, nineteen had been killed or wounded, eight or ten had gone to the rear with badly wounded men, and one had stumbled into a deep hole in the woods and had seriously hurt himself. There were no ambulances or stretcher bearers to take the injured to field hospitals; when men were wounded on the line, their companions often fell out to carry them to the rear without permission from their officers. Ammunition soon ran low, no orders or support were forthcoming from headquarters, and Colonel Hildebrand was nowhere to be found. Lieutenant Dawes wryly speculated that when the brigade commander saw his regiments driven back, "he assumed that their usefulness was at an end, and rode away and tendered his services to General [John A.] McClernand for staff duty." Everything was utter confusion: command and control deteriorated rapidly in the thick woods, Union lines bent and dissolved, and Confederate fire seemed to come from all directions at once. When one volunteer was hit in the shin by a spent ball, an officer ordered him to the rear, only to have him reappear a few minutes later. "As the line broke and began to drift through the brush," Dawes recalled, "this soldier came limping back and said, 'Cap, give me a gun. This blamed fight *aint got any rear*.'"[19]

After retreating deeper into the woods, Lieutenant Dawes and his companions eventually found Colonel Hildebrand sitting on his horse by a barn, watching the battle unfold. At first Dawes was relieved. "'Now, we are all right,' I said to our men, and directing them to lie down in a little gully I went to the colonel, and said, 'Colonel where is the brigade?'" Hildebrand shrugged and answered: "'I don't know; go along down that road and I guess you will find some of them. I saw [Lieutenant] Jack Henricle [of the 77th Ohio Infantry] out there just now.'" Dawes could scarcely believe the brigade commander's indifferent manner. "'Why don't you come with us, get the men together and do something?'" he suggested, with an impatience bordering on insubordination. "'Go along down that road,'" Hildebrand answered sharply. "'I want to watch this fight.'"[20] Perplexed, Dawes told his fellow officers what the colonel had said, and the exhausted group moved out again. Soon, as Hildebrand had predicted, they encountered Lieutenant Henricle of the 77th Ohio Infantry. The lieutenant's "arm and shoulder were covered with blood," Dawes recalled, "where a wounded man had fallen against him, his coat was torn by a bullet, his face was stained with powder, his lips were blackened by biting cartridges, he carried a gun. His eyes shone like fire. He was the man we long had sought." Dawes asked, "'Jack, where is the brigade?' He replied, 'Part of your regiment and part of ours are right down this way a little way.' I felt like falling on his neck and weeping for joy, but did not."[21] Having regained their bearings, Lieutenant Dawes and his men finally rejoined the fight. The next day, April 7, the Union army salvaged a critical strategic victory against their equally untried Confederate foes in the bloodiest battle fought on the North American continent to that date.

Largely because of the initiative and leadership of a handful of company-grade volunteer officers, the 53rd Ohio Infantry survived the apparent emotional breakdown of its commander, an almost total lack of even the most basic drill and training, and a subsequent rout on the first day at Shiloh. By their instinctive actions, these young men helped prevent a serious setback from becoming a major catastrophe. This sort of leadership paid out in spades. The 53rd Ohio went on to serve with great distinction in every major campaign in the West, compiling one of the finest combat records of the war. Lieutenant Dawes would be promoted to major and remained with the regiment until being severely wounded at Dallas, Georgia, in 1864; he was brevetted lieutenant colonel upon his discharge from the army.[22] Sergeant Major Stephenson was given a commission and took Dawes's old post as regimental adjutant in February 1863.[23] Captain Jones was promoted to colonel and given command of the 53rd Ohio; in 1864 he was promoted once more to brigadier general and commanded a brigade for the remainder of the war.[24] Captain Percy, a professor of engineering before the Civil War, accepted a staff position as a topographical engineer in 1863; he was killed by a Confederate sharpshooter while in the trenches near Atlanta in August 1864.[25] Corporal Voris of the 17th Illinois Infantry accepted a lieutenant's commission in the 47th U.S. Colored Troops, and his name is now engraved on the African American Civil War Memorial in Washington, D.C.[26] As for the disgraced Colonel Appler, he was relieved of command and cashiered from the army soon after Shiloh. He is scarcely mentioned in the 53rd Ohio Infantry's official history.[27]

Among the many lessons imparted by early battles like First Bull Run and Shiloh, citizen-officers discovered that combat was unpredictable and traumatizing, and even good volunteers would run away under fire if their officers did not know how to exercise control over them. Sergeant Cyrus F. Boyd of the 15th Iowa Infantry, who earned a lieutenant's commission in 1863, recalled the panic that flowed through the Union army after facing enemy fire on the first day at Shiloh and officers' impotence to stop fleeing volunteers. "The woods were full of Infantry, cavalry, Artillery and all arms of the service were flying toward the River in countless numbers. Men yelled as they passed us 'Don't go out there' 'You'll catch hell' 'We are all cut to pieces' 'We are whipped.'" Hapless citizen-officers tried to rally their men and stem the tide, but to no avail. "There was also Infantry officers with swords drawn and trying to head off the flying troops and make them halt," Boyd continued. "There was Cavalrymen galloping after men and threatening to shoot them if they did not *stop*. But I saw no one stop." The sergeant was just as inexperienced as the rest of his new regiment, and as they marched toward the sound of the guns, such sights struck fear into their hearts. "Here we were a new Regt which had never until this morning heard an enemies gun fire thrown in this *hell* of battle—without warning," Boyd wrote. "It was every man for himself. We knew nothing about orders or officers. Indeed the Companies now became all mixed up without organization." He reported that "[c]avalrymen were riding in all directions with drawn sabers and revolvers threatening to shoot and 'Cut mens heads off' if they did not stop and rally. Officers were coaxing praying and exhorting men for 'God's sake' to stop and all make a stand together." Most of these efforts to halt the panicked troops, Boyd believed, were pointless. "But in most cases their orders and appeals were not heard by these demoralized men who kept going like a flock of sheep. All the terrors of hell would not have stoped them until they got to the River."[28]

These painful initiations into Civil War combat reflected a hard reality of war that volunteers and citizen-officers had to reconcile early in the conflict. Battles were terrible events, and to survive them, changes were necessary. Many veterans of these early engagements never quite got over their first exposure to the horror of battle. A captain in the 18th Wisconsin Infantry was haunted for the rest of his life by what he saw at Shiloh; even long after the war, one particular moment in his first battle was seared into his memory. On the second day, when his regiment halted amid "a gory, ghastly scene," the Wisconsin officer recalled hearing a cry for help from a mound of Confederate corpses. "I went to a gory pile of dead human forms in every kind of stiff contortion," he remembered, and "I found there a rebel, covered with clotted blood, pillowing his head on the dead body of a comrade. Both were red from head to foot. The dead man's brains had gushed out in a reddish and grayish mass over his face. The live one had lain across him all that horrible, long night in the storm." The captain filled the Confederate's canteen, but with his regiment preparing to move out, he had no choice but to leave the man to his fate. "'Forward!,' shouted the Colonel; and 'Forward!' was repeated by the officers," the Wisconsin officer recalled. "I left him."²⁹

Sergeant Boyd was also sickened by Shiloh's unexpected slaughter. His diary of the battle's second day presents a nightmarish portrait of an inexperienced volunteer's first traumatic encounter with combat. "Farther on the dead and wounded became more numerous," Boyd wrote of an overrun Confederate battery that he and his regiment had marched past. "I saw five *dead* Confederates all killed by one six pound solid shot—no doubt from one of our cannon They had been behind a log and all in a row The ball had raked them as they crouched behind the log (no doubt firing at our men)," he wrote. Boyd was unsparing in his description of the tableau. "One of them had his *head* taken off One had been struck at the right shoulder and his chest lay open. One had been cut in two at the bowels and nothing held the carcass together but the spine. One had been hit at the thighs and the legs were torn from the body." The final body was the worst sight; it "was piled up into a mass of skull, arms, some toes and the remains of a butternut suit." To Boyd, these enemy bodies were almost unrecognizable as people; the terrible destructive fire had turned men into debris, instantaneously erasing their humanity and reducing them to a heap of bone and tissue. "Some are torn all to pieces leaving nothing but their heads or their boots," he wrote. "Pieces of clothing and *strings of flesh* hang on the limbs of the trees round them—and the faithful horses have *died in the harness* right by the cannon. Some of them are torn to quarters by the bursting shells and their swollen bodies are already filling the air with a deadly odor." The carnage was not restricted to the enemy, though. "I saw one Union man leaning against a tree with a violin tightly grasped in his left hand," Boyd continued. "He had been dead some time and had no doubt been instantly killed.... I counted 26 dead battery horses on a few square rods of ground and the men were lying almost in heaps Blue and gray sleep together." The Iowan struggled to impose some measure of meaning on the bloodshed. "Oh my God! Can there be anything in the *future* that *compensates* for this slaughter," he wondered.³⁰

To endure the vast physical, psychological, intellectual, emotional, and moral challenges of combat, inexperienced citizen-officers and volunteers had to insulate themselves from the horrors of war; they had to harden themselves against such suffering if they hoped to survive physically and psychologically intact. As the anonymous officer of the 18th Wisconsin Infantry wrote of Shiloh, "After the battle was over, we, formerly citizens who had never seen, or heard the hiss of bullet, gathered the mangled corpses of those we had known at home and joked with the day before—friends who were as full of life, hope, and ambition as ourselves—and buried them in blankets, or sent them home in boxes, with as little concern as possible, and went immediately to joking and preparing to fight again." This swift and strange transformation from innocent civilian to hardened veteran after a single battle mystified him, even after the war was just a memory. "What spirit or principle was it that in one day gave us all the indifference and stoicism of veterans?" he wondered.[31]

Citizen-officers made the mental transition from civilian to veteran because their obligations as commanders, and their survival in combat, demanded it. By nature of their positions and military authority, company-grade officers were expected to serve as living examples for the volunteers they led and to behave in battle as they expected their men to behave. Those who hoped to be effective combat leaders therefore had to first master themselves, to habituate themselves to the horror of the battlefield and field hospital, and to compel or persuade their volunteers to instinctively obey them or else compromise their ability to carry out their essential military function. Learning war required citizen-soldiers to consider the meaning of the conflict and their place in it, to discard or modify unrealistic preconceptions about combat and its aftermath, and to imagine their place in the military hierarchy, often at the expense of long-cherished ideals, habits, and customs. Citizen-officers' part in this mental evolution was doubly difficult. Not only did leaders have to facilitate their volunteers' often-rocky transition from citizen to soldier, they also had to establish and maintain their military authority while overcoming their own fears and doubts. This could prove to be a lonely exercise, given the inevitable sense of isolation and distinctiveness incipient in the command relationship. It could also be a lethal proposition for inexperienced leaders seeking to win the approval of skeptical volunteers.[32]

In his provocative study of courage and the Civil War combat experience, historian Gerald E. Linderman asserts the primacy of that value in the making of effective combat leadership and emphasizes its persistence in the face of defeat, disillusionment, and experience. Most pertinent to Civil War combat leadership, Linderman argues, volunteers felt that personal character, not rank or authority, constituted the essential distinction between officers and volunteers. Therefore, citizen-officers were expected to prove their entitlement to obedience through the effectiveness of their leadership. Courage, in this equation, served as a source of currency. Command was therefore a transactional arrangement in which officers were required to accumulate courage as a form of currency through individual instances of bravery or excellence, with their volunteers providing them increasing returns of obedience with each investment.[33] Linderman's transactional conception of courage is particularly apposite in the first years of the war, when citizen-officers and volunteers alike were new to the business of war. As he rightly observes, courage's importance declined over time as acts of bravery became commonplace. Volunteers transformed into veterans with combat experience, and valor that might have impressed them in 1862 no longer held the same power in later years.[34]

While Linderman's assessment is compelling, and displays of conspicuous courage were assuredly important to establishing citizen-officers' military authority and credibility as leaders, the place of physical bravery in the pantheon of Civil War officer ideals should not be overstated, nor should the physical and moral cost of brazen acts of battlefield courage be underestimated. The lives of many gifted and effective citizen-officers were prematurely and unnecessarily snuffed out because these men placed too high a currency on the necessity of acts of physical courage in asserting effective leadership. Actually, a brave officer was far less important to his men than a good officer; that is, raw courage was almost useless if it brought about the destruction of a competent officer who otherwise embodied the necessary characteristics of an effective and inspirational leader. And, while acts of conspicuous courage could leave lasting impressions on volunteers, particularly if performed at critical moments, their long-term effects were often ephemeral at best. The true leadership benefit of an officer's acts of bravery was to demonstrate his personal character to the men and to convince them that he was an authority figure worthy of trust, respect, and obedience. Courage, however nuanced, fluid, and multifaceted, represented only a portion of the indispensable values, characteristics, and behaviors that citizen-officers were required to display to secure their authority and provide effective combat leadership. Just as competence, confidence, a convincing command presence, and a strong personal connection between officers and volunteers were critical to preserving trust and ensuring obedience in camp and on the march, these same values were as indispensable as bravery for effective combat leadership.

That is not to say that citizen-soldiers were indifferent to their officers' courage or lack thereof. Volunteers would accept many of a citizen-officer's flaws and shortcomings, but they would not willingly follow a coward into combat. The only failing that was certain to cripple the leadership effectiveness of a company commander, according to Union officer August V. Kautz, was a perception of cowardliness among his men. "[H]e may be deficient in any one or more traits or qualifications, yet hope for success, except courage," Kautz cautioned; "he cannot have his courage questioned and expect to succeed as an officer." Even then, an officer paralyzed by fear could redeem his cowardly reputation by earning the regard of his volunteers and fellow officers in battle. "But with courage he only needs the opportunity to achieve the respect and consideration of his companions and superiors, in spite of all bans and clouds under which he may rest."[35] Thus positioned as a legitimate authority over his volunteers, an officer could properly claim the moral right to lead his men into danger and expect that they would follow him. Moreover, a courageous officer, by assuming risks above and beyond those of his men, secured enough credibility to establish himself as a moral leader for his company and a figure worthy of esteem and obedience. As Captain Charles P. Mattocks of the 17th Maine Infantry wrote to his mother after the Battle of Chancellorsville: "You are well aware that it is the legitimate ambition of a soldier to obtain notice for services upon the field of battle. I shall never feel guilty for what I may gain in that matter. Political intrigue and personal influence may bring you the *straps*, but give me a chance like that of sunday and the other 4 days."[36]

While acts of conspicuous courage were the quickest path to establishing credibility, they were also the most hazardous and entailed extreme personal risks, ones that became abundantly clear early in the war. There is a multitude of ways to define courage in battle; one historian has aptly described it as "a supreme imperturbability in the face of death," which is "the ultimate gift in war."[37] Few Civil War citizen-officers epitomized the notion of total courage, along with its dark side, better than Confederate artillery officer William R. J. Pegram. A bespectacled prodigy who, by age twenty-three, had risen from lieutenant to colonel in the Army of Northern Virginia, Pegram was widely admired as one of the Confederacy's most gifted and daring officers. The bellicose young gunner had a flair for the dramatic, informing his men on one occasion, "A soldier should always seek the most desperate post that is to be filled," and on another inspired them by wrapping himself in his battery's battle flag and walking calmly back and forth amid enemy fire.[38]

Pegram reassured his family that such dangerous behavior was necessary for officers; all he could do was to perform his duty and rely upon divine providence to shield him from death. "I again got in a very hot place, and was unfortunate enough to lose Lieut. [Mercer] Featherstone and two men killed, and twelve wounded," he told his sister after the Battle of Cedar Mountain in August 1862, "but an ever merciful God again took me under His protection and brought me safely through the fight." The unfortunate Lieutenant Featherstone was decapitated by a Union artillery shell aimed at Pegram's battery. The round passed through both the lieutenant and his horse, lodging in the body of another nearby horse, where it "then exploded, tearing him to atoms," leaving Pegram and his men to recover the dead officer's body from the bloody mess.[39] During the engagement, Union marksmen singled out Pegram as the battery's commander and deliberately focused their fire on him; all of their shots miraculously missed, though only just. "I received four bullet holes through the skirt of my coat," he told his sister. "One sharp shooter took deliberate aim at me eight or ten times, and missed me. How is it possible to shew gratitude adequate to such divine mercy?" As a devout Christian, Pegram saw these experiences as a sign of divine favor. "What have I to fear from Yankee bullets and shells, as long as I am under His protection?" he marveled. "Ask Mother to cheer up, and remember that we are all under His protection."[40] But Pegram's good fortune eventually ran out. After innumerable daring exploits during the war, he was mortally wounded in April 1865 at the Battle of Five Forks, just days before the Army of Northern Virginia's final surrender at Appomattox Court House.[41]

Pegram's bravery was widely admired by his superiors, his fellow officers, and many of his own volunteers. Major General Henry Heth, for example, wrote that Pegram "was one of the few men, who, I believe was supremely happy in battle."[42] One well-worn anecdote holds that Confederate volunteers once declared of Pegram, "There's going to be a fight, for here comes that damned little man with the spec.'s!"[43] At a meeting of veterans after the war, Captain William Gordon McCabe, Pegram's friend and adjutant, fondly conjured a vision of the "boy-colonel riding along some crimson field, the sweet austerity of his grave face lit up with the joy of battle, as he was greeted by the hoarse cheering of his batteries."[44] Another veteran explained: "There was a certain magnetism about Willie Pegram that impressed all who came into his presence with his truly noble character. Never excited, possessing at all times that perfect equipoise so much to be prized in a commander, he embodied all the qualities of a soldier."[45]

These grand images of reckless heroism and coolness under fire conceal a grimmer aspect of this brand of aggressive courage. In 1863 one volunteer complained that Pegram was "a perfect gentleman and is moreover a fine officer, though *rather* too fond of fighting. In fact, he has been known to beg to be allowed to take his batt'n into a fight." His men somehow always seemed to find themselves at the perilous forefront of the army, even when they were assigned reserve positions far from the chance of enemy contact. Consequently, Pegram's batteries often suffered high casualties. "[S]uch chances as a batt'n *happening* to be in front after marching some or two or three hundred miles in extreme rear is rather extraordinary are they not."[46] Pegram's eagerness for battle may have won him glory, but it also fostered discontent in some of his volunteers, who believed their commander was profligate with their lives in pursuit of glory. At Cedar Mountain, when Pegram volunteered his battery to move into an extremely exposed position, his volunteers muttered with disapproval. This led him to take the extraordinary step of demanding that his men explicitly declare whether or not they intended to follow him into combat. If a minority expressed their disapproval, he proposed, they would be permitted to transfer to a new unit; if a majority disapproved, Pegram offered to resign his commission on the spot and return to the ranks as a private soldier. The volunteers, either shamed or inspired by this demonstration, unanimously chose to remain under his command.[47]

While displays of reckless courage could make a new citizen-officer's reputation, and quickly, officers of William Pegram's raw bravery were exceptional. Most citizen-officers did not know precisely how they would react when put to the first test of combat, but they were certain that their honor and reputation depended upon their performance. Therefore, many officers facing enemy fire for the first time were almost desperate to prove their coolness in battle, not only to their volunteers but also to their families and to themselves. Lieutenant Oliver Wendell Holmes Jr. of the 20th Massachusetts Infantry, a unit dubbed the "Harvard Regiment" because so many of its members were graduates of that institution, wrote proudly of his bravura performance in his first encounter with the enemy at Ball's Bluff in October 1861. While recovering from a dangerous chest wound received in the engagement, Holmes told his mother, "I felt and acted very cool and did my duty I am sure—I was out in front of our men encouraging 'em on when a spent shot knocked the wind out of me & I fell." His sense of relief and satisfaction is almost palpable in this account; he had faced enemy fire and lived through the test. After this close call, the young lieutenant roused himself from the ground and decided to press his luck again. "I crawled to the rear a few paces & rose by help of the 1st Sergt; & the Colonel who was passing said 'That's right Mr Holmes—Go to the Rear' but I felt that I couldn't without more excuse, so up I got and rushed to the front where hearing the Col. cheering the men on I waved my sword and asked if none would follow me when down I went again by the Colonel's side." This time the lieutenant was not so fortunate. "The first shot (the spent ball) struck me on the belly below where the ribs separate & bruised & knocked the wind out of me—The second time I hope only one ball struck me entering the left & coming out behind the right breast."[48] Seriously hurt, Holmes was at last carried from the field. He eventually recovered and returned to his company, his courage thoroughly established with his volunteers, his fellow officers, and himself.

Sometimes an officer's display of serenity under fire could make a greater impression on his volunteers than raw bravery. Union volunteer Abner R. Small of the 16th Maine Infantry remembered a remarkable instance of a battery commander's coolness at the Battle of Fredericksburg in December 1862. "Captain [James A.] Hall, sitting his superb horse as calmly as if on parade, was watching closely the work of his battery," Small recalled. "Now and then he shouted remarks to Colonels Root and Tilden, who reined their mounts near by, and they shouted replies. Interrupting the conversation, a solid shot came hurtling between the captain and the colonels and hit with a mighty thud a caisson of the battery, smashing it and exploding the magazine in a howling ball of flame." A more excitable officer would have panicked or sought cover, Small believed, but instead, "Captain Hall looked annoyed." The captain "got down deliberately from his horse, walked over to one of his guns, and sighted it; raised his hand, and an iron missile sped for the mark; a crash and a roar, and in the midst of a rebel battery there was a sudden upheaval of bursting shells, wheels, splinters, and human flesh." With the irritating Confederate guns neutralized, Small marveled, "The captain returned to his horse, mounted, and went on with the interrupted talk."[49]

By the fall of 1862, citizen-officers understood how a composed demeanor was necessary to maintain control over their companies on the battlefield. If an officer erred by making an untoward display of emotion during combat, he could spark a disastrous panic in his men. In the official report of his regiment's action at the Battle of Antietam, Captain Thomas M. Garrett of the 5th North Carolina Infantry described how an excitable junior officer's outburst during combat spread panic among the ranks of his company. Garrett, temporarily in command of his uneasy regiment, described how a fellow officer let his emotions conquer his composure. "Captain [T. P.] Thomson, Company G, came up to me, and in a very excited manner and tone cried out to me, 'They are flanking us! See, younder's a whole brigade!'" reported Garrett. "I ordered him to keep silence and return to his place. The men before this were far from being cool, but, when this act of indiscretion occurred, a panic ensued, and, despite the efforts of file-closers and officers, they began to break and run." Garrett was conscious that any intimation of cowardice in the official reports would destroy Thomson's military reputation, and so he was careful to qualify this untoward behavior as a product of excitement, not of fear. Nevertheless, Thomson's brief indiscretion highlighted that officer's shortcomings as a combat leader. "I have employed this language in regard to Captain Thomson's conduct because he remained upon the ground and exerted himself to rally the men," Garrett explained, "and, while it manifests clearly a want of capacity to command, my observation of him did not produce a conviction that it proceeded from a cowardly temper."[50] Questions of bravery or cowardice aside, Captain Garrett's damning report on his regiment's action at Antietam illustrates the lessons learned in the first years of the war, a maturing process that had begun to take place in the junior-officer corps of both armies by late 1862. Having gone through several major engagements, the citizen-officers of 1862 and early 1863 naturally had a far greater understanding of the requirements for effective combat leadership than at the start of the war. They had learned that good commanders had to do far more than look impressive and be recklessly brave under fire; they had to constantly attune themselves to the condition, emotions, and well-being of their companies and labor incessantly to maintain the fighting effectiveness of their volunteers at all times. Even the slightest slip could compromise their ability to maintain control on the battlefield.[51]

Though citizen-officers hoped that they would face battle with courage or coolness, waiting for their first engagement could prove an agony of uncertainty and self-doubt. Much of officers' free time in camp or on the march early in the war was devoted to worrying about battle's unknown trials, an essential element of the process of self-mastery. In action an officer's reputation, status, and manhood were at stake; to fail the test of leadership was, to some, a fate worse than death. Sometimes inexperienced officers coped with their fears by compartmentalizing their anxieties about courage and combat to master their emotions. Lieutenant Robert Gould Shaw of the 2nd Massachusetts Infantry spoke of the death of his friend, Theodore Winthrop, at the Battle of Big Bethel in 1861 and decided that the only way to conquer his own fears of a similar fate was simply to accept the possibility of death and leave it to fate. "I have thought a great deal about poor Winthrop," Shaw wrote to his mother. "I think that, if he had expected it, he would not have been sorry, excepting for the sake of his family. Some remarks I heard him make in Washington led me to think so. I find that thinking continually of the possibility of getting hit accustoms one so to the idea, that it doesn't seem so bad, after all."[52] Lieutenant Stephen David Clements of the 41st Georgia Infantry tried a different approach and relied on a fanciful metaphor, casting his sweetheart as a guardian angel watching over him for signs of cowardice. He imagined her ethereal presence simultaneously ensuring his safety and urging him to bravery on her behalf. In a letter to the young lady in the fall of 1861, he sought to convince her that when the inevitable first test of his courage came, he would not shame her. "How I thought you would like to accompany me on my dangerous & hard duties as my guardian spirit to admonish me of danger & direct me what to do: but no, you must go for another *purpose,* you seem not to be satisfied of my *bravery,* & you want to *scare me* if possible." The Georgia lieutenant promised the young lady that if only she had the power to accompany him into battle in spirit form, he would be able to draw strength and courage from her ghostly presence. "You might succeed had you the power to metamorphose yourself & follow me unknown, tho' I might show signs of fear still I think I should have presence of mind & be able to behave myself discreetly in danger," Clements assured her. "I do not profess to be brave," he confessed, "but in a battle or wherever my services may be needed, I believe I shall be found at my post in my right mind. Yet no one knows beforehand how he will act or what will be his feelings in a battle. When I pass thro' one unhurt, then I can tell you."[53]

The comfort of loved ones could be a powerful influence on inexperienced citizen-officers, particularly when managing their fears about their first combat. As inexperienced captain Simeon C. Wilkerson of the 18th Alabama Infantry wrote to his new bride in June 1863: "One of my friends told me he did not think he would stand a heavy fire from the enemy as well if he was a married man as he could [k]now that he has no wife to care for. I told him I thought I would stand a heavy fire better now than I would before I was married. I have more to fight for now than I had then," he explained. "I have always thought I had rather get killed than disgrace myself by running away while in an engagement. Now I had rather suffer a thousand deaths than have it said that Miss Nannie Byson married a young Capt who was cowardly enough to leave his command when he found that his life was endangered." Wilkerson saw the regard of his wife as a source of both comfort and motivation. "I know you would feel better to know that I fell at my post than you would to know I left it disgracefully," he added. "I am not anxious to be tryed, but hope I will not be found wanting when the test comes."[54]

The mere perception of cowardice could result in calamitous penalties for offending citizen-officers, as the 1863 case of Captain Henry C. Sweet vividly illustrates. Sweet, a company commander in the 105th Ohio Infantry, was the butt of a nasty prank that led to his public humiliation and dismissal from the army. While the captain led a scouting party, Indiana volunteer William Bluffton Miller registered in his diary, "some of [Sweet's] Boys put up a job on him. He left camp and went to a house to stay and the Boys put on Some citizens clotheing and went and captured him and Scared him by saying they were going to kill him but if he would tell how many men was in Halls command and all other information they wanted then break his Sword they would release him." Fearing for his life and thinking his supposed captors were Confederate partisans, Sweet did as he was told. The pranksters let him go, and the clueless officer "then come to camp telling what a terible fight he had with the 'Rebbs.' The Boys returned to camp and heard his Story and then told theirs and he was arrested." When the magnitude of Sweet's offense became clear, he "was brought out in front of the Brigade and the Shoulder Straps and Buttons cut off him." Miller pitied the captain but explained: "He was not liked by his men and they thought he was a coward and wanted to get rid of him. The[y] succeeded nicely as his sentence was that the Straps and buttons should be cut off of him. He [was] dismissed from the Service and sent across the Ohio River." Miller seems to have felt a twinge of regret about the captain's humiliation but, like other citizen-soldiers, had no sympathy for cowardly officers. "He was a nice looking young man and I felt sorry for him to think how he had disgraced himself," confessed Miller. "But this is no place for a coward and they better get away soon for I think the time is not far away when a man will have to Show his collors. If he cant face the enemy he better go home."[55]

Officers with a religious bent often managed their fear by relying upon divine providence to protect them in combat. In 1864 Captain Robert E.

Park of the 12th Alabama Infantry reflected upon the third anniversary of his enlistment and thought it a miracle that he had survived. "But despite the innumerable dangers I have passed through, through God's mercy I am still alive, and able and willing to confront the enemies of my country. Will I be spared to see another anniversary? The Omniscient One only can tell."[56] Lieutenant William Fielding Baugh of the 61st Virginia Infantry likewise declared that he did not fear for his personal safety but dreaded death simply because it would take him from his wife's loving embrace; his main solace was in his Christian faith. "The idea of being killed from you made me feel timid at first," he told her in the summer of 1862, "but after meditation I think I can submit myself to the fortunes of war and trust to a kind Providence for protection." Baugh firmly believed that a just God would not be so cruel as to separate two lovers whose feelings were so deep and true. "Surely I will be spared to come home again for I love you so dearly," he mused.[57]

Like Baugh, Lieutenant Matthew S. Austin of the 5th New Jersey Infantry was confident that his faith would preserve him in combat. "I have never doubted that my God would save me from the death of a battle-field, and from harm—for which I ever pray," Austin wrote to his mother in April 1863. "I say I ought not to doubt or waver in my faith, as I have the best evidence of God's goodness and care for his creatures, in my most remarkable preservation, in health, and from the dangers which have surrounded me, for the entire time I have been in the service. I enter upon all duties in the strong belief God guides ever, and for His own honor and glory."[58] Cynics might dismiss these declarations as naïve sentimentalism, as defensive rationalization, or as mere brave posturing. Indeed, acceptance, indifference, or the comforting assurances of loved ones at home could not ward off the bullets of the enemy nor spare citizen-officers and volunteers from the cruel, seemingly random ways in which death or injury could find them on the battlefield. Nevertheless, untried men who feared failing their first tests of leadership could, and did, draw comfort from many sources, and these efforts, along with the spiritual and emotional solace of faith and family, played critical roles in helping inexperienced officers master their fears before their first combat experiences.

The easiest way for citizen-officers to conquer their fears about death or failure in combat was simply to experience, and survive, their first engagement. Lieutenant Henry C. Lyon of the 34th New York Infantry, for example, described his sense of relief when his unit did not come apart at the seams in its first fight. "I will simply say that it was our first time in the 'fire' and although we came out scorched I thank God that we stood the test," the officer wrote to his brother in June 1862 after the Battle of Fair Oaks. "I confess that before the hour of trial came, I sometimes questioned in my mind and even doubted our Regt. if she ever came into a hand to hand conflict wit[h] the Enemy." Lyon was quick to correct any misconception that he questioned his volunteers' bravery; he merely wondered if his regiment would maintain discipline in the chaos of battle. "Not that I doubted the courage of the men individually for I believe no braver or better material exists in any Regt. than does in our own—But there was a doubt or mistrust of abilities somewhere or somehow through the whole Regt. that seemed to make us feel that in case of action every man would, as it were, fight on his own hook." The lieutenant feared that "there would be no unity in case of which there would be no strength and which is equally destructive to a Co., a Regt., or an Army.—But our surmises appeared to be unfounded for without boasting I shall state I do think that under the circumstances no Regt. has done better." Lyon attributed his unit's performance to the bonds of trust forged between its citizen-officers and volunteers. "Confidence in Commanders and in fellow soldiers is every thing in a Battle," he proclaimed. "A false movement producing a stampede will cause a panic that will appall the bravest-heart.—It is not when the enemy charges up on us, that we are the most frightened. It is when from some cause or other some of our own men run, that will make a soldier pale and act cowardly, if anything will." Lyon was proud of his volunteers' steadiness in their first engagement, and rightly so. "But thank fortune we had no such conduct in our Co. at least every man stood firm at his post giving and receiving fire like old veterans. In some instances displaying courage and heroism that would do credit to 'Napoleons Old Guard.'"[59]

Citizen-officers, as Lyon discovered, were set apart from the volunteers they led in battle; the degree of that distinctiveness and separation varied and increased with every advance up the military hierarchy. But even the least experienced lieutenant in a Civil War company was different from an enlisted volunteer. A citizen-officer possessed, by virtue of his commission and the authority that went with it, a status apart from the most grizzled veteran in the ranks. Furthermore, junior officers were the seedbed of higher command; most generals in both armies served as company-grade officers either before or during the war and understood that soldiers had to have confidence in their combat leaders' abilities. Whether officers rose, fell, or remained in place, and often whether they and their men lived or died, depended on their combat leadership abilities and the bonds of trust between them and their men. Combat clarified the need for competent, confident leadership, forcing volunteers to confront their innate resistance to officers' authority and reconfigure elements of the citizen-soldier mentality. In the citizen armies of the Civil War, military discipline and the persistent egalitarianism of the citizen-soldier ethos were often at odds and would remain so throughout the conflict. But the deadly campaigns of 1861, 1862, and early 1863 wrought a change in the volunteers; after their first engagements, they swiftly learned that an officer's sensitivity and respect were poor substitutes for competence, composure, leadership, and discipline in ensuring their survival on the battlefield. Citizen-officers likewise came to understand that self-mastery, while essential to combat leadership, was often insufficient to maintain control over panicked troops in moments of crisis. What was most needed, they learned, was discipline.

Historian David Herbert Donald argues that Confederate volunteers in particular never really modified their persistent citizen-soldier ethos, despite the experiences of war. He also maintains that Confederates clung fiercely to their independence and rejected the regular-army model of discipline advocated by their citizen-officers. "[T[he distinctive thing about the Confederate army," Donald posits, "is that Southern soldiers never truly accepted the idea that discipline is necessary to the effective functioning of a fighting force."[60] While it is true that both Confederate and Union volunteers fiercely resisted officers' encroachments on their prerogatives as citizens and equals, the traditional narrative of universally insubordinate, undisciplined Civil War citizen-soldiers barely held in check by their harried amateur officers is overly simplistic. In fact, the transformation of discipline in the armies defies easy generalizations or clear progressions and varied considerably from company to company—indeed, from volunteer to volunteer. A significant amount of informality sometimes existed between citizen-officers and their men as is to be expected among men who shared community relationships, kinship ties, and social connections before the war. Additionally, regular officers in both armies lamented the lack of discipline in their volunteers throughout the conflict.[61] Even so, there is scant evidence to indicate that the so-called Johnny Reb was more consistently unruly than was Billy Yank or, as Donald maintains, that he never accepted discipline as necessary. In fact, recent studies of discipline in the Union army show that Northern volunteers resisted officers' efforts to control them just as stubbornly and persistently as their Confederate counterparts and that Union authorities were forced to alter their adherence to the stern code of the regular army to maintain order among the volunteers.[62] And while overall discipline in the Confederate armies fluctuated throughout the war and eroded in the last two years as the tide turned against the South, this may be attributed to many complex factors in addition to a generalized culture of indiscipline. Brutal and continuous campaigning, a hopelessly inefficient supply system, and a junior-officer corps bled dry through casualties and attrition all helped contribute to Confederate discipline problems.[63]

It is a mistake to consider Civil War volunteers' indiscipline as a monolith, unchanged and unalterable. Such a view overlooks the fundamental shifts in mentality that took place among many citizen-soldiers on both sides once they had experienced combat in earnest. By the spring and summer of 1862, Union and Confederate citizen-officers' opinions of discipline and the citizen-soldier ethos had begun to evolve. In a July 1862 letter written by Lieutenant William Henry Harrison Lewis of the 16th Mississippi Infantry in the aftermath of the Seven Days' Campaign, he described how the men of his company had begun to accept that discipline was an indispensable component of the command relationship between officers and volunteers. "Brother John ... has been ... in command of the company," he wrote of his elder brother, a captain and company commander in the 16th Mississippi. "Brother John is more popular than of old—that is, the company having experienced in the later battles the result of want of discipline and, seeing the evil consequent thereof, appreciate his strictness."[64] That same summer Union citizen-officers were noticing a similar change in attitude among their men. "It is pleasant to see how differently the men feel towards their officers since we have been under fire together," Lieutenant Shaw of the 2nd Massachusetts Infantry wrote to his sister in June 1862 after his regiment's action in the First Battle of Winchester. Shaw, though a volunteer officer, had been an ardent critic of the citizen-soldier ethos among his men; at last, it seemed, his efforts to discipline his troops were paying off. "They appreciate the advantages of strict discipline now. Quincy heard one say, 'I notice how we didn't shoot any of our officers.' 'No,' said another, 'we need them to take care of us in a fight.'"[65] Captain George Thomas Blakemore of the 23rd Tennessee Infantry described similar changes toward drill and discipline he observed in his volunteers in June 1862. "[W]e are drilling very hard," Blakemore wrote in his diary from the Army of Mississippi's camp near Tupelo, Mississippi, and "the disciplian of the army is very rigid indeed, I say tis more so now than it ever has been since the war commenced."[66] Long after the war, Henry F. Lyster of the 2nd and 5th Michigan Infantry was still struck by the transformation in the citizen-soldier ethos he observed after battle. He recalled that the "soldier of '61 was full of life and patriotism, his ardor undampened by the stern discipline and reverses of the war." In contrast, Lyster observed: "The soldier of '65 was inured to hardship and adversity, and hoped less, but fought and accomplished more. The period of romance had changed to a period of system and endurance."[67]

The transformative years of 1862 and 1863 had antecedents in the long months before. Between the advent of war in April 1861 and the first major campaigns of the spring of 1862, most volunteer units had had the opportunity to learn the art of soldiering and to do so under the tutelage of the same company officers they enlisted with. This extended training period paid dividends, enabling green volunteers and citizen-officers to puzzle out the intricacies of military protocol, drill, and combat; to grow accustomed to each other in camp and in the field; and to acclimate themselves to the alien environment of army life.[68] While volunteers preserved and maintained their citizen-soldier resistance to authority throughout the war, it is also apparent that on both sides, many volunteers' conceptions of military hierarchy and discipline changed once they experienced battle in earnest. Along with emphasizing the importance of competent junior-officer leadership, particularly in fostering discipline, early engagements exposed grave regimental and company-grade combat leadership deficits in both armies. These experiences highlighted the shortcomings of the officer-election system in producing consistently effective company-grade leaders and spurred planners on both sides to action. By the summer of 1862, both armies had begun to implement officer-examination boards. The application of standards and training, along with valuable experience accrued in combat, led to a gradual improvement in the combat and command abilities in the junior-officer corps of both the Union and Confederate armies.[69]

Moreover, many citizen-officers exposed to combat gained a deeper understanding of the challenges and requirements of command. The 1862 reorganizations helped both Union and Confederate volunteers to realize that their officer-election systems were not producing adequate combat leaders, so officers too began to modify their understanding of the citizen-soldier ethos. By 1863, volunteers understood that competence, discipline, and composure were the most essential characteristics for successful citizen-officers rather than status or popularity. "We were well drilled in Hardee's Tactics, but had never been under fire before," Private Isaac Gordon Bradwell of the 31st Georgia Infantry remembered of the formative early years of combat. As for citizen-officers, he observed, "it was but natural in the great confusion and noise that they should make some mistakes. Two years later there were hundreds of private soldiers who could have managed better. Indeed, the whole thing now seems to me that it might have been more wisely conducted with greater success, and smaller loss."[70]

As citizen-officers confronted the immense difficulties and danger of their task, the lessons of combat leadership came at a terrible cost. Historians have spilled much ink describing and debating the destructiveness of Civil War combat, arguing over whether and how tactics, technology, training, and a host of other factors contributed to the bloodletting. Combat unquestionably took a severe toll upon Civil War armies, and the unexpected horror of the first two years of war took many volunteers by surprise. No single group in either army paid a steeper price in action than did company-grade volunteer officers. They often depended upon personal example, boldness, demonstrations of character, and instinctual or acquired leadership skills to secure their volunteers' obedience, rather than mere force, intimidation, or coercion. Citizen-officers and volunteers, Union and Confederate alike, were fond of repeating, and often mangling, an old adage from a British riflemen of the Napoleonic Wars: "[O]ur men had divided the officers into two classes; the 'come on' and the 'go on,'" and as an enlisted man once told an officer, "The words 'go on' don't befit a leader, Sir."[71] Historian Richard Holmes perhaps sums up this idea best: "It is a fundamental truth that a military leader will not succeed in battle unless he is prepared to lead from the front and to risk the penalties of doing so. This need to lead from the front is as relevant to unpleasant tasks off the battlefield as to dangerous ones on it."[72] The axiom applies equally to the citizen armies of the Civil War.

These expectations, along with the duties and requirements of company command, resulted in devastating casualty rates among junior officers, particularly among Confederates. In his landmark study of the Army of Northern Virginia, historian Joseph T. Glatthaar estimates that nearly a quarter of all officers in that army were killed in action, and four out of five either were killed or were wounded at least once. Confederate officers, he finds, were twice as likely to die as their enlisted volunteers.[73] In the research sample of 2,592 volunteer junior officers drawn from thirty-three regiments, Union junior officers suffered a 43-percent casualty rate between April 1861 and April 1865, while Confederate junior officers sustained a 47-percent casualty rate during the same period.[74] For comparison, recent estimates of the overall casualty rates for all Union soldiers are 16 percent and for all Confederate soldiers, 31 percent.[75] Confederate junior officers in the research sample suffered their heaviest casualties in 1862, with about 37 percent of their total wartime losses occurring in that year. Union officers also sustained heavy casualties in 1861 through 1863 but did not suffer their greatest losses until 1864. Both Union and Confederate junior officers sustained greater casualty rates than did enlisted men. Overall, Confederates in the sample sustained casualties at a higher rate than their Union counterparts in every year of the war, though both sides suffered nearly equal losses in 1863.[76]

There are several explanations for why company-grade citizen-officer casualties were so extreme in comparison to enlisted volunteers. First, successful company-level combat leadership was closely related to the efficiency and effectiveness of citizen-officers in their battlefield roles, and to be effective in a command role, these men had to be seen, heard, and obeyed by their volunteers. In the chaos, noise, and smoke of combat, this required captains and lieutenants to maintain a conspicuous presence along the firing line and on the march. This may seem an obvious point, but the simple fact is that being a company officer in a Civil War engagement required a great deal of personal courage. The trappings of office that so many young citizen-officers coveted—sword, sash, shoulder straps, and gilded braid—served a dual, and often deadly, purpose in battle. This regalia of rank helped identify them to their men as battlefield leaders and set them apart as command figures with military authority that was to be looked to, trusted, and obeyed under fire. These accoutrements also served to make officers tremendously, sometimes frighteningly, vulnerable to sharp-eyed enemy snipers across the battlefield, as their casualty rates attest. In June 1862 the Confederate Adjutant and Inspector General's Office permitted officers to remove their uniform jackets bearing gilded sleeve braids and, when in the field, to wear a plain gray jacket with a less gaudy collar rank insignia.[77] The Union army also recognized the obvious dangers posed by conspicuous officer insignia and followed suit but did not make allowances for them until late 1864—not coincidentally, the year of the Siege of Petersburg and of the heaviest casualties among Union officers in the sample. General Orders No. 286, issued by the Adjutant General's Office on November 22,

1864, specified that officers "serving in the field are permitted to dispense with shoulder-straps and the prescribed insignia of rank on their horse equipments." Gilded shoulder straps could be replaced by a subdued version of the standard rank insignia, and other accoutrements that would distinguish officers from enlisted men were dropped from the lists of required items. "Officers are also permitted to wear overcoats of the same color and shape as those of the enlisted men of their command. No ornaments will be required on the overcoats, hats, or forage caps; nor will sashes or epaulettes be required."[78]

Second, the physical position of company officers in combat often exposed them even further to targeted enemy fire. Union and Confederate regulations and the tactical manuals used by both armies provided specific guidelines for company-grade officers' battlefield obligations before, during, and after action. In most battlefield situations a captain's post was at the forefront of his company. In the line-of-battle formation, the usual combat formation for a unit under fire, the captain's place was on the extreme right front of the line, with lieutenants posted at intervals two paces behind the firing line to serve as file closers. While in column formation, company officers usually marched beside their troops at regular intervals. If a captain wished to change his company's formation, deploy skirmishers, coordinate its movements with the battalion or regiment, or divide it into platoons, the lieutenants and noncommissioned officers would see to it that the captain's orders were executed by shifting their positions accordingly. These movements further singled out company officers from their volunteers while under enemy fire, making them obvious targets.[79]

Third, to lead effectively, company officers had to demonstrate their willingness to ignore danger blithely, which often required them to move to the deadliest positions in the line and expose themselves to enemy fire to inspire their soldiers. The command radius of a company officer in combat was often limited by how loud he could call out orders or get the attention of his men, and so an officer's battlefield location and visibility to fire could vary greatly, depending on the tactical situation. Company officers labored mightily to master the complexities of drill, maneuver, and tactics set out in the drill books, but they could not change the difficult fact that their command role in combat left them exceptionally vulnerable to enemy bullets and shells.[80] After the Battle of Gettysburg, as the war ground into its third year, both sides recognized that the tidy formations and the clockwork precision mandated by antebellum tactical manuals did little to mitigate the advantages possessed by a foe armed with rifled muskets who assumed the tactical defensive and who knew that killing enemy officers conferred a great military and moral advantage.[81]

Company officers' battlefield roles were also distinctive from enlisted men in another respect. Civil War combat was a harrowing experience for any volunteer, but company combat command placed unique demands on citizen-officers. If judged solely on the tactical manuals and official after-action reports of the time, it appears that company officers were almost mechanical in battle; they seem to transmit and execute orders like cogs in a machine, managing their companies' rhythms of firing, reloading, and marching like the connective tissue in an organism. It is true that a large component of a company officer's combat role was mechanistic in nature, an impression reinforced by their descriptions of tediously poring over tactics manuals, studying the manners and comportment of regular officers, and running their companies through weeks of mind-numbing drill. It would be a mistake, however, to view company-grade officers as mere automatons in combat. The most fundamental, and perhaps the most underappreciated, role of a company officer in action was emotional rather than technical in nature. Effective company officers were not only the instructors and commanders of their men but also served as the moral center of gravity for the volunteers in their companies, the heart and soul of Civil War armies' most basic military unit. In other words, citizen-officers played the indispensable part of emotional touchstone in the stress and terror of battle, and their command persona became the source of inspiration for their volunteers in moments of fear, confusion, and crisis.

Newly promoted lieutenant John Quincy Adams Campbell of the 5th Iowa Infantry described the emotional role of company command after his first engagement in the Battle of Iuka in September 1862. "During the battle I was acting as Lieutenant," Campbell set out in his diary. "My duty was to cheer and encourage the men, and aid the company commander in managing the company. For a time I turned *exhorter* and plead[ed] and cheer with an earnestness (I perhaps might say enthusiasm) that seriously affected my diseased throat. I was utterly unconscious of danger, and although the dead and dying were dropping at my feet, I felt no emotion nor sorrow—there was a strange, unaccountable lack of *feeling* with me that followed me through the entire action." Realizing that his volunteers looked to him for his example, Campbell forced himself to remain calm and focused during the engagement. "Out of a battle and in a battle, I find myself two different beings," he mused. "During a part of the fight, I assisted the boys in loading by taking out their cartridges and tearing them, ready for loading. Corporal Banks was wounded while receiving a cartridge from my hand. Private Shelley was shot dead and dropped at my feet. Private Smail fell dead at my feet on my left, grasping hold of me as he fell."[82] Despite all this death and destruction, Campbell maintained his composure and managed to preserve his company.

Captain David Norton of the 42nd Illinois Infantry described a similar capacity to switch off his fears and project an aura of calm courage during an 1862 skirmish near Nashville, Tennessee. "My company was employed as skirmishers," Norton wrote in his diary, "and one of my boys fired twice at a Rebel without hitting him, and I was a little mad at it, and took a rifle from one of my boys and shot at him myself. I hit him in the leg, and he was carried back to the rear into the woods." In the same entry he reported: "At the time it was said, I was under a perfect storm of balls, & charging up a hill to drive the enemy skirmishers from behind a hedge, to allow our artillery to advance across an open field while the Secesh were covered by the hedge. I can't account for their not hitting some of us." Norton made a conscious decision to put himself in harm's way, risking life and limb to provide a brave example to his soldiers. This proved immensely successful in the engagement. "According to tactics," he confessed, "I should have been in [the] rear of my skirmishers, but when the balls began to fly pretty freely, it seemed cowardly for me to stay in the rear and order my men to go forward when it appeared to be certain death to enter that open field. So I went up on the line, & every man said he would keep as near the enemy as I [did]. I advanced on the run & drove the Secesh from their position."[83]

Volunteers expected their officers to interpret the chaos and uncertainty of battle and to calmly translate it into problems with understandable solutions by virtue of their training, experience, and natural leadership ability. They also demanded that their leaders not require anything of them that they were unwilling to do themselves. After the 1862 Battle of Chantilly, for example, Lieutenant George Washington Whitman of the 51st New York Infantry described how his willingness to snatch up a musket and fight by their sides heartened his shaken volunteers. "Our men broke a little at the first volley but we soon rallied them and then began about as sharp a fight as I ever wish to see," he wrote to his mother afterward. "As soon as the action commenced I took a rifle from one of our men who had been shot and I took 8 or 10 cartridges from some of the wounded and had a few shots on my own hook which seemed to encourage the men very much."[84] Whitman knew that his volunteers' eyes were on him in combat, constantly evaluating his abilities, his courage, and his bearing. Effective combat leaders were always conscious of the effects of their words and actions in battle, and the wise ones used their actions to their best advantage.

Like Whitman, Captain William Francis Bartlett of the 20th Massachusetts Infantry recognized the importance of his manner and words under fire. "Well the first volley came and the balls flew like hail," Bartlett wrote of his company's action during the 1861 Battle of Ball's Bluff. "The whizzing of balls was a new sensation. I had read so much about being under fire and flying bullets that I was curious to experience it." The captain was amazed by the withering fire the Confederates threw at his men and swiftly realized that his volunteers would likely break and run if he did not display brave leadership. "[The enemy] fired beautifully, too," he continued, "their balls all coming low, within from one to four feet of the ground. The men now began to drop around me.... Those that were lying down, if they lifted their foot or head it was struck. One poor fellow near me was struck in the hip while lying flat, and rose to go to the rear, when another struck him on the head, and knocked him over." Despite the fearsome volume of enemy fire, Bartlett rose from his covered position and began working his way through the company. "I felt that if I was going to be hit, I should be, whether I stood up or lay down," he explained, "so I stood up and walked around among the men, stepping over them and talking to them in a joking way, to take away their thoughts from the bullets, and keep them more self possessed." Bartlett did not expect himself to display such nerve in combat. "I was surprised at first at my own coolness. I never felt better, although I expected of course that I should feel the lead every second, and I was wondering where it would take me." He continued to joke with his men as enemy balls flew around them, teasing one man for his luck at avoiding fire and scolding another for getting his uniform dirty while lying in the grass. The captain's fearlessness under fire had the desired effect on his men. "The different companies began to wilt away under this terrible fire," Bartlett described. "Still there was no terror among the men; they placed implicit confidence in their officers (I refer to our regiment particularly), and you could see that now was the time they respected and looked up to them."[85]

Displaying this sort of effective combat leadership at the company level, while essential, could be an immensely complex task for Civil War citizen-officers. Enlisted volunteers on the firing line had a straightforward part to play in battle. A Civil War infantryman's primary responsibilities were to load and fire their muskets on command, to maintain their formation and maneuver as ordered, and to not flee from the enemy; cavalrymen and artillerymen performed different duties but had a similar mandate to fight the enemy and to follow their officers' orders. While enlisted volunteers' focus in combat was usually external, toward the enemy, and their mental energy was largely devoted to loading, firing, marching, and obeying their officers' commands, the demands on company officers were considerably more difficult. On the battlefield they focused simultaneously on the enemy and his movements; on the orders, queries, and demands for information issuing from higher echelons of command; and on the company's status and effectiveness. Captains and lieutenants had to comprehend and execute the orders of their battalion, regimental, or brigade commanders with alacrity and precision. They had to act wisely and decisively when orders were confusing, vague, or simply unavailable. In order to maintain their volunteers' military effectiveness, officers had to oversee mundane but essential tasks such as ensuring their soldiers had sufficient water in their canteens, ammunition for their muskets, rations, equipment, and stretcher bearers. They had to maintain fire discipline, preserve alignments, keep order in the ranks, and see to the disposition of stragglers, casualties, the panicked, the enraged, and the exhausted. Above all, officers had to lead on the field with the same mixture of authority, composure, and compassion that their volunteers expected of them in camp. They were not only military leaders but also custodians of their men, with an immense number of critical responsibilities to manage while under fire and often in deadly circumstances. The best company officers were able to cultivate these acquired skills into instinct; the worst never mastered their duties and found themselves overwhelmed by the responsibilities of command.

By December 1862 Captain John William De Forest of the 12th Connecticut Infantry felt that he could articulate the unique challenges of company-grade Civil War combat leadership. "I have discovered why officers are in general braver than soldiers," he wrote. "The soldier is responsible for himself alone, and so is apt to think of himself alone. The officer is responsible for his company, and so partially forgets his own peril." As such, De Forest struck upon the essence of junior-officer combat leadership in the Civil War and the difference between soldiering in the ranks and commanding troops in battle. An officer's responsibilities extended not only to his own duties and self-preservation but also to the well-being and military obligations of the men under his command. "His whole soul is occupied with the task of keeping his ranks in order," De Forest explained, "and it is only now and then that he takes serious note of the bullets and shells." In a sense, then, the burden of command could even become a welcome distraction from the raw fear of combat that every soldier going into battle had to face. "It would demand a good deal of courage, I think, to be a mere looker-on in a battle," De Forest concluded.[86]

Even for company-grade officers who lived through the first years of the war, successfully managing these myriad demands could take a heavy psychological toll. Writing to his parents from the "field of battle" in June 1862, Oliver Wendell Holmes Jr. attempted to describe the indescribable as he surveyed the carnage after the Battle of Fair Oaks. "It is singular with what indifference one gets to look on the dead bodies in gray clothes wh. lie all around—(or rather did—We are burying them today as fast as we can—) As you go through the woods you stumble constantly, and, if after dark, as last night on picket, perhaps tread on the swollen bodies already fly blown and decaying, of men shot in the head back or bowels—Many of the wounds are terrible to look at—especially those fr. fragments of shell."[87] The lieutenant's subsequent description of his participation in the Battle of Glendale a month later has a feverish, kaleidoscopic quality; his account perfectly encapsulates the immense stress and confusion of Civil War combat at the company level. "[A]fternoon terribly thirsty (hardly any water to be had) came up double quick onto field of action (knapsacks on backs) Nelson's Farm," Holmes wrote to his parents. "Forward in line (whole battalion front) better than the Regt. generally does it on drill—*Whang* goes a shell two men drop in Co G." As Holmes's unit began to take casualties, the volunteers in the ranks called out each one to their company commander. "'Captain! Noonan's hit,'" one cried. "'No Matter, Forward Guide Right,'" Holmes heard the captain answer. "We go forward passing a deserted battery the dead lying thick round it," he reported, "and then begins to the deuce of a time."[88]

The Confederate fire was so ferocious, Lieutenant Holmes told his parents, that a sister regiment simply crumbled and began to flee. "[T]he Mich. 7th on our left breaks & runs *disgracefully*," he wrote, adding, "(private) they lay it to Col. [Ira R.] Grosvenor who they say showed the white feather." Fortunately, the 20th Massachusetts Infantry held firm, mainly because it had no clear avenue for a retreat. "We were flanked & nearly surrounded and that saved us," Holmes explained to his parents. With retreat impossible, and with confusion gripping the Union lines, the lieutenant and his fellow officers did what they could to impose order on the chaos. "After that we couldn't avoid confusion and what with stragglers of other Regts &c. didn't form a good line." The company's losses were heavy, and fire discipline quickly broke down. "In our Co. the loss in those known to be wounded was 1/5 to 1/4 the Co. The guns got so hot & dirty we couldn't load or fire more than 2/3 of 'em." Holmes was candid about his fear and exhaustion during the experience, and the panicked comments of some fellow officers did little to relieve his vexation. "The anxiety has been more terrible than almost any past experience," he wrote, "but through all I kept pretty lively only getting down when on the last of our march I was told by Cheerful birds like Tremlett & co that we *must* surrender or be cut to pieces within 36 hours." Holmes described the casualties among the officers, many whom were his good friends, in stark, clipped language. "Poor Lowell was hit just as Willy Putnam was & had to be left behind—beyond doubt dead. Patten hit in leg. Abbott lies w'd in arm. Muller wounded & missing Palfrey bruised not hurt N. P. Hallowell cut on the side not hurt. I was awfully frightened about him," he confessed. "I'm in comm'd of [Companies] E. & G. I'm too tired that is too mentally inefficient to write well," Holmes admitted, "but I've sent 2 notes before including a leaf of my pocket book written some time ago to you in case I was ever killed."[89]

In the war's first years, citizen-officers led through examples of courage, resiliency, and self-sacrifice. Convincing demonstrations of these values served as the foundation for the command relationship in volunteer companies. Drill, discipline, and the shared hardships of combat also served to strengthen the bonds required to maintain an effective command relationship between officers and their men.[90] Historians have found, however, that these values became less effective in securing volunteers' obedience over time; even after years of sustained combat and shared hardships, citizen-officers' personal examples and the bonds forged in battle were, in some cases, insufficient to secure the compliance of their troops.[91] Some officers learned the importance of coercion in their very first battle. Lieutenant Carter's regular-army command abilities proved vital in keeping his wavering company intact at the First Battle of Bull Run. Despite the Union army's failures on that field, the young company officer's leadership techniques were an ideal demonstration of effective company-grade command. Through a combination of threats, persuasion, and inspiration, Carter and his fellow regular officers managed to keep their unit together in their first engagement. "When we first went into action," he reported, "our men—who are mostly recruits—seemed inclined to back out, but we stationed ourselves behind them and threatened to shoot the first man that turned." Yet threats of physical violence alone were not enough to inspire Carter's company. "We then talked to them," he added, "told them they were the mainstay of the brigade, and finally, after having rested a little (although still under fire), we moved up in very good style."[92] Carter's regular-army leadership style at First Bull Run was a mixture of persuasion, inspiration, and coercion. This combination of methods later proved invaluable to inexperienced citizen-officers learning the techniques of combat command; more importantly, it served as a blueprint for command and control on the battlefield.[93] After 1862, both the Union and Confederate armies resorted to more-drastic steps to coerce compliance and preserve mastery over resisting volunteers. Both sides employed details or provost guards to round up deserters and stragglers and bring them in for court-martial and possible execution. In cases of desertion under fire, both Union and Confederate troops were sometimes ordered to open fire on routed friendly units or even to bayonet comrades who showed signs of wavering during assaults.[94]

Reflecting on the Confederate performance in the Battle of Shiloh, corps commander Major General Braxton Bragg believed that his citizen-officers' inexperience, particularly their inability to prevent volunteers from straggling or fleeing, had prevented the Army of Mississippi from winning a decisive victory. The best solution to the problem, in his mind, was for the officers to employ more-systematic coercion techniques in combat. In his report of the engagement, Bragg maintained, "The want of proper organization and discipline, and the inferiority in many cases of our officers to the men they were expected to command, left us often without system or order; and the large proportion of stragglers resulting weakened our forces and kept the superior and staff officers constantly engaged in the duties of file-closers." Volunteers' tendency to break ranks in search of plunder exacerbated the problem of straggling. "Especially was this the case after the occupancy of each of the enemy's camps, the spoils of which served to delay and greatly to demoralize our men." Nevertheless, Bragg believed the lost victory had imparted some important lessons to the troops. "In this result we have a valuable lesson, by which we should profit—never on a battle-field to lose a moment's time, but leaving the killed, wounded, and spoils to those whose special business it is to care for them, to press on with every available man, giving a panic-stricken and retreating foe no time to rally, and reaping all the benefits of a success never complete until every enemy is killed, wounded, or captured."[95]

On December 4, 1862, just days before the Battle of Prairie Grove in northwestern Arkansas, Confederate major general Thomas C. Hindman issued detailed instructions to his officers on how they and their men should conduct themselves in combat. These instructions, which his subordinate officers were to read aloud to their troops, echo many of the concerns expressed by Bragg; Hindman was neither circumspect about how he wished for his volunteers to behave in battle nor delicate about what he expected his officers to do if their troops did not meet these expectations. The general's first order of business was to instruct his enlisted men on the importance of fire discipline. "Never fire because your comrades do; nor because the enemy does; nor because you happen to see the enemy; nor for the sake of firing rapidly. Always wait till you are certainly within the range of your gun," Hindman ordered, "then single out your man, take deliberate aim, as low down as the knee, and fire." Hindman took a pragmatic approach to combat; he had no grand illusions about chivalry and instructed his troops to aim for enemy officers at every opportunity. "When occasion offers, be certain to pick off the enemy's officers, especially the mounted ones, and to kill his artillery horses." The Confederate commander also made it abundantly clear what would happen to those men who failed to obey their officers' orders, who straggled, or who fled in battle. "Do not break ranks to plunder. If we whip the enemy, all he has will be ours; if not, the spoil will be of no benefit to us. Plunderers and stragglers will be put to death upon the spot. File-closers are especially charged with this duty. The cavalry in rear will likewise attend to it."[96] Though Hindman's orders brim with fierce determination and confidence in his volunteers, his reference to file closers was doubtless intended for effect, and as a warning. His instructions also demonstrate the importance of coercion as a method for maintaining discipline in combat.

The tactical manuals used by both armies prescribed the use of file closers in companies; their use, while customary, was also potentially the most draconian method for implementing coercion in battle. The 1863 *U.S. Infantry Tactics* manual defined file closers as "[t]he officers and non-commissioned officers of a company, whose habitual position is two places behind the rear rank," but it was more or less silent about their function in battle.[97] Practically speaking, these men were under orders to use force to prevent enlisted volunteers on the firing line from fleeing; file closers imposed their will either through the threat of punishment or, when necessary, the use of deadly force. Officers and men who served in this capacity were understandably reluctant to describe specific instances of cowardice among their volunteers. With its shameful connotations of cowardice, compulsion, and brute force, citizen-officers on both sides did not often discuss this onerous duty in their letters, diaries, or reports. The term "file closer" appears a mere seventeen times among the thousands of official documents published in the 128 volumes of the *Official Records,* and historians have all but ignored the vital role of such men on the battlefield.[98] Even so, file closers were a critical part of the coercive element of Civil War company command and grew in importance when volunteers were unresponsive to citizen-officers' efforts to persuade their obedience.

Despite their general reticence on the matter, some citizen-officers did contain in their letters noteworthy descriptions of the role and importance of file closers in combat early in the war. Lieutenant Holmes of the 20th Massachusetts Infantry remarked upon the critical role of file closers in maintaining the integrity of his company in action and rather proudly described his own efforts to maintain order through force. "Once when *entre nous* the right of Lowell's Co begun to waver a little and fall back," he wrote of his regiment's participation in the Seven Days' Campaign of June and July 1862, "our left stood and didn't give an inch—But really as much or rather more is due to the file closers than anything else." Holmes was responsible for overseeing his company's file closers in the engagement; most of them were noncommissioned officers known to be authoritative, dependable, and steady under fire. "I told 'em to shoot any man who ran," Holmes informed his parents, "and they lustily buffeted every hesitating brother—I gave one (who was cowering) a smart rap over the backsides with the edge of my sword—and stood with my revolver & swore I'd shoot the first man who ran or fired against orders." Apparently, this heavy-handed approach to battlefield discipline had the desired effect. "Well we licked 'em and this time there was the maneuvering of a battle to be seen," Holmes boasted, "splendid and awful to behold; especially as the dusk allowed us to see clearly the lines of flames from the different Regts as they fired."[99] Union colonel Nelson Taylor, commanding the 72nd New York Infantry at the Battle of Malvern Hill in July 1862, also remarked on the effectiveness of the company file closers in his regiment. "During this action no man left the ranks," Taylor grimly reported after the battle. "The dead lay where they fell, and the wounded were laid by the file-closers just in rear of the line. The men kept perfectly closed up, and obeyed with alacrity every order. Of the conduct of all, officers and men, I can speak but in terms of commendation. It was most praiseworthy."[100]

As the fortunes of war turned against the Confederacy, its commanders reiterated the importance of file closers in maintaining combat discipline. By early 1865, General Robert E. Lee believed the need for effective file closers in his beleaguered Army of Northern Virginia was so pressing that he included detailed instructions for their use in general orders to his troops. During the Siege of Petersburg in February 1865, Lee instructed his corps commanders to conduct competency evaluations of the company officers and noncommissioned officers in his regiments. "Such of the former as shall be reported deficient in intelligence, coolness, and capacity," he ordered, "will be brought before examining boards, and those of the latter so reported will be reduced to the ranks. Appointments to fill vacancies among the non-commissioned officers will be made from those soldiers of the company most distinguished for courage, discipline, and attention to duty." Furthermore, "The whole number of file-closers in each company shall be one for every ten men, and for this purpose lance appointments will be given, if necessary, to men of the character above described, who will be required to wear a distinctive badge." Lee was particularly concerned with ensuring that they knew their duties and were men of proven competence and character. "The file-closers will be carefully instructed in their duties by the regimental commanders," he continued, "and vacancies will be filled as they occur among the non-commissioned and lance officers from the best and most tried soldiers of the company." In a circular accompanying the orders, Lee ordered his commanders to "[i]mpress upon your officers that discipline cannot be attained without constant watchfulness on their part. They must attend to the smallest particulars of detail. Men must be habituated to obey, or they cannot be controlled in battle, and the neglect of the least important order impairs the proper influence of the officer."[101]

Lee was explicit about the file closers' duties to avoid any confusion on the matter. "On the march they will be required to prevent straggling and be held responsible for the presence of their respective squads of ten. In action they will keep two paces behind the rear rank of their several squads, the non-commissioned and lance officer with loaded guns and fixed bayonets. They will be diligently instructed to aid in preserving order in the ranks and enforcing obedience to commands, and to permit no man to leave his place unless wounded, excused in writing by the medical officer of the regiment, or by order of the regimental commander." In an ominous turn the general explicitly authorized file closers to enforce combat discipline with deadly force if required. "For this purpose they will use such degree of force as may be necessary. If any refuse to advance, disobey orders, or leave the ranks to plunder or to retreat, the file-closer will promptly cut down or fire upon the delinquents. They will treat in the same manner any man who uses words or actions calculated to produce alarm among the troops." Lee concluded his orders by emphasizing how essential combat discipline was to the survival of the army. "Justice to the brave men who remain at their posts, no less than the success to our arms, demands that this order be rigorously executed, and it will be enjoined upon file-closers that they shall make the evasion of duty more dangerous than its performance."[102]

Coercion, discipline, and other stern command techniques that enabled citizen-officers to achieve mastery over their volunteers in battle—while effective—could breed great resentment in camp and on the march. Private John Davis Billings of the 10th Independent Battery, Massachusetts Light Artillery, wryly recalled, "Many a wearer of shoulder-straps was to be shot by his own men in the first engagement" because of these perceived outrages against their rights as citizens. "But," he added, "somehow or other, when the engagement came along there seemed to be Rebels enough to shoot without throwing away ammunition on Union men." Billings believed that the loudest agitators who boasted of their intentions to shoot their officers in battle also tended to be shirkers, cowards, or deserters, for "about that time too the men, who in more peaceful retreats were so anxious to shoot their own officers, could not always be found, when wanted, to shoot more legitimate game."[103] Lieutenant Shaw, seeking to soothe his sister who had read a newspaper story about volunteers threatening to shoot their officers, told her the story of the youthful Captain Charles Redington Mudge of his own 2nd Massachusetts Infantry. Mudge was wounded during the First Battle of Winchester in 1862, and though at the time he was apparently not well liked by some of his volunteers, they rushed to save the officer's life when he fell leading them. "They carried [Mudge]," Shaw wrote to his sister, "and dragged him in a waggon, and dressed his wound. At Charlestown, they got hold of a Secession Doctor, and stood guard over him while he examined the Captain's leg." There was no reason to fear for the officers' safety, Shaw reassured his sister; soldiers may have grumbled about their commanders, but in the end, combat created a unifying effect that often tended to overcome their grievances.[104]

Combat emphasized the importance of personal loyalty between junior officers and enlisted men and could quickly render grievances and resentments inconsequential; as the old witticism goes, the prospect of death tended to concentrate the mind wonderfully. Union and Confederate soldiers, despite the requirements of regulations and the imposition of army discipline, still bounded the terms of their service based on a relationship of mutual dependence with their officers. These bonds could become so strong under the pressures of combat that the natural divide between citizen-officers and volunteers meant little, especially when death intervened. The 17th Maine Infantry's Captain Mattocks described the death of an enlisted man in his company after Chancellorsville in May 1863 in wrenching terms. "One of my Corporals—a splendid young man—who had his life torn away by a shell, died after much but patient suffering yesterday morning," Mattocks told his mother soon after. "He was a genuine martyr, and felt that he was really dying for his country. Another must soon follow him, and a third was shot dead upon the field. My noble company—and it is a noble one—which I have successfully protected against disease I find I can not shield against such carnage as this."[105] This relationship worked in the reverse as well. William Henry Harrison Clayton of the 19th Iowa Infantry lamented the death of a particularly caring company officer he and his comrades thought was recovering from his wounds. "We knew that Lieut. Kent was severely wounded but did not know that he was dead until this spring," Clayton wrote from New Orleans in 1864. "We learned from one of the 3rd Iowa Cav., Thos. Pace of Pittsburg, that he died. The boys all mourn his loss, there was not one of the company but what liked him. He was always joking with some one, and would do anything in his power to please us."[106] Citizen-officers could not lead without, at a minimum, the tacit consent of their volunteers, and any who placed his life and reputation in the hands of troops who neither trusted nor respected him faced perilous prospects indeed. On the other hand, a citizen-officer not only depended upon the consent of his soldiers to establish his command authority but also relied upon these bonds of personal loyalty and respect for his very survival.

The bonds of combat and the trauma of death also drew fellow leaders together. Robert Gould Shaw described the heartbreaking sight of brother officers dead on the field after the savage battle of Cedar Mountain in August 1862. "The first man I recognized was [Captain Richard D.] Cary," wrote Shaw. "He was lying on his back with his head on a piece of wood. He looked calm and peaceful, as if he were merely sleeping; his face was beautiful, and I could have stood and looked at it a long while." As the lieutenant wandered the field littered with corpses, he found the bodies of four other friends, all company officers in his regiment. "Captain [William B.] Williams we found next. Then [Captain Richard Chapman] Goodwin, [Captain Edwin Gardner] Abbott, and [Captain Stephen George] Perkins. They had all probably been killed instantly, while Cary lived until two o'clock P.M. of the next day." Shaw could not help lingering over one of his dead friends. "His was the only dead body I have ever seen that it was pleasant to look at, and it was beautiful.... All these five were superior men; every one in the regiment was their friend. It was a sad day for us, when they were brought in dead, and they cannot be replaced."[107] Citizen-officers formed deep bonds of comradeship with their fellow officers in combat; connections that were both fragile and essential. When these were destroyed in death, it created a void that could have a devastating emotional effect upon those left behind.

The emotional connections forged in combat, along with persuasion and coercion, when employed effectively in combination could move volunteers to feats of courage and self-sacrifice that seem almost unbelievable to the modern eye. Accounts of such exploits are too numerous to repeat here, but one such episode is particularly evocative of the manner of bravery and composure that Civil War volunteers valued so highly in their citizen-officers. By the Battle of Gettysburg in July 1863, twenty-four-year-old Charles Mudge had risen from company command to serve as the lieutenant colonel of the 2nd Massachusetts Infantry; his example on that field demonstrates the awful price for citizen-officers and volunteers who attempted the impossible in combat. On the final morning of the battle, Mudge received orders from brigade headquarters to prepare an assault on a strong Confederate position at the base of Culp's Hill. The plan required his volunteers to cross Spangler's field, an open meadow with very little natural cover, and strike enemy troops dug in behind captured Union breastworks. Mudge knew the enterprise was likely to fail, and so to ensure that he had not misunderstood the orders, he asked the courier to repeat them. Sadly, there had been no miscommunication, and the orders were explicit: the 2nd Massachusetts would cross the field and storm the enemy works immediately, despite the obvious risks. "Well," Mudge is said to have remarked, "it is murder, but it's the order." He formed his volunteers, unfurled the regimental flags, and ordered the troops to advance. "Up, men, over the works! Forward, double quick!" he urged them, drawing his sword, moving to the front of the regiment, and leading the attack.[108] As feared, the 2nd Massachusetts charged across the deadly open field and straight into a blistering Confederate fire. In a matter of minutes, the regiment sustained 137 casualties, and of the twenty-two company and regimental officers leading the attack, twelve were killed or wounded. Among the dead was Lieutenant Colonel Mudge, shot through the throat while leading from the front. The 2nd Massachusetts's ill-fated effort at Gettysburg was later explained as a regrettable mistake and attributed to the fog of war.[109]

Such trials during the conflict's first few years, while costly, drew officers and volunteers closer together as comrades and clarified volunteers' priorities about their military service. As Private Billings observed well afterward, "in justice to both officers and privates, that the first two years of the war, when the exactions of the service were new, saw three times the number of punishments administered in the two subsequent years; but, aside from the getting accustomed to the restraints of the service, campaigning was more continuous in the later years, and this kept both mind and body occupied." Combat and the shared misery of campaigning helped bridge the gap between officers and men, while discipline enabled them to fight the enemy more effectively. "It is inactivity which makes the growler's paradise," Billings observed. "Then, in the last years of the war the rigors of military discipline, the sharing of common dangers and hardships, and promotions from the ranks, had narrowed the gap between officers and privates so that the chords of mutual sympathy were stronger than before, and trivial offences were slightly rebuked or passed unnoticed."[110] Upper-level commanders could provide a great deal of inspiration for their soldiers, but only the captains and lieutenants stood shoulder to shoulder with the enlisted men on the firing line. Company officers shared their volunteers' peril, personally looked after their welfare, served as an example of bravery and resiliency, and quite often died as a result. They had to have a strong will, relentless optimism, unflappable composure, and the simple but ineffable ability to maintain control over themselves and their men in unimaginable circumstances. The first years of combat and campaigning forced recalcitrant citizen-soldiers to come to terms with their place in the military hierarchy. Though discipline remained a serious concern in both armies, the hard realities of combat helped volunteers keep their grievances against officers in perspective. As the war entered its final years, the nature of combat and the character of the junior-officer corps continued to evolve, but the combat-leadership lessons citizen-officers learned in the first battles deeply informed the manner in which they led, fought, and died throughout the remainder of the conflict.

6

Maturation of the Volunteer Junior Officer Corps

In the winter of 1863, Captain Henry Thweatt Owen of the 18th Virginia Infantry still dreamed about Gettysburg. Five months earlier, on July 3, 1863, at about 2 o'clock in the afternoon, Owen and his regiment had trudged up the slope of Cemetery Ridge with Garnett's Brigade of Pickett's Division in the Army of Northern Virginia's doomed frontal assault against the Army of the Potomac's center. Under a merciless sun and after two days of brutal combat, nine well-disciplined and well-led infantry brigades, fifteen regiments in all, crossed nearly a mile of gently undulating fields into an inferno. General Lee had hoped that the assault would drive the Union II Corps from its commanding position on the high ground and break the army's weakened center. This was not to be. The intense Confederate artillery barrage preceding the attack covered the ridge in smoke but did little to weaken the Union troops dug in behind breastworks and low stone walls. Well-placed artillery and thousands of steady rifle muskets were trained on the space between the two armies; Owen and his comrades knew they had been ordered to march straight onto a killing ground. More than half of the 12,500 Confederates who made the assault later known as Pickett's Charge were killed or wounded in the space of a single hour. Of the fifteen regiments involved in the attack, eleven were commanded by former cadets of the Virginia Military Institute; all eleven of these officers became casualties.[1] Owen's regiment alone lost twenty-nine of its thirty-one officers; every officer and volunteer in his Company C, except Owen himself and one other man, were struck by enemy metal during the charge.[2]

Captain Owen somehow returned to the Confederate lines unscathed, but the memory of that murderous day continued to torment him. In his dream the captain found himself caught up in a monumental battle that felt instantly familiar. He saw the hazy shapes of Pennsylvania's landscape before him and realized he was reliving the disastrous final attack on Cemetery Ridge. "We were advancing in line of battle upon the enemy[;] troops on my right and left shot dead away as far as the eye could see all pressing on the fearful conflict," he told his wife in December 1863. "I could hear the fearful reports of five batteries of cannon and the perpetual roar of fifty thousand muskets while a dark cloud of smoke hung over the field mantling everything as the gloom of dusky sunset. Far away to the front I saw the dim outlines of lofty hills, broken rocks, and lofty precipices which resembled Gettysburg." With the surreal sense of awareness that sometimes accompanies dreams, Owen understood where he was and what was happening, but something was amiss in the tableau. "As we advanced further I found we were fighting that great battle over again and I saw something before me like a thin shadow which I tried to go by but it kept in front of me and whichever way I turned it still appeared between me and the enemy," Owen continued. "Nobody else seemed to see or notice the shadow which looked as thin as smoke and did not present myself to the enemy distinctly thru' it." The apparition deeply unsettled the captain, and he tried to get away from it. "I felt troubled and oppressed but still the shadow went out before me. I moved forward in the thickest of the fray trying to loose sight of it and went all through the Battle of Gettysburg again with the shadow ever before me and between me and the enemy." Still the ghostly form dogged Owen's steps, "and when we came out beyond the danger of shot it spoke and said to me 'I am the Angel that protected you. I will never leave nor forsake you.' The surprise was so great that I awoke and burst into tears." He was overwhelmed by the emotions the strange dream stirred in him: gratitude over his good fortune at living through the battle, but guilt that he had survived when so many of his comrades had not. "What had I done," Owen wondered, "that should entitle me to such favours beyond tho' hundreds of brave and reputed good men who had fallen on that day leaving widowed mothers and widowed wives, orphan children and disconsolate families to mourn their fates?"[3]

Though many were only just coming to realize it, by late 1863 the experience of two-and-a-half years of war had caused a change in company-grade volunteer officers. For Owen and others who fought in it, the Civil War was a fundamentally damaging experience. Officers and surgeons of the period did not possess the same understanding of psychological battle injuries in the same way that modern physicians do, but the shock and sustained trauma of extended campaigning nevertheless took a heavy toll on citizen-officers and volunteers. Many would continue to suffer from their experiences, in both tangible and intangible ways, for the rest of their lives.[4] The physical and psychological costs of learning, assuming, and exercising military authority while subjecting themselves to the immense hazards of combat leadership weighed heavily upon these men. Some, like Henry Owen, were haunted by their experiences and struggled to find meaning in the carnage; leading their volunteers into such death and destruction only seemed to increase this burden. Many interpreted the war's shattering effects, and their role in the damage, through the prism of their Christian faith. Like their enlisted volunteers, officers sought a sense of order in the malignant randomness of the battlefield and ascribed their survival, or the deaths and injuries of comrades and fellow officers, to God's inscrutable purpose.[5]

For Lieutenant Edgar L. Bumpus of the 33rd Massachusetts Infantry, the prospect of death was the catalyst for a religious epiphany. Bumpus, writing to a clergyman acquaintance in March 1864, described how the perils of his duties led him to prepare his soul for eternity. "It is over one year since I began to think of the welfare of my soul," he wrote. "The regiment was on Picket (this was while we was at Stafford Court House Va) I was alone in my tent when the question came up in my mind, are you prepared to meet your last Judge? are you prepared to lead men in the charge? and have you prepared yourself in case you should be killed? Why should you not be condemned without one plea?" These questions tormented Bumpus, and he sought comfort in religious faith. "I could not rest, before morning I determined to find rest and there was only one way, to acknowledge Christ, and to throw myself at his feet. For I had his promis[e] that a[l]though your sins are as crimson yet they shall be as white as wool." Seeking reassurance, the anxious young lieutenant searched out comrades whom he knew to be devoted believers. "I conversed with three good men Johnson of Co K Crockett Co E and Burrage of Co H. All three of them have fallen in the cause of their Country[.] They were Christerns, and was prepared to meet their God. Two of them Burrage and Crockett was killed out-right. Johnson Lived 3 or 4 days." Bumpus had little opportunity to mourn his dead comrades. "I could not visit [Johnson] for we was busily engaged throwing up rifle pits, and erecting batteries. He died happy was cheerful to the last, and had no fear when he crossed the river, he was received by the angles with joy. May his ashes rest in peace."⁶ Like his three friends, Bumpus died in action, killed at the Battle of Resaca in May 1864.⁷

Other citizen-officers struggling with the damage of war assumed a state of numbness or emotional detachment, sometimes taking a fatalistic approach to the disillusionment and destruction they endured.⁸ In May 1864 Lieutenant Charles Harvey Brewster, adjutant of the 10th Massachusetts Infantry, described his veterans' jaded indifference to seeing human remains as they marched over the old Chancellorsville battlefield. "[W]e passed over the battle ground of last year," Brewster wrote to his mother, and "there were lots of human skulls and bones lying [on] top of the ground and we left plenty more dead bodies there to decay and bleach to keep thier grim company. [T]he woods we have fought over both there and here are strewn with the dead bodies of both parties who lay as they fell unburied," he noted. "I cannot give you an idea of half the horrors I have witnessed and yet so common have they become that they do not excite a feeling of horror."⁹ That same month Confederate officer Columbus Sykes of the 43rd Mississippi Infantry described the carnage at the Battle of Pickett's Mill with a peculiar combination of horror, detachment, and gratitude to God. "On Friday evening the 27th, the enemy charged Granbury's and Lowrey's brigades of Cleburne's division," he told his wife two days after the battle. "I walked over the battlefield in Cleburne's front yesterday evening. The Yankee loss was terrific—the spectacle was revolting—the ground was almost literally covered with their dead. They were lying piled so thick that I could, had I chosen, have walked over a large portion of the field on their mutilated bodies," Sykes wrote with a strange exuberance. "Their loss was unquestionably and I think without exaggeration 15 or 20 to our one. The disparity is wonderful and can only be attributed to the over-ruling Providence of God."¹⁰ Union captain Levi Bird Duff tried to articulate the emotional devastation of battle and his subsequent efforts to process the savagery all around him. "We see men killed here by hundreds and thousands, we soon forget however that death has been among us; but the slain are remembered at home and years will not remove the sorrow and anguish of their death," he wrote in 1863. "I have to make out to-day a list of the casualties in my company since it entered the service and when I came to write May 31 1862 I said to myself, that was a day of calamity to us. When I looked at the long list of men who went down in the fearful struggle of that day I could scarcely refrain from weeping," he admitted to his wife. Moreover, the lingering emotional trauma of death and destruction affected not only company officers but regimental leaders as well. "When after the battle of Fair Oaks Col McKnight was informed that [several company officers] were killed & that one half of his regiment was lost he exclaimed that he was ruined," Duff lamented of his regiment's admired commander. "Then & there his spirit was broken; he has never since shown himself to be the man he was before."[11]

Only a certain callousness could permit participants to endure such trauma. Callousness to the widespread anguish of the war's final years was not confined to the armies, though, as some citizen-officers discovered. In June 1864 Confederate captain Richard W. Corbin observed the widespread suffering in Richmond's military hospitals and noted that the emotional numbness so common among the volunteers seemed to have seeped into the civilian populace as well. "Almost at every step my gaze is met by the sight of trains of poor fellows maimed and mutilated by the brutal mercenaries of the North. Such is the pitch of callousness to which men and women have arrived here, after witnessing for three bloody years all the horrors of war, that now they eye these miserable objects with apparent indifference." The staff officer was careful to explain that he detected no malice in the residents' disaffection; it was, he believed, a coping mechanism similar to that of the volunteers and officers in the field. "This indifference does not arise, I am sure, from any dullness of sensibility; these people have shown too often by their acts of devotion how good their hearts are, for me to suspect that their feelings are at all dead." Fatalism and emotional distance served as barriers against the trauma facing soldiers and civilians alike, he surmised. "No, I think that as they are prepared for the same fate, that it comes from a wish not to render themselves miserable by an exhibition of compassion which would be of no use to the objects of it," concluded Corbin.[12]

Nearly three years of combat had punished the junior-officer corps on both sides, mentally, physically, and emotionally. Yet the campaigns during that time also served to transform them into something quite unlike their early war selves. Those company-grade leaders who survived were in many ways quite different from the officers of 1861 and 1862. Despite the devastating losses among Southern officers during the first two years of the war, by the end of 1863 Jefferson Davis felt the previously amateurish Confederate officer corps had at last been tempered into an effective instrument. "Though we have lost many of the best of our soldiers and most patriotic of our citizens (the sad but unavoidable result of the battles and toils of such a campaign as that which will render the year 1863 ever memorable in our annals)," the president assured the Confederate Congress in December of that year, "the Army is believed to be in all respects in better condition than at any previous period of the war. Our gallant defenders, now veterans, familiar with danger, hardened by exposure, and confident in themselves and their officers, endure privations with cheerful fortitude and welcome battle with alacrity." Despite defeats at Gettysburg, Vicksburg, and Chattanooga, Davis believed that the army's essential self-confidence stemmed in large part from improvements among the citizen-officers who led the volunteers. "The officers, by experience in field service and the action of examining boards in relieving the incompetent," he maintained, "are now greatly more efficient than at the commencement of the war. The assertion is believed to be fully justified that, regarded as a whole, for character, valor, efficiency, and patriotic devotion, our Army has not been equaled by any like number of troops in the history of war."[13]

As citizen-officers struggled to cope with the damaging effects of combat, the identity of company-grade leadership in both armies had changed by 1864. Many of the volunteer captains and lieutenants commissioned in the war's first years were dead, maimed, imprisoned, or had resigned from the service. Those who survived into 1864 tended to move up the ladder of military hierarchy; company-grade officers of proven ability seldom lingered in that position for long, given the voracious need for competent and effective regimental and brigade commanders in both armies. The attrition rates among citizen-officers at company grade were, like their casualty rates, extreme. In the research sample Confederate junior officers experienced a 43-percent attrition rate resulting from promotions, transfers, and resignations between April 1861 and April 1865. In other words, approximately 43 percent of company-grade Confederates in the sample resigned, transferred, or were promoted out of their company during the war. More than 30 percent of them resigned or otherwise left the army, while about 13 percent transferred or were promoted out of their companies. The attrition rate among sample Confederate junior officers who served in the Trans-Mississippi and western theaters was, at 42 percent, slightly lower than the 44-percent rate among those in the East. Union junior officers in the sample suffered even higher rates of attrition than their Confederate counterparts. Among the sampled officers, 53 percent resigned, transferred, or were promoted out of their companies between April 1861 and April

1865. Of these, about 17 percent were promoted or transferred out, while just over 36 percent either resigned or otherwise lost their commission. Some 15 percent of Union junior officers serving in the Trans-Mississippi and western theaters were promoted out of their companies, while 17.5 percent of those in the East left their companies by promotion.[14]

The resulting void in company-grade leadership opened up positions for enlisted volunteers who aspired to command. It is difficult to generalize about the overall quality of junior officers in 1864 and 1865, though judging by the resiliency and effectiveness of their leadership, it seems that a combination of experience, training, and discipline paid long-term dividends among the junior-officer corps on both sides. Given the substantial turnover among these leaders due to casualties, resignations, and promotions from 1862 onward, the identity of both the Union and Confederate company-grade officers was often in a state of flux. Late in the war such officers in both armies were former privates or noncommissioned officers with extensive experience in the ranks. New company-grade citizen-officers promoted in the Civil War's final years may have lacked the polish, education, or prestige of their early war predecessors, but most brought significant experience to their positions, along with an intrinsic understanding of the mentality of their enlisted volunteers. Union and Confederate leaders placed a premium on ability as the primary criteria for rewarding talented or experienced enlisted volunteers with commissions late in the war. Yet sometimes that advancement came at a steep personal price, and former enlisted men felt overwhelmed by the change in responsibilities. In July 1864 Sergeant James Litton Cooper of the 20th Tennessee Infantry won a commission but came to regret it. After receiving three wounds and performing numerous acts of bravery under fire, the sergeant received a commission as a staff officer to reward his gallantry during the Atlanta Campaign. "On the 18th of July I received my promotion to Aid[e]," he recalled in 1865. "The letter from [Brig.] Gen [Robert C.] Tyler in regard to it said, for meritorious conduct, was the position given. Very flattering indeed." Cooper's account of his first day as an officer highlights the abject condition of the Army of Tennessee late in the war. "On the 23d I was ordered upon duty as Aid[e], at B[r]igade Headquarters, and mounted on a mule from which the owner had been killed the day previous. Under these cheering auspices I commenced my oath as a 'staff officer.'" Embarrassed, Cooper eventually exchanged his mule for a horse and uneasily assumed his new commission, but he never fully adjusted to life as an officer.[15]

Though some late-war citizen-officers elevated from the ranks felt uneasy with their new status and responsibilities, others took great pride and pleasure in their promotions. William Cowper Nelson was an enlisted man in the 17th Mississippi Infantry in 1862; by 1863 he was a staff officer in the Army of Northern Virginia and enthused about the vast improvement in his circumstances. "The duties of my position as Ordnance Officer are very light," Nelson wrote to his mother, "and so I have plenty of time for the duties of the Adjutant General's Department. The Generals' sons have not arrived as yet, and it is probable that I will continue to perform 'Double-duty' for several weeks to come, but there is a vast difference between soldiering as a private, and as an officer, I serve a long apprenticeship however, and I think am somewhat entitled to a little ease now."[16] Union volunteer Henry Clay Matrau, only sixteen years old when he enlisted, was commissioned as a lieutenant in 1864 and given command of a company in the 6th Wisconsin Infantry, part of the famous Iron Brigade. "Scince I wrote last to you I have advanced another step in the line of promotion," the young man informed his parents soon after. "I have received my commission as 1st Lieutenant of Co G and am now commanding officer of the company. You see, my father and mother, that I have arisen step by step to my present position as an officer in the U.S. Army. It has been by my own efforts, too, for I belong to a strange reg't from a strange state and the friend's I have now in the reg't I have gained scince the war began." Matrau was careful to qualify his satisfaction by describing the difficulty of his ascension from the ranks. "I am rather proud, more for your sakes than my own, that I am able to present so clear a record of my services and I believe that my Parents will be proud of their son. I dont wish to be thought any egotistical in thus speaking of myself but there ain't many that know how hard it is for a private to rise, as I have, from the lowest rank in the army to that of a commissioned Officer, with no help but my own right hand."[17]

By early 1864 both armies could draw on months or years of combat experience, training, and mutual trust to endure the ordeal of battle. Experienced citizen-officers and volunteers knew each other's strengths and weaknesses, and the men rewarded their officers' effective leadership with loyalty, resiliency, and obedience, at least on the battlefield. Desertion, conscription, casualties, and attrition battered both sides, but the nucleus of experienced volunteers and officers at the heart of the Union and Confederate armies had learned much about the art of soldiering. For many, combat had peeled away the fragility of their civilian selves, discarding those unable or unwilling to conform to war's harsh demands. Historians have described this operation in turns as a hardening, an annealing, or an immunizing process. The stolidity of late-war volunteers and citizen-officers had largely superseded the early war sense of grandeur, spectacle, and glory. These veterans had seen too much that repudiated such naive conceptions; war had become a vast and irresistible force they must endure and, if fortunate, survive.[18] Days after his regiment was ravaged at the Battle of Gettysburg, Captain Henry Livermore Abbott encapsulated this paradoxical mixture of sorrow and stoicism in a letter to his father. Abbot, whose 20th Massachusetts Infantry had lost ten of thirteen officers and 117 of 231 enlisted volunteers in the battle, likened his gutted regiment to a mechanism. "Indeed with only two officers beside myself remaining, I can't help feeling a little spooney when I am thinking," he wrote to his father, "& you know I am not at all a lachrymose individual in general. However I think we can run the machine." The captain could indeed "run the machine," and he would fall while leading his regiment in the Battle of the Wilderness in May 1864.[19]

Combat, citizen-officers found, stripped away irrelevancies and exposed inner character, and for those who survived into the war's final years, this unforgiving process could be a revelation. Volunteers who seemed to have little potential for military excellence could, under duress, exceed all their officers' expectations to the contrary. Lieutenant William Henry Harrison Lewis described the unforeseen results of war's refining process to his mother in August 1863. "War is a strange scale for measuring men and brings forth strange developments in the character of men," he observed, "who to all appearance in civic life are men of courage and sterling worth. You remember how disgracefully this unfortunate young fellow acted when returning to the army with me at New Orleans. Well, would you ever have thought he would make a reliable soldier? No, never! Well, he made as good a soldier as there was in the regiment, cool and brave in battle and always on hand and never shirking duty in camp." Lewis contrasted the young man's unexpected excellence with other volunteers, who in civilian life seemed to possess all the necessary components to make brave soldiers but who failed when put to the test. "Compare this soldier with others who occupied honorable positions in society . . . , and as soldiers there is no comparison."[20]

For the citizen-armies of 1864, all their skill, experience, and ability would be required to endure the trials ahead. With his ascension to the command of the Union armies, Lieutenant General Ulysses S. Grant implemented his plan to put a swift end to the Confederacy through a vast coordinated strategic effort of concentration that only promised to increase the tempo of destruction.²¹ Citizen-officers sensed these changes; they knew the war would not go on forever, and some now thought they could detect a terrible crescendo coming that spring. Charles Brewster attempted to describe to his sister the sense of foreboding he felt in April 1864, on the eve of the Federal campaign to destroy the Confederate army in Virginia. "We are expecting a mighty hard time when the campaign opens and shall probably see a great many tired and hungry days but we shall think nothing of that if we can only whip these Rebs. I think I could go another month without anything to eat if I knew that was to be the result." The wryness in the lieutenant's missive did not mask his sense of impending dread at what he described as the end of days. "I suppose we have a larger Army than ever before and so no doubt has Lee and the shock of battle will be terrible when the two armies meet. [O]ld Sheldon of Haydenville, Emmilines father would say that it was the Armageddon prophesied in Scripture and the end of the world was certainly coming immediately. I imagine that if he could be there he would think it had come sure."²²

The campaigns of early 1864 proved as costly as Brewster feared. Captain George A. Bowen of the 12th New Jersey Infantry, formerly a sergeant, provided a nightmarish account of hand-to-hand fighting during the Battle of Spotsylvania Court House. Bowen's regiment marched into battle through a driving rain and formed up for a daybreak assault on the Confederate salient known as the Mule Shoe. "[W]e moved forward across an open piece of ground," the captain wrote in his diary, "an Officer on the Division Staff telling us to 'give a cheer and double quick as there was a line of battle in our front.' We did as directed and rushed up to the enemys position which was a strong line of earthworks with a line of abatis in its front; this we were obliged to destroy ere we could get to their line of battle." Bowen, commanding Company C, leaped into the Confederate earthworks with another officer and began clearing a path for his volunteers. "The assault had been a surprise and we captured the line of works with 3,000 prisoners 28 pieces of artillery and 2 Gen Officers." He decided to exploit this unexpected advantage and ordered his men to keep going, but the Union troops were soon forced to withdraw to the trenches. "[W]e halted and turned their works against them," Bowen continued, "and now commenced the most stubborn fight of my experience, it was almost a hand to hand fight in fact it was at times, the enemy made charge after charge right up to the muzzle of our guns only to be repulsed again and again this continued without interruption all day long and until 2 or 3 oclock of the morning." According to the captain, "the attacks were impetuous the resistance was stubborn. When we crossed the entrenchments was at an angle and here was the great slaughter of the day." This was the infamous Bloody Angle, where nearly twenty-four hours of savage hand-to-hand combat left mounds of Union and Confederate corpses in the contested trenches. "[I]t has been the worst day I have as yet seen," an exhausted Bowen tersely concluded.[23]

Lieutenant Brewster was also at the Bloody Angle, and his description of the carnage there is unstinting. "We went in at six o'clock yesterday morning," he wrote the day after the engagement, "and came out about the same time this morning." Crouched in the filth of the Spotsylvania trenches, an exhausted Brewster scrawled a poignant letter describing the experience to his sister. "I am writing this seated in the mud covered with blood + dirt and powder," he explained. "[Yesterday] we went up to hold the enemys rifle pits and redoubts and had not been there long before the enemy charged them." The lieutenant was disgusted at the poor performance of some Union troops who "broke and ran like sheep without firing a gun" as the first Confederate counterattack struck their position. "[T]he Rebels came into the same rifle pit with us and commenced an enfilading fire before we knew they were there," he explained, "and we had any quantity of men killed and wounded in much less time than it takes to tell of it." The casualties among Brewster's 10th Massachusetts Infantry were severe, particularly among the company officers. "Capt Weatherill was hit as were Capt Knight Capt Johnson Capt Gilmore + Geo Bigelow also Major Parker and his horse was riddled with bullets + killed. Lieut Munyan was also wounded." In the ensuing pandemonium Brewster lost track of many of his people. "I do not know how many men we have lost yet as we have not got but about 30 muskets with us this morning and some of the Officers are missing yet. [B]oth flagstaffs were hit three times and the state flag was cut short off."

The memory of that miserable night in the trenches haunted Brewster. "I cannot begin to tell you the horrors I have seen," he confessed, "but I must wait to tell you about the campaign when I get home there is to[o] much of it, the incidence [sic] crowd upon me so and I have but a little time and it is commencing to rain." The ferocity of the combat at the Bloody Angle was unlike anything the officer had ever seen. "[O]ur men fought the Rebels close to the other side of the breast works and knocked thier [sic] guns aside, and jumped up on the work and shot them down." In the rainy darkness Brewster could not see the terrible results of this intense combat, but first light revealed the awful outcome. "I saw this morning the other side of the pit and the Rebels are piled up in heaps 3 or 4 deep and the pit is filled with them piled up dead and wounded together," he wrote to his sister. "I saw one completely trodden in the mud so as to look like part of it and yet he was breathing and gasping." Overwhelmed, Brewster concluded: "[I]t was bad enough on our side of the breast work but on thiers it was awful. [S]ome of the wounded were groaning and some praying but I cannot write more this morning."[24]

As the savage campaigns of 1864 ground on, even the most hardened participants were appalled at their intensity and human cost. After seeing the slaughter at Cold Harbor in June 1864, Confederate staff officer Richard Corbin wondered if the enemy had gone mad. Describing the bloody failure of the Union army's frontal assault against entrenched Confederates, the captain wrote to his father:, "Everything indicates that this is the supreme effort of the North to crush out the South. Never has their fighting been characterized by such desperation and recklessness. Their battalions have been repeatedly hurled against the Southern breastworks with unwonted impetuosity and dash, but each time they have reeled back in disorder and cut to pieces." Corbin could not reconcile how such profligacy with human life could come from a civilized people. The Cold Harbor carnage seemed inhuman, somehow, the horrible spectacle resembling a product of insanity rather than reason. "I have not spoken to a single soldier here who was not convinced that the Yankee courage in the recent battles has been screwed up by means of the strongest whiskey," he declared. "One of them who was slightly wounded in one of those engagements told me that some of the Yankees were so drunk when they charged that they could hardly stand upon their legs, and that they would roll harmlessly into the entrenchments, and there allow themselves to be disarmed." Corbin believed that "[i]n some cases they were so mad with liquor that they would throw away their muskets and run into the cannon's mouth." Sickened by such wanton butchery, Corbin placed blame for the bloodshed at the feet of barbarous Yankee politicians. "Nothing is too bad for these miscreants in Washington," he fumed. "They now cap the climax by hurrying their own men into eternity when beastly drunk. Horrible, horrible."[25]

Only resiliency ensured that citizen-officers could endure such trials and continue to exercise effective leadership. The acquired resiliency of the battle line, sustained and reinforced by citizen-officers' confidence, experience, and discipline, enabled volunteers to tolerate the terrifying morass of the Civil War's final two years.[26] The bonds of affection and mutual support formed between citizen-officers and volunteers over years of campaigning were essential to maintaining that resiliency, but they could also be a liability if not properly contained and managed. Even outstanding combat leaders could struggle with this harsh and paradoxical requirement. "We are soon going to start on the coming campaign," Henry Abbott wrote to his mother in March 1864 on the eve of the Overland Campaign. "We shall have by long odds the greatest battle ever fought on this continent. Every battle grows worse and this corps lost 45 percent at Gettysburg, it will probably lose 50 percent this time, that is about 15,000." The captain knew the odds, but he also realized that effective combat leadership required him to suppress these emotions and, when militarily necessary, order his men to their possible deaths. Still, the truth of the matter left him sick at heart. "It makes me sad to look on this gallant regiment which I am instructing and disciplining for slaughter," he brooded, "to think that probably 250 or 300 of the 400 who go in, will get bowled out."[27] Confederate Robert E. Park's sense of compassion, perhaps oddly, extended to the enemy. A captain in the 12th Alabama Infantry, he nevertheless decried the "fearful butchery" of Grant's "drunken soldiers—his European hirelings" after the Battle of Spotsylvania Court House in 1864. "[Grant's] recklessness in sacrificing his hired soldiery, therefore, seems to me to be heartless and cruel in the extreme," Park mused in his diary. "He looks upon his soldiers as mere machines—not human beings—and treats them accordingly."[28] Citizen-officers like Abbott and Park had to learn how to shield themselves from the toxic emotional consequences of ordering their volunteers to risk life and limb, day after day, with no end in sight. Only by suppressing their natural tendency toward compassion could officers risk the lives of the men they lived among and led and still command with resolve.

Nevertheless, as the war entered its final act, volunteers and their officers recognized that the inevitable carnage of earlier campaigns, if unchecked, would eventually bring about their obliteration. Many reconciled the necessity of prudent combat leadership with their earlier expectations of conspicuous courage accompanying the privileges of an officer's commission. On the battlefield enemy fire did not discriminate between the excellent and the mediocre, and seemingly random bullets or capricious fragments of hot metal could snuff out the lives of outstanding leaders as well as incompetents or cowards. Such experiences brought great disillusionment, though also a pragmatic acceptance of reality. By 1864 many experienced volunteers fortunate enough to be led by good company-grade officers even came to resent the raw acts of conspicuous courage that had so impressed them earlier in the war.[29] During the Atlanta Campaign, for example, Major Robert P. Findley of the 74th Ohio Infantry chronicled his awareness of the relationship between effective combat leadership and battlefield prudence in his personal journal. "At the outset of the war, a man who would get behind a log or stone was jeered at by his fellows, and the officer who would have stood behind a tree on the skirmish line, cut off his [shoulder] straps to avoid being a target for sharpshooters, and not have exposed his person by standing upright and in exposed positions, would have been stigmatized as a coward," he explained. "But now, of the officer or soldier who won't take these precautions, if killed or wounded, the expressions of soldiers are 'I don't pity him, he had no business exposing himself unnecessarily.'" Findley, who had risen to the rank of major after company command, was dismayed that some of his fellow officers insisted on linking their effectiveness as leaders with their capacity to master fear by excessively exposing themselves to enemy fire. Such pointless heroism was not only reckless, he believed, but also placed their volunteers at risk. By foolishly squandering their lives for illegitimate, ineffective, or selfish reasons, citizen-officers deprived their men of essential leadership. Still, the heroic impulse toward conspicuous courage persisted among many late in the war. "Some yet have the idea that it will gain them a reputation for bravery and expose themselves accordingly," Findley wrote. "It is the duty of an officer to take every precaution to preserve his own life and that of his men, consistent with the performance of his duty, and if an officer will expose himself unnecessarily, he cannot consistently require care on the part of his men."[30]

Wise and experienced citizen-officers saw no shame in tempering reckless acts of battlefield valor with prudence, particularly if they felt they had sufficiently established their courage. Preparing for the Overland Campaign in late April 1864, Charles Brewster heard a rumor that his corps was to be placed in reserve. "I hope [it] is true," the lieutenant wrote to his sister, "although I suppose you will call that a cowardly wish but although we see a great many in print, we see very few in reality, of such desperate heroes that they had rather go into the heat of battle than not, when they can do their duty just as well by staying out, and when the reserves are called in they always get the toughest fighting."[31] The 3rd Minnesota Infantry's Captain C. C. Andrews agreed. "While a captain habituates himself to an indifference to danger, he should remember that it is a sacred duty to be prudent both of his own life and the lives of his men. The country needs every man, and cannot afford that a life should be wasted."[32] That is not to say that conspicuous acts of valor became less frequent later in the war; rather, in 1864 and 1865 the insights gleaned from earlier campaigning informed officers' battlefield decisions differently than in earlier years and demonstrated the value of prudence in combat.

Yet late-war officers' calculated acts of courage could, if properly employed, inspire even the most jaded volunteers to extraordinary efforts in combat. In May 1864 Confederate William H. S. Burgwyn took part in the storming of Union positions at the Battle of Proctor's Creek during the Bermuda Hundred Campaign. The lieutenant led a company of his 35th North Carolina Infantry in the morning assault and described his feelings of terror and exhilaration in his diary later that evening. "As soon as the word 'charge' was given I sprang upon the parapet, waved my hat and yelled with all my might as soon as I could cross the ditch in front," he wrote. "I ran ahead of the regiment, waved my hat, and called on the men to follow and nobly did they come though the enemy's sharpshooters fired as fast as possible from rifles that shot seven times in succession, and though the line was considerably disorganized from crossing the ditch and going through the thick underbrush not a man faltered." Determined to rally his troops, Burgwyn leaped into action. "About three hundred yards from our breastworks and fearing that the enemy fire and the bad ground might throw them into confusion, I seized the colors of the 51st North Carolina Regiment and called on the men to follow." The young officer pressed onward until he reached the Union earthworks. "Mounting them and waving the colors I jumped on the other side and pushed forward closely followed by the men with their color bearer and their colonel at their head." Several of the Federals tried to shoot Burgwyn down. "As soon as they perceived me four aimed their pieces at me but I falling down at the time, partly from sheer exhaustion and to prevent them from shooting me, their balls missed me but one passed through my hat brim." He picked up the flag and resumed his charge. "Rising again and with a shout I ran past the pits and the Yankees surrendered by crowds. I had just time then to hand the colors to a color bearer when I fell down again almost fainting and a severe fit of vomiting seized me," he confessed.[33]

Moments of emotional exaltation in battle could lead volunteers to abandon discipline, ignore their officers, and throw caution to the wind; only good leadership or good fortune could salvage such situations. Captain John William De Forest of the 12th Connecticut Infantry described such an instance at the Third Battle of Winchester in September 1864. His regiment was eager to charge a vulnerable enemy but had been ordered to halt; the 12th Connecticut "was still rocking back and forth, fluctuating between discipline and impulse," De Forest wrote. In front of them appeared a mounted staff officer, "a dashing young fellow in embroidered blue shirt, with trousers tucked into his long boots," De Forest recalled. The staff officer "pointed to the wood with his drawn sabre. It was a superb picture of the equestrianism of battle; it was finer than any scene by Horace Vernet or Wouwerman." With that simple gesture, "[t]he whole regiment saw him and rejoiced in him; it flung orders to the winds and leaped out like a runaway horse. The wood was carried in the next minute," wrote De Forest. Fortunately, this momentary lapse in combat discipline did not result in a disaster, though it certainly could have.[34]

Citizen-officers in both armies continued to wrestle with problems resulting from their volunteers' indiscipline during the war's final years. There is a key distinction, however, between combat discipline and broader military discipline in the camps, on the drill fields, and on the march. Though the citizen-soldier ethos underwent continual modification and adaptation throughout the conflict, late-war volunteers on both sides never abandoned their democratic identities. Their fundamental conceptions of military service—voluntariness, temporariness, indiscipline, egalitarianism, and democratic prerogatives—altered, adapted, and bent but did not break under the strain of military discipline and the pressures of necessity. By 1864 experienced volunteers appreciated the absolute importance of discipline in combat, if not in camp; they had seen too much of battle by then to believe otherwise. As historian Joseph T. Glatthaar observes of Confederate volunteers, "Officers may not have inculcated the level of discipline that ex-Regulars sought in camp, but these volunteers executed some of the most outstanding feats on foot in American military history, and their consistent level of achievement is unsurpassed in national annals."[35] The same may be said of Union citizen-officers who may have coveted the stern authority of their regular-army counterparts but had to settle for a détente with their undisciplined volunteers.[36] Union and Confederate officers rarely, if ever, managed to replicate regular-army military discipline among their citizen-soldiers, and their attempts to do so often met with resistance and failure. But the combat records and sheer endurance of Union and Confederate volunteers alike attest to the excellence of their battlefield performance. These achievements would have been impossible without effective combat discipline.[37]

Just as the contours of battlefield leadership, citizen-officer courage, and discipline evolved during the war's final years, the nature of combat itself was also changing by 1864. Costly and ineffective early war frontal assaults illustrated the vast difficulties of attacking enemy troops in entrenched positions. Though commanders in both armies persisted in conducting sanguinary charges into the conflict's final years, the ineffectiveness of frontal attacks at Kennesaw Mountain, Cold Harbor, Franklin, and elsewhere continued to demonstrate the hazards of assaulting enemy entrenchments. Some forward-thinking officers attempted to modify their tactical doctrine, attacking in columns instead of the traditional linear formations or engaging in covering fire and coordinated rushes toward defensive positions.[38] The innovative Union brigadier general Emory Upton, for instance, employed a coordinated approach to assaulting fixed positions at Spotsylvania Court House in May 1864, yet despite initial success, the effort ultimately failed because of a lack of support.[39] Confederate major general Patrick Ronayne Cleburne organized company-sized units of sharpshooters and experimented with various tactical attack formations as early as 1862; indeed, in his fatal assault on the Union works at the Battle of Franklin in November 1864, Cleburne employed columns of brigades until just before contact in an attempt to minimize the damage from enemy fire.[40] Such tactics were neither new to Civil War commanders nor unique to 1864 and 1865, but even these innovations would hardly have been achievable for troops without combat discipline and effective leadership perfected through awful experience.[41]

Late-war battles posed significant challenges for company-grade citizen-officers. Extended periods of continuous contact between the armies, coupled with the exceptionally difficult terrain characterizing many of these engagements, made combat especially confused and hard to manage.[42] At the Battle of Chickamauga in September 1863, for example, Lieutenant Albion W. Tourgée of the 105th Ohio Infantry explained the problems of negotiating the wilderness of northern Georgia along with the peculiar challenges it presented to regimental and company officers attempting to control their volunteers in combat. "No one seemed to know where our position was," he remembered of the first day's fighting. "All was doubt and uncertainty." The arduous terrain aggravated the existing command-and-control problems. As Tourgée described: "The ground was wooded, broken with low, transverse hills and irregular knolls. The woods were open, but grown here and there with baffling stretches of dense underbrush. There were a very few small fields and indistinct roads.... It was the worst possible region in which to maneuver an army, being without landmarks or regular slopes, and so thickly wooded that it was impossible to preserve any alignment." Even worse, the lieutenant and his fellow officers often operated while cut off from corps, division, and even brigade headquarters, and regiments or companies had little idea what they were supposed to do or where they needed to be. "Besides, there seemed to be, as we know there was, an utter lack of fixed and definite plan, and a woeful ignorance of the field," Tourgée recalled. "Soldiers are quick to note such things, and one of the [regiment], seeing a group of officers in consultation, said he guessed they were 'pitching pennies to decide which way the brigade should front.'"[43] The woods and brambles were so thick at Chickamauga, Tourgée noted, that "[t]here was no chance to use artillery save at close range. On our whole front there was hardly a place where a range of three hundred yards could be secured. Communication between the flanks was almost impossible." Union and Confederate commanders' attempts to assert control over the battlefield were further hampered by a mind-numbingly complex network of backwoods paths, faint trails, impenetrable underbrush, and hidden gullies. "The winding roads were full of lost staff-officers," Tourgée wrote. "The commander of a regiment rarely saw both flanks of his command at once. Even companies became broken in the thickets, and taking different directions were lost to each other." Even years after the battle, Tourgée could make little sense of Chickamauga. "Confusion reigned even before the battle began. It is folly to attempt to unravel the tangled web of that two days' fight. Even the part a single regiment took is almost untraceable."[44]

George Bowen described the bewildering fighting in the May 1864 Battle of the Wilderness in similar terms. The Wilderness was arguably an even more confusing environment for a large battle than Chickamauga, and the officers and volunteers who experienced it were often left to fend for themselves in the confusion. Captain Bowen's 12th New Jersey Infantry marched into battle "over the ground that had been fought over the day before," he wrote in his diary, "where we seen the results of the fight in great winrows of dead both of our own men and the enemy proving how fierce had been the assualt and how stubborn the resistence." Bowen's regiment pursued the Confederates through the junglelike terrain of the Wilderness until "the enemy made a stand and our Right Flank becoming exposed, and at the same time they received reinforcements of fresh troops they soon found the gap on our right and our flank and came very near surrounding us, and then began a fearful slaughter." The tide of battle quickly turned against the Federals, and as "the Regt on our right gave way exposing us to a murderous fire we tried to stand it but it was more than human power could do and we were forced to fall back which we did contesting the ground inch by inch losing many men in killed and wounded and prisoners." Junior leaders' composure and initiative were absolutely essential when command and control broke down, as it often did in the Wilderness. During his regiment's fighting withdrawal, Bowen's stubborn volunteers dissolved into pockets of platoons, squads, and individuals, firing blindly into the thick woods and hoping to reach the safety of Union lines before they were cut off and annihilated. "[I]n the retreat through the brush our organization became broken and our whole Corps became broken up into squads who were fighting on their own account," recalled Bowen. After rallying whatever friendly troops he could find, the captain helped lead the makeshift group back into the fight in time to fend off a Confederate assault. "To[o] much credit cannot be given the men who held this part of the line," Bowen concluded, "as they were not organized brigades or Regt but the squads who had been fighting in the woods and were of all Regt Brigades without their officers. This ended the fighting for the day, our loss both in Officers and men had been fearful."[45]

Late-war fighting in rough terrain placed exceptional demands upon junior officers because of the isolation and independence inherent in such duties. At the Battle of New Hope Church in late May 1864, Lieutenant Ralsa C. Rice of the 125th Ohio Infantry recounted feelings of extreme isolation in his command responsibilities on the skirmish line. Rice described the forbidding landscape of northern Georgia as "a wilderness but little superior to that at Chickamauga" and believed the Confederates had chosen "seclusion as a means of defense; their works, at least so far as we came into contact with them, were invariably hidden by brush and thickets. A long time was spent in locating their lines so that our approaches might comply as near as possible with their general contour. Our experiences in developing the enemy," he wryly remembered, "had caused an invention of tactics not laid down in 'Hardee.'" With his company commander absent, the lieutenant was placed in command of his regiment's skirmish line before the battle and told to get orders from the 105th Ohio Infantry's second in command, Major Joseph Bruff. Rice remembered his instructions were "to advance until the enemy's main line was encountered and then hold our position. The bugle would sound the signals. I ventured to ask if we must comply with the regular skirmish drill. 'Take your own way, so long as you get there,' said the major." Rice's task was an arduous one, given the problematic terrain of the battlefield and the confused command situation it caused. "At the beginning, brush, brambles and briars must be gotten through," he recalled, "then an open woods with gradual descent of ground for 300 yards, then brush again. On our emerging from the brush we saw the line we were to relieve but a short distance away, engaged in dodging bullets coming from, as near as we could make out, the thicket further down." Rice's orders to his skirmishers were succinct. "'Every man for himself,'" he told them. "'Each man must be his own reserve. Take advantage of everything offering protection. We have not a man to spare.'"

Lieutenant Rice and his skirmishers advanced into the woods, pushing out ahead of their regiment. Eventually, Rice ordered his men to halt on the edge of an open field in sight of a Confederate position along a high bluff. "The Johnnies on the bluff above our boys were making target of us," he remembered. "On looking out I saw one of these fellows loading his gun. How I longed for my old Springfield, if only for a moment." Taking cover behind a tree, the lieutenant called on one of his sergeants for help. "I placed my hat on the end of a stick and put it out past the tree," Rice wrote. "The ruse brought a bullet, making the bark fly. We sprang out, the sergeant took good aim and fired," killing the enemy marksman. After climbing the heights, Rice assembled his men behind a large fallen tree. "With no recall or orders to fall back," he wrote, "we remained here until dark." The skirmishers spent a sleepless night watching shells burst in the dark woods; the memory remained with the citizen-officer and his volunteers long after the war was over. "Long and continuous shooting had made our nerves impervious to such sounds—even the loud tone of the cannons passed unnoticed," Rice remembered. "But I very much doubt if we could ever get used to any sudden nocturnal outbreak."[46]

Though leading skirmishers in deep woods or broken terrain was a challenge, some officers learned to enjoy the exercise. Captain Charles W. Wills of the 103rd Illinois Infantry was ebullient about the skirmishing near Dallas, Georgia, during the Atlanta Campaign. In his diary entry of May 27, 1864, Wills declared: "I tell you this was exciting. My men all stood like heroes (save one), and some of them did not fall back when I wanted them to.

The bush was so thick that we could hardly get through in any kind of line." Death could come suddenly in the dense woods, and two of Wills's volunteers were felled by enemy fire before they knew what hit them. "Gustine and Suydam were about 20 feet on my left when they were shot," wrote the captain, "but I couldn't see them. The Rebels were not 15 feet from them. I had 31 men on the line, and nine killed and wounded, and one prisoner, is considerable of a loss. They took six more of Company K prisoners, but three of them got off." Despite the heavy casualties, Wills remained enthusiastic about the experience. "I don't think anyone can imagine how exciting such a fracas as that is in thick brush," he concluded.[47]

While some citizen-officers seemed to thrive on the confusion of battle, others had a far different outlook. Union captain John W. Tuttle of the 3rd Kentucky Infantry, for instance, described the Army of the Tennessee's chaotic attempts to reinforce the Union XX Corps's failed assaults during the Battle of New Hope Church. "Marched at 9 A.M. in the direction of Dallas," he wrote. "Hooker ran into the rebs and fought them all evening. Our Division formed in line of battle a little before dark then moved two or three miles to the left. Was unable to get my horse over the steep cliffs and ravines so I got lost from my regt. and indeed from my Division." Disoriented in the dark woods, Tuttle got an eye-opening display of his army in chaos. "Met thousands of wounded and stragglers. The rain came down in torrents and it was truly heart rending to hear the groans of the wounded all along for miles as I searched for my regt. Thousands were crowding forward to relieve those who had been fighting—Infantry, Cavalry and Artillery, without the slightest regard to organization for that was impossible. Those relieved came back in swarms, some carrying or leading their wounded comrades." To make matters even worse, officers were notably absent in the turmoil, and nobody seemed able to impose any order. "Sometimes a battery would run through the ranks of the Infantry scattering the men in every direction and again some unlucky horseman would ride into a batch of wounded men. All was hurry and confusion and nearly everybody was swearing at the top of his voice." Tuttle thought it was a bad omen for the Union effort to take Atlanta. "If the rebs had known our condition it would have been an easy matter to have stampeded even the sturdy veterans of the 4th corps."[48]

Composure and initiative demonstrated by citizen-officers late in the war was always essential in the chaotic conditions of combat, but decisive company-grade leadership in small-unit actions could prevent a dangerous tactical situation from turning into a disastrous one. In an engagement at

Rocky Face Ridge in February 1864, Lieutenant John S. Stubbs of the 42nd Georgia Infantry helped turn back a Union assault through decisiveness and sheer nerve. The Georgians were deployed along the crest of a high ridge as skirmishers, with instructions to keep an eye out for an expected Union advance. Colonel Robert J. Henderson, the regiment's commander, stationed two of his companies at the base of the ridge under Captain J. T. Mitchell and held two others as a reserve under Lieutenant Stubbs. Before leaving the reserve behind, the colonel explained that if the forward picket line was attacked, Stubbs would be responsible for providing support. As the 42nd Georgia's official historian wrote, Henderson "impressed upon Lt. Stubbs both the probability of an attack on that part of the line, and the importance of holding it. He closed his directions with this statement: 'I charge you, whatever you do, do not let Mitchell be driven in.'"[49] With this sharp warning ringing in his ears, Stubbs and his reserve companies settled in to wait for the anticipated Union attack. In a few moments a brigade of Michigan and Illinois volunteers began probing the 42nd Georgia's advanced positions. As soon as he heard muskets firing along the picket line, Stubbs ordered his reserve companies forward to reinforce the position; when he reached Mitchell and his pickets, he repeated the colonel's orders that "the line must be held at all hazards." Unfortunately, Mitchell was in no condition to obey. An enemy bullet had torn an artery in the captain's arm, and he was in danger of bleeding to death. He told Stubbs to take charge of the line so he could go to the rear and find a surgeon. The lieutenant, perhaps unnerved at the sudden responsibility, protested that he was too junior to take command, and since another officer on the line was senior to him, the responsibility should pass to him. Mitchell had no time to argue, however, and once again told Stubbs to take charge. With no other choice, and with the approaching brigade threatening to overwhelm the Georgians' ragged line, Stubbs agreed. The lieutenant brought up his two reserve companies, "sandwiched between Capt. Mitchell's" just behind the crest of the hill, and unleashed a volley. When the Union attackers hesitated under the fire, Stubbs saw an opportunity and "ordered the entire line forward, and with a yell they moved to charge." The Confederates' unexpected appearance took the Federals by surprise; they fell back, leaving the wounded commander of the 10th Michigan Infantry behind to be captured. Stubbs, who would later be promoted to captain, took the Union officer's sword as a trophy and proudly bore it for the remainder of the war.[50]

Confusing or cluttered terrain, chaotic tactical conditions, disorder behind the lines, and breakdowns in battlefield command and control were not peculiar to the Civil War's final two years, nor were skirmishing, loose-order formations, or the increased reliance on junior-officers' initiative and decisiveness in confused combat situations. But effective combat performance in the battles of 1864 and 1865 required strong company-grade leadership, experienced volunteers exuding personal initiative and combat discipline, and a command relationship between officers and men founded on trust and the acceptance of military authority.[51] The confusing nature of many of these late-war engagements illustrates the problems citizen-officers had to overcome. The terrain of the battlefields of 1864 and 1865 was no more confusing than that of 1862 and 1863, as the jumbled landscapes of 1862 battles like Shiloh and Fair Oaks illustrate. But when presented with confusing or disorienting battlefield conditions and with little guidance from superiors, the burden for maintaining control in many late-war engagements often devolved upon company-grade officers. Loose-order formations compounded this difficulty. Fortunately, many of the captains and lieutenants of 1864 could draw upon the lessons of prior experience, as well as instincts honed over several years of campaigning, to make sense of these challenges. Often this simply meant that they had to adapt to fluid, rapidly evolving circumstances with flexibility and creativity, relying on experience and trust, rather than on their superiors' instructions, as their primary guide. In addition, as volunteers became more self-sufficient and experienced, citizen-officers altered their combat-leadership roles. Company-grade officers leading veteran citizen-soldiers could afford to turn their combat focus outward, devoting their energies toward managing battlefield circumstances and tactical factors. As they came to trust and rely upon the discipline and experience of their troops, officers were able to occupy themselves less with their custodial role, somewhat easing the burdens of company command in combat.[52]

Despite these improvements at the company level, errors at the brigade, division, or corps level could lead to costly consequences. The imperative to obey, regardless of the price, led to many wasteful and pointless attacks. These mistakes could be extremely damaging to volunteers' morale. In turn, needless wastage of lives undermined citizen-officers' confidence in their commanders' judgment. Captain John W. Lavender of the 4th Arkansas Infantry, for example, resented what he considered absurd orders to assault an impossible Union position during the Battle of Ezra Church on July 28, 1864. Lavender was certain the effort would fail, yet he and his men were compelled to obey the directive no matter what. "It was Extreamely warm and we had to advance some Distance through an open Field," Lavender recalled, "[t]he Federal Brest works being in the Edge of the Woods Just out side the Field. When our lines Entered the open Field some three Hundred yards From their works they opened a terific Fire of Shells & Small arms on our line." His volunteers had experienced enough combat to understand the peril of a slow and deliberate advance across open ground against an entrenched position. "We held our fire and advanced [as] rapedly as possible," Lavender wrote. "When aboute half way we opened fire and advanced in Double Quick time." Unfortunately, the Confederates' efforts were in vain. "We got near the works but our Fire done Them but Little Damage as they was Protected by Splendid Earth works and was literally mowing our men Down," wrote Lavender. "So our lines was Forced to fall back or all be killed. We fell Back with fearful loss, the worst we had in any one Battle During the war for the number of men ingaged in it.... [N]early all the Field oficers of the Brigade [were lost] and a great Many company officers." The pointlessness of the assault was almost as destructive to the volunteers' spirit as enemy fire was to their ranks. "This Battle Discouraged our men Badly as they could never understand why they Should have been Sent in to such a Death Trap to be Butchered up with no hope of gaining any thing," Lavender lamented. "If we had succeeded in takeing that one Point we never could have held it but Such is War."[53]

Citizen-officers tried to shield their men from the devastating consequences of foolish orders, though in a practical sense there was usually little they could do. Captain James L. Burkhalter of the 86th Illinois Infantry, upon receiving orders that his Company F would help lead the XIV Corps's direct attack on impregnable Confederate positions at Kennesaw Mountain in 1864, poured out his anger in his diary. "So much for the foolish dream of our soldiers who thought that our few days in reserve presaged a new status as a pet brigade. Pet my foot. *Rested for the slaughter would be more like it.*" Burkhalter could do nothing except prepare his men for the hopeless frontal assault up what would later be known as Cheatham Hill. "The stupidity of this order is enough to paralyze me. However, I obeyed the orders so far as related to getting ready. This amounted to having plenty of ammunition, a musket, and to divest the men of all surplus baggage and equipment. But the role of Judas is more than I can swallow and must here acknowledge myself as altogether too skeptical to have the least confidence in the success of the enterprise." The captain decided that his best option, as company commander, was to keep his opinions to himself. "I think it far better not to give the plan of operation to my men, lest I gag on my own words and reveal that I have the horrors, which, in turn, would give them the horrors too. I consider the folly of this undertaking of itself sufficient notice for their own peace of mind." Burkhalter survived, though the attack on Cheatham Hill, as expected, was a bloody failure.[54]

The accrued experience of extended campaigning informed citizen-officers expectations, and effective leaders knew just how much they could ask of their men. When an officer sensed that his volunteers had reached their limits of suffering, he had to exercise the good judgment not to push them further or else risk their physical or moral obliteration. Those leaders who endured the campaigns of 1864 and 1865 employed a complex calculus for striking this difficult balance. Historian Wayne Wei-Siang Hsieh, for instance, attributes the Army of the Potomac's failure to inflict a decisive defeat on the Army of Northern Virginia during the 1864 Overland Campaign on, in part, the inadequate leadership of Grant's subordinates. "Unfortunately, the leadership ranks of the Federal eastern army continued to compare poorly to the Army of Northern Virginia," he maintains. "This absence of a strong cohort of corps and division commanders in the Army of the Potomac contributed as much to the Overland campaign's stalemate as did the increasing power of fieldworks." Moreover, Hsieh argues, in 1864 the Army of the Potomac "had the numbers and material support necessary to overcome that defensive advantage, if properly commanded and led," and its dreadful losses during the campaign "show more than enough fighting spirit among the army's humblest ranks," a disparity he attributes to poor corps and division leadership.[55]

While Hsieh is certainly correct that combat leadership is essential to battlefield success, historians should also remember that no matter how talented the generals, there was a physical and psychological limit to what Civil War citizen armies could endure in the combat. As any junior officer charging the Confederate entrenchments at Cold Harbor would have known, when volunteers reached the limits of their endurance, they could not be coerced into going further, except to their deaths. But this was something company-grade officers had to discover for themselves. Captain Andrews of the 3rd Minnesota Infantry explained: "Acquainted as he must necessarily be with his men, the captain best knows what they are capable of accomplishing. He knows whether or not they will fight valiantly. Hence, his determination to hold a position or encounter an equal or greater force must be based upon this knowledge."⁵⁶ As George Bowen's account of the futile Union assaults at Cold Harbor in 1864 attests, taking the Confederate position was simply too much to ask of his volunteers; when they recognized the futility of the attempt, they simply refused to continue. "Just at daybreak we advanced on the enemys works capturing their outposts and advanced to within a few yards of their main line, but we were overpowered and outnumbered and we fell back.... The order was again given to charge but the men positively refused to attempt another assault, notwithstanding all we could do in the way of driving or exhortation." Even remaining prone in one place was tantamount to suicide, as the Confederates lobbed artillery shells onto the prone men. "One shell exploded in our Regt at this time killing seven (7) men including Capt McCrumb and wounding several others," Bowen wrote. Pinned to the ground by heavy enemy fire and exposed to a burning sun, the Federals dug in where they could and held on until night. To make matters even worse, the volunteers had to leave their casualties strewn across the field for fear of enemy fire. "All our dead and wounded of the morning are still lying where they fell as it has been certain death for a wounded man to stir during the daylight," the captain concluded. "[A]fter dark a number of our men were got off by their comrades crawling on their bellies and dragging them off as they dare not rise up."⁵⁷

Lieutenant Ambrose G. Bierce served as a topographical engineering officer during the Atlanta Campaign, and his account of the unsuccessful Union assault at Pickett's Mill on May 27, 1864, is a starkly sensitive exploration of the limits of Civil War volunteers' endurance in battle. "Early in my military experience I used to ask myself how it was that brave troops could retreat while still their courage was high," he wrote. "As long as a man is not disabled he can go forward; can it be anything but fear that makes him stop and finally retire? Are there signs by which he can infallibly know the struggle to be hopeless?" Bierce was a veteran who had participated in numerous actions by 1864, but still he struggled with these questions. "In this engagement, as in others, my doubts were answered as to the fact; the explanation is still obscure," he admitted. "In many instances which have come under my observation, when hostile lines of infantry engage at close range and the assailants afterward retire, there was a 'dead-line' beyond which no man advanced." Bierce believed this invisible boundary marked the full extent of what volunteers' minds and bodies could endure in combat. He had an obstructed view of the engagement and marveled at how this battle seemed to assume a life of its own. "Most of our men fought kneeling as they fired," he wrote, "many of them behind trees, stones and whatever cover they could get, but there were considerable groups that stood." As the momentum surged back and forth, no one really seemed to be in control. Individual acts of bravery were common, Bierce remembered, and were often suicidal. "Frequently the dim figure of an individual soldier would be seen to spring away from his comrades, advancing alone toward that fateful interspace, with leveled bayonet. He got no farther than the farthest of his predecessors." Bierce estimated "that a third [of the Union dead] were within fifteen paces, and not one within ten [of the Confederate line]." The "dead-line" of combat, he believed, served as the primary indicator for participants to find the limits of their capacity for suffering. Moreover, the decision whether to advance or to flee came not from officers, but from the senses and instincts of common soldiers. "No command to fall back was given, none could have been heard. Man by man, the survivors withdrew at will, sifting through the trees into the cover of the ravines, among the wounded who could drag themselves back; among the skulkers whom nothing could have dragged forward." Bierce ascribed an almost supernatural restorative property to the dubious protection of a fence; the prospect of even minimal cover seemed to buoy the volunteers' morale far out of proportion to its actual benefits. "As the disorganized groups fell back along this fence on the wooded side, they were attacked by a flanking force of the enemy moving through the field in a direction nearly parallel with what had been our front.... But already our retreating men, in obedience to their officers, their courage and their instinct of self-preservation, had formed along the fence and opened fire." The makeshift protection arrested the Union retreat. "The apparently slight advantage of the imperfect cover and the open range worked its customary miracle: the assault, a singularly spiritless one, considering the advantages it promised and that it was made by an organized and victorious force against a broken and retreating one, was checked."[58]

When officers and volunteers pushed themselves beyond their capacity to endure, they risked annihilation. At the Siege of Petersburg in June 1864, the 1st Maine Heavy Artillery experienced the costliest engagement of any single Civil War regiment, and through a combination of bravery and inexperience was almost annihilated in a matter of moments. The 1st Maine, an artillery unit in name only, was actually an oversized infantry regiment composed of members of the former 18th Maine Infantry and of garrison troops who previously served in the Washington defenses. On

June 18 the regiment's commander, Colonel Daniel Chaplin, led his volunteers in a poorly conceived charge against Confederate works; it was an effort that horrified observers were certain would fail.[59] "There was probably not a staff officer in Mott's division who had seen those lines that did not feel that the undertaking was well nigh impossible at this hour," wrote Lieutenant Horace H. Shaw, the unit's regimental historian who also served as Chaplin's aide during the attack, "but the First Maine officers and men were soldiers. The first duty of a soldier is obedience to orders. When this order came they obeyed it with alacrity." The sight of the field itself was enough to dishearten the volunteers. "Five hundred yards across an open field in plain sight of the enemy, within easy range of their artillery posted along their works a mile in length and across the river in position to rake the field, they must run before they could reach the enemy's lines," wrote Shaw. He believed that in this instance the combat experience of the Army of Potomac's tough veterans supporting his regiment served as an impediment rather than an advantage, and if circumstances had been otherwise, his inexperienced comrades might have had a chance to succeed. "If the attack had been made promptly by our troops all along the line as ordered," Shaw observed, "the enemy would have had plenty to attend to in their immediate front. But the veteran troops on the right and left had not forgotten their experience in assailing breastworks at the Wilderness, at Spottsylvania, and at Cold Harbor. They did indeed rush forward at the order, but the fire was so terrific in their faces that they fell back into their breastworks." Unfortunately, the Maine volunteers surged ahead without the support they expected. "The enemy's firing along their whole line was now centered into this field," remembered Shaw. "The earth was literally torn up with iron and lead. The field became a burning, seething, crashing, hissing hell, in which human courage, flesh, and bone were struggling with an impossibility, either to succeed or to return with much hope of life." The outcome of such an attack was predictably dire. "[I]n ten minutes those who were not slaughtered had returned to the road or were lying prostrate upon that awful field of carnage."[60]

Having begun the charge with 900 men, the 1st Maine Heavy Artillery left 7 officers and 108 men dead on the field, with another 25 officers and 464 men wounded; another 19 would die of their wounds, and 1 man was taken prisoner. These casualties represented over 68 percent of the regiment, the largest loss of men or officers in any one unit on any one day of battle in the Civil War.[61] Brigadier General Philippe Régis de Trobriand knew that someone had blundered but was unsure whom to blame for the catastrophic charge. "The assault had no possible chance of success. It had to cross an open space three times as great as that generally assigned to charges of this sort.... They went as far as it was possible to go, melting away to the sight in a stream of blood, and strewing the ground with their dead and wounded." De Trobriand's eyewitness account of the assault was understandably tinged with bitterness. "These deplorable mistakes took place only too often during the war," he explained. "It may have been that a corps commander too readily accepted the erroneous report of a volunteer officer of his staff. Eager for success, he gave the order to charge, without himself verifying the condition of affairs." Once this first error had been committed, de Trobriand observed, the chain of events was nearly impossible to stop. "The general of division has not always the moral courage to venture to object to such an order. The brigade commander, clearly seeing that it is a question of the useless destruction of one more of his regiments, can take it upon himself to comment upon it to his immediate superior, who will probably reply: 'I know that as well as you do; but what can I do about it? The order is peremptory; it must be obeyed.' It is obeyed, and a regiment is massacred."

General de Trobriand asserted that the 1st Maine's virtual annihilation so disheartened its commander that the officer's death soon afterward was a foregone conclusion. "Colonel Chaplin escaped in the butchery; but it struck him a mortal blow, from which he did not recover," the general recalled. "His men belonged to the same neighborhood with him. He had organized them; he had led them from the forests of Maine. They were his great family." De Trobriand maintained that witnessing the deaths of so many of his volunteers and officers damaged Chaplin so much that he resigned himself to perish in battle. "When [Chaplin] saw them sacrificed under his eyes," the general remembered, "a melancholy discouragement took hold on him. Sombre presentiments besieged him. He was surrounded by phantoms." Chaplin fell to a Confederate sharpshooter on August 17, nearly a month to the day after his regiment's near-obliteration at Petersburg. "I regretted his death without being surprised at it, as I expected it," de Trobriand wrote. "He was a doomed man." Believing the colonel was marked for death, de Trobriand attempted to describe the sense of doom he believed he could see in certain officers and men. "Its imprint is fugitive, and yet appears sometimes in the looks, at the bottom of which one divines the trembling of the soul soon about to depart," he observed, "sometimes in the smile, in which appear the fleeting shadows of a cloud which does not belong to the earth; sometimes in certain movements as if worn out." But the mark of death also could manifest in a feigned optimism or manic, unsettling vigor. "Sometimes, on the contrary, the finger of death is shown by a feverish energy without reason, forced laughter, jerky movements," de Trobriand mused. Nonetheless, he concluded, most doomed men did not comprehend the fate that awaited them. "I am far from contending that all those who are about to die are marked," he concluded. "On the contrary, the immense majority march on to death without the least previous indication of the fate awaiting them."[62]

For officers who survived annihilation in the final battles of the Civil War, the enticements of home, family, and the restoration of their civilian selves proved a powerful motivation to set aside their hard-won military authority. Like the citizen-soldier ideal of Cincinnatus returning to his fields, these men longed for the day when they could hang up their sword and, symbolically if not literally, take up the plow once more. Indeed, this finite commitment to military service is one of the key distinctions between citizen-officers and their regular-army counterparts. George Washington's "fatal, but necessary Operation of War," the voluntary, temporary aspect of citizen-officers' military service, remained steadfast throughout the Civil War; when the great task was finished, most citizen-officers wanted nothing more than to return to their peacetime lives.[63] The lure of home and family could be a potent incentive for them to set aside their martial selves and return to civilian life.

The emotional pressure to leave behind their military identities and return to their homes and families could be intense. In some cases veteran volunteers themselves pressured loved ones to avoid unnecessary military service, particularly as the war reached its terrible crescendo in 1864 and 1865. "One thing more," the 28th Massachusetts Infantry's Peter Welsh warned his brother in 1864, "never for heavens sake let a thought of enlisting in this army cross your mind." He urged his younger brother, "it is right and the duty of citizens and those who have lived long enough in this country to become citizens to fight for the maintainence of law order and nationality but the country has no claim on you and never bring upon yourself the dangers and hardships of a soldiers life where the country nor cause has no claim on your service[.]"[64] At times these pressures could manifest themselves in extreme ways. In February 1865 Mamie Stanton was unconvinced that her husband, Lieutenant Courtland G. Stanton of the 21st

Connecticut Infantry, actually intended to return home when his term of service expired. Mamie had heard a rumor that he planned to reenlist in the army; desperately, she threatened to commit suicide should he choose to remain in the military. "Hope you will not get your mind so much taken up that you will forget all about home, Mother and 'Mamie' and re-enlist," she wrote to him. "Most every one says you will but I don't believe it. I guess Mother is a little afraid you will for she was telling yesterday of something she was going to get Ben to do 'if Court re-enlists' but I cannot think of it." Then Mamie delivered her ultimatum. "If you should enlist for three years more I should have no desire to live any longer and I certainly think I should commit suicide for I would not pass another such three years for all the world to be separated from you and you in so much danger." Attempting to justify her rash declaration, she appealed to his sympathy. "*[T]hink* of it—a life that is so much dearer to me than my own in such danger and the long waiting and suspence between hope and fear. It is bad enough to endure the separation from one so dear to me, for so long a time, but if I was sure of your coming home alive and well it would be nothing to this, and I must endure it six months longer." Mamie held out a frantic hope that her husband would eventually return to her unharmed. "Thank God it is so near over, and you are still spared. But you'll never re-enlist will you? [F]or 'Mamie's' sake you will come home. Court if you should re-enlist I should know that you had ceased to love me and that I don't believe. Forgive me for thinking of such a thing, but people frighten me when they say they 'know you will re-enlist.' They'll see."[65] These threats must have worked, for Stanton did as his wife wished and declined to reenlist.

For many, however, the enticements or pressures of home and family could not trump their dedication to the cause for which they fought. Lieutenant George W. Squier of the 44th Indiana Infantry was emphatic about his duty as an officer and his commitment to victory, and he had no patience for those who returned to their families before the rebellion was crushed. "If I could have my way, every man subject to military duty in the northern states would have a musket placed in their hands in less than thirty days, and I would not deal very gently with them either. [I] would like to command a company of those conscripts. It would do me good to bring the cowardly snakes to time to show them [the] beauties of soldiering." To Squier, his duty was a noble calling; nothing less than the preservation of the Republic and the eradication of slavery would justify terminating his military service. In ill health by 1864, it was within his rights to tender his resignation, and many of his fellow officers in similar circumstances did precisely that, a fact that dismayed him. "When I see men of my acquaintance homeward bound, it is with difficulty that I keep from getting in a perfect panic to go to[o]," Squier explained to his wife, "but I think of the maxim 'let thy fair wisdom not thy passion sway.'" The war had taken on a higher purpose for him, a purpose he tried to explain. "I feel now moore as though we were contending for something real, something tangable than ever before, and were it not for my bad health, am not sure but that I should consider it my duty to stay in the service until the great object was attained." Hardship and danger were obstacles to be overcome, Squier believed, and true patriots would not hide behind such excuses when their country needed them. "For surely one' s obligation does not cease as long as the necessity exists, and the government surely has a claim on every able bodied loyal man until the great end is attained, the mighty work accomplished, and the redemption of the enthralled complete, and we become not only in name but in reality a free people," he declared. The war would not be complete until " we can consistently claim that America ofers an asylum for the opressed of all nations, not excluding even Africa, until even the despised negro can find safety and liberty under [the] broad folds of the American banner."[66]

To some the war was, or became, an epiphany, a crusade to ensure human equality initiated by President Lincoln's decision to issue the Emancipation Proclamation in 1862. Levi Duff, a captain in the 105th Pennsylvania Infantry, articulated these passionate feelings to his wife shortly after news of the proclamation reached him in Virginia. "It [the Emancipation Proclamation] struck us like a thunder-clap at least it did me, for I thought that Lincoln was firmly chained to the fatal jugernaut of Border state influence. . . . I had already begun to fear that another revolution would be necessary to rid this country of the incubus of slavery. But to my surprise & gratification there is now a better prospect before." Duff, an ardent abolitionist, saw his misgivings about Lincoln's commitment to ending slavery swept away by the president's decision to emancipate the enslaved persons residing within the resisting Southern states. For such officers, a war for emancipation was life altering, and the cause of emancipation suffused their entire mentality and approach to the conflict. "But a few days ago I would see the end of the rebellion only in the triumph of Southern arms & in the success of their confederacy," Duff exulted. "I could see beyond only continuous strife between two nations, contiguous & without natural boundaries dividing them—embitter[ed] in their feelings towards each other by a long

& bloody war. And still slavery existed to degrade and brutalize the black man, & to curse with its blighting influence the white man. But one thing was needed to throw sunshine on this dark picture, but one thing was necessary to be done to give us permanent & prosperous peace—to do justice to the black man, whose wrongs stand in our light."[67]

For officers like Captain Duff, emancipation was a powerful catalyst and represented a small step toward expiation of the country's original sin of slavery. "The President's proclamation is not a recompense for their long withheld rights," he cautioned. "It is no atonement for our long continued brutality & wrong—we can make no atonement for this—we can offer no recompense for that, we can only say to our enslaved brethren rise up & be free & ask God to forgive us for having held them in slavery from generation to generation." But by making the war about emancipation, President Lincoln also rescued Duff's flagging enthusiasm for the cause of Union. "Many times during the last few months I thought I was almost committing a crime in exposing my life for a government which knew no law of action but wrong to a weak and despised race," he confessed. "More than once did I think of throwing down my sword & returning home. But I was encouraged to continue by the reflection that this war—whether intended to be so or not—must prove more or less disastrous to slavery—& I trusted that God was working out some grand result which it was not proper for us to know then. I am glad now that I did not turn back. I am encouraged to go forward by this last just & righteous act of the President." Further, the Emancipation Proclamation clarified the complexities of the war for Captain Duff and breathed new life into his determination to see the conflict through to victory. "I now know for what I am fighting—for what I am periling my life and all I hold dear," he declared. "And I know too that whether I live or die the great result will be attained—the rebellion will be conquered, slavery will be abolished, & we will have a government of which we may be proud—one which—freed from the foul blot of slavery—will give us dignity among the nations of the world."[68]

On the other hand, many other Union citizen-officers were less concerned with such weighty issues. Some simply came to enjoy military life, and a few even considered making their applications for appointments to the regular army when their terms of volunteer service concluded. U.S. Army officials knew they had a wealth of talent and experience to draw from among the volunteer officer corps as the Civil War wound down, and they occasionally invited outstanding citizen-officers who considered making the military their profession to apply for postwar commissions. In June 1865 Henry Matrau was one of those who liked the army well enough to consider it for a career but believed that he would have trouble passing the mandatory boards of examination. "I did not wish to remain in the service," the captain informed his parents. "I knew that although I can drill a Company & understand the tactics as well as any Volunteer officer in the service who never had an opportunity to study & has learned everything by practice, that although I can get the commanding officer of my regiment to testify as to my ability to handle a company of men in battle, yet I could not pass the examination from the fact that I have got the practice and not the theory."[69]

Matrau's concerns were not unique. Transitioning from volunteer service to the professional officer corps was not an easy task and required significant dedication. Lieutenant George W. Yates of the 4th Michigan Infantry, for example, was not dissuaded by the numerous difficulties of pursuing a regular-army commission after the war. Yates rose from the ranks to serve as adjutant of his regiment and, later on detached service, as a staff officer in Missouri to Major General Alfred Pleasanton. When the 4th Michigan was mustered out of service in 1864, the lieutenant was told that he too would have to leave the army. Yates was an excellent officer, having been brevetted to higher rank for bravery in battle, and was dismayed that he might have to give up his military ambitions. In a letter to the Adjutant General's Office, Yates begged for special consideration. "If I am to be mustered out, what shall I do to be continued in the service?" he pleaded. "I am very much attached to General Pleasonton, and he desires that I may remain with him. What will it be necessary for me to do to continue in my present position after the 20th inst.?" Yates presented his case for retaining his commission in impassioned, patriotic terms. "I entered the service as a private with a desire to continue in it so long as the war should last—I still desire to serve to the best of my ability so long as there is an armed Rebel in the land, and shall feel very much chagrined if mustered out at what appears to be the crisis of our troubles."[70] His request was initially denied, but after the intervention of Pleasanton and a number of sympathetic superior officers, the young volunteer secured a commission in the 45th Missouri Infantry and, a month later, in the 13th Missouri Cavalry. After the war Yates entered his coveted place in the U.S. Army as a captain, only to die in 1876 with George Armstrong Custer's 7th Cavalry at the Battle of the Little Bighorn.[71]

Men such as Matrau and Yates, however, were exceptional. Most citizen-officers longed for a return to civilian life once the war ended, and many began planning their homecoming as soon as the end of their service was in sight. "I live in hopes that the war is fast drawing to a close & then I trust that I will be among the number to return home safe & sound," Union lieutenant John H. Black wrote to his wife in March 1865. "It will then be you & I who will rejoice, and live together happily & not quarrel," he promised. Apparently, Black had heard rumors of marital discord among other couples in his town and worried that he would return to similar unpleasantness. "That town of yours appears to be quite a place for the men & women to quarrel & fight," he ventured. "I cannot imagine what possesses them to quarrel so much. I trust you & I will live to set them an example how man & wife should live."[72] Captain William H. Lambert of the 33rd New Jersey Infantry described his eagerness to leave military service soon after the Confederate surrender. He wrote to a friend, "I hope to be home, if the war is actually terminated by the end of July at the furthest, and then to doff forever the uniform of the soldier." Lambert then turned to another important matter—namely, asking his friend to secure a book of poetry for a young woman he intended to pursue when he mustered out. "I wish to present to a lady friend of mine a copy of Tennyson's Poems and I wish you to procure it for me. . . . I want you to purchase the handsomest complete edition of Tennyson you can find."[73] For Black, Lambert, and other citizen-officers eager to return to civilian life, the end of their military service could not come fast enough.

Even so, many Union volunteer officers savored final victory and were overwhelmed by the national display of gratitude for their sacrifices at the Grand Review of the Armies of the Republic in Washington, D.C. Lieutenant Francis M. Guernsey of the 32nd Wisconsin Infantry explained the intensity of this emotional outpouring in a vivid letter to his wife. "[N]one of us expected such a glorious welcome as we received from the grateful people," he told her. "Fannie I cant begin to describe how we soldiers felt when we saw how the Nation threw open her arms and how warmly she welcomed us home, our work ended and the Union preserved." For Guernsey and his fellow officers and volunteers, the Grand Review marked the end of a long and deadly ordeal, and the thanks of the nation affirmed the righteousness of their cause. "[E]very mans heart was big with emotion we knew that our long years of suffering and hardships had now a glorious end," wrote the lieutenant, "and that we should soon go home to our loved ones and enjoy the fruits of our hard years of labor and danger, our national honor vidicated [sic], a pleashure to our friends, a Terror to our foes."[74]

For Confederate citizen-officers, their final years and months in service were utterly different. These men endured defeat with a jumble of optimism, denial, defiance, hatred, and eventually a dawning sense of shame and despair. Some led their volunteers to adopt public resolutions of patriotic resolve in the war's final months, declaring their intention to continue the fight no matter what the odds. Others loudly proclaimed their faith in Southern invincibility and the rightness of their cause while emphasizing the unbreakable spirit of the dwindling Confederate armies. Fasting, prayer, and national days of religious reflection on the South's dire circumstances also provided some with spiritual comfort, but these measures could do little to alter the painful realities of late 1864 and 1865.[75] Historian Peter S. Carmichael describes some Confederate officers during the war's final year as "a group of young men so driven by hatred, so infused with religious zeal, and so fearful of enduring the humiliation of defeat, that they lost touch with the military situation facing the Confederacy."[76] Only the most fanatical or self-deluded among the junior officers truly believed that the South would recover military victory in the spring of 1865, yet many persisted in this belief until the very end. Captain Charles Frederic Bahnson, a staff officer serving in North Carolina in April 1865, described this dogged faith in final victory, declaring in a letter to his father that God would rescue the Confederacy and punish the enemy. "The victims [of alleged Union atrocities] are members of the finest families of our good old State; great-great indeed are their trials, and nobly have many borne up beneath the iron heel of despotism, bidding us go on and conquer!" he wrote. "Does it not appear to you, my dear father, that a good and all-wise God, can never protect such a cause—such fiendish acts—and that in spite of all the gloomy fears that pervade our breasts at present, will make us come out successfully, and reward our wearied efforts with success, giving us freedom and independence for our reward!" Bahnson affirmed that he would do his duty and remain true to the cause, no matter what the personal cost. "Let come what will, I will strive not to falter, but push boldly on to attain that end, for which we have so long been struggling."[77]

Others struggled to decipher the meaning of defeat, remaining defiant even as their situations became hopeless. C. Irvine Walker, a staff officer in the Army of Tennessee, railed against what he saw as an unnecessary surrender and wondered what the future would hold. "I knew that as soon as [Joseph E.] Johnston capitulated the whole Cis Miss. dept. was at the mercy of the enemy," he wrote in his diary, "so it would not be long before

I was captured. I had no hopes of carrying on a guerilla warfare for a cause and in a country which was abandoned by the Government, which was surrounded by a mob of thieves and plunderers." Walker burned with rage at the behavior of the crumbling Confederate government. "I have never been more disgusted than with the conduct of our high officials in the late turn of affairs. They have escaped to the Trans. Miss. Dept laden with plunder, carrying off all the gold of the Treas. Dept. which should have been distributed among the soldiers who have fought and bled for a ruined cause."[78] Walker was left with few options save surrender; his beaten army was at the mercy of the hated enemy, and his primary remaining desire was for home and for peace. "Now that the matter is settled I am anxious to be out of the way of this mob," he recorded on May 1, 1865. "I never felt so mortified in my life as this morning when I went into the presence of the Yankee Officers to sign my parole. I was introduced to the gentlemen, but only saluted very formally, trying to look as dignified as possible. Some officers took their hands upon being presented, but I would have been shot before I would have done it." Walker was defiant to the last, maintaining his firm belief that victory would somehow be achieved. "They have forced me to yield to the U.S. Gov., but have not changed my feelings towards it in the slightest degree," he wrote. "I feel and will always feel the same hatred to them, however events may compel me to hide it. I shall I believe live to see the Independence of the C.S. yet."[79]

 Confederate officers dealing with their army's defeat had the additional burden of maintaining an optimistic veneer for their men, if for no other reason than simply to keep up their soldiers' spirits and to preserve the military integrity of their units. Motivating their volunteers to endure in the war's final years could be an immensely difficult task for these officers. Many experienced soldiers disdained what they felt were hollow appeals to their patriotism, and those who did not desert particularly resented the interference of leaders whom they believed had an imperfect understanding of the army and its sacrifices. As John Booker of the 38th Virginia Infantry wrote in the spring of 1864, "I believe the health of the soldiers here [is] very good though they all seem to be low spirited. They think the time is drawing nigh when they will be called upon again to meet there enemies on the field again. And to think that there is no relief for them but that they have got to still remain in the field." Booker's company officers tried to persuade their disheartened volunteers to reenlist for the duration of the war, and they met with some success; that is, until more-senior officials intervened. "The Governor came out the other day and made us a speech and tried to get the men to re-enlist for the war, and when he had quit speaking the Colonel had us all in line and then had the Colors carried to the front and then told all the men that he wanted all who were determined to be freemen to step out on the line with the Colors and all who were willing to be slaves for their enemies to stand fast and I reckon there were about one third of the men went on line with the Colors and the rest stood fast." Booker was among those who declined to step forward. "I didn't intend to re-enlist nor I was not willing to be a Slave for my enemies and I didn't go on line with the re-enlisted," he explained, "and I didn't wish to be in either line."

Booker believed that the officer had entirely misread his volunteers. "The colonel thought by telling the men what he did he would get all the men to come on line with the Colors and be considered re-enlisted," he explained. But by this time in the war, such a demonstration was hardly sufficient to persuade the hard-bitten veterans of the 38th Virginia Infantry. "Though they have passed a bill to hold us in service and I don't know what good it will do for us to re-enlist," Booker groused. "I am of the opinion that if we were to re-enlist it would have a bad effect on our leading men. It looks like our leading men thinks we are willing to stay and fight all the time and never get tired, and I believe that as long as we will stay here and express a willingness to stay here our leading men will keep the war up." The Virginian did not wish to encourage Confederate officials to prolong the war unnecessarily and blamed them for refusing to seek a peaceful settlement with the enemy. "I believe that we might have had peace before this time if our head leading men would have tried," he complained.[80]

With defeat came vast uncertainty about the future. Unlike their Union counterparts, Confederate citizen-officers were in a precarious position after the surrender; the thought of living as a defeated people in a land ravaged by war was hardly appealing. "I can't see into the future at all," C. Irvine Walker lamented in his diary after the Army of Tennessee's capitulation in North Carolina. "Everything seems blank before me. I can't tell what will be the condition of our country and what course to pursue for myself. Whether duty calls me to remain here, or leave my home to seek one in another land." Walker was unclear about what his responsibilities to the Confederate cause would be after surrender. "The question of what is my duty is a perplexing one, and I don't feel like settling it until I can receive the advice of those nearest and dearest to me, and after mature deliberation." He could see few viable options for himself and his comrades. "I do not like the prospects of living under Yankee rule, and if I consulted my feelings, I would not remain a day in So. Ca. that I can avoid. But how can I get away? Where in the wide world can we go? Where can we wind around us the associations of relatives and friends?" Still, Walker remained a defiant proponent of the cause of Southern independence and was willing to carry on the war, if possible. "I believe that the struggle for southern liberty and independence is not yet over," he declared. "We are temporarily crushed, overpowered—but we will rise, phoenix like from our ashes, and yet achieve our freedom and nationality."[81]

Unrepentant in defeat, Confederate officers like Walker harbored deep emotional wounds and an inexorable determination to see their cause justified. From this vast well of bitterness would spring many of the authors of the "Lost Cause," the architects of the defeat of Reconstruction (the so-called Redemption), and the captains in an ongoing effort to preserve white supremacy through the application of violence and racial terror across the postwar South. Others, weary of war and longing to salvage their pride and sense of identity, joined with their Northern counterparts to reshape the memory of the war and in some cases to infuse it with a reconciliationist meaning. Occasionally, former Confederate officers pursued commissions in the U.S. Army. Many, though, simply returned to their homes and farms, hoping to recover some semblance of what they had lost and managing their wounds as best as they could. Those who could no longer bear to live with the memories of their experiences sometimes elected to leave the South forever.[82]

For Union and Confederate citizen-officers returning home after the Civil War, there was no systematic method to reincorporate themselves into the fabric of their civilian lives. They went to peace in much the same way as they had gone to war—with little guidance or instruction, armed mainly with their instincts, natural aptitude, and the capacity to adapt to uncertain and changing circumstances. Fortunate former officers could rely upon their families and communities for comfort and recast the memories of war to fit the demands of peace. With time and distance, they could temper their memories through a pall of nostalgia, consoling themselves with a glorious narrative of comradeship, excitement, and noble sacrifice, though unwittingly complicating subsequent generations' efforts to unravel the true meaning of their experiences. Military conflict altered American society, redefined citizens' ideological expectations of themselves and their fellow citizens, and altered their relationship to the state. As Americans on both sides adapted their cherished traditions and identities to survive, citizen-officers and volunteers came to see the value of order, hierarchy, technical and military competence, and most importantly, how those regularizing characteristics could clash with their cherished citizen-soldier ethos. While the Spanish-American War of 1898 would once again see the use of state volunteers in national service, American citizen-soldiers never went to war on the same scale or led in the same way as they did during the Civil War. Nevertheless, the volunteer image remained an image of considerable potency for postwar Americans; volunteers remained, in Major General John A. Logan's words, "the pivotal point upon which the security of our people and the perpetuation of their liberties so safely rest."[83]

Epilogue

"I have been thinking over the past four years within the past two days," Lieutenant Charles F. Lee of the 55th Massachusetts Infantry (Colored) wrote in July 1865. "[I]t is almost impossible for me to realize that so much has been accomplished as a nation," he confessed to his mother and sister. "[W]e have done more in four short years than any other ever did in twenty but at what a fearful cost.... [Y]et I do not believe there are many (if any) who would, even were it in their power, call back those who have given their lives for their country." Lee, who experienced combat as both an enlisted soldier and as a company-grade officer of African American volunteers, reflected on his service with a mixture of amazement and humility. "[W]hen I look back and see what others have done, I am ashamed of the little part it has been my fortune to perform, and there is only one satisfaction about it, which is this: I would willingly have done more had it been in my power."[1] Lee's letter reflects the sense of wonder many citizen-officers and volunteers felt at the sweeping national changes wrought by the Civil War. One and a half centuries later, we are still unraveling the complex legacy that conflict and the part citizen-officers and volunteers played in forging that legacy.

Citizen-officers' Civil War experiences helped shape the subsequent military policy of the United States, and the challenges they faced, and often overcame, helped set the stage for the transformation of the American volunteer system in later decades. Despite the best efforts of postwar reformers like Emory Upton to repair its manifest shortcomings, the volunteer system survived for three decades after Appomattox. The Spanish-American War marked the beginning of the end for the state militia system, however. Inevitable tensions between U.S. Army and National Guard officers arose as training and organizational defects in the volunteers became abundantly clear. These problems led postbellum army planners to rehash their arguments against the utility and competence of volunteers and citizen-officers. Secretary of War Elihu Root, embracing the reforms proposed by Upton's adherents, instituted an energetic program of reforms. The Dick Act of 1903 aimed to remedy longstanding problems with the volunteer system, and Root's measures brought state militias under federal authority. These reforms also required militia units to conform to the U.S. Army's organizational structure and incentivized these mandates through federal financial support. By the first decades of the twentieth century, volunteers represented only a small percentage of the national military force in comparison to regulars, reservists, and federal draftees. The vast citizen armies of the Civil War, with their elected officer corps and uneven training practices, were no more.[2]

Citizen-officers' Civil War experiences also illustrate the painful lessons that conflict imparted to its participants. On closer examination these lessons provide striking insights into how the Civil War, and wars generally, can alter deeply held ideals and longstanding traditions. Officers grew into their avocation, and volunteers gradually modified their expectations about the citizen-soldier ethos. This change reveals a haphazard, often incomplete, and occasionally traumatic evolution from green civilians to hardened veterans who were, if not quite professional soldiers, then at least something resembling professionals more than amateurs. Former private Isaac Gordon Bradwell of the 31st Georgia Infantry, his perspective seasoned by time and understanding, used his twilight years to reflect on this deadly education. "We had the 'grit' then," the aging veteran remembered of himself and his comrades in the first years of the conflict, "but we lacked experience, which we, officers and privates, learned then and afterwards." The only way to remedy this deficiency, Bradwell discovered, was by surviving long enough to apply the lessons learned. "The want of this on the part of our officers cost us dearly," he lamented, "and our loss could never be restored, for the flower of our regiments were killed or rendered unfit for further military service."[3] Early battles like Shiloh and First Bull Run made the hazards of incompetent leadership and inexperience abundantly clear to participants and observers alike. Without effective company-grade leaders, untried volunteers had little chance to survive combat and even less to become effective soldiers. With effective officers, they at least had a fighting chance.

As Civil War volunteers and citizen-officers educated themselves about how to survive in combat, their difficult experience altered them. With knowledge, intuition, and understanding, those who survived underwent a unique hardening process. Novice officers learned to lead by example, through persuasion and shared sacrifice, and with conspicuous courage, demonstrations of virtue, and convincing authority. Inexperienced volunteers adjusted their antebellum expectations about independence, egalitarianism, and discipline to fit their new reality. Later campaigns disclosed an overall improvement of the quality of company-grade officers on both sides, though at a horrendous cost in casualties and attrition. Combat discipline in both the Union and Confederate armies gradually but steadily improved as did citizen-officers' attempts to employ innovative tactics to husband the lives of their volunteers. With experience, they also began to realize that there were practical limitations to what their men could hope to achieve in combat. Prudent officers took these lessons to heart; ineffective, oblivious, or incompetent ones did not, such men jeopardizing their authority and foolishly risking their own lives as well as the lives of their volunteers.

The evolution of junior-officer leadership and the citizen-soldier ethos during the war required volunteers to reevaluate and reconcile their conceptions of military service within the restrictions imposed by the conflict. Citizen-officers found themselves in positions of authority for a variety of reasons: some were chosen because of their education or their family's reputation, others for their charisma or popularity among their comrades, still others because of their competence, experience, or temperament. Some ultimately proved cowardly or incompetent, while others demonstrated great courage and natural leadership. In the process citizen-officers developed their own distinctive culture within the armies. As fusions of the citizen-soldier and the professional, with regularizing tendencies that borrowed elements from both worlds, citizen-officers learned to lead through instinct, initiative, and improvisation. In applying these difficult lessons, company-grade citizen-officers faced a difficult quandary. Many were inexperienced amateurs desperate for any expert guidance. On the one hand, they could choose to emulate the examples of professional officers of the regular army by instilling discipline in volunteers, aspiring to military precision and efficiency, and assuming many of the alien, if effective, characteristics of the West Pointers. On the other hand, citizen-officers were products of the same ideological heritage as their enlisted volunteers and shared the same established electoral tradition or democratic ethos from antebellum society. The regular-army model and the citizen-soldier ethos were often at odds, and citizen-soldiers found their beliefs thrown into question by the exigencies of war and the need to make volunteer armies efficient and cohesive. Like the commanders of Xenophon's Ten Thousand, Union and Confederate citizen-officers also had to consider a vast array of complicated, often competing demands as they navigated the difficult terrain of their elusive military authority. The Civil War had different meanings in victory and defeat; peace represented something very different for the officers of the Union than it did for Confederates. Officers and volunteers nevertheless managed to retain the duality of their shared citizen-soldier ethos. Their determination is a testament not only to the power of the republican traditions and civic identities at the heart of their American identities but also to the compelling ways that ideas—and ideals—shape the course of history.

APPENDIXES

A Note on the Research Sample

The research data for this study are derived from two separate samples with overlapping composition. All of the units represented include officers for whom I have writings or other manuscript materials and whom I could identify through census data or military records. The demographic sample consists of 150 subjects—seventy-five Union and seventy-five Confederate volunteer junior officers who held a company-grade commission of second lieutenant, first lieutenant, or captain for a term of at least one year between 1861 and 1865. Union members of the demographic sample include officers from Connecticut, Indiana, Iowa, Maine, Maryland, Massachusetts, Michigan, Missouri, New Jersey, New York, Ohio, Pennsylvania, Vermont, and Wisconsin. Confederate members of the demographic sample include officers from Alabama, Arkansas, Florida, Georgia, Kentucky, Louisiana, Maryland, Mississippi, North Carolina, South Carolina, Tennessee, Texas, and Virginia. Census data for the demographic sample were drawn from the Eighth Census of the United States. Supplementary biographical information was obtained from the Compiled Service Records of Confederate Soldiers, Record Group 109, and the Compiled Service Records of Volunteer Union Soldiers, Record Group 94, with additional information drawn from the postwar regimental histories and company rosters cited in the bibliography.

The research sample for junior officer casualty and attrition data consists of 2,592 Union and Confederate company-grade officers representing volunteer infantry units in service for more than twelve consecutive months between 1861 and 1865. Members of the demographic sample were also included in the casualty and attrition sample. I chose to look at officers of infantry units for casualty and attrition data for three main reasons. First, the vast majority of Civil War combat troops served as infantry, and while it is impossible to reconstruct a "typical" officer for study, I believe that volunteer infantry officers' experiences provide a good sense of what the junior officer experience was like. Second, because of the large numbers of junior officers serving in these types of units, casualty and service records for volunteer infantry officers of company grade were most readily available for analysis. Third, rosters for these units were the most accessible and verifiable, an essential requirement for researchers, particularly given the spotty availability of Confederate regimental records.

The Union portion of the casualty and attrition sample consists of seventeen regiments—seven that served primarily in the western or Trans-Mississippi theaters and ten that served mainly in the eastern theater. More soldiers and officers served in the eastern theater than in the western or Trans-Mississippi theaters, and so I have weighted the sample to reflect this. The states represented in the Union casualty and attrition sample are Connecticut, Illinois, Indiana, Iowa, Maine, Massachusetts, Minnesota, Missouri, New Jersey, New York, Ohio, Pennsylvania, Vermont, and Wisconsin. The sample also includes the 43rd U.S. Colored Troops, whose officers were primarily Pennsylvanians. The Confederate portion of the casualty and attrition sample consists of sixteen regiments: seven whose main service was in the western or Trans-Mississippi theaters and nine that served mainly in the eastern theater. The states represented in the Confederate casualty and attrition sample are Alabama, Arkansas, Florida, Georgia, Kentucky, Louisiana, Mississippi, North Carolina, South Carolina, Tennessee, Texas, and Virginia.

I have defined "casualties" as captains or lieutenants killed in action, wounded in action, missing in action, taken prisoner, or having died in service, which includes victims of illness, accidents, or undetermined causes. Overall, junior officer deaths by illness and accident were extremely infrequent in comparison to combat-related injuries in the sample; furthermore, specific causes of junior officer deaths or injuries while in service were not always (or even often) indicated in regimental and company records. In deciding which regiments to include in the casualty and attrition sample, I purposely chose to include several famous units alongside more obscure or even unknown ones so as not to favor regiments that sustained exceptionally high casualties. Data for the casualty and attrition sample were drawn from the Compiled Service Records of Confederate Soldiers, Record Group 109, and the Compiled Service Records of Volunteer Union Soldiers, Record Group 94, with additional information obtained from the postwar regimental histories and rosters cited in the bibliography.

APPENDIX 1

Antebellum Professions and Slaveholding of Junior Officers

ANTEBELLUM PROFESSIONS OF UNION JUNIOR OFFICERS

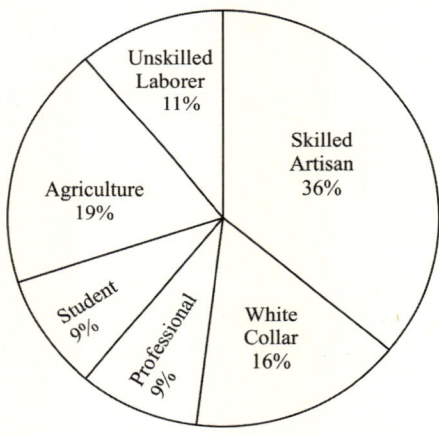

ANTEBELLUM PROFESSIONS OF CONFEDERATE JUNIOR OFFICERS

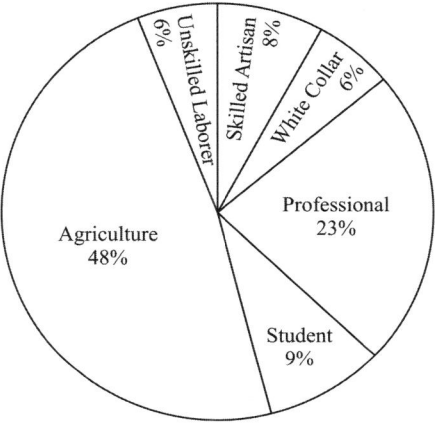

SLAVEHOLDING OF CONFEDERATE JUNIOR OFFICERS

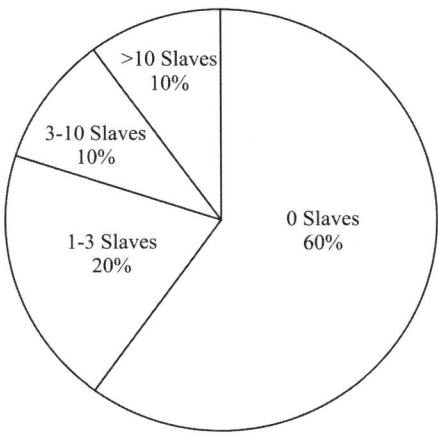

APPENDIX 2
Defining Characteristics of Junior Officers

AGE OF JUNIOR OFFICERS

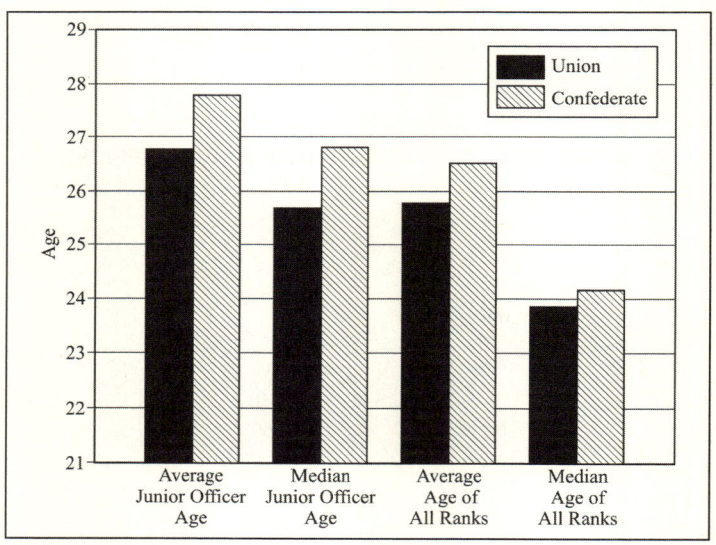

Defining Characteristics of Junior Officers | 229

HOUSEHOLD WEALTH OF JUNIOR OFFICERS

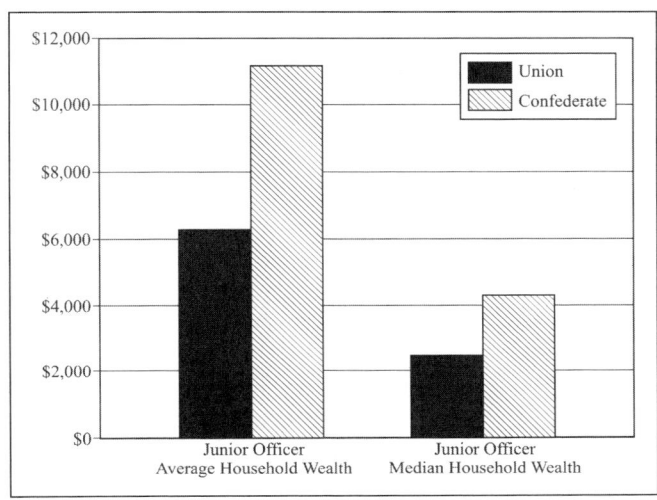

MARITAL STATUS OF JUNIOR OFFICERS

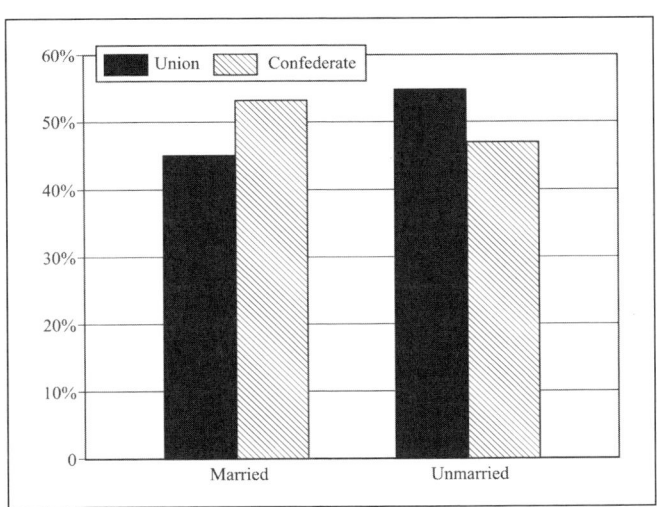

NUMBER OF CHILDREN OF JUNIOR OFFICERS

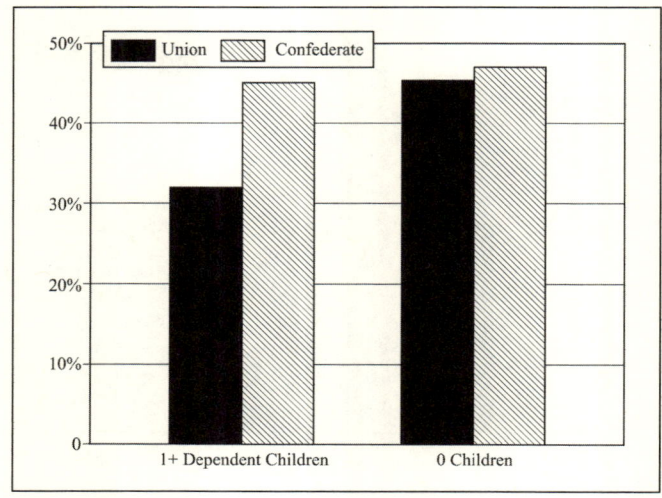

APPENDIX 3
Junior Officer Casualties, Union

UNION CASUALTIES, 1861

	115 IL	53 OH	33 IA	21 MO	10 IN	7 IL	13 CT	19 ME	18 CT	40 NY	2 MA	43 USCT	103 PA	8 NJ	8 VT	1 MN	6 WI	Total
APR	–	–	–	–	–	–	–	–	–	–	–	–	–	–	–	0	–	–
MAY	–	–	–	–	–	–	–	–	–	–	0	–	–	–	–	0	–	–
JUN	–	–	–	–	–	–	–	–	–	0	0	–	–	–	–	0	–	–
JUL	–	–	–	–	–	0	–	–	–	0	0	–	–	–	–	14	2	16
AUG	–	–	–	–	–	0	–	–	–	0	0	–	–	–	–	0	0	0
SEP	–	–	–	–	0	1	–	–	–	0	0	–	0	0	–	0	0	1
OCT	–	–	–	–	0	0	–	–	–	0	0	–	0	0	–	0	0	0
NOV	–	–	–	–	0	0	0	–	–	0	0	–	0	0	–	0	0	0
DEC	–	–	–	–	0	0	0	–	–	0	0	–	0	0	–	0	0	0
Total	–	–	–	–	0	1	0	–	–	0	0	–	0	0	–	14	2	17

UNION CASUALTIES, 1862

	115 IL	53 OH	33 IA	21 MO	10 IN	7 IL	13 CT	19 ME	18 CT	40 NY	2 MA	43 USCT	103 PA	8 NJ	8 VT	1 MN	6 WI	Total
JAN	–	–	–	–	3	0	0	–	–	0	0	–	0	0	–	0	0	3
FEB	–	–	–	0	0	1	0	–	–	0	0	–	0	0	0	0	0	1
MAR	–	–	–	0	2	0	0	–	–	0	0	–	0	0	0	0	0	2
APR	–	–	–	1	0	4	0	–	–	0	0	–	0	0	0	0	1	6
MAY	–	–	–	3	1	0	0	–	–	0	6	–	1	2	0	0	0	13
JUN	–	–	–	0	1	0	0	–	–	1	0	–	1	2	3	2	0	10
JUL	–	–	–	0	0	0	0	–	–	0	0	–	1	0	3	1	0	5
AUG	–	–	–	0	0	0	0	0	0	2	22	–	0	1	0	0	7	32
SEP	0	1	–	0	0	0	0	0	0	0	8	–	0	0	5	6	19	39
OCT	0	0	0	0	0	5	0	1	0	0	1	–	0	0	0	1	1	9
NOV	0	0	0	0	0	0	0	0	0	0	0	–	0	0	1	0	0	1
DEC	0	0	0	0	0	0	0	0	0	2	1	–	2	1	0	1	1	8
Total	0	1	0	4	7	10	0	1	0	5	38	–	5	6	12	11	29	129

UNION CASUALTIES, 1863

	115 IL	53 OH	33 IA	21 MO	10 IN	7 IL	13 CT	19 ME	18 CT	40 NY	2 MA	43 USCT	103 PA	8 NJ	8 VT	1 MN	6 WI	Total
JAN	0	0	0	0	0	0	0	0	0	0	0	–	0	0	0	0	0	0
FEB	0	0	0	0	0	1	0	0	0	0	0	–	0	0	0	0	0	1
MAR	2	0	0	0	0	0	0	0	0	0	0	–	0	0	1	0	0	3
APR	0	1	0	0	0	0	4	0	0	0	0	–	0	0	0	0	0	5
MAY	0	0	0	0	0	0	0	0	0	1	10	–	0	1	2	0	0	14
JUN	0	0	0	1	0	0	4	0	6	0	3	–	0	0	6	0	0	20
JUL	0	0	3	0	0	0	0	20	0	3	17	–	0	1	0	16	19	79
AUG	0	0	0	0	0	0	0	0	0	0	0	–	0	1	0	9	0	10
SEP	9	0	0	0	11	0	0	0	0	0	0	–	0	0	0	0	0	20
OCT	0	0	0	1	1	0	0	0	0	0	0	–	0	0	0	3	0	5
NOV	0	1	0	0	1	0	0	0	0	1	0	–	0	0	0	0	0	3
DEC	0	0	0	0	0	0	0	0	0	0	0	–	0	0	0	1	0	1
Total	11	2	3	2	13	1	8	20	6	5	30	–	0	3	9	29	19	161

UNION CASUALTIES, 1864

	115 IL	53 OH	33 IA	21 MO	10 IN	7 IL	13 CT	19 ME	18 CT	40 NY	2 MA	43 USCT	103 PA	8 NJ	8 VT	1 MN	6 WI	Total
JAN	0	0	0	0	0	0	0	0	0	0	0	–	0	0	0	0	0	0
FEB	0	0	0	0	0	0	0	1	0	0	0	–	0	0	0	0	0	1
MAR	0	0	0	0	0	1	0	0	0	0	0	0	0	0	0	0	0	1
APR	0	0	7	0	0	0	1	0	0	0	0	0	22	0	0	0	0	30
MAY	2	3	1	0	0	3	0	12	1	8	1	1	0	2	0	0	19	53
JUN	0	0	0	0	1	0	0	3	6	5	2	0	0	0	0	0	6	23
JUL	0	0	1	0	1	0	0	2	4	0	2	9	0	0	0	0	5	24
AUG	0	4	0	0	0	0	0	0	0	0	1	0	0	0	0	0	3	8
SEP	0	0	0	0	0	0	1	0	0	1	1	0	0	0	6	0	0	9
OCT	2	0	0	0	–	4	0	0	0	0	0	4	0	0	15	0	0	25
NOV	0	0	0	0	–	0	0	0	0	0	0	2	0	0	0	0	0	2
DEC	0	1	0	0	1*	0	2	0	0	0	1	0	0	0	1	0	0	6
Total	4	8	9	0	3	8	4	18	11	14	8	16	22	2	22	0	33	182

*Died of wounds after discharge

UNION CASUALTIES, 1865

	115 IL	53 OH	33 IA	21 MO	10 IN	7 IL	13 CT	19 ME	18 CT	40 NY	2 MA	43 USCT	103 PA	8 NJ	8 VT	1 MN	6 WI	Total
JAN	0	0	0	0	–	0	0	0	0	0	0	0	0	0	0	0	0	0
FEB	0	0	0	0	–	0	0	1	0	0	0	0	0	0	0	0	5	6
MAR	0	0	0	0	–	0	0	0	0	0	7	0	0	0	0	0	5	12
APR	0	1*	0	1	–	0	0	2	0	0	0	0	0	2	0	0	1	7
Total	0	1*	0	1	0	0	0	3	0	0	7	0	0	2	0	0	11	25

*Died of wounds in 1866

TOTAL UNION CASUALTIES, 1861–65

	115 IL	53 OH	33 IA	21 MO	10 IN	7 IL	13 CT	19 ME	18 CT	40 NY	2 MA	43 USCT	103 PA	8 NJ	8 VT	1 MN	6 WI	Total
Sample	49	48	66	77	51	76	56	88	43	60	87	36	78	83	112	61	112	1,183
Casualties	15	12	12	7	23	20	12	42	17	24	83	16	27	13	43	54	94	514
Rate (%)	30.6	25.0	18.2	7.7	45.1	26.3	21.4	47.7	39.5	40.0	95.4	44.4	34.6	15.7	38.4	88.5	83.9	43.5

CASUALTY SUMMARY, UNION JUNIOR OFFICERS

West/Trans-Mississippi units: 115 IL, 53 OH, 33 IA, 21 MO, 10 IN, 7 IL, 13 CT
East units: 19 ME, 18 CT, 40 NY, 2 MA, 43 USCT, 103 PA, 8 NJ, 8 VT, 1 MN, 6 WI

Total Union Junior Officers in Sample
423 (West/Trans-Mississippi)
760 (East)
1,183 (Total)

Total Casualties
101 (West/Trans-Mississippi)
413 (East)
514 (Total)

Casualty Rate
23.9% (West/Trans-Mississippi)
54.3% (East)
43.4% (Total)

APPENDIX 4
Junior Officer Attrition, Union

UNION PROMOTIONS AND RESIGNATIONS, 1861–65

	115 IL	53 OH	33 IA	21 MO	10 IN	7 IL	13 CT	19 ME	18 CT	40 NY	2 MA	43 USCT	103 PA	8 NJ	8 VT	1 MN	6 WI	Total
Sample	49	48	66	77	51	76	56	88	43	60	87	36	78	83	112	61	112	1,183
POC	9	10	10	7	13	13	3	7	3	11	35	4	6	10	13	19	25	198
RES	22	24	23	34	21	31	16	49	15	32	24	6	28	40	17	9	40	431
Rate (%)	63.3	70.8	50.0	53.2	66.7	57.9	33.9	63.6	41.9	71.7	67.8	27.8	43.6	60.2	26.8	45.9	58.0	53.2

POC: Promoted or transferred out of company

RES: Resigned, reduced to ranks, dismissed, cashiered, or discharged prior to 1865

ATTRITION SUMMARY, UNION JUNIOR OFFICERS

West/Trans-Mississippi units: 115 IL, 53 OH, 33 IA, 21 MO, 10 IN, 7 IL, 13 CT
East units: 19 ME, 18 CT, 40 NY, 2 MA, 43 USCT, 103 PA, 8 NJ, 8 VT, 1 MN, 6 WI

Attrition from Promotion
65 (West/Trans-Mississippi)
133 (East)
198 (Total)

Attrition Rates from Promotion
15.4% (West/Trans-Mississippi)
17.5% (East)
16.7% (Total)

Attrition from Resignation
171 (West/Trans-Mississippi)
260 (East)
431 (Total)

Attrition Rates from Resignation
40.4% (West/Trans-Mississippi)
34.2% (East)
36.4% (Total)

Total Attrition from Promotion and Resignation
236 (West/Trans-Mississippi)
393 (East)
629 (Total)

Total Attrition Rates from Promotion and Resignation
55.8% (West/Trans-Mississippi)
51.7% (East)
53.2% (Total)

APPENDIX 5

Junior Officer Casualties, Confederate

CONFEDERATE CASUALTIES, 1861

	42 GA	20 TN	4 AR	5 KY	10 SC	6 MS	3 LA	45 VA	22 NC	17 VA	21 GA	14 AL	47 AL	2 FL	3 AR	26 NC	Total
APR	–	–	–	–	–	–	–	–	–	–	–	–	–	–	–	–	–
MAY	–	–	–	–	–	–	0	0	–	–	–	–	–	–	0	0	–
JUN	–	0	–	–	–	–	0	0	–	0	0	–	–	–	0	0	–
JUL	–	0	–	–	0	–	0	0	0	4	0	–	–	0	0	0	4
AUG	–	0	0	–	0	0	5	2	0	0	0	0	–	0	0	0	7
SEP	–	0	0	–	0	0	0	0	0	0	0	0	–	0	0	0	0
OCT	–	0	0	0	0	0	0	0	0	0	0	0	–	0	0	0	0
NOV	–	0	0	0	0	0	0	0	0	0	1	0	–	0	0	0	1
DEC	–	0	0	0	0	0	0	0	1	0	0	0	–	0	0	0	1
Total	–	0	0	0	0	0	5	2	1	4	1	0	–	0	0	0	13

CONFEDERATE CASUALTIES, 1862

	42 GA	20 TN	4 AR	5 KY	10 SC	6 MS	3 LA	45 VA	22 NC	17 VA	21 GA	14 AL	47 AL	2 FL	3 AR	26 NC	Total
JAN	–	4	1	–	0	–	0	0	0	0	0	0	–	0	1	0	6
FEB	–	0	0	–	0	1	0	0	0	0	0	0	–	0	0	0	1
MAR	0	0	0	1	0	0	2	0	0	0	0	0	–	0	0	3	6
APR	0	7	0	4	0	11	0	0	0	0	0	2	–	0	0	0	24
MAY	0	0	0	0	0	0	1	0	6	15	0	2	0	28	0	0	52
JUN	4	0	0	0	0	0	0	0	3	10	2	16	0	11	0	0	46
JUL	2	0	0	0	0	0	0	0	2	0	1	0	0	0	0	0	5
AUG	0	0	0	0	0	0	0	0	3	3	6	2	9	0	0	0	23
SEP	0	0	0	0	0	0	15	4	0	5	5	0	7	4	6	0	46
OCT	0	0	1	0	0	0	1	0	1	0	0	0	0	0	0	0	3
NOV	0	0	0	0	0	0	0	0	1	0	0	0	0	0	0	0	1
DEC	2	9	5	6	8	0	1	0	1	0	0	0	0	0	0	0	32
Total	8	20	7	11	8	12	20	4	17	33	14	22	16	43	7	3	245

CONFEDERATE CASUALTIES, 1863

	42 GA	20 TN	4 AR	5 KY	10 SC	6 MS	3 LA	45 VA	22 NC	17 VA	21 GA	14 AL	47 AL	2 FL	3 AR	26 NC	Total
JAN	0	0	0	1	0	0	0	0	0	0	1	0	0	0	0	0	2
FEB	0	0	0	2	0	0	0	0	0	0	0	0	0	0	0	0	2
MAR	0	0	0	0	0	0	0	0	1	0	1	0	0	0	0	0	2
APR	0	0	3	0	0	0	2	0	1	0	1	0	0	1	1	0	9
MAY	0	0	0	0	0	1	4	0	6	0	3	0	0	4	0	0	18
JUN	0	2	0	0	0	0	5	1	0	0	1	1	1	2	0	0	13
JUL	2	0	1	0	0	0	7	0	6	4	6	1	9	20	13	7	76
AUG	0	0	0	0	0	0	0	2	1	0	0	0	0	1	0	0	4
SEP	0	9	5	0	4	0	0	0	1	0	1	1	4	2	9	0	36
OCT	0	0	0	1	0	0	0	1	0	0	0	0	1	0	0	1	4
NOV	0	0	0	1	2	0	0	0	0	0	0	1	0	1	0	0	5
DEC	0	0	1	2	0	0	0	0	0	0	2	0	0	0	0	0	5
Total	2	11	10	7	6	1	18	4	16	4	16	4	15	31	23	8	176

CONFEDERATE CASUALTIES, 1864

	42 GA	20 TN	4 AR	5 KY	10 SC	6 MS	3 LA	45 VA	22 NC	17 VA	21 GA	14 AL	47 AL	2 FL	3 AR	26 NC	Total
JAN	0	0	0	0	0	0	0	0	0	1	0	0	0	0	0	0	1
FEB	2	0	0	0	0	0	0	0	0	0	0	0	0	1	0	0	3
MAR	0	0	1	0	0	0	0	0	0	0	0	0	0	0	0	0	1
APR	0	0	1	0	0	0	0	0	0	0	1	0	0	0	0	0	2
MAY	3	0	1	0	1	1	0	10	0	0	4	1	11	1	13	6	52
JUN	0	2	0	1	0	0	0	24	0	0	2	1	3	3	0	0	36
JUL	3	2	3	0	18	1	0	0	1	0	3	2	0	0	3	0	36
AUG	3	3	2	0	0	1	0	1	0	0	1	0	0	0	0	0	11
SEP	0	2	0	0	1	0	0	15	0	0	3	0	1	0	1	0	23
OCT	0	0	0	0	0	0	0	2	0	0	0	0	3	0	2	0	7
NOV	2	3	0	0	4	1	0	0	0	0	0	0	0	0	0	0	10
DEC	2	4	2	0	0	0	0	0	0	0	0	0	0	0	0	0	8
Total	15	16	10	1	24	4	0	52	1	1	14	4	18	5	19	6	190

CONFEDERATE CASUALTIES, 1865

	42 GA	20 TN	4 AR	5 KY	10 SC	6 MS	3 LA	45 VA	22 NC	17 VA	21 GA	14 AL	47 AL	2 FL	3 AR	26 NC	Total
JAN	0	0	0	0	0	0	0	0	0	0	0	0	0	0	0	0	0
FEB	0	0	0	0	0	0	0	0	0	0	0	0	0	0	0	0	0
MAR	1	0	0	0	0	0	0	4	0	5	2	0	0	0	0	0	12
APR	0	0	0	0	0	0	0	0	29	0	3	0	0	0	2	0	34
Total	1	0	0	0	0	0	0	4	29	5	5	0	0	0	2	0	46

TOTAL CONFEDERATE CASUALTIES, 1861–65

	42 GA	20 TN	4 AR	5 KY	10 SC	6 MS	3 LA	45 VA	22 NC	17 VA	21 GA	14 AL	47 AL	2 FL	3 AR	26 NC	Total
Sample	56	82	70	59	100	101	82	113	112	100	82	80	86	96	97	93	1,409
Casualties	26	47	27	19	38	17	43	66	64	47	50	30	49	79	51	17	670
Rate [%]	46.4	57.3	38.6	32.2	38.0	16.8	52.4	58.4	57.1	47.0	61.0	37.5	57.0	82.3	52.6	18.3	47.6

CASUALTY SUMMARY, CONFEDERATE JUNIOR OFFICERS

West/Trans-Mississippi units: 42 GA, 20 TN, 4 AR, 5 KY, 10 SC, 6 MS, 3 LA
East units: 45 VA, 22 NC, 17 VA, 21 GA, 14 AL, 47 AL, 2 FL, 3 AR, 26 NC

Total Confederate Junior Officers in Sample
550 (West/Trans-Mississippi)
859 (East)
1,409 (Total)

Total Casualties
217 (West/Trans-Mississippi)
453 (East)
670 (Total)

Casualty Rate
39.5% (West/Trans-Mississippi)
52.7% (East)
47.6% (Total)

APPENDIX 6

Junior Officer Attrition, Confederate

CONFEDERATE PROMOTIONS AND RESIGNATIONS, 1861–65

	42 GA	20 TN	4 AR	5 KY	10 SC	6 MS	3 LA	45 VA	22 NC	17 VA	21 GA	14 AL	47 AL	2 FL	3 AR	26 NC	Total
Sample	56	82	70	59	100	101	82	113	112	100	82	80	86	96	97	93	1,409
POC	4	18	2	11	7	9	10	8	5	44	10	10	7	14	20	5	184
RES	9	18	30	31	36	35	13	23	38	15	17	30	31	31	40	30	427
Rate (%)	23.2	43.9	45.7	71.2	43.0	43.6	28.0	27.4	38.4	59.0	32.9	50.0	44.2	46.9	61.9	37.6	43.4

POC: Promoted or transferred out of company
RES: Resigned, reduced to ranks, dismissed, cashiered, or discharged prior to 1865

ATTRITION SUMMARY, CONFEDERATE JUNIOR OFFICERS

West/Trans-Mississippi units: 42 GA, 20 TN, 4 AR, 5 KY, 10 SC, 6 MS, 3 LA
East units: 45 VA, 22 NC, 17 VA, 21 GA, 14 AL, 47 AL, 2 FL, 3 AR, 26 NC

Attrition from Promotion
61 (West/Trans-Mississippi)
123 (East)
184 (Total)

Attrition Rates from Promotion
11.1% (West/Trans-Mississippi)
14.3% (East)
13.1% (Total)

Attrition from Resignation
172 (West/Trans-Mississippi)
255 (East)
427 (Total)

Attrition Rates from Resignation
31.3% (West/Trans-Mississippi)
29.7% (East)
30.3% (Total)

Total Attrition from Promotion and Resignation
233 (West/Trans-Mississippi)
378 (East)
611 (Total)

Total Attrition Rates from Promotion and Resignation
42.4% (West/Trans-Mississippi)
44.0% (East)
43.4% (Total)

APPENDIX 7
Aggregate Casualties of Union and Confederate Junior Officers

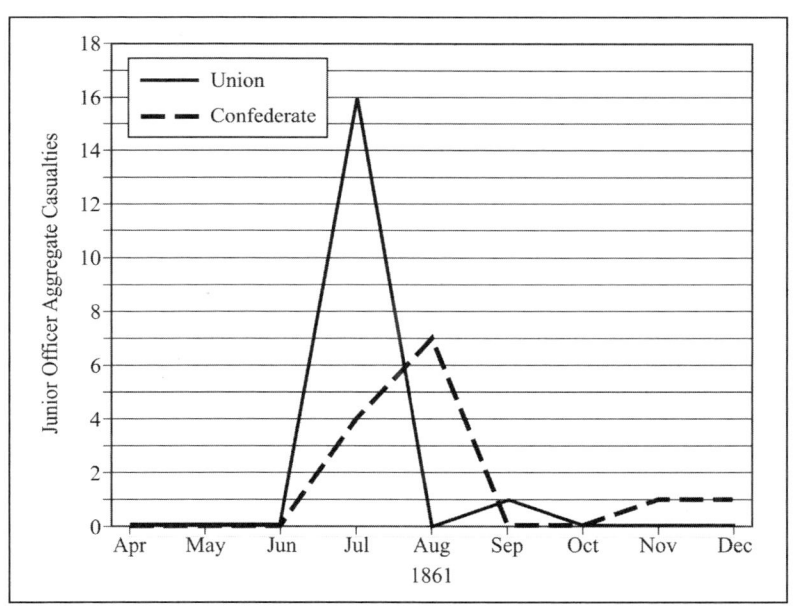

AGGREGATE CASUALTIES OF JUNIOR OFFICERS, 1862

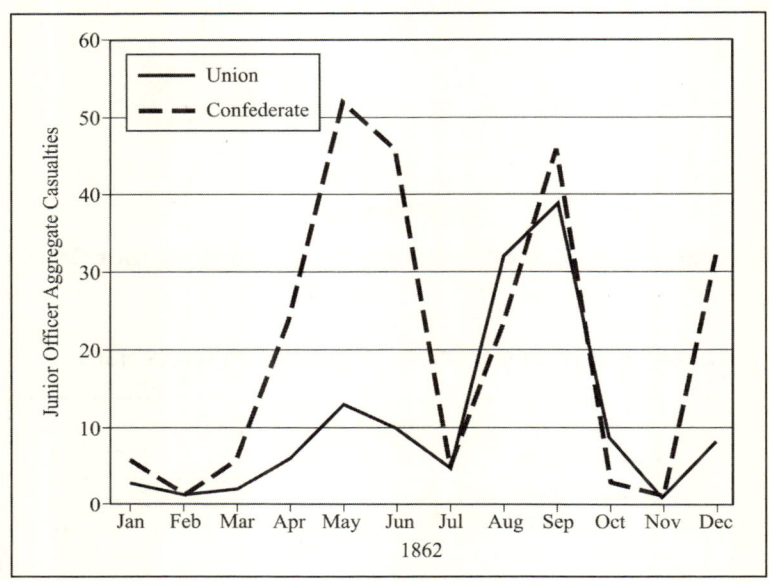

AGGREGATE CASUALTIES OF JUNIOR OFFICERS, 1863

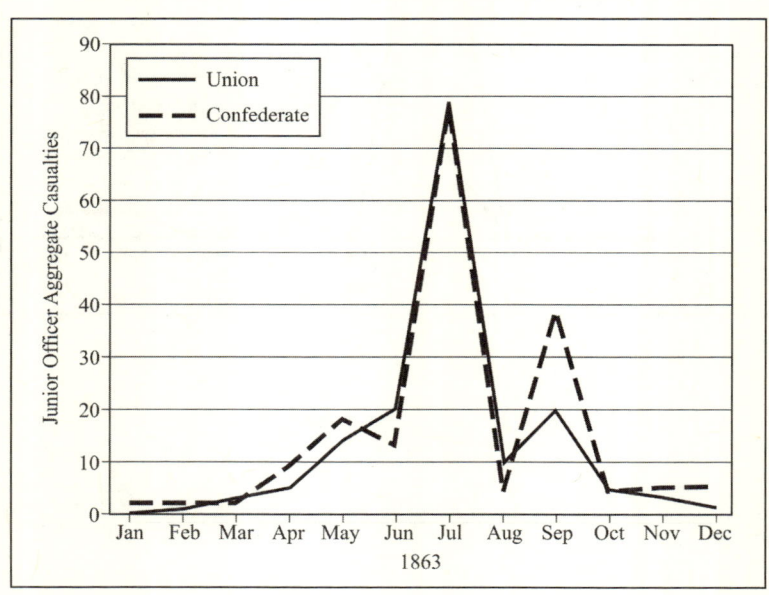

AGGREGATE CASUALTIES OF JUNIOR OFFICERS, 1864

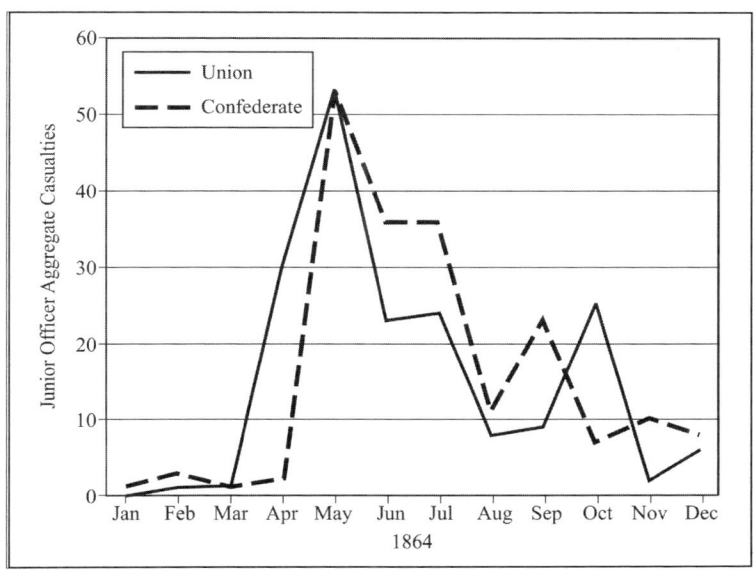

AGGREGATE CASUALTIES OF JUNIOR OFFICERS, 1865

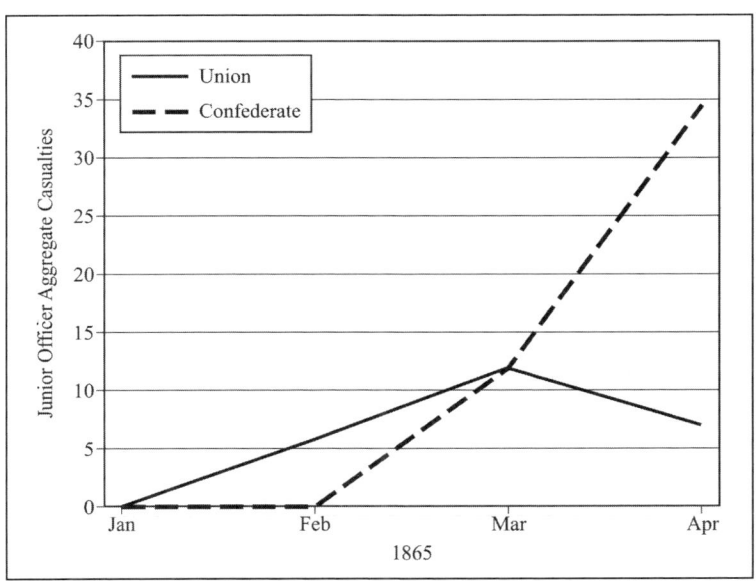

AGGREGATE CASUALTIES OF JUNIOR OFFICERS, 1861–65

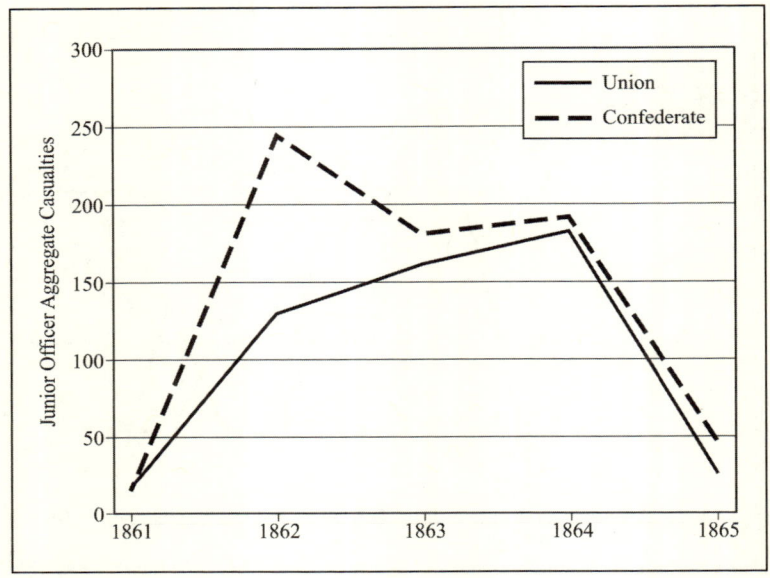

NOTES

Abbreviations

1861 *C.S. Regulations*	Confederate States War Department, *Army Regulations Adopted for Use in the Confederate States . . .* (New Orleans: Bloomfield & Steel, 1861)
1861 *U.S. Regulations*	U.S. War Department, *Revised Regulations for the Army of the United States, 1861* (Philadelphia: J. G. L. Brown, 1861)
CSR-Confederate	Compiled Service Records of Confederate Soldiers, Record Group 109, National Archives and Records Administration, Washington, D.C.
CSR-Union	Compiled Service Records of Volunteer Union Soldiers, Record Group 94, National Archives and Records Administration, Washington, D.C.
JLNC	John L. Nau Civil War Collection, Houston, Tex.
MOC	Eleanor Brockenbrough Library, Museum of the Confederacy, Richmond, Va.
OR	U.S. War Department, *The War of the Rebellion: A Compilation of the Official Records of the Union and Confederate Armies,* 70 vols. in 128 parts (Washington, D.C.: Government Printing Office, 1880–1901)
TSLA	Tennessee State Library and Archives, Nashville
USAMHI	U.S. Army Military History Institute, Carlisle Barracks, Pa.
VHS	Virginia Historical Society, Richmond

Preface

1. Xenophon, *Anabasis,* 1:118–19. Also see Rood, *American Anabasis.*
2. For a survey of the historiography of common soldiers in the Civil War, see Sheehan-Dean, "Blue and Gray in Black and White," 9–30. McPherson, *For Cause and Comrades,* illustrates historians' propensity to blur distinctions between officers and common soldiers.

On the historiographical value of examining Civil War soldiers' motivations and experiences, see Cain, "'Face of Battle' Needed," 5–27; and Glatthaar, "'New' Civil War History," 339–69. For a critique of the "band of brothers" concept of group cohesion and combat motivation, see Hamner, *Enduring Battle,* and "Why Do Soldiers Fight?," 10–12. Also see Phillips, "Battling Stereotypes," 1407–25.

3. Bartholomees, *Buff Facings and Gilt Buttons;* Jones, *Right Hand of Command;* and Krick, *Staff Officers in Gray,* focus exclusively on Union and Confederate staff officers. In *Maryland's Blue & Gray,* Kevin Ruffner takes a biographical approach and analyzes only officers from Maryland. Robert Price's "Leadership in the Civil War" is an unpublished study of Civil War officer leadership and command written from a serving military officer's perspective, but it is the only work of its kind to appear in the last fifty years.

4. For a straightforward popular survey of Civil War officers, see Davis, *Rebels & Yankees.* For soldier studies that explore certain aspects of the junior officer–enlisted man command relationship, see Linderman, *Embattled Courage,* and Hess, *Union Soldier in Battle.* Lorien Foote and Steven Ramold have both produced detailed works on discipline in the Union army, but ideology, leadership, and command relationships are mostly beyond the scope of their studies. Among the best works dealing with Civil War junior officers is Peter S. Carmichael's *Last Generation,* but Carmichael discusses Confederate officers' wartime experiences in only one full chapter. Because of the unique focus of his study, he leaves many questions about the citizen-soldier ethos—combat, officer culture and professionalization, the influence of the regular-army model, and the evolution of citizen-officer leadership—unaddressed. In his monumental study of the Confederate Army of Northern Virginia, Joseph T. Glatthaar describes the development of Confederate leadership and officer culture within that force, but by necessity his discussion is limited in scope and content. Carmichael and Glatthaar confine their examinations to Confederate officers in one army; nevertheless, both serve as starting points for this study of Union and Confederate company-grade citizen-officers.

1. Ideological Origins of the Volunteer Junior Officer Corps

1. George Washington, "Address to the New York Provincial Congress," June 26, 1775, in *Papers,* 41. Washington's statement echoes the 1647 address of Oliver Cromwell's soldiers to the English Parliament: "On becoming soldiers we have not ceased to be citizens." Address, "Humble Representation," Oliver Cromwell's soldiers to the English Parliament, [1647], in Andrews, *Columbia Dictionary of Quotations,* 52.

2. Washington, "Address to the New York Provincial Congress," 41; Samet, *Willing Obedience,* 17–18.

3. Higginson, "Regular and Volunteer Officers," 349.

4. On Higginson's Civil War experiences, see Meyer, *Colonel of the Black Regiment.*

5. Thornton, *Politics in a Slave Society;* Holt, *Political Crisis of the 1850s;* Bond, *Political Culture in the Nineteenth-Century South;* Morrison, *Slavery and the American West;* Pocock, *Machiavellian Moment,* 507.

6. Cunliffe, *Soldiers and Civilians,* 40–41; Shy, *People Numerous and Armed,* 251–52; Winders, *Mr. Polk's Army,* 73; Herrera, "Self-Governance and the American Citizen as Soldier," 23; Hsieh, *West Pointers and the Civil War,* 12–15.

7. Morgan, *Birth of the Republic,* 73; Wood, *Radicalism of the American Revolution,* 341–42; Smith, *No Party Now,* 47; Herrera, "Guarantors of Liberty and Republic," 24–27.

8. Lawson, *Patriot Fires*, 8.
9. *Philadelphia Public Ledger*, June 7, 1861.
10. Royster, *Destructive War*, 145–48; Dew, *Apostles of Disunion*, 74–75; Fox-Genovese and Genovese, *Mind of the Master Class*, 71.
11. *Atlanta Southern Confederacy*, June 25, 1861.
12. Royster, *Destructive War*, 175–76.
13. Hahn, *Roots of Southern Populism*, 119; Bond, *Political Culture in the Nineteenth-Century South;* McCurry, *Masters of Small Worlds*, 266–70; Higginbotham, "Martial Spirit in the Antebellum South," 6–13; Selesky, *War and Society in Colonial Connecticut*, 201; Rowe, *Bulwark of the Republic*, ix–xiii, 134; Skeen, *Citizen Soldiers in the War of 1812*, 41, 56–58, 182; Laver, "Rethinking the Social Role of the Militia," 777–816; Forgie, *Patricide in the House Divided*, 207–12.
14. Bailyn, *Ideological Origins of the American Revolution*, 301–19; Wood, *Creation of the American Republic*, 65–70; McCoy, *Elusive Republic*, 57–65; Appleby, *Liberalism and Republicanism in the Historical Imagination*, 285–87; Rodgers, "Republicanism," 19; Sandel, *Democracy's Discontent*, 5–6; Kloppenberg, *Virtues of Liberalism*, 61; Onuf, *Jefferson's Empire*, 54.
15. Weigley, *American Way of War*, 13–17; Weigley, *Towards an American Army*, 1–9; Leach, *Arms for Empire*, 192; Mahon, *Militia and the National Guard*, 14–34.
16. Cress, "Radical Whiggery on the Role of the Military," 42–43; Harrington, "Commonwealth of Oceana," in *"Commonwealth of Oceana" and "A System of Politics,"* 9–10; Pocock, "Machiavelli, Harrington, and English Political Ideologies," 553–56, 559–62; Pocock, "James Harrington and the Good Old Cause," 46; Pocock, "Civic Humanism and Its Role in Anglo-American Thought," in *Politics, Language, and Time*, 85–88, 90–94; Banning, "Quarrel with Federalism," 34–36.
17. Herrera, "Self-Governance and the American Citizen as Soldier," 21–52. The first Militia Act, enacted in May 1792, granted the president the authority to call state militias into federal service "whenever the United States shall be invaded, or be in imminent danger of invasion from any foreign nation or Indian tribe." Act of May 8, 1792, ch. 33, *Statutes at Large of the United States*, 1:271–74. On the role of the militia in antebellum society, see Stauffer, "Volunteer or Uniformed Companies in the Antebellum Militia," 108–16; McCreedy, "Palladium of Liberty"; and Pitcavage, "Equitable Burden."
18. Kettner, *Development of American Citizenship*, 208; Brooks, "Social and Cultural Dynamics of Soldiering in Hood's Texas Brigade," 546–47; Noe, *Reluctant Rebels*, 110–12; Wood, *Creation of the American Republic*, 483–99; Morgan, *Challenge of the American Revolution*, 211–18; Bailyn, *Ideological Origins of the American Revolution*, 161–75.
19. Lofgren, "Compulsory Military Service under the Constitution," 76–79; Pitcavage, "Equitable Burden," 246–86; Shy, *People Numerous and Armed*, 32, 252.
20. Tocqueville, *Democracy in America*, 1:370.
21. Kolenda, "What Is Leadership?," 16; DeBuse, "Citizen-Officer Ideal," 9–10, 13–16.
22. Hillyard, *Cincinnatus and the Citizen-Servant Ideal*, 81–86.
23. Richard, *Founders and the Classics*, 55–56, 68, 70–72, 94, 109; Wills, *Cincinnatus;* Higginbotham, *Washington and the American Military Tradition;* Stagg, "Freedom and Subordination," 572.
24. John Adams to [William Tudor], June 24, 1776, in Adams, *Works*, 3:411.
25. Patrick Henry, "Henry's Speech in the Virginia Ratifying Convention [1788]," in Elliot, *Debates in the Several State Conventions*, 3:162.

26. Richard, *Founders and the Classics*, 70–72.
27. Broadwater, *George Mason*, 68–69.
28. George Mason, "Remarks on Annual Elections for the Fairfax Independent Company," [Apr. 1775], in Mason, *Papers*, 1:229–30.
29. Ibid.
30. Ibid.
31. Doyle, *Aristocracy and Its Enemies*, 99–130.
32. Royster, *Revolutionary People at War*, 349.
33. Weigley, *Towards an American Army*, 13–22.
34. Cunliffe, *Soldiers and Civilians*, 223–30; Huntington, *Soldier and the State*, 167–69; Nye, "Western Masculinities in War and Peace," 417–38.
35. Wood, *Radicalism of the American Revolution*, 304; Andrew Jackson, First Annual Message, Dec. 8, 1829, in Richardson, *Compilation of the Messages and Papers of the Presidents*, 2:449. On the relationship between the citizen-soldier tradition and the emerging regular army, see Coffman, "Duality of the American Military Tradition," 967–80; Kohn, *Eagle and Sword*, 279–82; Mahon, *Militia and the National Guard*, 3; Bailyn, *Ideological Origins of the American Revolution*, 62–63; Jacobs, *Beginning of the U.S. Army*; and Crackel, *Mr. Jefferson's Army*. A strain of the historiography of the antebellum U.S. Army has deemphasized the role of Jacksonian democratic thought and classical republican ideology in the development of a professional officer class. Nevertheless, ideology powerfully shaped American citizens' conception of the "proper" place of a standing army and of its leaders. See Volpe, "Origins of the Frémont Expeditions," 245–63; Childress, "Army in Transition"; Weigley, *United States Army*, 144–72; Prucha, *Sword of the Republic;* Watson, *Jackson's Sword;* and Watson, *Peacekeepers and Conquerors*.
36. Hsieh, *West Pointers and the Civil War*, 13; Pitcavage, "Equitable Burden," 231–35; Morgan, *Inventing the People*, 160–67.
37. Anderson, *People's Army*, vii, 39, 155–61, 178; Coffman, "Duality of the American Military Tradition," 967–80.
38. Thomas Barclay Diary, Jan. 13, 1848, in Peskin, *Volunteers*, 236.
39. Jefferson Davis, Second Inaugural Address, Feb. 22, 1862, in *Jefferson Davis, Constitutionalist*, 9:543.
40. Wood, *Radicalism of the American Revolution*, 304.
41. Watson, *Liberty and Power*, 49–53. Also see Wettemann, *Privilege vs. Equality*.
42. Morgan, *Inventing the People*, 302. For a contrary view on the power of egalitarianism, see Pessen, "Egalitarian Myth and the American Social Reality,'" 989–1034.
43. Tocqueville, *Democracy in America*, 1:62; Watson, *Liberty and Power*, 32–33.
44. Morgan, *Inventing the People*, 153–73; Waldstreicher, *In the Midst of Perpetual Fetes*, 156–60.
45. Watson, *Liberty and Power*, 43.
46. Skelton, *American Profession of Arms*, 89–90. Also see Haber, *Quest for Authority and Honor in the American Professions*, and Bledstein, *Culture of Professionalism*.
47. Hsieh, *West Pointers and the Civil War*, 19–25; Stagg, "Freedom and Subordination," 544–45, 571–72; Elting, *Amateurs, to Arms!*, 6–8.
48. Skelton, *American Profession of Arms*, 134; Hsieh, *West Pointers and the Civil War*, 12; Cunliffe, *Soldiers and Civilians*, 154–56.
49. Skelton, *American Profession of Arms*, 194–95.
50. Ibid., 181.

51. Ibid., xiv–xvi; Moten, *Delafield Commission*, 107; Ball, *Army Regulars on the Western Frontier*.

52. Stagg, "Freedom and Subordination," 571–72.

53. Hsieh, *West Pointers and the Civil War*, 20–25; Smith, *Engineering Security*; Linn, *Echo of Battle*; Wooster, *American Military Frontiers*.

54. Watson, "Manifest Destiny and Military Professionalism," 493; Skelton, *American Profession of Arms*, 36–41; Wettemann, "A Part or Apart," 193–217.

55. Weigley, *Towards an American Army*, 13–16, 22; Hsieh, *West Pointers and the Civil War*, 16, 25.

56. George Gordon Meade to [his wife], Nov. 27, 1846, in Meade, *Life and Letters*, 1:162–63.

57. Ibid.

58. Bauer, *Mexican War*, 101–102, 220–21. Also see Levinson, *War within War*, and Johnson, *Gallant Little Army*.

59. Daniel Harvey Hill Diary, Dec. 1846, in Hill, *Fighter from Way Back*, 28.

60. George B. McClellan to [his mother], Nov. 14, 1846, in McClellan, *Mexican War Diary and Correspondence*, 38–39.

61. George B. McClellan to [his mother], Dec. 5, 1846, ibid., 49.

62. Theodore Laidley to My dear Father, Apr. 11, 1847, in Laidley, *"Surrounded by Dangers of All Kinds,"* 62.

63. Theodore Laidley to My dear Father, Oct. 24, 1847, ibid., 120.

64. Foos, *Short, Offhand, Killing Affair*, 93.

65. Kenly, *Memoirs of a Maryland Volunteer*, 77, 165.

66. Robert Anderson Diary, Jan. 28, 1847, in Anderson, *Artillery Officer in the Mexican War*, 17 (emphasis in original).

67. George Gordon Meade to [his wife], July 9, 1846, in Meade, *Life and Letters*, 1:109–10.

2. Creation of the Civil War Junior Officer Corps

1. Taliaferro N. Simpson to Richard F. Simpson, Feb. 6, 1860, in Everson and Simpson, *Far, Far from Home*, xv–xvi.

2. Taliaferro N. Simpson to Dear Home Folks, Jan. 15, 1863, ibid., 171–72.

3. Eicher and Eicher, *Civil War High Commands*, 55. The Provisional Confederate Congress authorized the creation of a regular army on March 6, 1861, but this force was never completely implemented. Act of Mar. 6, 1861, ch. 26, *Statutes at Large of the Provisional Government Confederate States*, 45–46; *OR*, ser. 4, 1:127–31.

4. Higginson, "Regular and Volunteer Officers," 349.

5. Donald, *Lincoln*, 296, 301, 305; Eicher and Eicher, *Civil War High Commands*, 55. Under the amended Militia Act of 1792, the president had the authority to call for troops from the states, and the War Department determined each state's troop quota. Governors and citizens then decided if they would comply with the president's requests. Act of May 8, 1792, ch. 33, *Statutes at Large of the United States*, 1:271–74. Also see Wilson, *Business of Civil War*, 38.

6. Eicher and Eicher, *Civil War High Commands*, 71.

7. Coffman, *Old Army*, 92; Davis, *Rebels & Yankees*, 29; Newell and Shrader, *Of Duty Well and Faithfully Done*, 53–54; Weinert, *Confederate Regular Army*.

8. Orr, "'All Manner of Schemes and Rascalities,'" 101–102; Wade, "Roads to the Top," 157 63.

9. Adjutant General's Office, General Orders No. 15, May 4, 1861, in U.S. War Department, *General Orders Affecting the Volunteer Force* (1862), 1:1; Act of July 22, 1861, ch. 9, *Statutes at*

Large of the United States, 12:270; Eicher and Eicher, *Civil War High Commands,* 66. General Orders No. 110, issued on April 29, 1863, set the standards for Union volunteer regiments after 1863. See *OR,* ser. 3, 3:175.

10. 1861 *Army Regulations.*

11. Boatner, *Civil War Dictionary,* 610–12.

12. Adjutant General's Office, General Orders No. 15, May 4, 1861, in U.S. War Department, *General Orders Affecting the Volunteer Force* (1862), 1:1.

13. Act of July 22, 1861, ch. 9, *Statutes at Large of the United States,* 12:268–71. Section 10 of this act specifies that "when vacancies occur in any of the companies of volunteers, an election shall be called by the colonel of the regiment to fill such vacancies, and the men of each company shall vote in their respective companies for all officers as high as captain, and vacancies above captain shall be filled by the votes of the commissioned officers of the regiment, and all officers so elected shall be commissioned by the respective Governors of the States, or by the President of the United States."

14. Act of Aug. 6, 1861, ch. 57, sec. 3, *Statutes at Large of the United States,* 12:318.

15. Act of Feb. 28, 1861, ch. 22, *Statutes at Large of the Provisional Government of the Confederate States,* 43–44; *OR,* ser. 4, 1:117.

16. Act of Dec. 11, 1861, ch. 9, *Statutes at Large of the Provisional Government of the Confederate States,* 223–24; *OR,* ser. 4, 1:825–26.

17. Act of Apr. 16, 1862, ch. 31, *Statutes at Large of the Confederate States,* 1:29–32; *OR,* ser. 4, 1:1095–97; Shaw, "Confederate Conscription and Exemption Acts," 368–405; Moore, *Conscription and Conflict in the Confederacy,* 256–70; Escott, *Military Necessity,* 170.

18. Act of Apr. 16, 1862, ch. 31, *Statutes at Large of the Confederate States,* 1:32.

19. Murdock, *One Million Men,* 22, 49. To help compensate for its impending manpower shortage in the spring of 1862, the Union relied at first on the Militia Act of July 17, 1862, which permitted the recruitment of black soldiers into the army, albeit with lower pay than white volunteers. Ibid., 111; Act of July 17, 1862, ch. 200, secs. 19–21, *Statutes at Large of the United States,* 12:594–97.

20. Geary, *We Need Men,* 104–108.

21. Upton, *Military Policy,* 460.

22. Ibid., 469–70.

23. John H. Black to Dear Jennie, July 21, 1862, John H. Black Papers, Document DL0756, JLNC.

24. Robert H. Miller to My Dear Mother, Feb. 14, 1862, in Connor, "Letters of Lieutenant Robert H. Miller," 70–71.

25. Coffman, "Duality of the American Military Tradition," 970.

26. *OR,* ser. 4, 2:948.

27. George Gordon Meade to [his wife], Nov. 24, 1861, in Meade, *Life and Letters,* 1:231.

28. *OR,* ser. 4, 2:1001.

29. Robert E. Lee to My Dear Sir, Dec. 24, 1861, in *OR,* ser. 1, 6:350.

30. [Gov. John A. Andrew] to [Sen. Charles Sumner] and [Sen. Henry Wilson], Aug. 3, 1861, in Gordon, *Organization and Early History of the Second Mass. Regiment of Infantry,* 28.

31. *OR,* ser. 1, 43(1):757.

32. *New York Times,* Aug. 1, 1861.

33. Joseph E. Brown to Hon. James A. Seddon, secretary of war, May 30, 1863, in Brown and Seddon, *Correspondence,* 3.

34. Upton, *Military Policy,* 233–35, 275.

35. Wilder Dwight to Dear Mother, Sept. 7, 1861, in Dwight and Dwight, *Life and Letters of Wilder Dwight*, 97–98 (emphasis in original).

36. Ruffin Thomson to [his father], Jan. 10, 1861, quoted in Wiley, *Johnny Reb*, 20.

37. Joseph J. Hoyle to My Dear wife, Oct. 2, 1862, in Hoyle, *"Deliver Us from This Cruel War,"* 71.

38. Marshall, *Army Life*, 55.

39. James Henry Langhorne to My Dear Aunt Nannie, Oct. 19, 1861, Langhorne Family Papers, VHS.

40. Emerson, "Leadership and Civil War Desertion," 26.

41. Henry Perkins Goddard to My own dear Sister, Aug. 10, 1862, in Goddard, *Good Fight That Didn't End*, 43–44.

42. Henry Perkins Goddard, 14th Regiment Connecticut Volunteer Infantry, CSR-Union, microfilm 535, reel 7.

43. Charles Frederic Bahnson to Dear Father, Sept. 25, 1862, in Chapman, *Bright and Gloomy Days*, 33–34.

44. Henry L. Graves to [his mother], May 7, 1862, quoted in Wiley, *Johnny Reb*, 20.

45. Fleharty, *Our Regiment*, 9.

46. Sydnor, *American Revolutionaries in the Making*, 103–104.

47. For an explanation of the sources, methodology, and composition of the research sample, see "Notes on the Research Sample."

48. See Appendix 2, Figure 2.1. Historian James M. McPherson finds that for all Union recruits, both officers and enlisted men, their average age at enlistment was 25.8 years old, and their median age at enlistment was 23.9 years. For all Confederates, he finds the average age at enlistment to be 26.5 years old, and the median age to be 24.2 years. McPherson, *For Cause and Comrades*, viii. Historian Joseph T. Glatthaar finds the average and median ages of Confederate officers of all ranks in the Army of Northern Virginia to be 27.2 and 23 years old, respectively. Glatthaar, *Soldiering in the Army of Northern Virginia*, 85–86.

49. See Appendix 2, Figures 2.3–2.4. Glatthaar finds that 37.8 percent of the Army of Northern Virginia's officers were married and 37.2 percent had children. Glatthaar, *Soldiering in the Army of Northern Virginia*, 85–86.

50. See Appendix 2, Figure 2.2. Glatthaar finds that Confederate officers in the Army of Northern Virginia had an average family wealth of $14,917 and a median family wealth of $3,000. To date, no similar statistical portrait of the Union officer corps is available. Ibid., 86–87.

51. See Appendix 1, Figures 1.1–1.2. McPherson finds that 84.2 percent of Union officers had professional, white-collar, or skilled-artisan occupations prior to the Civil War, while only 43.4 percent of Union enlisted men came from such backgrounds. In his sample 89.5 percent of Confederate officers of all ranks had professional, white-collar, skilled-artisan, or planter occupations, while 44 percent of Confederate enlisted men had similar antebellum occupations. McPherson, *For Cause and Comrades*, 181–82. Glatthaar finds that 91.5 percent of Confederate officers of all ranks in the Army of Northern Virginia had professional, white-collar, skilled-artisan, or planter occupations before the war. He also finds that 49.5 percent of Army of Northern Virginia officers resided in slaveholding households in 1860, of which 25.4 percent contained between three and ten slaves. In the Confederacy as a whole, 24.9 percent, or one in every four households, held slaves. Glatthaar, *Soldiering in the Army of Northern Virginia*, 86–88.

52. Poague, *Gunner with Stonewall*, 4 (emphasis in original).

53. Robert Gould Shaw to Dear Father, Aug. 13, 1861, in Shaw, *Blue-Eyed Child of Fortune,* 126.

54. Clark, *Histories of the Several Regiments and Battalions from North Carolina,* 1:221–22.

55. Marshall, *Army Life,* 53–55.

56. Henry A. Buck Diary, Jan. 20, 1862, quoted in Wiley, *Billy Yank,* 24.

57. Robert Gould Shaw to My dear Sue, Aug. 15, 1861, in Shaw, *Blue-Eyed Child of Fortune,* 128–32.

58. Upton, *Military Policy,* 260.

59. Act of July 22, 1861, ch. 9, sec. 10, *Statutes at Large of the United States,* 12:270. On June 25, 1864, concerned with institutional corruption and incompetence, Congress required that all quartermaster and commissary officers appear before boards of examination to determine their fitness. Act of June 25, 1864, ch. 149, ibid., 13:181–82.

60. Levi Bird Duff to [Harriet Nixon], Feb. 13, 1862, in Duff, *To Petersburg with the Army of the Potomac,* 38.

61. Foote, *Gentlemen and the Roughs,* 10n16.

62. William Preston Johnston to Sir, July 15, 1862, in *OR,* ser. 1, 10(1):780–81.

63. Adjutant and Inspector General's Office, General Orders No. 36, May 17, 1862, in Confederate States War Department, *General Orders . . . 1862,* 48; Adjutant and Inspector General's Office, General Orders No. 39, May 26, 1862, ibid., 52–53.

64. Act of Oct. 13, 1862, ch. 57, *Statutes at Large of the Confederate States of America,* 2:85.

65. William Preston Johnston to Sir, July 15, 1862, in *OR,* ser 1, 10(1):780–81.

66. Jefferson Davis to the Senate and House of Representatives, Aug. 18, 1862, in Richardson, *Compilation of the Messages and Papers of the Confederacy,* 236–37.

67. Jefferson Davis to the Senate and House of Representatives, Oct. 8, 1862, ibid., 257–59.

68. Samuel W. Melton to James A. Seddon, Nov. 11, 1863, in *OR,* ser. 4, 2:948.

69. James C. Bates to Dear Mary, May 10, 1862, in Bates, *Texas Cavalry Officer's Civil War,* 117 (emphasis in original).

70. Krick, *Staff Officers in Gray,* 10–14; Bartholomees, *Buff Facings and Gilt Buttons,* 123–46; Jones, *Right Hand of Command,* 15–32.

71. Ayling, *Yankee at Arms,* xii, 18 (Jan. 8, 1862).

72. Juliette A. Kinzie to Abraham Lincoln, June 16, 1864. Available at *Abraham Lincoln Papers at the Library of Congress,* Manuscript Division (Washington, D.C.: American Memory Project, [2000–02]), http://memory.loc.gov/cgi-bin/query/r?ammem/mal:@field%28DOCID +@lit%28d3379000%29%29, accessed Sept. 21, 2010 (emphasis in original).

73. Henry K. Burgwyn Jr. to [his mother], May 11, 1862, in Burgwyn, *Captain's War,* 3n6; Henry K. Burgwyn Jr. to [his father], May 20, 1862, ibid.; William H. S. Burgwyn to My dear Parents, May 6, 1862, ibid., 3.

74. On political friendship and patronage in the antebellum era, see Altschuler and Blumin, *Rude Republic,* 117–18. On partisan politics and officer promotions in the Union armies, see Orr, "'All Manner of Schemes and Rascalities,'" 81–103.

75. Favill, *Diary of a Young Officer,* 193 (Sept. 21, 1862).

76. John W. Harris to Dear Ma, Feb. 26, 1862, John W. Harris Letters, TSLA.

77. Robert H. Miller to My Dear Mother, Feb. 20, 1862, in Connor, "Letters of Lieutenant Robert H. Miller," 73 (emphasis in original).

78. Nelson Chapin to Dear Elizabeth, Dec. 14, 1861, Nelson Chapin Correspondence, Civil War Times Illustrated Collection, USAMHI.

79. Soldier [Henry Perkins Goddard], "Justice in the Army," *Washington (D.C.) National Republican,* Mar. 30, 1862, in Goddard, *Good Fight That Didn't End,* 11–12.

80. Fleharty, *Our Regiment,* 9.

81. Brown, *Fourth Regiment of Minnesota Infantry,* 21–22.

82. McCarthy, *Detailed Minutiae of Soldier Life,* 38.

83. Watson, *Liberty and Power,* 46; Herrera, "Guarantors of Liberty and Republic," 24; Rahe, *Inventions of Prudence,* 177–79.

84. Brown, *Fourth Regiment of Minnesota Infantry,* 22.

85. Theophilus Perry to Dear Harriet, Sept. 4, 1862, in Perry, *Widows by the Thousand,* 22–23.

86. Nathaniel Lowe to My *Own* Dear Jen, July 3, 1863, Nathaniel Lowe Papers, Document DL1046.6, JLNC.

87. Soldier [Henry Perkins Goddard], "Justice in the Army," *Washington (D.C.) National Republican,* Mar. 30, 1862, in Goddard, *Good Fight That Didn't End,* 11–12.

88. Favill, *Diary of a Young Officer,* 12 (Apr. 21, 1861).

89. Charles Morfoot to Dear family, Feb. 27, 1863, Charles Morfoot Papers, Document DL1081.19, JLNC; Charles Morfoot, 101st Regiment Ohio Volunteer Infantry, CSR-Union, microfilm 552, reel 76.

90. Dobak, *Freedom by the Sword,* 15.

91. Chauncey H. Cooke to Dear Mother, Apr. 10, 1863, in Cooke, *Badger Boy in Blue,* 46.

92. Higginson, "Regular and Volunteer Officers," 349.

93. Act of Feb. 17, 1864, ch. 58, *Statutes at Large of the Confederate States,* 4:204; Glatthaar, *General Lee's Army,* 199. Gen. Robert E. Lee put an optimistic gloss on the Confederacy's elimination of officer elections: "The recent law abolishing the system of elections, and opening the way to promotion to all who distinguish themselves by the faithful discharge of duty, affords a new incentive to officers and men." *OR,* ser. 1, 46(2):1247–48. Officer elections fell into disuse in both the Union and Confederate armies after 1863, as appointments and promotions became the de facto method for advancement. The Union army abandoned the officer-election system earlier, but the Confederacy was the first to officially abolish the policy. Griffith, *Battle Tactics,* 96.

94. On the tensions and complexities in antebellum participatory democracy, see Ryan, *Civic Wars;* Smith, *Dominion of Voice;* Sinha, *Counterrevolution of Slavery;* Huston, *Land and Freedom;* Voss-Hubbard, *Beyond Party;* Formisano, *For the People;* Neem, *Creating a Nation of Joiners;* and Volk, "Perils of 'Pure Democracy,'" 641–79.

95. On the nineteenth-century international discussion of democracy and its limits, see Kahan, *Liberalism in Nineteenth-Century Europe.* On officer elections and the bonds between officers and volunteers, see Hamner, *Enduring Battle,* 129. On politics in the Union high command, see Goss, *War within the Union High Command.*

3. The Challenges of Company Leadership

1. Herrera, "Guarantors of Liberty and Republic," 14–15; Hill, *Minute Man in Peace and War;* Riker, *Soldiers of the States;* Derthick, *National Guard in Politics;* Laver, *Citizens More than Soldiers;* Weigley, *Towards an American Army;* Hagen and Roberts, *Against All Enemies;* Kemble, *Image of the Army Officer in.*

2. Higginson, "Regular and Volunteer Officers," 349.

3. Ibid., 351.

4. Watson, "Manifest Destiny and Military Professionalism," 471.

5. Skelton, *American Profession of Arms;* Huntington, *Soldier and the State;* Cunliffe, *Soldiers and Civilians;* Kohn, *Eagle and Sword;* Symonds, "Improvised Army at War," 155–71.

6. Bettersworth and Silver, *Mississippi in the Confederacy,* 1:178.

7. Glatthaar, *General Lee's Army,* 194.

8. Ramold, *Baring the Iron Hand,* 35–36.

9. S. Millet Thompson Diary, Sept. 17, 1862, in Thompson, *Thirteenth Regiment of New Hampshire Volunteer Infantry,* 3.

10. Levi Bird Duff to [Harriet Nixon], Dec. 10, 1861, in Duff, *To Petersburg with the Army of the Potomac,* 29.

11. Higginson, "Regular and Volunteer Officers," 351.

12. Ibid., 350.

13. Ibid.

14. Avant, "From Mercenary to Citizen Armies," 42; Skelton, *American Profession of Arms,* 87–89; Linderman, *World within War,* 205–10; Skelton, "West Point and Officer Professionalism," 22–37.

15. Samuel A. Craig Diary, Feb. 5, 1862, Civil War Times Illustrated Collection, USAMHI.

16. Higginson, "Regular and Volunteer Officers," 351.

17. Avant, "From Mercenary to Citizen Armies," 46.

18. Porter, *One of Morgan's Men,* 115.

19. Cadets from the Georgia Military Institute and Virginia Military Institute were instrumental in training Confederate volunteers in 1861. See Conrad, *Young Lions,* 37–42; Bohannon, "Cadets, Drillmasters, Draft Dodgers, and Soldiers," 5–29; and Andrew, *Long Gray Lines.*

20. Higginson, "Regular and Volunteer Officers," 351.

21. Many editions and revisions to both Confederate and Union regulations appeared over the course of the war, though it appears that the 1861 versions were the most widely used. See 1861 *C.S. Regulations;* 1861 *U.S. Regulations;* and Craighill, *Army Officer's Pocket Companion.*

22. Higginson, "Regular and Volunteer Officers," 349–50.

23. Andrews, *Hints to Company Officers,* 47–48.

24. The literature concerning company-grade military leadership has flourished since the late twentieth century. For a small sampling, see Clarke, *Guidelines for the Leader and the Commander;* Marshall, *Officer as Leader;* Collins, *Common Sense Training;* Buck and Korb, *Military Leadership;* Malone, *Small Unit Leadership;* Flanagan, *Before the Battle;* Van Creveld, *Command in War;* Nye, *Challenge of Command;* Christopher D. Kolenda, ed., *Leadership: The Warrior's Art* (Carlisle, Pa.: Army War College Foundation Press, 2001); U.S. Department of the Army, *Military Leadership;* and Moten, *Army Officers' Professional Ethic.*

25. The first comprehensive resource describing the role and duties of Civil War officers was August V. Kautz's *The 1865 Customs of Service for Officers of the Army* (1866). Written in 1865 and published just after the Civil War, this book is a distillation of U.S. Army regulations, rules, and customs concerning the leadership and military duties of both regular and volunteer officers. Though it was not available during the war, the book provides information that is a good general representation of the customs and regulations governing both Union and Confederate officers. C. C. Andrews, a captain in the 3rd Minnesota Infantry, wrote his brief but insightful *Hints to Company Officers on their Military Duties* in 1862 while imprisoned in Georgia and published it late in the war. Also see Wood, *Civil War Generalship,* 22.

26. Holmes, *Acts of War*, 340–53.
27. Higginson, "Regular and Volunteer Officers," 350.
28. Ibid., 348.
29. Ibid., 352 (emphasis in original).
30. Shannon, *Organization and Administration of the Union Army*.
31. A. R. H. Ranson to My dear Henry, June 4, 1861, A. R. H. Ranson Papers, Document DL1311.003, JLNC.
32. John Alexander Dale to Dear Brother, Oct. 15, 1862, John Alexander Dale Papers, Document DL0853.001, ibid.
33. Kautz, *Company Clerk*.
34. William Bluffton Miller Diary, May 17, 1863, in Miller, *Fighting for Liberty and Right*, 92.
35. Davis, *Rebels & Yankees*, 44–46.
36. Hannibal Paine to Dear Sister, Feb. 24, 1863, Hannibal Paine Papers, TSLA.
37. John Quincy Adams Campbell Diary, Nov. 8, 1863, in Campbell, *The Union Must Stand*, 130.
38. Henry Newton Comey Diary, June 8, 1863, in Comey, *Legacy of Valor*, 121.
39. Moran, *Anatomy of Courage*, 166–67.
40. William Bluffton Miller Diary, May 25, 1863, in Miller, *Fighting for Liberty and Right*, 93–94.
41. Giles, *Rags and Hope*, 48.
42. William Bluffton Miller Diary, May 10, 1863, in Miller, *Fighting for Liberty and Right*, 89.
43. Willoughby Babcock to [unnamed correspondent], Aug. 16, 1861, in Babcock, *Selections*, 71.
44. William Bluffton Miller Diary, June 4, 1863, in Miller, *Fighting for Liberty and Right*, 96.
45. Thomas Reese Lightfoot to Dear Cousin, May 29, 1861, in Burnett, "Letters of Three Lightfoot Brothers," 389. Also see Bonner, *Mastering America;* Woodward, *Marching Masters*, 37–42.
46. Linderman, *Embattled Courage*, 56.
47. Foote, "Rich Man's War, Rich Man's Fight," 270.
48. Higginson, "Regular and Volunteer Officers," 350 (emphasis in original).
49. Bull, *Soldiering*, 118.
50. Brooks, "Social and Cultural Dynamics of Soldiering in Hood's Texas Brigade," 548.
51. Fleharty, *Our Regiment*, 8 (emphasis in original).
52. Albert Livingston to My Dear Parents, Mar. 24, 1864, Albert Livingston Papers, MOC.
53. Ripley, *Vermont Riflemen*, 108.
54. Marshall, *Army Life*, 55.
55. James M. Williams to My dear little wife, Feb. 28, 1862, in Williams, *From That Terrible Field*, 41–42.
56. James M. Williams to My dear Lizzie, Mar. 18, 1862, ibid., 48–49.
57. John Mark Smither to My Dear Uncle, July 24, 1864, in Parker, *Touched by Fire*, 93–95.
58. John Mark Smither, CSR-Confederate, microfilm 227, reel 34.
59. Martin V. B. Richardson to Dear Sister, Dec. 2, 1861, Martin V. B. Richardson Papers, Document DL0286, JLNC.
60. Stephenson, *Civil War Memoir*, 40.
61. Willoughby Babcock to [unnamed correspondent], Apr. 29, 1861, in Babcock, *Selections*, 46.

62. Willoughby Babcock to [unnamed correspondent], May 8, 1861, ibid.
63. Levi Bird Duff to [Harriet Nixon], Aug. 20, 1861, in Duff, *To Petersburg with the Army of the Potomac,* 15.
64. Francis M. Guernsey to My Dear Fanny, Jan. 23, 1863, Francis M. Guernsey Papers, Document DL0301.37, JLNC.
65. Robert E. Park Diary, July 1, 1863, in Park, "Twelfth Alabama Infantry," 243.
66. Keegan, *Mask of Command,* 316.
67. Samuel A. Craig Diary, Feb. 5, 1862, Civil War Times Illustrated Collection, USAMHI (emphasis in original).
68. Robert Gould Shaw to My dear Effie, Apr. 16, 1862, in Shaw, *Blue-Eyed Child of Fortune,* 191.
69. Charles O. Musser to Dear Sister, Aug. 24, 1863, in Musser, *Soldier Boy,* 82.
70. Brooks, "Social and Cultural Dynamics of Soldiering in Hood's Texas Brigade," 547. Also see Bledsoe, "Homecircle," 22–43.
71. Carter, *Four Brothers in Blue,* 134; John J. Thompson, 22nd Massachusetts Volunteer Infantry, CSR-Union, microfilm 544, reel 40.
72. Lorenzo A. Miears Memoir, 19, Garland County Historical Society, Hot Springs, Ark.
73. Glatthaar, *General Lee's Army,* 25–26, 188–89.
74. Andrews, *Hints to Company Officers,* 52.
75. Howell, *Henderson County, Texas,* 75–76.
76. William Henry Harrison Clayton to Dear Brother, Aug. 27, 1864, in Clayton, *Damned Iowa Greyhound,* 117–18 (emphasis in original).
77. Charles O. Musser to Dear Father, Feb. 3, 1863, in Musser, *Soldier Boy,* 24.
78. An enrollment act of March 3, 1863, required the consolidation of the companies of any regiment whose strength fell below half of the maximum number prescribed by law. *OR,* ser. 3, 3:91.
79. Richard Byrnes, 28th Massachusetts Volunteer Infantry, CSR-Union, microfilm 544, reel 6.
80. Peter Welsh to My dear wife, May 13, 1863, in Welsh, *Irish Green and Union Blue,* 95.
81. Peter Welsh to My dear wife, Sept. 19, 1863, ibid., 124–25.
82. Peter Welsh to My dear wife, Apr. 14, 1864, ibid., 150.
83. Ibid., 150n2.
84. Edward Lee to My dear Mother, Mar. 12, 1862, Lewis Leigh Collection, USAMHI (emphasis in original).
85. John Beatty Diary, Sept. 26, 1861, in Beatty, *Citizen-Soldier,* 70.
86. John Beatty Diary, Oct. 6, 1861, ibid., 76.
87. Wilson, *History of a Volunteer Regiment,* 15.
88. William Bluffton Miller Diary, June 4, 1863, in Miller, *Fighting for Liberty and Right,* 96.
89. Samuel Storrow Diary, Oct. 26, 1864, Samuel Storrow Journals, MS 192, Woodson Research Center, Rice University, Houston, Tex.
90. Ibid., Nov. 8, 1864.
91. Carmichael, *Last Generation,* 150–51.
92. Richard Corbin to My Dear Mother, June 8, 1864, in Corbin, *Letters of a Confederate Officer,* 52–53.
93. Foote, *Gentlemen and the Roughs,* 122; Mitchell, *Vacant Chair,* 52, 158.
94. A. L. Harrington to [his brother], June 13, 1864, quoted in Wiley, *Johnny Reb,* 242.

95. Robert Dickinson to Dear Amanda, May 7, 1862, Robert Dickinson Papers, Document DL1236, JLNC.

96. George Anderson Mercer Diary, Oct. 30, 1862, 64–65, Southern Historical Collection, Louis Round Wilson Special Collections Library, University of North Carolina, Chapel Hill.

97. Favill, *Diary of a Young Officer,* 49 (July–Dec. 1861).

98. Robert Gould Shaw to Dearest Mother, Dec. 25, 1861, in Shaw, *Blue-Eyed Child of Fortune,* 168–69 (emphasis in original).

99. Brother Charles to Dear Sister, Oct. 18, 1862, Miscellaneous Civil War Papers, Document DL0065, JLNC.

100. James Newell Lightfoot to Dear Uncle, June 5, 1861, in Burnett, "Letters of Three Lightfoot Brothers," 391.

101. William Henry Harrison Clayton to Dear Brother, Nov. 13, 1862, in Clayton, *Damned Iowa Greyhound,* 26–27.

102. Levi Bird Duff to [Harriet Nixon], Aug. 13, 1861, in Duff, *To Petersburg with the Army of the Potomac,* 13–14.

103. Levi Bird Duff to [Harriet Nixon], Aug. 20, 1861, ibid., 15.

104. Richard Corbin to My Dear Mother, June 8, 1864, in Corbin, *Letters of a Confederate Officer,* 53.

105. Higginson, "Regular and Volunteer Officers," 350.

106. William Bluffton Miller Diary, May 15, 1863, in Miller, *Fighting for Liberty and Right,* 91.

107. Higginson, "Regular and Volunteer Officers," 348.

4. Citizen-Officer Culture

1. Henry Perkins Goddard to Dear Mother, Sept. 26, 1862, in Goddard, *Good Fight That Didn't End,* 64–65.

2. William R. J. Pegram to My Dear Jennie, Apr. 3, 1862, Pegram-Johnson-McIntosh Papers, VHS.

3. Skelton, *American Profession of Arms,* 167–69; Peskin, *Winfield Scott and the Profession of Arms,* 58–59; Wetteman, *Privilege vs. Equality,* 45–72; Watson, "Professionalism, Social Attitudes, and Civil-Military Accountability"; Watson, "Continuity in Civil-Military Relations and Expertise," 221–50; Molloy, "Technical Education and the Young Republic"; Morrison, *"Best School in the World";* Skelton, "Commanding Generals and the Question of Civil Control," 153–72. On the development of institutional culture in armed forces, see Wilson, "Defining Military Culture," 11–41.

4. On the similarities of Union and Confederate leadership, doctrine, tactics, and equipment, and why these similarities may have contributed to battlefield equilibrium during the Civil War, see Perello, *Quest for Annihilation,* and Hsieh, *West Pointers and the Civil War.*

5. Oliver Wendell Holmes Jr. to My Dear Old Dad, Mar. 29, 1863, in Holmes, *Touched with Fire,* 90–91 (emphasis in original).

6. Small, *Road to Richmond,* 12–13.

7. William R. J. Pegram to My Dear Jennie, Oct. 7, 1862, Pegram-Johnson-McIntosh Papers, VHS.

8. Levi Bird Duff to [Harriet Nixon], Dec. 10, 1861, in Duff, *To Petersburg with the Army of the Potomac,* 29.

9. Committee of the Regimental Association, *Thirty-Fifth Massachusetts*, 220.

10. Donald, "Confederate as a Fighting Man," 178–93; Brooks, "Social and Cultural Dynamics of Soldiering in Hood's Texas Brigade," 535–72; Glatthaar, *General Lee's Army*, 186–99; Ramold, *Baring the Iron Hand*, 43–78; Gallagher, *Union War*, 124, 158–62.

11. *OR*, ser. 4, 2:1001.

12. *Statutes at Large of the United States Congress*, 38th Cong., 1st Sess., June 25, 1864, Ch. 149, 181–82.

13. Haughton, *Training, Tactics, and Leadership*, 119.

14. John William De Forest to [his wife], May 23, 1862, in De Forest, *Volunteer's Adventures*, 23.

15. William Bluffton Miller Diary, May 14, 1863, in Miller, *Fighting for Liberty and Right*, 91; Harrison H. Wheeler Service Record, Index to Compiled Service Records of Volunteer Union Soldiers Who Served in Organizations from the State of Ohio, 75th Regiment Ohio Volunteer Infantry, RG 94, NARA, microfilm 540, reel 82; James W. Swaney Service Record, ibid.

16. John William De Forest to [his wife], May 23, 1862, in De Forest, *Volunteer's Adventures*, 23.

17. Kautz, *1865 Customs of Service*, 19.

18. Newell and Shrader, *Of Duty Well and Faithfully Done*, 70–73; Eicher and Eicher, *Civil War High Commands*, 71; Weigley, *United States Army*, 199; Spiller, "From Hero to Leader," 196.

19. Coffman, *Old Army*, 92; Davis, *Rebels & Yankees*, 29; Newell and Shrader, *Of Duty Well and Faithfully Done*, 70–73.

20. Bartholomees, *Buff Facings and Gilt Buttons*, 123–41; R Jones, *Right Hand of Command*, 15–20; Newell and Shrader, *Of Duty Well and Faithfully Done*, 70.

21. Graves, "'Dry Books of Tactics,'" 50–61, 173–77; Graves and Frederiksen, "'Dry Books of Tactics' Re-Read," 64–65.

22. Hardee, *Rifle and Light Infantry Tactics* (1855); Casey, *Infantry Tactics*; Gibbon, *Artillerist's Manual*; McWhiney and Jamieson, *Attack and Die*, 49–58; Hsieh, *West Pointers and the Civil War*, 82–90.

23. Adjutant General's Office, General Orders No. 15, May 4, 1861, in U.S. War Department, *General Orders Affecting the Volunteer Force* (1862), 1:1; Act of July 22, 1861, ch. 9, sec. 10, *Statutes at Large of the United States*, 12:270; Eicher and Eicher, *Civil War High Commands*, 66; *OR*, ser. 3, 3:175. Artillery batteries were typically commanded by captains, and two-gun sections within the battery were led by lieutenants.

24. Kautz, *1865 Customs of Service*, 223–24.

25. Ibid., 224.

26. Butterfield, *Camp and Outpost Duty for Infantry*, 114 (emphasis in original).

27. Kautz, *1865 Customs of Service*, 225.

28. Ibid., 231.

29. Andrews, *Hints to Company Officers*, 29.

30. Union and Confederate regulations were nearly identical concerning the responsibilities of company officers and the routines of camp, garrison, and campaign. See 1861 *U.S. Regulations*, Art. XXVIII, 39; and 1861 *C.S. Regulations*, Art. XXVIII, 24.

31. 1861 *U.S. Regulations*, Art. XXVIII, 39; 1861 *C.S. Regulations*, Art. XXVIII, 24.

32. 1861 *U.S. Regulations*, Art. XIII, 21; 1861 *C.S. Regulations*, Art. XIII, 10.

33. 1861 *U.S. Regulations*, Art. XXXII, 58–61; Art. XXXIII, 61–65; and Art. XXXVI, 84–87; 1861 *C.S. Regulations*, Art. XXXIII, 48–51; and Art. XXXVI, 71–75.

34. Wilbur Fisk to [unnamed correspondent], Nov. 25, 1864, Civil War Times Illustrated Collection, USAMHI.

35. Genovese, "Chivalric Tradition in the Old South," 180–98; Carmichael, *Last Generation,* 59–61; Berry, *All That Makes a Man,* 171–72; Wyatt-Brown, *Southern Honor,* 26–29, 89–102; Rotundo, *American Manhood,* 232–35; Carnes and Griffen, *Meanings for Manhood,* 190–92; Nye, "Western Masculinities in War and Peace," 417–38. On antebellum class, professions, and gentlemanliness, see Bowman, *At the Precipice.*

36. James B. Griffin to My Darling Wife, July 11, 1861, in McArthur and Burton, *Gentleman and an Officer,* 98–99.

37. Stiles, *Four Years under Marse Robert,* 110.

38. William McKnight to Dear Wife, Jan. 12, 1863, in McKnight, *Do They Miss Me At Home?,* 42. Historian Michael Barton, in his study of Civil War volunteers and their writings, finds that citizen-soldiers and officers on both sides of the conflict esteemed the personal qualities of virtue, morality, and integrity even more than kindness, friendliness, competence, or courage. See Barton, *Goodmen,* 24, 35–36.

39. George W. Browning to [Cinda Browning], n.d., George W. Browning Papers, Document DL0152.43, JLNC.

40. Alfred E. Doby to My Darling Wife, Jan. 15, 1863, Alfred E. Doby Letters, MOC.

41. S. Millet Thompson to [Emma A. Griffin], May 22, 1863, S. Millet Thompson Papers, Document DL0799, JLNC.

42. Judith Farrer Watkins to Dear Capt. Clements, Feb. 21, 1864, Cary Family Papers, VHS.

43. George M. Lalane Diary, Feb. 14, 1864, MOC.

44. Ibid., Mar. 8, 1864.

45. Robert H. Dungan to Sir, [n.d.], 1864, Samuel Thompson Buchanan Letters, VHS.

46. Watson B. Smith to Dear Father, Sept. 1, 1863, Watson B. Smith Papers, Document DL1119, JLNC.

47. Kautz, *1865 Customs of Service,* 19–20.

48. Glatthaar, *General Lee's Army,* 194.

49. Ramold, *Baring the Iron Hand,* 124.

50. Levi Bird Duff to [Harriet Nixon], Nov. 13, 1861, in Duff, *To Petersburg with the Army of the Potomac,* 27–28.

51. Alexander Swift "Sandie" Pendleton to My Dear Lella, Apr. 16, 1863, Alexander Swift Pendleton Papers, Document DL0476, JLNC.

52. Samuel Storrow Diary, Nov. 25, 1864, Samuel Storrow Journals, MS 192, Woodson Research Center, Rice University, Houston, Tex.

53. According to both the Union and Confederate Articles of War: "No officer or soldier shall send a challenge to another officer or soldier, to fight a duel, or accept a challenge if sent, upon pain, if a commissioned officer, of being cashiered; if a non-commissioned officer or soldier, of suffering corporeal punishment, at the discretion of a court-martial." 1861 *U.S. Regulations,* Art. XXV, 489; 1861 *C.S. Regulations,* Art. XXV, 178. On dueling among Civil War officers, see Huff, "Last Duel in Arkansas," 36–49; Wyatt-Brown, *Southern Honor;* Foote, *Gentlemen and the Roughs,* 78, 94–119; and Frevert, *Men of Honour.*

54. "Introduction," in Babcock, *Selections,* 69.

55. Kautz, *1865 Customs of Service,* 20.

56. James P. Douglas to Dear Sallie, Dec. 10, 1861, in Douglas, *Douglas's Texas Battery,* 22–23.

57. George W. Browning to My Dear Wife, Oct. 19, 1863, George W. Browning Papers, Document DL0152.67, JLNC.

58. Charles G. Blake to My dear Judith, Aug. 8, 1863, Charles G. Blake Papers, Document DL0603, ibid.

59. Ibid. (emphasis in original).

60. John Hampden Chamberlayne to My dear friend, July 17, 1862, John Hampden Chamberlayne Papers, VHS.

61. John Hampden Chamberlayne to My dear Mother, Nov. 11, 1862, ibid.

62. Courtland G. Stanton to Dear Mamie, Dec. 3, 1864, Courtland G. Stanton Papers, Document DL0011.102, JLNC.

63. George Washington Whitman to Dear Mother, Apr. 12, 1862, in Whitman, *Civil War Letters,* 50.

64. Robert Gould Shaw to Dear Mother, May 19, 1861, in Shaw, *Blue-Eyed Child of Fortune,* 101.

65. Brother Charles to Dear Sister, Oct. 18, 1862, Miscellaneous Civil War Papers, Document DL0065, JLNC.

66. George Washington Whitman to Dear Mother and all the rest, Apr. 27, 1862, in Whitman, *Civil War Letters,* 51 (emphasis in original).

67. Boatner, *Civil War Dictionary,* 624. On the controversies over black soldiers' pay in the Union army, see Glatthaar, *Forged in Battle,* 169–76.

68. Joseph J. Hoyle to My Dear wife, Apr. 16, 1863, in Hoyle, *"Deliver Us from This Cruel War,"* 105 (emphasis in original).

69. E. L. Coleman to Dear Friend, Feb. 5, 1862, E. L. Coleman Papers, MOC (emphasis in original).

70. Theodore Preston Kellogg to Dear Sarah, Jan. 19, 1862, Theodore Preston Kellogg Papers, Document DL0200, JLNC.

71. Goss, *Recollections of a Private,* 73.

72. John William De Forest to [his wife], Oct. 1, 1862, in De Forest, *Volunteer's Adventures,* 48–49.

73. Woodward, *Marching Masters,* 80–88.

74. Alexander Swift "Sandie" Pendleton to My Dear Lella, Apr. 16, 1863, Alexander Swift Pendleton Papers, Document DL0476, JLNC.

75. William H. S. Burgwyn Diary, Feb. 1, 1863, in Burgwyn, *Captain's War,* 56; William H. S. Burgwyn to Dear Mother, Jan. 5, 1863, ibid., 57; Glatthaar, *General Lee's Army,* 309–14; Carmichael, "'We Were the 'Men.'"

76. Ujanirtus Allen to [Susan Allen], Apr. 18, 1862, in Allen, *Campaigning with "Old Stonewall,"* 86.

77. Ujanirtus Allen to [Susan Allen], Apr. 27, 1863, ibid., 229.

78. 1861 *U.S. Regulations,* Art. XIII, 24; 1861 *C.S. Regulations,* Art. XIII, 17.

79. George Washington Whitman to Dear Mother, Apr. 12, 1862, in Whitman, *Civil War Letters,* 50.

80. Clark, *Histories of the Several Regiments and Battalions from North Carolina,* 1:220–21.

81. James B. Griffin to My Dearest Wife, Feb. 2, 1862, in McArthur and Burton, *Gentleman and an Officer,* 148. On the importance of honor and reputation among elite white Southern men, see Wyatt-Brown, *Southern Honor,* and Ayers, *Vengeance and Justice.*

82. James H. Gillam to Dear Companion, Dec. 30, 1862, James H. Gillam Papers, USAMHI.

83. On the utility of the symbols of office in enforcing discipline in the Union army, see Foote, *Gentlemen and the Roughs,* 152, 158–59. Foote notes that angry volunteers occasionally challenged their citizen-officers to fistfights on the condition that the latter first remove their rank insignia.

84. "The sword and sword-belt will be worn upon all occasions of duty, without exception." 1861 *U.S. Regulations,* Art. LI, 483. Also see 1861 *C.S. Regulations,* Art. XIII, 11.

85. "An officer under arrest will not wear a sword, or visit officially his commanding or other superior officer, unless sent for; and in case of business, he will make known his object in writing." 1861 *U.S. Regulations,* Art. XXVII, 39; 1861 *C.S. Regulations,* Art. XXVII, 30.

86. Keegan, *Mask of Command,* 4.

87. Thomas Blackburn Rodgers Memoir, Pennsylvania 140th Infantry Regimental Papers, Brake Collection, USAMHI.

88. Wilbur Fisk to [unnamed correspondent], Nov. 25, 1864, Civil War Times Illustrated Collection, USAMHI.

89. Ibid.

90. John W. Harris to Dear Ma, Aug. 30, 1863, John W. Harris Papers, TSLA.

91. Henry Clay Matrau to My Dear Parents, Oct. 30, 1864, in Matrau, *Letters Home,* 98–99.

92. 1861 *U.S. Regulations,* Art. XLII, 171; and Art. XLIII, 245–46; 1861 *C.S. Regulations,* Art. XLII, 129. Due to Confederate supply problems and material shortages by 1864, regulations permitted officers to draw a private's allowance of clothing and rations if needed. Adjutant and Inspector General's Office, General Orders No. 28, Mar. 6, 1864, in Confederate States War Department, *General Orders . . . 1864,* 42–43.

93. George Washington Weston to My Dearest Emelia, Mar. 3, 1863, George Washington Weston Papers, Document DL1412.24, JLNC (emphasis in original).

94. Arliskas, *Cadet Gray and Butternut Blue,* 70–72.

95. Courtland G. Stanton to Dear Mamie, Nov. 4, 1864, Courtland G. Stanton Papers, Document DL0011.100, JLNC (emphasis in original).

96. Charles J. Mills to Dear Mother, Jan. 21, 1864, Charles J. Mills Letters, USAMHI.

97. George Washington Whitman to Dear Mother, June 1, 1862, in Whitman, *Civil War Letters,* 53–54.

98. Arthur L. Conger to Miss Edgerly, [n.d.], 1864, Arthur L. Conger Papers, USAMHI.

99. Wright, *Language of the Civil War,* 59.

5. The Early War Combat Experience

1. John Pelham to [his father], July 23, 1861, *Jacksonville (Ala.) Republican,* Aug. 8, 1861.
2. Thomas J. Goree to Dear Uncle Pleas, Aug. 2, 1861, in Goree, *Longstreet's Aide,* 28.
3. J. A. McPherson to [the editors], July 22, 1861, *Fayetteville (N.C.) Observer,* July 29, 1861.
4. John Pelham to [his father], July 23, 1861, *Jacksonville (Ala.) Republican,* Aug. 8, 1861.
5. Baylor, *Bull Run to Bull Run,* 22.
6. Hennessy, *First Battle of Manassas,* 63–64.
7. Curtis, *Bull Run to Chancellorsville,* 42–45.
8. John S. Ellis to [unnamed correspondent], Aug. 2, 1861, *San Francisco Bulletin,* Aug. 20, 1861.
9. Thomas J. Goree to Dear Uncle Pleas, Aug. 2, 1861, in Goree, *Longstreet's Aide,* 27.
10. Eugene Carter to [his father], [n.d.], 1861, in Carter, *Four Brothers in Blue,* 9.

11. Curtis, *Bull Run to Chancellorsville,* 42–45.

12. McDonough, *Shiloh,* 175; Frank and Reaves, *"Seeing the Elephant,"* 140–47.

13. Duke, *Fifty-Third Ohio Volunteer Infantry,* 2.

14. McDonough, *Shiloh,* 91; Cunningham, *Shiloh and the Western Campaign of 1862,* 135.

15. Dawes, "My First Day under Fire at Shiloh," 4:4.

16. Ibid., 5–11 (emphasis in original).

17. Dawes mistakenly remembers Cpl. William M. Voris as "A. C. Voris." William M. Voris, 17th Regiment Illinois Volunteer Infantry, CSR-Union, microfilm 539, reel 93.

18. Dawes, "My First Day under Fire at Shiloh," 11–12.

19. Ibid., 13–14 (emphasis in original).

20. Ibid., 16–17.

21. Ibid., 17.

22. Duke, *Fifty-Third Ohio Volunteer Infantry,* 250–51; Ephraim Cutler Dawes, 53rd Regiment Ohio Volunteer Infantry, CSR-Union, microfilm 552, reel 25.

23. Duke, *Fifty-Third Ohio Volunteer Infantry,* 293–94; William B. Stephenson CSR, 53rd Regiment Ohio Volunteer Infantry, CSR-Union, microfilm 552, reel 104.

24. Duke, *Fifty-Third Ohio Volunteer Infantry,* 247–48; Wells S. Jones, 53rd Regiment Ohio Volunteer Infantry, CSR-Union, microfilm 552, reel 56.

25. Duke, *Fifty-Third Ohio Volunteer Infantry,* 255–56; James R. Percy, 53rd Regiment Ohio Volunteer Infantry, CSR-Union, microfilm 552, reel 83; Dawes, "Hero of the War," 298.

26. William M. Voris, 17th Regiment Illinois Volunteer Infantry, CSR-Union, microfilm 539, reel 93; William M. Voris, 47th U.S. Colored Troops, ibid., microfilm 589, reel 89; Plaque C-60, African American Civil War Memorial, Washington, D.C.

27. Jesse J. Appler, 53rd Regiment Ohio Volunteer Infantry, CSR-Union, microfilm 552, reel 3; Duke, *Fifty-Third Ohio Volunteer Infantry,* 90.

28. Boyd, *Civil War Diary,* 30–32 (Apr. 7, 1862; emphasis in original).

29. "Captain H.," in Moore, *Civil War in Song and Story,* 64 (emphasis in original).

30. Boyd, *Civil War Diary,* 37–38 (Apr. 7, 1862; emphasis in original).

31. "Captain H.," in Moore, *Civil War in Song and Story,* 64.

32. Holmes, *Acts of War,* 341–42; Linderman, *Embattled Courage,* 22–23, 44–60.

33. Linderman, *Embattled Courage,* 34, 44–45; Hess, *Union Soldier in Battle,* 95–96.

34. Linderman, *Embattled Courage,* 156–58.

35. Kautz, *1865 Customs of Service,* 19.

36. Charles P. Mattocks to Dear Mother, May 10, 1863, in Mattocks, *"Unspoiled Heart,"* 31 (emphasis in original).

37. Moran, *Anatomy of Courage,* 188.

38. Carmichael, *Lee's Young Artillerist,* 63, 78.

39. Ibid., 56.

40. William R. J. Pegram to My Dearest Jennie, Aug. 14, 1862, Pegram-Johnson-McIntosh Papers, VHS.

41. Carmichael, *Lee's Young Artillerist,* 166.

42. Heth, *Memoirs,* 195.

43. Wise, "Boy Gunners of Lee," 156.

44. McCabe, "Address to the Annual Reunion of Pegram's Battalion, . . . 1886," 6.

45. Goolsby, "Col. William Johnston Pegram," 271.

46. Fleet, *Green Mount,* 262.

47. Carmichael, *Lee's Young Artillerist,* 63.
48. Oliver Wendell Holmes, Jr., to My Dear Mother, Oct. 23, 1861, in Holmes, *Touched with Fire,* 13.
49. Small, *Road to Richmond,* 65.
50. *OR,* ser. 1, 19(1):1043–45.
51. Linderman, *Embattled Courage,* 47–50.
52. Robert Gould Shaw to Dearest Mother, June 16, 1861, in Shaw, *Blue-Eyed Child of Fortune,* 109.
53. Stephen D. Clements to [Mary Catherine (Holmes) Clements], [n.d.], 1861, Cary Family Papers, VHS (emphasis in original).
54. Simeon C. Wilkerson to My Dear Wife, June 20, 1863, Simeon C. Wilkerson Papers, Document DL1339, JLNC.
55. William Bluffton Miller Diary, May 12, 1863, in Miller, *Fighting for Liberty and Right,* 90; Henry C. Sweet, 15th Regiment Ohio Volunteer Infantry, CSR-Union, microfilm 552, reel 107.
56. Park, "Diary," 372–73 (June 12, 1864).
57. William Fielding Baugh to My Dearest Pinkie, Aug. 3, 1862, William F. Baugh Letters, VHS.
58. Matthew S. Austin to My Dear Mother, Apr. 24, 1863, Matthew S. Austin Papers, Document DL0956.5, JLNC.
59. Henry C. Lyon to Brother Sam, June 24, 1861, in Lyon, *"Desolating This Fair Country,"* 119–21.
60. Donald, "Confederate as a Fighting Man," 180–81; Donald, "Died of Democracy," in Hattaway and Jones, *Why the North Won the Civil War,* 81–92.
61. Linderman, *Embattled Courage,* 42–43; Glatthaar, *General Lee's Army,* 176–77; Ramold, *Baring the Iron Hand,* 377. Ramold finds that indiscipline in some Union regiments had reached nearly uncontrollable levels by 1863.
62. Foote, *Gentlemen and the Roughs;* Ramold, *Baring the Iron Hand,* 395.
63. Glatthaar, *General Lee's Army,* 438.
64. William Henry Harrison Lewis to Dear Mother, July 30, 1862, in Evans, *16th Mississippi Infantry,* 94–95.
65. Robert Gould Shaw to My Dear Susie, June 6, 1862, in Shaw, *Blue-Eyed Child of Fortune,* 207.
66. George Thomas Blakemore Diary, June 26, 1862, George Thomas Blakemore Papers, TSLA.
67. Lyster, "Recollections of the Bull Run Campaign," 17.
68. Weitz, "Drill, Training, and the Combat Performance of the Civil War Soldier," 276–77.
69. Glatthaar, *General Lee's Army,* 197–99; Foote, *Gentlemen and the Roughs,* 10n16.
70. Bradwell, *Under the Southern Cross,* 63–64.
71. Costello, *Adventures of a Soldier,* 151.
72. Holmes, *Acts of War,* 341–42.
73. Glatthaar, *General Lee's Army,* 196–99. No comparable casualty study currently exists for the Union officer corps.
74. See Appendixes 3–7.
75. Faust, *This Republic of Suffering,* 274n2.
76. See Appendixes 3, 5, and 7. Union armies, like their Confederate counterparts, also demanded courageous officers willing to demonstrate leadership by examples of physical cour-

age and technical proficiency. See, for example, Catton, "Union Discipline and Leadership," 18–25.

77. C.S. War Department, Circular, June 3, 1862, in Field and Robin Smith, *Uniforms of the Civil War,* 269.

78. Adjutant General's Office, General Orders No. 286, Nov. 22, 1864, in U.S. War Department, *General Orders Affecting the Volunteer Force* (1864), 4:170.

79. For detailed instructions for the precise positions of company officers in various formations, see Hardee, *Rifle and Light Infantry Tactics* (1862), 89–102. On the hazards and difficulties of Civil War officers engaging in linear battlefield tactics, see Hamner, *Enduring Battle,* 30–31, 40–41, 62.

80. Muir, *Tactics and the Experience of Battle in the Age of Napoleon,* 190–92. The hazards of regimental and company command were not unique to Civil War armies. Company-grade officers in the armies of the Napoleonic Wars faced similar dangers, with French, British, and Allied infantry officers sustaining disproportionately greater casualties than did their enlisted men.

81. McWhiney and Jamieson, *Attack and Die,* 99–111; Hess, *Rifle Musket in Civil War Combat,* 198–208, 213–15. Hess disagrees with McWhiney and Jamieson about the influence of the rifled musket on the tactics and deadliness of Civil War battles, arguing that these weapons were far less destructive than historians have previously believed. Nevertheless, after 1863 commanders seem to have been more hesitant to make frontal assaults against entrenched enemy positions than in 1861–62, with the 1864 assaults at Cold Harbor, Kennesaw Mountain, and Franklin among the notable exceptions.

82. John Quincy Adams Campbell Diary, Sept. 20, 1862, in Campbell, *The Union Must Stand,* 60.

83. David W. Norton Diary, Nov. 12, 1862, quoted in Sword, *Courage under Fire,* 21.

84. George Washington Whitman to Dear Mother, Sept. 5, 1862, in Whitman, *Civil War Letters,* 61–62.

85. William Francis Bartlett to My Dear Mother, Oct. 25, 1861, in Palfrey, *Memoir of Wm. F. Bartlett,* 23–24 (emphasis in original).

86. John William De Forest to [his wife], Dec. 7, 1862, in De Forest, *Volunteer's Adventures,* 75.

87. Oliver Wendell Holmes Jr. to Dear Parents, June 2, 1862, in Holmes, *Touched with Fire,* 47.

88. Oliver Wendell Holmes Jr. to My Dear Mother and Father, July 5, 1862, ibid., 58–60 (emphasis in original).

89. Ibid.

90. Historian Mark A. Weitz finds that the incessant drill exercises of the Civil War's infantry-heavy armies not only instilled combat discipline in volunteers but also served to bind them together psychologically. "Close order marching drew upon a primitive human behavioral form of sociality. Training and marching in unison bonded men together in a unique way and created a special sense of cooperativeness and of belonging among men sharing a common danger. Close order drill and training made professionals out of the amateurs. It transformed the mass of civilians into men inured to war, a change undergone by the Civil War recruits." Weitz, "Drill, Training, and the Combat Performance of the Civil War Soldier," 271.

91. McPherson, *For Cause and Comrades,* 48–51; Linderman, *Embattled Courage,* 43–56. Lorien Foote argues that wealthy, elite Union citizen-officers, the so-called "Brahmins" of

Massachusetts, tended to use harsh forms of discipline and coercion in their regiments even in 1861, far earlier than most Civil War volunteer units. Foote, "Rich Man's War, Rich Man's Fight," 285. Also see Miller, "Brahmins under Fire:," 75–109; and Meier, *Nature's Civil War,* 134.

92. Eugene Carter to [his father], [n.d.], 1861, in Carter, *Four Brothers in Blue,* 9.

93. Hamner, *Enduring Battle,* 123; Wood, *Civil War Generalship,* 14.

94. McPherson, *For Cause and Comrades,* 50; Radley, *Rebel Watchdog,* 102–108; Linderman, *Embattled Courage,* 171. Also see Marrs, "Desertion and Loyalty in the South Carolina Infantry," 47–65; Weitz, *More Damning than Slaughter;* and Emerson, "Leadership and Civil War Desertion," 20–21.

95. *OR,* ser. 1, 10(1):469–70.

96. Ibid., 22(1):83.

97. U.S. War Department, *U.S. Infantry Tactics,* 426.

98. Garrison, *Amazing Civil War,* 155. Garrison characterizes Civil War officers' reluctance to speak about file closers in combat as a "conspiracy of silence."

99. Oliver Wendell Holmes, Jr., to Dear Parents, June 2, 1862, in Holmes, *Touched with Fire,* 51–52 (emphasis in original).

100. *OR,* ser. 1, 11(2):145–46.

101. General Orders No. 4, ibid., 46(2):1249–50.

102. Ibid.

103. Billings, *Hardtack and Coffee,* 152.

104. Robert Gould Shaw to My Dear Susie, June 6, 1862, in Shaw, *Blue-Eyed Child of Fortune,* 207. Civil War "fragging," or the deliberate targeting of officers by their own troops, remains a difficult subject for modern historians to address; such incidents undoubtedly occurred, but documentation is often scarce.

105. Charles P. Mattocks to Dear Mother, May 10, 1863, in Mattocks, *"Unspoiled Heart,"* 31.

106. William Henry Harrison Clayton to Dear Father, Mother, and Brothers, July 24, 1864, in Clayton, *Damned Iowa Greyhound,* 101–102.

107. Robert Gould Shaw to Dearest Mother, Aug. 12, 1862, in Shaw, *Blue-Eyed Child of Fortune,* 231.

108. Gordon, *Organization and Early History of the Second Mass. Regiment of Infantry,* 13–17.

109. Pfanz, *Gettysburg—Culp's Hill & Cemetery Hill,* 350.

110. Billings, *Hardtack and Coffee,* 154.

6. Maturation of the Volunteer Junior Officer Corps

1. Stewart, *Pickett's Charge,* 266; Hess, *Pickett's Charge,* 335.

2. Henry Thweatt Owen to my dear Wife, Dec. 21, 1863, in Owen, *War of Confederate Captain Henry T. Owen,* 111.

3. Ibid., 111–13.

4. Holmes, *Acts of War,* 255; Dean, *Shook over Hell;* Miller, "Confederate Amputees and the Women Who Loved (or Tried to Love) Them," 301–20; Shaffer, *After the Glory.*

5. Faust, *This Republic of Suffering,* 14–31.

6. Edgar L. Bumpus to Rev. L. R. Eastman Jr., n.d., Edgar L. Bumpus Papers, Document DL0583.6, JLNC.

7. Edgar L. Bumpus, 33rd Regiment Massachusetts Volunteer Infantry, CSR-Union, micro-

film 554, reel 5.

8. Linderman, *Embattled Courage*, 252–57; Hess, *Union Soldier in Battle*, 103–105.

9. Charles Harvey Brewster to Dear Mother, May 11, 1864, in Brewster, *When This Cruel War Is Over*, 295.

10. Columbus Sykes to My Dear Darling, May 29, 1864, in Strayer and Baumgartner, *Echoes of Battle*, 123.

11. Levi Bird Duff to [Harriet Nixon Duff], Jan. 1, 1863, in Duff, *To Petersburg with the Army of the Potomac*, 102.

12. Richard W. Corbin to My Dear Father, June 10, 1864, in Corbin, *Letters of a Confederate Officer*, 52–53. Along with increased religiosity, disillusionment, and emotional distancing, citizen-officers and volunteers experienced a vast spectrum of emotional reactions to the trauma of combat. Dean, *Shook over Hell*, 53–69.

13. Jefferson Davis to the Senate and House of Representatives, Dec. 7, 1863, in Richardson, *Compilation of the Messages and Papers of the Confederacy*, 369–70.

14. See Appendixes 4 and 6.

15. James Litton Cooper Memoir, 43, TSLA. Though Cooper was apparently promoted to captain in the war's final months, it is unclear from surviving records when or if he ever officially mustered in at that rank. Alderson, "Civil War Diary of Captain James Litton Cooper," 141–73.

16. William Cowper Nelson to My Dearest Mother, Feb. 22, 1863, in Nelson, *Hour of Our Nation's Agony*, 118–19.

17. Henry Clay Matrau to My Dear Parents, Oct. 30, 1864, in Matrau, *Letters Home*, 98–99.

18. Linderman, *Embattled Courage*, 240–45.

19. Henry Livermore Abbott to My Dear Papa, July 6, 1863, in Abbott, *Fallen Leaves*, 186; Henry Livermore Abbott, 20th Regiment Massachusetts Volunteer Infantry, CSR-Union, microfilm 544, reel 1.

20. William Henry Harrison Lewis to [his mother], Aug. 22, 1863, in Evans, *16th Mississippi Infantry*, 198–99.

21. McPherson, *Battle Cry of Freedom*, 721–22; Royster, *Destructive War*, 332–36; Grimsley, *And Keep Moving On*, 161–64.

22. Charles Harvey Brewster to Dear Mary, Apr. 30, 1864, in Brewster, *When This Cruel War Is Over*, 290.

23. George A. Bowen, 12th Regiment New Jersey Volunteer Infantry, CSR-Union, microfilm 550, reel 2; George A. Bowen Diary, May 12, 1864, George A. Bowen Papers, USAMHI.

24. Charles Harvey Brewster to Dear Mary, May 13, 1864, in Brewster, *When This Cruel War Is Over*, 295–96.

25. Richard W. Corbin to My Dear Father, June 10, 1864, in Corbin, *Letters of a Confederate Officer*, 52–53.

26. Hess, *Union Soldier in Battle*, 113–17; Glatthaar, *General Lee's Army*, 421–24.

27. Henry Livermore Abbott to My Dear Mother, Mar. 27, 1864, in Abbott, *Fallen Leaves*, 241.

28. Park, "Diary," 372 (June 10, 1864).

29. Linderman, *Embattled Courage*, 156–60.

30. Robert P. Findley Journal, June 2, 1864, in *Xenia (Ohio) Torch-Light*, July 6, 1864, quoted in Strayer and Baumgartner, *Echoes of Battle*, 153.

31. Charles Harvey Brewster to Dear Mary, Apr. 30, 1864, in Brewster, *When This Cruel War Is Over*, 290–91.

32. Andrews, *Hints to Company Officers*, 58.

33. William H. S. Burgwyn Diary, May 16, 1864, in Burgwyn, *Captain's War*, 143.

34. De Forest, *Volunteer's Adventures*, 187.

35. Glatthaar, "Dynamic for Success and Failure," 72.

36. Ramold, *Baring the Iron Hand*, 78.

37. Weitz, "Drill, Training, and the Combat Performance of the Civil War Soldier," 270.

38. Ibid., 288; Mahon, "Civil War Infantry Assault Tactics," 63–64. Mahon argues that Civil War troops employed covering fire techniques in assaults on fortifications as early as 1862.

39. Fitzpatrick, "Emory Upton," 102–108; *OR*, 36(1):660–68; Matter, *If It Takes All Summer*, 160–62.

40. Weitz, "Shoot Them All," 333; Jacobson and Rupp, *For Cause & For Country*, 248.

41. Weitz, "Drill, Training, and the Combat Performance of the Civil War Soldier," 289; Nosworthy, *Bloody Crucible of Courage*, 258–79.

42. Nosworthy, *Bloody Crucible of Courage*, 521–32.

43. Tourgée, *Story of a Thousand*, 217–18.

44. Ibid., 218–19.

45. George A. Bowen Diary, May 6, 1864, George A. Bowen Papers, USAMHI.

46. Rice, *Yankee Tigers*, 99–105.

47. Charles W. Wills Diary, May 27, 1864, in Wills, *Army Life of an Illinois Soldier*, 249–50.

48. John William Tuttle Diary, May 25, 1864, in Tuttle, *Union, the Civil War, and John W. Tuttle*, 186–87.

49. Calhoun, *42d Regiment Georgia Volunteers*, 37; John S. Stubbs, CSR-Confederate, microfilm 226, reel 58; Robert J. Henderson CSR, ibid., reel 28; J. T. Mitchell CSR, ibid., reel 43.

50. Calhoun, *42d Regiment Georgia Volunteers*, 37.

51. Mahon, "Civil War Infantry Assault Tactics," 62.

52. Moseley, "Evolution of the American Civil War Infantry Tactics," 369; McWhiney and Jamieson, *Attack and Die*, 100–101; Griffith, *Battle Tactics*, 155; Haughton, *Training, Tactics, and Leadership;* Grimsley, "Surviving Military Revolution," 74–91; Hess, *Rifle Musket in Civil War Combat*, 173. For a discussion of the postwar lessons of 1864 and 1865, see Jamieson, *Crossing the Deadly Ground*.

53. Lavender, *War Memoirs*, 97–99, copy in Arkansas Historical Commission, Little Rock.

54. James L. Burkhalter Diary, June 27, 1864, in Litvin, "Captain Burkhalter's Georgia War," 497–98 (emphasis in original); James L. Burkhalter, 86th Regiment Illinois Volunteer Infantry, CSR-Union, microfilm 539, reel 12.

55. Hsieh, *West Pointers and the Civil War*, 186–87.

56. Andrews, *Hints to Company Officers*, 60.

57. George A. Bowen Diary, June 3, 1864, George A. Bowen Papers, USAMHI.

58. "The Crime at Pickett's Mill," in Bierce, *Ambrose Bierce's Civil War*, 45–48.

59. Whitman and Turner, *Maine in the War for the Union*, 458–71.

60. Shaw and House, *First Maine Heavy Artillery*, 121–22.

61. Ibid., 455–72.

62. Ibid., 141–42.

63. George Washington, "Address to the New York Provincial Congress," June 26, 1775, in *Papers*, 41.

64. Peter Welsh to Dear brother Frank, Apr. [?], 1864, in Welsh, *Irish Green and Union Blue*, 155.

65. Mary Stanton to My own Dear Court, Feb. 24, 1865, Courtland G. Stanton Papers, Document DL0011.140, JLNC.

66. George W. Squier to [his wife], Sept. 4, 1864, in Squier, *This Wilderness of War,* 78. On Union soldiers, emancipation, and motivation, see Manning, *What This Cruel War Was Over,* and White, *Emancipation, the Union Army, and the Reelection of Abraham Lincoln.*

67. Levi Bird Duff to [Harriet Nixon Duff], Sept. 26, 1862, in Duff, *To Petersburg with the Army of the Potomac,* 75–76.

68. Ibid.

69. Henry Clay Matrau to Dear Father and Mother, June 6, 1865, in Matrau, *Letters Home,* 120–21.

70. George W. Yates to Sir, June 3, 1864, George W. Yates Papers, Document DL0002.2, JLNC.

71. George W. Yates, 4th Regiment Michigan Volunteer Infantry, CSR-Union, microfilm 545, reel 48; George W. Yates, 45th Regiment Missouri Volunteer Infantry, ibid., microfilm 390, reel 54; George W. Yates, 13th Regiment Missouri Volunteer Cavalry, ibid.; Donovan, *Terrible Glory,* 309.

72. John H. Black to My Dear Wife, Mar. 15, 1865, John H. Black Papers, Document DL0785, JLNC.

73. William H. Lambert to My Dear George, Apr. 28, 1865, William H. Lambert Papers, Document DL0480, ibid.

74. Francis M. Guernsey to My dear Fannie, May 26, 1865, Francis M. Guernsey Papers, Document DL0301_90, ibid. On the contested meanings of the Grand Review, see Gallagher, *Union War,* 7–32.

75. Phillips, *Diehard Rebels,* 162–65; Noll, *Civil War as a Theological Crisis,* 18.

76. Carmichael, *Last Generation,* 207; Power, *Lee's Miserables,* 291, 302–15. Power notes that Confederate accounts from the spring of 1865 are considerably scarcer than those from earlier in the war, largely because of the swiftness and intensity of military events during that period.

77. Charles Frederic Bahnson to My Dear Father, Apr. 6, 1865, in Chapman, *Bright and Gloomy Days,* 172.

78. C. Irvine Walker Diary, Apr. 29, 1865, in Walker, *Great Things Are Expected of Us,* 175.

79. C. Irvine Walker Diary, May 1, 1865, ibid., 176.

80. John Booker to My Dear Cousin, Mar. 1, 1864, John and James Booker Civil War Letters, University of Virginia, Charlottesville.

81. C. Irvine Walker Diary, May 2, 1865, in Walker, *Great Things Are Expected of Us,* 176.

82. Foner, *Reconstruction,* 429–36; Foster, *Ghosts of the Confederacy,* 11–35; Blight, *Race and Reunion,* 98–139; Gallagher, "Shaping Public Memory of the Civil War," 39–63; Leeman, *Redemption,* 24–25; Budiansky, *Bloody Shirt,* 56; Sommerville, "'Will They Ever Be Able to Forget?,'" 321–39; Holberton, *Homeward Bound.*

83. Logan, *Volunteer Soldier of America,* 615.

Epilogue

1. Charles F. Lee to Dear Mother & Josie, July 1, 1865, Charles F. Lee Papers, Document DL0423, JLNC.

2. Cosmas, *Army for Empire,* 324–26; Militia Act of 1903, 32 Stat. 775 (1903); Jamieson, *Crossing the Deadly Ground.*

3. Bradwell, *Under the Southern Cross,* 63–64.

BIBLIOGRAPHY

Archival Sources

BUTLER CENTER FOR ARKANSAS STUDIES, LITTLE ROCK

Arkansas Civil War Materials Collection
Charles H. Atkins Collection
John A. Mitchell Civil War Letters
Munger Family Civil War Letters
Benjamin Palmer Collection
Edward A. Potter Jr. Civil War Collection
Jefferson Robinson Civil War Diary
Smith Family Papers
James Sykes Civil War Letters
John Talbut Civil War Letters
George W. Taylor Civil War Diary
United Daughters of the Confederacy, Arkansas Division Collection
James A. Williamson Letters

ELEANOR BROCKENBROUGH LIBRARY, MUSEUM OF THE CONFEDERACY, RICHMOND, VA.

Bateman Family Collection
Charles C. Baughman Collection
Beauchamp-West Family Collection
Breedin-Coleman Family Collection
Bryan Family Collection
Clack-Livingston Family Collection
Coggill-Mitchell Family Collection
E. L. Coleman Papers
Confederate Regulations Collection
Cutchin-Hodsden Family Collection

Dabney Family Collection
Deas-Archer Family Collection
Alfred E. Doby Letters
Ellyson-Hotchkiss Family Collection
Finley Family Collection
Hunt-Morgan-Hill Family Collection
Hunter Family Collection
George M. Lalane Diary
Leake Family Collection
Albert Livingston Papers
Macgill Family Collection
Mason Family Collection
Moody Family Collection
Morris Family Collection
John S. Mosby Collection
Joseph Mullen Papers
Robert P. Myers Papers
Nelson-Overbey Family Collection
Nicholls-Clopton Family Collection
Pilcher-Wilkerson Family Collection
Richwood-Cameron Family Collection
Rules of the Examination, Confederate States War Department
Seward Family Collection
Smith-Johnson Family Collection
Storey Family Collection
Sullivan Family Collection
Surghnor-Joiner Family Collection
Thom Family Collection
Thomas Family Collection
Tompkins Family Collection
Williams Family Collection
J. Christopher Winsmith Papers

GARLAND COUNTY HISTORICAL SOCIETY, HOT SPRINGS, ARK.

Lorenzo A. Miears Memoir

JOHN L. NAU CIVIL WAR COLLECTION, HOUSTON, TEX.

William B. Alexander Papers
Josiah Anderson Papers

Matthew S. Austin Papers
John H. Black Papers
Charles G. Blake Papers
George W. Browning Papers
Edgar L. Bumpus Papers
Amos S. Collins Papers
Lafayette Calhoun Cooper Papers
John Alexander Dale Papers
William Wirt Daugherty Papers
Robert Dickinson Papers
Warren F. Dodge Papers
Gilbert Malleson Elliot Papers
Amos F. Garrison Papers
Alvin H. Griswold Papers
Francis M. Guernsey Papers
John T. Gwyn Papers
George S. Hawley Papers
Charles Hill Papers
Samuel J. Keller Papers
Theodore Preston Kellogg Papers
Samuel Noble King Papers
William H. Lambert Papers
Charles F. Lee Papers
Nathaniel Lowe Papers
John McLauchlan Papers
Miscellaneous Civil War Papers
Charles Morfoot Papers
Alexander Swift Pendleton Papers
Joseph H. Prime Papers
A. R. H. Ranson Papers
Martin V. B. Richardson Papers
Thomas H. Riddle Papers
Nathaniel Robie Papers
George W. Rockwood Papers
William L. Savage Papers
Watson B. Smith Papers
David Smolk Papers
Courtland G. Stanton Papers
William A. Stephens Papers
S. Millet Thompson Papers
George Washington Weston Papers

Henry Wetzel Papers
Nathan S. Wheeler Papers
Simeon C. Wilkerson Papers
Wesley P. Winans Papers
Richard Kirtland Woodruff Papers
Benjamin T. Wright Papers
George Washington Wright Papers
George W. Yates Papers

LIBRARY OF CONGRESS, MANUSCRIPT DIVISION, WASHINGTON, D.C.

Abraham Lincoln Papers. Available online through the American Memory Project, [2000–2002], http://memory.loc.gov/ammem/alhtml/alhome.html. Accessed September 21, 2013.

LIBRARY OF VIRGINIA, RICHMOND

Denoon Family Papers
Grimsley Family Papers
Henry Thweatt Owen Papers
Rives Family Papers
John F. Sale Papers

NATIONAL ARCHIVES AND RECORDS ADMINISTRATION, WASHINGTON, D.C.

Compiled Military Service Records of Volunteer Union Soldiers, Record Group 94
Compiled Service Records of Confederate Soldiers, Record Group 109
U.S. Bureau of the Census. Eighth Census of the United States. Microfilm 653

SOUTHERN HISTORICAL COLLECTION, LOUIS ROUND WILSON SPECIAL COLLECTIONS LIBRARY, UNIVERSITY OF NORTH CAROLINA, CHAPEL HILL

George Anderson Mercer Diary

TENNESSEE STATE LIBRARY AND ARCHIVES, NASHVILLE

John J. Blair Papers
George Thomas Blakemore Papers
Bostick Family Papers
Nathan Brandon Papers
U. T. Brown Papers
Andrew Jackson Campbell Diary

Achilles V. Clark Papers
James Litton Cooper Memoir
James Lowery Davis Papers
Eugene Frederic Falconnet Memoir
Alfred Tyler Fielder Papers
John Davis Floyd Papers
George A. Gordon Papers
Richard Cross Gordon Papers
James A. Hall Papers
John W. Harris Letters
James A. Madding Papers
John William McCord Papers
Perry Franklin Morgan Papers
Bradford Nichol Papers
John Piney Oden Papers
F. J. Paine Papers
Hannibal Paine Papers
William E. Sloan Papers
Walter Kibell Wendel Papers
Thomas Black Wilson Diary

U.S. ARMY MILITARY HERITAGE INSTITUTE, CARLISLE, PA.

Timothy Bateman Diary
George A. Bowen Papers
Arthur L. Conger Collection
Radford Eugene Mobley Letters
Curtis C. Pollack Letters

Anders Collection

Hezekiah Clock Letters

Brake Collection

Samuel G. Boone Memoir, 88th Pennsylvania Infantry Regimental Papers
Francis Bacon Jones Papers, 88th Pennsylvania Infantry Regimental Papers
Thomas Blackburn Rodgers Memoir, 140th Pennsylvania Infantry Regimental Papers

Civil War Miscellaneous Collection

Jonas Denton Elliott Letters
John D. Fish Letters

Dayton E. Flint Letters
James H. Gillam Letters
John D. Hill Letters
Silas W. Kelly Letters
Charles B. Loop Letters
M. Edgar Richards Letters

Civil War Times Illustrated Collection

Nelson Chapin Correspondence
Samuel A. Craig Diary
Wilbur Fisk Letters
Jacob Heffelfinger Diaries
Thomas Hodgkins Papers
Joseph J. Scroggs Diary
Henry Richard Swan Letters

Harrisburg Civil War Round Table Collection

Benjamin F. Ashenfelter Papers
Albert B. Cree Letters
Andrew Knox Letters
Charles J. Mills Letters

Leigh Collection

Sylvester H. Brown Letter
Henry G. Cannon Papers
Willard S. Chapin Papers
Walter Kempster Letter
Edward Lee Letters
David W. Low Letters
Patrick Nolan Letter
Frank M. Phelps Letters
John P. Shaw Letter
Nelson V. Stanton Letters
John Ed Thompson Letters

UNIVERSITY OF VIRGINIA, CHARLOTTESVILLE

Barnes Family Papers
John and James Booker Civil War Letters
John Cowper Granbery Papers

Asa Holland Papers
Micajah Woods Papers

VIRGINIA HISTORICAL SOCIETY, RICHMOND

Aylett Family Papers
Bagby Family Papers
William Fielding Baugh Papers
Samuel Thompson Buchanan Letters
Cary Family Papers
John Hampden Chamberlayne Papers
Clayton Family Papers
James Lindsey Coghill Papers
Giles Buckner Cooke Papers
Edmundson Family Papers
Thomas Claybrook Elder Papers
Richard F. Eppes Papers
John Walter Fairfax Papers
Hankins Family Papers
Edwin Harmon Papers
Samuel Horace Hawes Papers
James Hays Papers
Headquarters Papers, Army of Northern Virginia
Ambrose Powell Hill Papers
Hobson Family Papers
Keiley Family Papers
Keith Family Papers
Clinton M. King Papers
Langhorne Family Papers
Osmun Latrobe Diary
Leyburn Family Papers
James Wellington Lineberger Papers
Joseph Banks Lyle Papers
Joseph Richard Manson Papers
George Marshall McDowell Papers
David Gregg McIntosh Papers
Meade Family Papers
William Young Mordecai Papers
William T. Nelson Papers
Pegram-Johnson-McIntosh Papers
Richard Channing Price Papers

John Paul Jones Semmes Papers
Robert Augustus Stiles Papers
Franklin Stringfellow Papers
Talcott Family Papers
James Harrison Williams Papers
Gilbert Jefferson Wright Papers

WOODSON RESEARCH CENTER, RICE UNIVERSITY, HOUSTON, TEX.

Samuel Storrow Journals

Periodicals

Fayetteville (N.C.) Observer
Jacksonville (Ala.) Republican
New York Times
Philadelphia Public Ledger
San Francisco Bulletin
Southern Confederacy (Atlanta, Ga.)

Published Primary Sources

Abbott, Henry Livermore. *Fallen Leaves: The Civil War Letters of Major Henry Livermore Abbott*. Edited by Robert Garth Scott. Kent, Ohio: Kent State University Press, 1991.

Adams, John. *The Works of John Adams, Second President of the United States, with a Life of the Author*. Edited by Charles Francis Adams. 10 vols. Boston: Little, Brown, 1850–56.

Alderson, William T., ed. "The Civil War Diary of Captain James Litton Cooper, September 30, 1861, to January 1865." *Tennessee Historical Quarterly* 15 (June 1956): 141–73.

Alexander, Edward Porter. *Fighting for the Confederacy: The Personal Recollections of General Edward Porter Alexander*. Edited by Gary W. Gallagher. Chapel Hill: University of North Carolina Press, 1998.

Allen, Ujanirtus. *Campaigning with "Old Stonewall": Confederate Captain Ujanirtus Allen's Letters to His Wife*. Edited by Randall A. Allen and Keith S. Bohannon. Baton Rouge: Louisiana State University Press, 1998.

Ambrose, D. Lieb. *History of the Seventh Regiment Illinois Volunteer Infantry, from Its First Muster into the U.S. Service, April 25, 1861, to its Final Muster Out, July 9, 1865*. Springfield: Illinois Journal, 1868.

Anderson, Robert. *An Artillery Officer in the Mexican War, 1846–1847: Letters of*

Robert Anderson, Captain 3rd Artillery U.S.A. Edited by Eba Anderson Lawton. New York: G. P. Putnam's Sons, 1911.

Andrews, C. C. *Hints to Company Officers on their Military Duties.* New York: Van Nostrand, 1864.

Ayling, Augustus D ed. *A Yankee at Arms: The Diary of Lieutenant Augustus D. Ayling, 29th Massachusetts Volunteers.* Edited by Charles F. Herberger. Knoxville: University of Tennessee Press, 1999.

Babcock, Willoughby M., Jr. *Selections from the Letters and Diaries of Brevet-Brigadier General Willoughby Babcock of the Seventy-Fifth New York Volunteers, a Study of Camp Life in the Union Armies during the Civil War.* New York: University of the State of New York, 1922.

Barney, William L. *The Making of a Confederate: Walter Lenoir's Civil War.* New York: Oxford University Press, 2007.

Bates, James C. *A Texas Cavalry Officer's Civil War: The Diary and Letters of James C. Bates.* Edited by Richard Lowe. Baton Rouge: Louisiana State University Press, 1999.

Bates, Samuel P. *History of the Pennsylvania Volunteers, 1861–1865.* Harrisburg, Pa.: n.p., 1868–71.

Baylor, George. *Bull Run to Bull Run; or, Four Years in the Army of Northern Virginia.* Richmond, Va.: B. F. Johnson, 1900.

Beatty, John. *The Citizen-Soldier; or, Memoirs of a Volunteer.* Cincinnati: Wilstach, Baldwin, 1879.

Bettersworth, John K., and James W. Silver, eds. *Mississippi in the Confederacy.* 2 vols. Baton Rouge: Louisiana State University Press, 1961.

Bierce, Ambrose. *Ambrose Bierce's Civil War.* Edited by William McCann. New York: Wings Books, 1996.

Billings, John Davis. *Hardtack and Coffee; or, the Unwritten Story of Army Life.* Boston: G. M. Smith, 1888.

Boyd, Cyrus F. *The Civil War Diary of Cyrus F. Boyd, Fifteenth Iowa Infantry, 1861–1863.* Edited by Mildred Throne. Iowa City: State Historical Society of Iowa, 1953.

Bradwell, Isaac Gordon. *Under the Southern Cross: Soldier Life with Gordon Bradwell and the Army of Northern Virginia.* Compiled and edited by Pharris Deloach Johnson. Macon, Ga.: Mercer University Press, 1999.

Brewster, Charles Harvey. *When This Cruel War Is Over: The Civil War Letters of Charles Harvey Brewster.* Edited by David W. Blight. Amherst: University of Massachusetts Press, 1992.

Brown, Alonzo L. *History of the Fourth Regiment of Minnesota Infantry Volunteers during the Great Rebellion, 1861–1865.* St. Paul, Minn.: Pioneer, 1892.

Brown, Joseph E., and James A. Seddon. *Correspondence between Governor Brown and the Secretary of War, upon the Right of the Georgia Volunteers, in Confed-*

erate Service, to Elect Their Own Officers. Milledgeville, Ga.: Boughton, Nisbet, Barnes, & Moore, State Printers, 1863.

Bull, Rice C. *Soldiering: The Civil War Diary of Rice C. Bull*. Edited by K. Jack Bauer. San Rafael, Ca.: Presidio, 1977.

Burgwyn, William H. S. *A Captain's War: The Letters and Diaries of William H. S. Burgwyn, 1861–1865*. Edited by Herbert M. Schiller. Shippensburg, Pa.: White Mane, 1994.

Burnett, Edmond Cody. "Letters of Three Lightfoot Brothers, 1861–1864. Part I." *Georgia Historical Quarterly* 25 (1941): 371–400.

Burton, Joseph Q., and Theophilus F. Botsford. *Historical Sketches of the Forty-Seventh Alabama Infantry Regiment, C.S.A.* Tuscaloosa, Ala.: CSA Publishing, 1982.

Butterfield, Daniel. *Camp and Outpost Duty for Infantry*. 1862. Reprint, Mechanicsburg, Pa.: Stackpole, 2003.

Callaway, Joshua K. *The Civil War Letters of Joshua K. Callaway*. Athens: University of Georgia Press, 1997.

Calhoun, William Lowndes. *History of the 42d Regiment Georgia Volunteers, CSA States Army, Infantry*. Atlanta: n.p., 1900.

Campbell, John Quincy Adams. *The Union Must Stand: The Civil War Diary of John Quincy Adams Campbell, Fifth Iowa Volunteer Infantry*. Edited by Mark Grimsley and Todd D. Miller. Knoxville: University of Tennessee Press, 2000.

Carpenter, George N. *History of the Eighth Regiment Vermont Volunteers, 1861–1865*. Boston: Deland & Barta, 1886.

Carter, Robert Goldthwaite. *Four Brothers in Blue; or, Sunshine and Shadows of the War of the Rebellion, a Story of the Great Civil War from Bull Run to Appomattox*. 1896. Reprint, Austin: University of Texas Press, 1975.

Casey, Silas. *Infantry Tactics, for the Instruction, Exercise, and Manoeuvres of the Soldier, a Company, Line of Skirmishers, Battalion, Brigade, or Corps D'Armee*. 3 vols. New York: D. Van Nostrand, 1862.

Chamberlayne, John Hampden. *Ham Chamberlayne—Virginian: Letters and Papers of an Artillery Officer in the War for Southern Independence, 1861–1865*. Wilmington, N.C.: Broadfoot, 1992.

Chapman, Charles Frederic. *Bright and Gloomy Days: The Civil War Correspondence of Captain Charles Frederic Bahnson, a Moravian Confederate*. Edited by Sarah Bahnson Chapman. Knoxville: University of Tennessee Press, 2003.

Clark, Reuben G. *Valleys of the Shadow: The Memoir of Confederate Captain Reuben G. Clark, Company I, 59th Tennessee Mounted Infantry*. Knoxville: University of Tennessee Press, 1994.

Clark, Walter ed. *Histories of the Several Regiments and Battalions from North Carolina in the Great War, 1861–'65*. 3 vols. Raleigh, N.C.: E. M. Uzzell, 1901.

Clayton, Henry Harrison ed. *A Damned Iowa Greyhound: The Civil War Letters of*

William Henry Harrison Clayton. Edited by Donald C. Elder. Iowa City: University of Iowa Press, 1998.

Collier, Calvin L. *"They'll Do to Tie To!": The Story of the Third Regiment, Arkansas Infantry, C.S.A.* Little Rock, Ark.: J. D. Warren, 1959.

Comey, Henry Newton, ed. *A Legacy of Valor: The Memoirs and Letters of Captain Henry Newton Comey, 2nd Massachusetts Infantry.* Edited by Lyman Richard Comey. Knoxville: University of Tennessee Press, 2004.

A Committee of the Regimental Association. *Thirty-Fifth Massachusetts: History of the 35thMassachusetts Volunteers, 1862–1865. With a Roster.* Boston: Mills, Knight, & Co., 1884.

Connor, Forrest P., ed. "Letters of Lieutenant Robert H. Miller to His Family, 1861–1862." *Virginia Magazine of History and Biography* 70 (January 1962): 62–91.

Cooke, Chauncey H. *A Badger Boy in Blue: The Civil War Letters of Chauncey H. Cooke.* Edited by William H. Mulligan Jr. Detroit: Wayne State University Press, 2007.

Cooke, John Esten. *Wearing of the Gray: Being Personal Portraits, Scenes, and Adventures of the War.* Baton Rouge: Louisiana State University Press, 1997.

Corbin, Richard. *Letters of a Confederate Officer to His Family in Europe during the Last Year of the War of Secession.* 1902. Reprint, Baltimore: Butternut and Blue, 1993.

Costello, Edward. *Adventures of a Soldier; or, Memoirs of Edward Costello, K.S.F.* London: Henry Colburn, 1841.

Cotton, John. *Yours Till Death: Civil War Letters of John W. Cotton.* Tuscaloosa: University of Alabama Press, 2003.

Craighill, William P. *The Army Officer's Pocket Companion.* New York: D. Van Nostrand, 1862.

Curtis, Newton Martin. *From Bull Run to Chancellorsville: The Story of the Sixteenth New York Infantry together with Personal Reminiscences.* New York: G. P. Putnam's Sons, 1906.

Cutrer, Thomas W., and T. Michael Parrish, eds. *Brothers in Gray: The Civil War Letters of the Pierson Family.* Baton Rouge: Louisiana State University Press, 2004.

Davidson, Greenlee. *Captain Greenlee Davidson, C.S.A.: Diary and Letters, 1851–1863.* Edited by Charles W. Turner. Verona, Va.: McClure, 1975.

Davis, Jefferson. *Jefferson Davis, Constitutionalist: His Letters, Papers, and Speeches.* Edited by Dunbar Rowland. 10 vols. Jackson: Mississippi Department of Archives and History, 1923.

Davis, Nicholas A. *Chaplain Davis and Hood's Texas Brigade: Being an Expanded Edition of the Reverend Nicholas A. Davis's the Campaign from Texas to Maryland, with the Battle of Fredericksburg.* Baton Rouge: Louisiana State University Press, 1999.

Dawes, Ephraim C. "A Hero of the War." In *G.A.R. War Papers: Papers Read before*

Fred C. Jones Post, No. 401, Department of Ohio, G.A.R., Volume 1, 293–98. Cincinnati, Ohio: Fred C. Jones Post 401, 1891.

———. "My First Day under Fire at Shiloh." In *Sketches of War History, 1861–1865: Papers Prepared for the Ohio Commandery of the Military Order of the Loyal Legion of the United States, 1890–1896,* edited by W. H. Chamberlin, 4:1–22. Cincinnati, Ohio: Robert Clarke, 1896.

Dawson, Francis Warrington. *Reminiscences of Confederate Service, 1861–1865*. Baton Rouge: Louisiana State University Press, 1993.

Dearing, Alfred Long. *The Diary of a Confederate Officer during the War and into the Reconstruction Period*. Athens: University of Georgia Press, 1954.

De Forest, John William. *A Volunteer's Adventures: A Union Captain's Record of the Civil War*. Edited by James H. Croushore. Baton Rouge: Louisiana State University Press, 1996.

Dickey, Luther S. *History of the 103d Regiment, Pennsylvania Veteran Volunteer Infantry, 1861–1865*. Chicago: n.p., 1910.

Douglas, Henry Kyd. *I Rode with Stonewall*. Chapel Hill: University of North Carolina Press, 1968.

Douglas, James Postell. *Douglas's Texas Battery, CSA*. Edited by Lucia Rutherford Douglas. Waco, Tex.: Texian, 1966.

Dubose, Henry Kershaw. *History of Company B, Twenty-First Regiment (Infantry) South Carolina Volunteers, Confederate States Provisional Army*. Columbia: University of South Carolina Press, 2009.

DuBose, William Porcher. *Faith, Valor, and Devotion: The Civil War Letters of William Porcher DuBose*. Edited by W. Eric Emerson and Karen Stokes. Columbia: University of South Carolina Press, 2010.

Duff, Levi Bird. *To Petersburg with the Army of the Potomac: The Civil War Letters of Levi Bird Duff, 105th Pennsylvania Volunteers*. Edited by Jonathan E. Helmreich. Jefferson, N.C.: McFarland, 2009.

Duke, John K. *History of the Fifty-Third Ohio Volunteer Infantry, during the War of the Rebellion 1861–1865. Together with More Than Thirty Personal Sketches of Officers and Men*. Portsmouth, Ohio: Blade Printing, 1900.

Dwight, Wilder, and Elizabeth Amelia Dwight. *Life and Letters of Wilder Dwight: Lieut.-Col. Second Mass. Inf. Vols*. Boston: Ticknor & Fields, 1868.

Dyer, Frederick H. *A Compendium of the War of the Rebellion: Compiled and Arranged from Official Records of the Federal and CSA Armies, Reports of the Adjutant Generals of the Several States, the Army Registers and Other Reliable Documents and Sources*. 3 vols. Des Moines, Iowa: Dyer, 1908.

Elliot, Jonathan, ed. *The Debates in the Several State Conventions on the Adoption of the Federal Constitution*. 2nd ed., 5 vols. Washington, D.C.: Printed for the Editor, 1836.

Evans, Robert G., comp. and ed. *The 16th Mississippi Infantry: Civil War Letters and Reminiscences*. Jackson: University Press of Mississippi, 2002.

Everson, Guy R., and Edward W. Simpson Jr., eds. *Far, Far from Home: The Wartime Letters of Dick and Tally Simpson, 3rd South Carolina Volunteers*. New York: Oxford University Press, 1994.

Favill, Josiah Marshall. *The Diary of a Young Officer Serving with the Armies of the United States during the War of the Rebellion*. Chicago: R. R. Donnelley & Sons, 1909.

Ferguson, Hubert L., ed. "Letters of John W. Duncan, Captain Confederate States of America." *Arkansas Historical Quarterly* 9 (Winter 1950): 298–312.

Fleet, Benjamin Robert. *Green Mount, a Virginia Plantation Family during the Civil War: Being the Journal of Benjamin Robert Fleet and Letters of His Family*. Edited by Betsy Fleet and John D. P. Fuller. Lexington: University Press of Kentucky, 1962.

Fleharty, S. F. *Our Regiment: A History of the 102d Illinois Infantry Volunteers*. Chicago: Brewster & Hanscom, 1865.

Floyd, Frederick Clark. *History of the Fortieth (Mozart) Regiment, New York Volunteers*. Boston: F. H. Gilson, 1909.

Foster, Samuel T. *One of Cleburne's Command: The Civil War Reminiscences and Diary of Capt. Samuel T. Foster, Granbury's Texas Brigade, CSA*. Edited by Norman D. Brown. Austin: University of Texas Press, 1980.

Gibbon, John. *The Artillerist's Manual*. New York: D. Van Nostrand, 1860.

Giles, Val C. *Rags and Hope: The Memoirs of Val C. Giles, Four Years with Hood's Brigade, Fourth Texas Infantry, 1861–1865*. Compiled and edited by Mary Lasswell. New York: Coward-McCann, 1961.

Goddard, Henry P. *The Good Fight That Didn't End: Henry P. Goddard's Accounts of Civil War and Peace*. Edited by Calvin Goddard Zon. Columbia: University of South Carolina Press, 2008.

Good, John J. *Cannon Smoke: The Letters of Captain John J. Good, Good-Douglas Texas Battery, CSA*. Compiled and edited by Lester Newton Fitzhugh. Hillsboro, Tex.: Hill Junior College Press, 1971.

Gordon, George Henry. *The Organization and Early History of the Second Mass. Regiment of Infantry: An Address*. Boston: Rockwell & Churchill, 1873.

Goree, Thomas J. *Longstreet's Aide: The Civil War Letters of Major Thomas J. Goree*. Edited by Thomas W. Cutrer. Charlottesville: University Press of Virginia, 1995.

Goss, Warren Lee. *Recollections of a Private: A Story of the Army of the Potomac*. New York: Thomas Y. Crowell, 1890.

Grayson, William John, and Elmer L. Puryear. "The Confederate Diary of William John Grayson." *South Carolina Historical Magazine* 63 (July 1962): 137–49.

———. "The Confederate Diary of William John Grayson (Continued)." *South Carolina Historical Magazine* 63 (October 1962): 214–26.

Grisamore, Silas T. *The Civil War Reminiscences of Major Silas T. Grisamore, C.S.A.* Edited by Arthur W. Bergeron. Baton Rouge: Louisiana State University Press, 1993.

Guerrant, Edward O. *Bluegrass Confederate: The Headquarters Diary of Edward O. Guerrant.* Edited by William C. Davis and Meredith L. Swentor. Baton Rouge: Louisiana State University Press, 1999.

Guiney, Patrick R. *Commanding Boston's Irish Ninth: The Civil War Letters of Colonel Patrick R. Guiney, Ninth Massachusetts Volunteer Infantry.* Edited by Christian G. Samito. New York: Fordham University Press, 1998.

Hardee, William J. *Rifle and Light Infantry Tactics; for the Exercise and Manoevres of Troops When Acting as Light Infantry or Riflemen.* 2 vols. Philadelphia: Lippincott, Grambo, 1855.

———. *Rifle and Light Infantry Tactics; for the Exercise and Manoevres of Troops When Acting as Light Infantry or Riflemen.* New York: J. O. Kane, 1862.

Haskell, John. *The Haskell Memoirs: The Personal Narrative of a Confederate Officer.* Edited by Gilbert E. Govan and James W. Livingood. New York: G. P. Putnam's Sons, 1960.

Heartsill, W. W. *Fourteen Hundred and 91 Days in the Confederate Army.* Jackson, Tenn.: McCowat-Mercer, 1954.

Heth, Henry. *The Memoirs of Henry Heth.* Edited by James L. Morrison Jr. Westport, Conn.: Greenwood, 1974.

Higginson, Thomas Wentworth. "Regular and Volunteer Officers." *Atlantic Monthly* 14 (September 1864): 348–57.

Hill, Daniel Harvey. *A Fighter from Way Back: The Mexican War Diary of Lt. Daniel Harvey Hill, 4th Artillery, USA.* Edited by Nathaniel Cheairs Hughes Jr. and Timothy D. Johnson. Kent, Ohio: Kent State University Press, 2002.

Holmes, Oliver Wendell, Jr. *Touched with Fire: Civil War Letters and Diary of Oliver Wendell Holmes, Jr.* Edited by Mark De Wolfe Howe. New York: Fordham University Press, 2000.

Horry County [S.C.] Historical Society. "South Carolina Tenth Regiment." *Independent Republic Quarterly* 32 (Spring 1998): 1–44.

Howell, H. Grady. *Going to Meet the Yankees: A History of the "Bloody Sixth" Mississippi Infantry, C.S.A.* Jackson, Miss.: Chickasaw Bayou, 1981.

Hoyle, Joseph J. *"Deliver Us from This Cruel War": The Civil War Letters of Lieutenant Joseph J. Hoyle, 55th North Carolina Infantry.* Edited by Jeffrey M. Girvan. Jefferson, N.C.: McFarland, 2010.

Kautz, August V. *The Company Clerk: Showing How and When to Make Out All the Returns, Reports, Rolls, and Other Papers, and What to Do with Them.* Philadelphia: J. B. Lippincott, 1865.

———. *The 1865 Customs of Service for Officers of the Army.* 1866. Reprint, Mechanicsburg, Pa.: Stackpole, 2002.

Kendall, John Smith. "Recollections of a Confederate Officer." *Louisiana Historical Quarterly* 29 (October 1946): 1041–1228.

Kenly, John R. *Memoirs of a Maryland Volunteer. War with Mexico, in the Years 1846–7–8.* Philadelphia: J. B. Lippincott, 1873.

Laidley, Theodore. *"Surrounded by Dangers of All Kinds": The Mexican War Letters of Lieutenant Theodore Laidley.* Edited by James M. McCaffrey. Denton: University of North Texas Press, 1997.

Lavender, John W. *The War Memoirs of Captain John W. Lavender, C.S.A. They Never Came Back: The Story of Co. F Fourth Arks. Infantry, Originally Known as the Montgomery Hunters, as Told by Their Commanding Officer.* Edited by Ted R. Worley. Pine Bluff, Ark.: Southern, 1956.

Litvin, Marvin, ed. "Captain Burkhalter's Georgia War." In *Voices of the Prairie Land,* 2:497–98. Galesburg, Ill.: Mother Bickerdyke Historical Collection, 1972.

Lyon, Henry C. *"Desolating This Fair Country": The Civil War Diary and Letters of Lt. Henry C. Lyon, 34th New York.* Edited by Emily N. Radigan. Jefferson, N.C.: McFarland, 1999.

Lyster, Henry F. "Recollections of the Bull Run Campaign after Twenty-seven Years." *A Paper Read before Michigan Commandery of the Military Order of the Loyal Legion of the United States, February 1, 1887.* Detroit: W. S. Ostler, 1888.

Manigault, Arthur Middleton. *A Carolinian Goes to War: The Civil War Narrative of Arthur Middleton Manigault, Brigadier General, C.S.A.* Edited by R. Lockwood Tower. Columbia: University of South Carolina Press, 1992.

Marshall, Albert O. *Army Life: From a Soldier's Journal.* Edited by Robert G. Shultz. Fayetteville: University of Arkansas Press, 2009.

Mason, George. *The Papers of George Mason, 1725–1792.* Edited by Robert A. Rutland. 3 vols. Chapel Hill: University of North Carolina Press, 1970.

Matrau, Henry. *Letters Home: Henry Matrau of the Iron Brigade.* Edited by Marcia Reid-Green. Lincoln: University of Nebraska Press, 1993.

Mattocks, Charles. *"Unspoiled Heart": The Journal of Charles Mattocks of the 17th Maine.* Edited by Philip N. Racine. Knoxville: University of Tennessee Press, 1994.

McBrien, D. D., and William Wakefield Garner. "Letters of an Arkansas Confederate Soldier (Part 1)." *Arkansas Historical Quarterly* 2 (March 1943): 58–70.

———. "Letters of an Arkansas Confederate Soldier (Part 2)." *Arkansas Historical Quarterly* 2 (June 1943): 171–84.

———. "Letters of an Arkansas Confederate Soldier (Part 3)." *Arkansas Historical Quarterly* 2 (September 1943): 268–86.

McCabe, W. Gordon. "Address to the Annual Reunion of Pegram's Battalion, . . . 1886." *Southern Historical Society Papers* 14 (1886): 5–34.

McCarthy, Carlton. *Detailed Minutiae of Soldier Life in the Army of Northern Virginia, 1861–1865.* 1882. Reprint, Lincoln: University of Nebraska Press, 1993.

McClellan, George B. *The Mexican War Diary and Correspondence of George B. McClellan.* Edited by Thomas W. Cutrer. Baton Rouge: Louisiana State University Press, 2009.

McKnight, William. *Do They Miss Me at Home?: The Civil War Letters of William McKnight, Seventh Ohio Volunteer Cavalry.* Edited by Donald C. Maness and H. Jason Combs. Athens: Ohio University Press, 2010.

McMurray, William Josiah. *History of the Twentieth Tennessee Regiment Volunteer Infantry, C.S.A.* Nashville, Tenn.: Publication Committee, 1904.

Meade, George Gordon. *The Life and Letters of George Gordon Meade: Major-General United States Army.* 2 vols. New York: Charles Scribner's Sons, 1913.

Meynier, Arthur. *Life and Military Services of Col. Charles D. Dreux.* New Orleans: E. A. Brandao, Printers, 1883.

Miller, William Bluffton. *Fighting for Liberty and Right: The Civil War Diary of William Bluffton Miller, First Sergeant, Company K, Seventy-Fifth Indiana Volunteer Infantry.* Edited by Jeffrey L. Patrick and Robert J. Willey. Knoxville: University of Tennessee Press, 2005.

Moore, Frank, ed. *The Civil War in Song and Story.* New York: P. F. Collier, 1889.

Moore, John W. *Roster of North Carolina Troops in the War between the States.* 2 vols. Raleigh, N.C.: Ashe & Gatling, 1882.

Moxley, William Morel. *Oh, What a Loansome Time I Had: The Civil War Letters of Major William Morel Moxley, Eighteenth Alabama Infantry, and Emily Beck Moxley.* Edited by Thomas W. Cutrer. Tuscaloosa: University of Alabama Press, 2002.

Musser, Charles O. *Soldier Boy: The Civil War Letters of Charles O. Musser, 29th Iowa.* Edited by Barry Popchock. Iowa City: University of Iowa Press, 1995.

Nelson, William Cowper. *The Hour of Our Nation's Agony: The Civil War Letters of Lt. William Cowper Nelson of Mississippi.* Edited by Jennifer W. Ford. Knoxville: University of Tennessee Press, 2007.

Nisbet, James C. *Four Years on the Firing Line.* Wilmington, N.C.: Broadfoot, 1987.

O'Brien, John. *Things Grew Beautifully Worse: The Wartime Experiences of Captain John O'Brien, 30th Arkansas Infantry, C.S.A.* Edited by Brian K. Robertson. Little Rock: Butler Center for Arkansas Studies, 2001.

Ohio Roster Commission. *Official Roster of the Soldiers of the State of Ohio in the War of the Rebellion, 1861–1865, Compiled under the Direction of the Roster Commission.* Akron, Ohio: Werner, 1886–95.

Owen, Henry T. *The War of Confederate Captain Henry T. Owen.* Edited by Kimberly Ayn Owen, Graham C. Owen, and Michael M. Owen. Westminster, Md.: Heritage Books, 2004.

Palfrey, Francis Winthrop. *Memoir of William Francis Bartlett.* Boston: Houghton, Osgood, 1879.

Park, Robert E. "Diary of Captain Robert E. Park, Macon, Georgia. Late Captain Twelfth Alabama Regiment, Confederate States Army." *Southern Historical Society Papers* 1 (1876): 370–86, 430–37.

———. "Diary of Captain Robert E. Park, Twelfth Alabama Regiment." *Southern Historical Society Papers* 2 (1876): 25–30, 172–80, 232–39, 306–15.

———. "The Twelfth Alabama Infantry, Confederate States Army." *Southern Historical Society Papers* 33 (1905): 193–296.

Parker, Eddy R., ed. *Touched by Fire: Letters from Company D, 5th Texas Infantry, Hood's Brigade, Army of Northern Virginia, 1862–1865*. Hillsboro, Tex.: Hill College Press, 2000.

Patterson, Edmund Dewitt. *Yankee Rebel: The Civil War Journal of Edmund Dewitt Patterson*. Edited by John Gilchrist Barrett. Knoxville: University of Tennessee Press, 2004.

Perry, Theophilus. *Widows by the Thousand: The Civil War Letters of Theophilus and Harriet Perry, 1862–1864*. Edited by M. Jane Johansson. Fayetteville: University of Arkansas Press, 2000.

Peskin, Allan, ed. *Volunteers: The Mexican War Journals of Private Richard Coulter and Sergeant Thomas Barclay, Company E, Second Pennsylvania Infantry*. Kent, Ohio: Kent State University Press, 1991.

Petty, Elijah P. *Journey to Pleasant Hill: The Civil War Letters of Captain Elijah P. Petty, Walker's Texas Division CSA*. Edited by Norman D. Brown. San Antonio: University of Texas, Institutes of Texan Culture, 1982.

Peyton, John William. *Eyewitness to War in Virginia, 1861–1865: The Civil War Diary of John William Peyton*. Edited by Walbrook D. Swank. Shippensburg, Pa.: Burd Street, 2003.

Poague, William Thomas. *Gunner with Stonewall: Reminiscences of William Thomas Poague*. Edited by Monroe F. Cockrell. Jackson, Tenn.: McCowat-Mercer, 1957.

Polley, Joseph B.. *A Soldier's Letters to Charming Nellie: The Correspondence of Joseph B. Polley, Hood's Texas Brigade*. Edited by Richard B. McCaslin. Knoxville: University of Tennessee Press, 2007.

Porter, John M. *One of Morgan's Men: Memoirs of Lieutenant John M. Porter of the Ninth Kentucky Cavalry*. Edited by Kent Masterson Brown. Lexington: University Press of Kentucky, 2011.

Rice, Ralsa C. *Yankee Tigers: Through the Civil War with the 125th Ohio*. Edited by Richard A. Baumgartner and Larry M. Strayer. Huntingdon, W.Va.: Blue Acorn, 1992.

Richardson, James D. comp. *A Compilation of the Messages and Papers of the Confederacy, including the Diplomatic Correspondence, 1861–1865*. Nashville, Tenn.: United States Publishing, 1905.

———. *A Compilation of the Messages and Papers of the Presidents, 1789–1897.* 10 vols. Washington, D.C.: Published by Authority of Congress, 1900.

Ripley, William Y. W. *Vermont Riflemen in the War for the Union, 1861–1865. A His-*

tory of Company F, First United States Sharp Shooters. 1883. Reprint, Rochester, Mich.: Grand Army, 1981.

Royse, Isaac Henry Clay. *History of the 115th Regiment, Illinois Volunteer Infantry*. Terra Haute, Ind.: n.p., 1900.

Seymour, William J. *The Civil War Memoirs of Captain William J. Seymour: Reminiscences of a Louisiana Tiger*. Edited by Terry L. Jones. Baton Rouge: Louisiana State University Press, 1997.

Shaw, Horace H., and Charles J. House. *The First Maine Heavy Artillery, 1862–1865*. Portland, Maine: n.p., 1903.

Shaw, James Birney. *History of the Tenth Regiment Indiana Volunteer Infantry: Three Months and Three Years Organizations*. Lafayette, Ind.: Committee on Publication of History, 1912.

Shaw, Robert Gould. *Blue-Eyed Child of Fortune: The Civil War Letters of Colonel Robert Gould Shaw*. Edited by Russell Duncan. Athens: University of Georgia Press, 1999.

Sheffey, John Preston. *Soldier of Southwestern Virginia: The Civil War Letters of Captain John Preston Sheffey*. Edited by James I. Robertson. Baton Rouge: Louisiana State University Press, 2007.

Small, Abner R. *The Road to Richmond: The Civil War Memoirs of Maj. Abner R. Small of the 16th Maine Vols.; with His Diary as a Prisoner of War*. Edited by Harold Adams Small. Berkeley: University of California Press, 1959.

Smith, John Day. *The History of the Nineteenth Regiment of Maine Volunteer Infantry, 1862–1865*. Minneapolis: Great Western Printing, 1909.

Spence, Alexander E. *Getting Used to Being Shot At: The Spence Family Civil War Letters*. Edited by Mark K. Christ. Fayetteville: University of Arkansas Press, 2003.

Sperry, Andrew F. *History of the 33d Iowa Infantry Volunteer Regiment, 1863–66*. Des Moines: Mills, 1866.

Sprague, Homer B. *13th Infantry Regiment of Connecticut Volunteers during the Great Rebellion*. Hartford, Conn.: Case, Lockwood, 1867.

Squier, George W. *This Wilderness of War: The Civil War Letters of George W. Squier, Hoosier Volunteer*. Edited by Julie A. Doyle, John David Smith, and Richard M. McMurry. Knoxville: University of Tennessee Press, 1998.

Starr, N. D., and T. W. Holman. *The 21st Missouri Regiment Infantry Veteran Volunteers. Historical Memoranda*. Fort Madison, Iowa: Roberts & Roberts, Printers, 1899.

Stephenson, Philip Daingerfield. *The Civil War Memoir of Philip Daingerfield Stephenson, D.D: Private, Company K, 13th Arkansas Volunteer Infantry and Loader, Piece No. 4, 5th Company, Washington Artillery, Army of Tennessee, CSA*. Edited by Nathaniel Cheairs Hughes Jr. Baton Rouge: Louisiana State University Press, 1998.

Stiles, Robert Augustus. *Four Years under Marse Robert.* New York: Neale, 1903.
Thompson, Ed Porter. *History of the Orphan Brigade.* Louisville, Ky.: Lewis N. Thompson, 1898.
Thompson, S. Millet. *Thirteenth Regiment of New Hampshire Volunteer Infantry in the War of the Rebellion, 1861–1865: A Diary Covering Three Years and a Day.* New York: Houghton Mifflin, 1888.
Tillman, James Adams. *A Palmetto Boy: Civil War–Era Diaries and Letters of James Adams Tillman.* Edited by Bobbie Swearingen Smith. Columbia: University of South Carolina Press, 2010.
Tocqueville, Alexis de. *Democracy in America.* 2 vols. 1835, 1840. Reprint, New York: Bantam Classics, 2004.
Tourgée, Albion Winegar. *The Story of a Thousand: Being a History of the Service of the 105th Ohio Volunteer Infantry, in the War for the Union from August 21, 1862, to June 6, 1865.* Buffalo, N.Y.: S. McGerald & Son, 1896.
Trout, Robert J., ed. *With Pen and Saber: The Letters and Diaries of J. E. B. Stuart's Staff Officers.* Mechanicsburg, Pa.: Stackpole, 1995.
Tunnard, W. H. *A Southern Record: The History of the Third Regiment Louisiana Infantry.* Baton Rouge: n.p., 1866.
Tuttle, John W. *The Union, the Civil War, and John W. Tuttle: A Kentucky Captain's Account.* Edited by Hambleton Tapp and James C. Clotter. Frankfort: Kentucky Historical Society, 1980.
Upton, Emory. *The Military Policy of the United States.* Washington, D.C.: Government Printing Office, 1912.
Walker, C. I. *Rolls and Historical Sketch of the Tenth Regiment, So. Ca. Volunteers, in the Army of the CSA States.* Charleston, S.C.: Walker, Evans, & Cogswell, Printers, 1881.
Walker, C. Irvine. *Great Things Are Expected of Us: The Letters of Colonel C. Irvine Walker, 10th South Carolina Infantry, C.S.A.* Edited by William Lee White and Charles Denny Runion. Knoxville: University of Tennessee Press, 2009.
Walker, William C. *History of the Eighteenth Regiment Conn. Volunteers in the War for the Union.* Norwich, Conn: n.p., 1885.
Washington, George. *The Papers of George Washington: Revolutionary War Series.* Edited by Philander D. Chase. Vol. 1. Charlottesville: University Press of Virginia, 1985.
Welsh, Peter. *Irish Green and Union Blue: The Civil War Letters of Peter Welsh, Color Sergeant, 28th Regiment, Massachusetts Volunteers.* Edited by Lawrence Frederick Kohl and Margaret Cossé Richard. New York: Fordham University Press, 1986.
Whitman, G. W. *The Civil War Letters of G. W. Whitman.* Edited by Jerome M. Loving. Durham, N.C.: Duke University Press, 1975.
Whitman, William E. S., and Charles H. Turner. *Maine in the War for the Union: A*

History of the Part Borne by Maine Troops in the Suppression of the American Rebellion. Lewiston, Maine: N. Dingley Jr., 1865.

Williams, James M. *From That Terrible Field: Civil War Letters of James M. Williams, Twenty-First Alabama Infantry Volunteers.* Edited by John Kent Folmar. Tuscaloosa: University of Alabama Press, 1991.

Wills, Charles W. *Army Life of an Illinois Soldier, including a Day by Day Record of Sherman's March to the Sea: Letters and Diary of the Late Charles W. Wills.* Compiled by Mary E. Kellogg. Washington, D.C.: Globe Printing, 1906.

Wilson, William. *The History of a Volunteer Regiment.* New York: Veteran Volunteer Publishing, 1891.

Wise, George. *History of the Seventeenth Virginia Infantry, C.S.A.* Baltimore: Kelly, Piet, 1870.

Wise, Jennings C. "The Boy Gunners of Lee." *Southern Historical Society Papers* 42 (1917): 152–73.

Wright, Gilbert. "Some Letters to His Parents by a Floridian in the Confederate Army." *Florida Historical Quarterly* 36 (April 1958): 353–72.

Xenophon. *The Anabasis.* Translated by Edward Spelman. 2 vols. New York: J. & J. Harper, 1834.

Government Publications

Confederate States War Department. *Army Regulations Adopted for Use in the Confederate States in Accordance with Late Acts of Congress: Revised from the Army Regulations of the U.S. Army, 1857, Retaining All That is Essential for the Officers of the Line, To Which is Added, an Act for the Establishment and Organization of the Army of the Confederate States of America; Also, Articles of War for the Government of the Army of the Confederate States of America.* New Orleans: Bloomfield & Steel, 1861.

———. *General Orders from Adjutant and Inspector General's Office, Confederate States Army, from January 1862 to December 1862.* Columbia, S.C.: Steampower Presses of Evans & Cogwell, 1864.

———. *General Orders from Adjutant and Inspector General's Office, Confederate States Army, from January 1, 1864 to July 1, 1864, Inclusive.* Columbia, S.C.: Evans & Cogwell, 1864.

The Statutes at Large of the Confederate States of America, Commencing with the First Session of the First Congress, 1862. 5 vols. Edited by James M. Matthews. Richmond, Va.: R. M. Smith, printer, 1862–64.

The Statutes at Large of the Provisional Government of the Confederate States of America, from the Institution of the Government, February 8, 1861, to Its Termination, February 18, 1862. Edited by James M. Matthews. Richmond, Va.: R. M. Smith, printer, 1864.

Statutes at Large of the United States of America, 1789–1873. 18 vols. Available online, American Memory Project, Library of Congress, http://memory.loc.gov/ammem/amlaw/lwsl.html.

U.S. Department of the Army. *Military Leadership.* FM 22-100. Washington, D.C.: Headquarters, Department of the Army, 1961. Available online, Internet Archive, https://archive.org/details/FM22-1001961.

U.S. War Department. *General Orders Affecting the Volunteer Force, Adjutant General's Office.* 3 vols. Washington, D.C.: Government Printing Office, 1862.

———. *General Orders Affecting the Volunteer Force, Adjutant General's Office.* 4 vols. Washington, D.C.: Government Printing Office, 1864.

———. *Revised Regulations for the Army of the United States, 1861.* Philadelphia: J. G. L. Brown, Printer, 1861.

———. *U.S. Infantry Tactics, for the Instruction, Exercise, and Manoevres of the United States Infantry, including Infantry of the Line, Light Infantry, and Riflemen.* Philadelphia: J. B. Lippincott, 1863.

———. *The War of the Rebellion: A Compilation of the Official Records of the Union and Confederate Armies.* 70 vols. in 128 parts. Washington, D.C.: Government Printing Office, 1880–1901.

Secondary Sources

Allardice, Bruce S. *Confederate Colonels: A Biographical Register.* Columbia: University of Missouri Press, 2008.

Allardice, Bruce S., and Lawrence Lee Hewitt. *Kentuckians in Gray: Confederate Generals and Field Officers of the Bluegrass State.* Lexington: University Press of Kentucky, 2008.

Altschuler, Glenn C., and Stuart M. Blumin. *Rude Republic: Americans and Their Politics in the Nineteenth Century.* Princeton, N.J.: Princeton University Press, 2000.

Anderson, Fred. *A People's Army: Massachusetts Soldiers and Society in the Seven Years' War.* New York: W. W. Norton, 1984.

Andrew, Rod. *Long Gray Lines: The Southern Military School Tradition, 1839–1915.* Chapel Hill: University of North Carolina Press, 2004.

Andrews, Robert, ed. *The Columbia Dictionary of Quotations.* New York: Columbia University Press, 1993.

Appleby, Joyce. *Liberalism and Republicanism in the Historical Imagination.* Cambridge, Mass.: Harvard University Press, 1992.

Arliskas, Thomas M. *Cadet Gray and Butternut Blue: Notes on Confederate Uniforms.* Gettysburg, Pa.: Thomas, 2006.

Avant, Deborah. "From Mercenary to Citizen Armies: Explaining Change in the Practice of War." *International Organization* 54 (Winter 2000): 41–72.

Ayers, Edward L. *Vengeance and Justice: Crime and Punishment in the 19th-Century American South.* New York: Oxford University Press, 1984.

Bailyn, Bernard. *The Ideological Origins of the American Revolution.* Cambridge, Mass.: Harvard University Press, 1967.

Ball, Durwood. *Army Regulars on the Western Frontier, 1848–1861.* Norman: University of Oklahoma Press, 2001.

Banning, Lance G. "Quarrel with Federalism: A Study in the Origins and Character of Republican Thought." Ph.D. diss., Washington University, 1971.

Bartholomees, J. Boone, Jr. *Buff Facings and Gilt Buttons: Staff and Headquarters Operations in the Army of Northern Virginia, 1861–1865.* Columbia: University of South Carolina Press, 1998.

Barton, Michael. *Goodmen: The Character of Civil War Soldiers.* University Park: Pennsylvania State University Press, 1981.

Bauer, K. Jack. *The Mexican War, 1846–1848.* Lincoln: University of Nebraska Press, 1992.

Berry, Stephen W., II. *All That Makes a Man: Love and Ambition in the Civil War South.* New York: Oxford University Press, 2003.

Bledsoe, Andrew S. "The Homecircle: Kinship and Community in the Third Arkansas Infantry, Texas Brigade, 1861–1865." *Arkansas Historical Quarterly* 71 (Spring 2012): 22–43.

Bledstein, Burton J. *The Culture of Professionalism: The Middle Class and the Development of Higher Education in America.* New York: W. W. Norton, 1976.

Blight, David W. *Race and Reunion: The Civil War in American Memory.* Cambridge, Mass.: Harvard University Press, 2001.

Boatner, Mark M., III. *The Civil War Dictionary,* Rev. ed. New York: Vintage Books, 1991.

Bohannon, Keith. "Cadets, Drillmasters, Draft Dodgers, and Soldiers: The Georgia Military Institute during the Civil War." *Georgia Historical Quarterly* 79 (1995): 5–29.

Bond, Bradley. *Political Culture in the Nineteenth-Century South: Mississippi, 1830–1890.* Baton Rouge: Louisiana State University Press, 1995.

Bonner, Robert E. *Mastering America: Southern Slaveholders and the Crisis of American Nationhood.* New York: Cambridge University Press, 2009.

Bowman, Shearer Davis. *At the Precipice: Americans North and South during the Secession Crisis.* Chapel Hill: University of North Carolina Press, 2010.

Broadwater, Jeff. *George Mason, Forgotten Founder.* Chapel Hill: University of North Carolina Press, 2006.

Brooks, Charles E. "The Social and Cultural Dynamics of Soldiering in Hood's Texas Brigade." *Journal of Southern History* 67 (August 2001): 535–72.

Buck, James H., and Lawrence J. Korb, eds. *Military Leadership.* Beverly Hills, Calif.: Sage, 1981.

Budiansky, Stephen. *The Bloody Shirt: Terror after Appomattox*. New York: Viking, 2008.

Cain, Marvin R. "A 'Face of Battle' Needed: An Assessment of Motives and Men in Civil War Historiography." *Civil War History* 28 (March 1982): 5–27.

Carmichael, Peter S. *The Last Generation: Young Virginians in Peace, War, and Reunion*. Chapel Hill: University of North Carolina Press, 2005.

———. *Lee's Young Artillerist: William R. J. Pegram*. Charlottesville: University Press of Virginia, 1995.

———. "'We Were the Men': The Ambiguous Place of Confederate Slaves in Southern Armies." July 20, 2008. Civil War Memory. http://cwmemory.com/2008/07/20/peter-carmichael-on-black-confederates-and-confederate-slaves/. Accessed April 7, 2013.

Carnes, Mark C., and Clyde Griffen, eds. *Meanings for Manhood: Constructions of Masculinity in Victorian America*. Chicago: University of Chicago Press, 1990.

Carp, Benjamin L. "Nations of American Rebels: Understanding Nationalism in Revolutionary North America and the Civil War South." *Civil War History* 48 (March 2002): 5–33.

Catton, Bruce. "Union Discipline and Leadership in the Civil War." *Marine Corps Gazette* 40, no. 1 (January 1956): 18–25.

Childress, David T. "The Army in Transition: The United States Army, 1815–1846," Ph.D. diss., Mississippi State University, 1974.

Clarke, Bruce C. *Guidelines for the Leader and the Commander*. Harrisburg, Pa.: Stackpole, 1966.

Coddington, Edwin B. *The Gettysburg Campaign: A Study in Command*. New York: Scribner's, 1968.

Coffman, Edward M. "The Duality of the American Military Tradition: A Commentary." *Journal of Military History* 64:4 (October 2000): 967–980.

———. *The Old Army: A Portrait of the American Army in Peacetime, 1784–1898*. New York: Oxford University Press, 1988.

Collins, Arthur S. *Common Sense Training: A Working Philosophy for Leaders*. Novato, Calif.: Presidio, 1978.

Connelly, Thomas Lawrence. *Army of the Heartland: The Army of Tennessee, 1861–1862*. 1967. Reprint, Baton Rouge: Louisiana State University Press, 2001.

———. *Autumn of Glory: The Army of Tennessee, 1862–1865*. 1971. Reprint, Baton Rouge: Louisiana State University Press, 2001.

Conrad, James Lee. *The Young Lions: Confederate Cadets at War*. Columbia: University of South Carolina Press, 2004.

Cosmas, Graham A. *An Army for Empire: The United States Army in the Spanish-American War*. College Station: Texas A&M University Press, 1998.

Cozzens, Peter. *The Shipwreck of Their Hopes: The Battles for Chattanooga*. Urbana: University of Illinois Press, 1996.

———. *This Terrible Sound: The Battle of Chickamauga.* Urbana: University of Illinois Press, 1996.

Crackel, Theodore J. "The Founding of West Point: Jefferson and the Politics of National Security." *Armed Forces and Society* 7, no. 4 (Summer 1981): 529–43.

———. "Jefferson, Politics, and the Army: An Examination of the Military Peace Establishment Act of 1802." *Journal of the Early Republic* 2, no. 1 (Spring 1982): 21–38.

———. *Mr. Jefferson's Army: Political and Social Reform of the Military Establishment, 1801–1809.* New York: New York University Press, 1987.

Cress, Lawrence Delbert. *Citizens in Arms: The Army and Militia in American Society to the War of 1812.* Chapel Hill: University of North Carolina Press, 1982.

———. "Radical Whiggery on the Role of the Military: Ideological Roots of the American Revolutionary Militia." *Journal of the History of Ideas* 40 (January–March 1979): 43–60.

Cunliffe, Marcus. *Soldiers and Civilians: The Martial Spirit in America, 1776–1865.* Boston: Little, Brown, 1968.

Cunningham, O. Edward. *Shiloh and the Western Campaign of 1862.* Edited by Gary D. Joiner and Timothy B. Smith. Havertown, Pa.: Casemate, 2009.

Daniel, Larry J. *Soldiering in the Army of Tennessee: A Portrait of Life in a Confederate Army.* Chapel Hill: University of North Carolina Press, 1991.

Davis, William C. *Rebels & Yankees: The Commanders of the Civil War.* London: Salamander, 1989.

Dean, Eric T. *Shook over Hell: Post-Traumatic Stress, Vietnam, and the Civil War.* Cambridge, Mass.: Harvard University Press, 1997.

DeBuse, Mark R. "The Citizen-Officer Ideal: A Historical and Literary Inquiry." M.A. thesis, Naval Postgraduate School, 2005.

Derthick, Martha. *The National Guard in Politics.* Cambridge, Mass.: Harvard University Press, 1965.

Dew, Charles B. *Apostles of Disunion: Southern Secession Commissioners and the Causes of the Civil War.* Charlottesville: University Press of Virginia, 2001.

Dobak, William A. *Freedom by the Sword: The U.S. Colored Troops, 1862–1867.* Washington, D.C.: Center of Military History, 2011.

Donald, David Herbert. "The Confederate as a Fighting Man." *Journal of Southern History* 25 (May 1959): 178–93.

———. *Lincoln.* New York: Simon & Schuster, 1996.

Donovan, James. *A Terrible Glory: Custer and the Little Bighorn—the Last Great Battle of the American West.* New York: Little, Brown, 2008.

Doyle, William. *Aristocracy and Its Enemies in the Age of Revolution.* Oxford: Oxford University Press, 2009.

Eicher, John H., and David J. Eicher. *Civil War High Commands.* Stanford: Stanford University Press, 2001.

Elting, John R. *Amateurs, to Arms! A Military History of the War of 1812*. Cambridge, Mass.: Da Capo, 1995.

Emerson, W. Eric. *Sons of Privilege: The Charleston Light Dragoons in the Civil War.* Columbia: University of South Carolina Press, 2005.

Emerson, William E. "Leadership and Civil War Desertion in the Twenty-Fourth and Twenty-Fifth Regiments North Carolina Troops." *Southern Historian* 17 (Spring 1996): 17–33.

Escott, Paul D. *Military Necessity: Civil-Military Relations in the Confederacy.* Westport, Conn.: Praeger Security International, 2006.

Estes, Claud. *List of Field Officers, Regiments, and Battalions in the Confederate Army, 1861 to 1865*. Macon, Ga.: J. W. Burke, 1912.

Faust, Drew Gilpin. *This Republic of Suffering: Death and the American Civil War.* New York: Vintage Books, 2008.

Field, Ron, and Robin Smith. *Uniforms of the Civil War: An Illustrated Guide for Historians, Collectors, and Reenactors.* Guilford, Conn.: Globe Pequot, 2005.

Fitzpatrick, David John. "Emory Upton: The Misunderstood Reformer." Ph.D. diss., University of Michigan, 1996.

Flanagan, Edward M. *Before the Battle: A Commonsense Guide to Leadership and Management.* Novato, Calif.: Presidio, 1985.

Foner, Eric. *Reconstruction: America's Unfinished Revolution, 1863–1877.* New York: HarperCollins, 1988.

Foos, Paul. *A Short, Offhand, Killing Affair: Soldiers and Social Conflict during the Mexican-American War.* Chapel Hill: University of North Carolina Press, 2002.

Foote, Lorien. *The Gentlemen and the Roughs: Manhood, Honor, and Violence in the Union Army.* New York: New York University Press, 2010.

———. "Rich Man's War, Rich Man's Fight: Class, Ideology, and Discipline in the Union Army." *Civil War History* 51 (September 2005): 269–87.

Forgie, George B. *Patricide in the House Divided: A Psychological Interpretation of Lincoln and His Age.* New York: W. W. Norton, 1979.

Formisano, Ronald P. *For the People: American Populist Movements from the Revolution to the 1850s.* Chapel Hill: University of North Carolina Press, 2008.

Foster, Gaines M. *Ghosts of the Confederacy: Defeat, the Lost Cause, and the Emergence of the New South, 1865–1913.* New York: Oxford University Press, 1988.

Fox-Genovese, Elizabeth, and Eugene D. Genovese. *The Mind of the Master Class: History and Faith in the Southern Slaveholders' Worldview.* New York: Cambridge University Press, 2005.

Frank, Joseph Allan. *With Ballot and Bayonet: The Political Socialization of American Civil War Soldiers.* Athens: University of Georgia Press, 1998.

Frank, Joseph Allan, and George A. Reaves. *"Seeing the Elephant": Raw Recruits at the Battle of Shiloh.* Westport, Conn.: Greenwood, 1989.

Frevert, Ute. *Men of Honour: A Social and Cultural History of the Duel.* Oxford: Oxford University Press, 1995.

Friend, Craig Thompson, and Lorri Glover, eds. *Southern Manhood: Perspectives on Masculinity in the Old South.* Athens: University of Georgia Press, 2004.

Gallagher, Gary W. *The Confederate War.* Cambridge, Mass.: Harvard University Press, 1999.

———. "Shaping Public Memory of the Civil War: Robert E. Lee, Jubal A. Early, and Douglas Southall Freeman." In *The Memory of the Civil War in American Culture,* edited by Alice Fahs and Joan Waugh, 39–63. Chapel Hill: University of North Carolina Press, 2004.

———. *The Union War.* Cambridge, Mass.: Harvard University Press, 2011.

Garrison, Webb B. *The Amazing Civil War.* Nashville, Tenn.: Rutledge Hill, 1998.

Geary, James W. *We Need Men: The Union Draft in the Civil War.* DeKalb: Northern Illinois University Press, 1991.

Genovese, Eugene D. "The Chivalric Tradition in the Old South." *Sewanee Review* 108 (Spring 2000): 180–98.

Gilmore, David D. *Manhood in the Making: Cultural Concepts of Masculinity.* New Haven, Conn.: Yale University Press, 1990.

Gindlesperger, James. *Seed Corn of the Confederacy: The Virginia Military Institute at New Market.* Shippensburg, Pa.: Burd Street, 1997.

Glatthaar, Joseph T. "A Dynamic for Success and Failure: Discipline, Cause, and Comrades in the Relationship between Officers and Enlisted Men in Lee's Army." In *The Struggle for Equality: Essays on Sectional Conflict, the Civil War, and the Long Reconstruction,* edited by Orville Vernon Burton, Jerald Podair, and Jennifer L. Weber, 59–75. Charlottesville: University Press of Virginia, 2011.

———. *Forged in Battle: The Civil War Alliance of Black Soldiers and White Officers.* New York: Free Press, 1990.

———. *General Lee's Army: From Victory to Collapse.* New York: Free Press, 2008.

———. "The 'New' Civil War History: An Overview." *Pennsylvania Magazine of History and Biography* 115 (July 1991): 339–69.

———. *Soldiering in the Army of Northern Virginia: A Statistical Portrait of the Troops Who Served under Robert E. Lee.* Chapel Hill: University of North Carolina Press, 2011.

Glover, Lorri. *Southern Sons: Becoming Men in the New Nation.* Baltimore: Johns Hopkins University Press, 2007.

Goolsby, J. C. "Col. William Johnston Pegram." *Confederate Veteran* 6 (June 1898): 271.

Goss, Thomas J. *The War within the Union High Command: Politics and Generalship during the Civil War.* Lawrence: University Press of Kansas, 2003.

Graves, Donald E. "'Dry Books of Tactics': U.S. Infantry Manuals of the War of 1812 and After." *Military Collector and Historian* 38 (Summer, Winter 1986): 50–61, 173–77.

Graves, Donald E., and John C. Frederiksen. "'Dry Books of Tactics' Re-Read: An Additional Note on U.S. Infantry Manuals of the War of 1812." *Military Collector and Historian* 39 (Summer 1987): 64–65.

Green, Jennifer R. *Military Education and the Emerging Middle Class in the Old South.* New York: Cambridge University Press, 2009.

Greenberg, Amy S. *Manifest Manhood and the Antebellum American Empire.* New York: Cambridge University Press, 2005.

Griffith, Paddy. *Battle Tactics of the Civil War.* New Haven, Conn.: Yale University Press, 1989.

Grimsley, Mark. *And Keep Moving On: The Virginia Campaign, May–June 1864.* Lincoln: University of Nebraska Press, 2002.

———. "Surviving Military Revolution: The U.S. Civil War." In *The Dynamics of Military Revolution, 1300–2050,* edited by Macgregor Knox and Williamson Murray, 74–91. Cambridge: Cambridge University Press, 2001.

Haber, Samuel. *The Quest for Authority and Honor in the American Professions, 1750–1900.* Chicago: University of Chicago Press, 1991.

Hagen, Kenneth J., and William P. Roberts, eds. *Against All Enemies: Interpretations of American Military History from Colonial Times to the Present.* New York: Greenwood, 1986.

Hagerman, Edward. *The American Civil War and the Origins of Modern Warfare: Ideas, Organization, and Field Command.* Bloomington: Indiana University Press, 1992.

Hahn, Steven. *The Roots of Southern Populism: Yeoman Farmers and the Transformation of the Georgia Upcountry, 1850–1890.* New York: Oxford University Press, 1983.

Hamner, Christopher H. *Enduring Battle: American Soldiers in Three Wars, 1776–1945.* Lawrence: University Press of Kansas, 2011.

———. "Why Do Soldiers Fight?" *Historically Speaking* (January 2012): 10–12.

Harrington, James. *"The Commonwealth of Oceana" and "A System of Politics."* Edited by J. G. A. Pocock. New York: Cambridge University Press, 1992.

Hattaway, Herman, and Archer Jones, eds. *Why the North Won the Civil War.* Rev. ed. New York: Touchstone, 1996.

Haughton, Andrew. *Training, Tactics, and Leadership in the Confederate Army of Tennessee: Seeds of Failure.* London and Portland, Ore.: Frank Cass, 2000.

Hennessy, John. *The First Battle of Manassas: An End to Innocence, July 18–21, 1861.* Lynchburg, Va.: H. E. Howard, 1989.

Herrera, Ricardo A. "Guarantors of Liberty and Republic: The American Citizen as Soldier and the Military Ethos of Republicanism, 1775–1861." Ph.D. diss., Marquette University, 1998.

———. "Self-Governance and the American Citizen as Soldier." *Journal of Military History* 65, no. 1 (January 2001): 21–52.

Hess, Earl J. *Field Armies and Fortifications in the Civil War: The Eastern Campaigns, 1861–1864*. Chapel Hill: University of North Carolina Press, 2005.

———. *In the Trenches at Petersburg: Field Fortifications and Confederate Defeat*. Chapel Hill: University of North Carolina Press, 2009.

———. *Pickett's Charge—The Last Attack at Gettysburg*. Chapel Hill: University of North Carolina Press, 2001.

———. *The Rifle Musket in Civil War Combat: Reality and Myth*. Lawrence: University Press of Kansas, 2008.

———. *The Union Soldier in Battle*. Lawrence: University Press of Kansas, 1997.

Higginbotham, Don. *George Washington and the American Military Tradition*. Athens: University of Georgia Press, 1985.

———. "The Martial Spirit in the Antebellum South: Some Further Speculations in a National Context." *Journal of Southern History* 58 (February 1992): 3–26.

Hill, Jim Dan. *The Minute Man in Peace and War: A History of the National Guard*. Mechanicsburg, Pa.: Stackpole, 1964.

Hillyard, Michael J. *Cincinnatus and the Citizen-Servant Ideal: The Roman Legend's Life, Times, and Legacy*. [Philadelphia]: Xlibris, 2001.

Holberton, William B. *Homeward Bound: The Demobilization of the Union & Confederate Armies, 1865–66*. Mechanicsburg, Pa.: Stackpole, 2001.

Holmes, Richard. *Acts of War: The Behavior of Men in Battle*. New York: Free Press, 1985.

Holt, Michael F. *The Political Crisis of the 1850s*. New York: W. W. Norton, 1983.

Howell, Kenneth Wayne. *Henderson County, Texas: An Antebellum History, 1846–1861*. Austin, Tex.: Eakin, 1999.

Hsieh, Wayne Wei-siang. *West Pointers and the Civil War: The Old Army in War and Peace*. Chapel Hill: University of North Carolina Press, 2009.

Huff, Leo E. "The Last Duel in Arkansas: The Marmaduke-Walker Duel." *Arkansas Historical Quarterly* 23 (Spring 1964): 36–49.

Huntington, Samuel P. *The Soldier and the State: The Theory and Practice of Civil-Military Relations*. Cambridge, Mass.: Harvard University Press, 1981.

Huston, Reeve. *Land and Freedom: Rural Society, Popular Protest, and Party Politics in Antebellum New York*. New York: Oxford University Press, 2000.

Jacobs, James Ripley. *The Beginning of the U.S. Army, 1783–1812*. Princeton, N.J.: Princeton University Press, 1947.

Jacobson, Eric A., and Richard A. Rupp. *For Cause & for Country: A Study of the Affair at Spring Hill and the Battle of Franklin*. Franklin, Tenn.: O'Moore, 2008.

Jamieson, Perry D. *Crossing the Deadly Ground: United States Army Tactics, 1865–1899*. Tuscaloosa: University of Alabama Press, 1994.

Jimerson, Randall C. *The Private Civil War: Popular Thought during the Sectional Conflict*. Baton Rouge: Louisiana State University Press, 1988.

Johnson, Timothy D. *A Gallant Little Army: The Mexico City Campaign*. Lawrence: University Press of Kansas, 2007.

Jones, R. Steven *The Right Hand of Command: Uses and Disuses of Personal Staffs in the Civil War*. Mechanicsburg, Pa.: Stackpole, 2000.

Kahan, Alan S. *Liberalism in Nineteenth-Century Europe: The Political Culture of Limited Suffrage*. New York: Palgrave Macmillan, 2003.

Keegan, John. *The Mask of Command*. New York: Penguin Books, 1987.

Kemble, Robert C. *The Image of the Army Officer in America*. Westport, Conn.: Greenwood, 1973.

Kettner, James H. *The Development of American Citizenship, 1608–1870*. Chapel Hill: University of North Carolina Press, 1978.

Kloppenberg, James T. *The Virtues of Liberalism*. New York: Oxford University Press, 1998.

Kohn, Richard H. *Eagle and Sword: The Federalists and the Creation of the Military Establishment in America, 1783–1802*. New York: Free Press, 1975.

Kolenda, Christopher D. "What Is Leadership? Some Classical Ideas." In *Leadership: The Warrior's Art,* edited by Christopher D. Kolenda, 3–26. Carlisle, Pa: Army War College Foundation Press, 2001.

Krick, Robert E. L. *Lee's Colonels: A Biographical Register of the Field Officers of the Army of Northern Virginia*. Alexandria, Va.: American Society for Training & Development, 1992.

———. *Staff Officers in Gray: A Biographical Register of the Staff Officers in the Army of Northern Virginia*. Chapel Hill: University of North Carolina Press, 2003

Laver, Harry S. *Citizens More than Soldiers: The Kentucky Militia and Society in the Early Republic*. Lincoln: University of Nebraska Press, 2007.

———. "Rethinking the Social Role of the Militia: Community-Building in Antebellum Kentucky." *Journal of Southern History* 68 (November 2002): 777–816.

Lawson, Melinda. *Patriot Fires: Forging a New American Nationalism in the Civil War North*. Lawrence: University Press of Kansas, 2005.

Leach, Douglas E. *Arms for Empire: A Military History of the British Colonies in North America, 1607–1763*. New York: Macmillan, 1973.

Leeman, Nicholas *Redemption: The Last Battle of the Civil War*. New York: Macmillan, 2006.

Levinson, Irving W. *War within War: Mexican Guerrillas, Domestic Elites, and the United States of America, 1846–1848*. Fort Worth: Texas Christian University Press, 2005.

Linderman, Gerald E. *Embattled Courage: The Experience of Combat in the American Civil War*. New York: Free Press, 1987.

———. *The World within War: America's Combat Experience in World War II.* Cambridge, Mass.: Oxford University Press, 1997.
Linn, Brian M. *The Echo of Battle: The Army's Way of War.* Cambridge, Mass.: Harvard University Press, 2007.
Lofgren, Charles A. "Compulsory Military Service under the Constitution: The Original Understanding." *William and Mary Quarterly,* 3rd ser., 33 (January 1976): 61–88.
Logan, John A. *The Volunteer Soldier of America.* Chicago: R. S. Peale, 1887.
Mahon, John K. "Civil War Infantry Assault Tactics." *Military Affairs* 25 (Summer 1961): 57–68.
———. *History of the Militia and the National Guard.* New York: Macmillan, 1983.
Malone, Dandridge. *Small Unit Leadership: A Common Sense Approach.* Novato, Calif.: Presidio, 1985.
Manning, Chandra. *What This Cruel War Was Over: Soldiers, Slavery, and the Civil War.* New York: Alfred A. Knopf, 2007.
Marrs, Aaron W. "Desertion and Loyalty in the South Carolina Infantry, 1861–1865." *Civil War History* 50 (March 2004): 47–65.
Marshall, S. L. A. *The Officer as Leader.* Harrisburg, Pa.: Stackpole, 1966.
Matter, William D. *If It Takes All Summer: The Battle of Spotsylvania.* Chapel Hill: University of North Carolina Press, 1988.
McArthur, Judith N., and Orville Vernon Burton. *A Gentleman and an Officer: A Military and Social History of James B. Griffin's Civil War.* New York: Oxford University Press, 1996.
McCoy, Drew R. *The Elusive Republic: Political Economy in Jeffersonian America.* Chapel Hill: University of North Carolina Press, 1980.
McCreedy, Kenneth Otis. "Palladium of Liberty: The American Militia System, 1815–1861." Ph.D. diss., University of California, Berkeley, 1991.
McCurry, Stephanie. *Masters of Small Worlds: Yeoman Households, Gender Relations, and the Political Culture of the Antebellum South Carolina Low Country.* New York: Oxford University Press, 1995.
McDonough, James L. *Shiloh: In Hell before Night.* Knoxville: University of Tennessee Press, 1977.
McPherson, James M. "Antebellum Southern Exceptionalism: A New Look at an Old Question." *Civil War History* 50 (December 2004): 418–33.
———. *Battle Cry of Freedom: The Civil War Era.* New York: Oxford University Press, 1988.
———. *For Cause and Comrades: Why Men Fought in the Civil War.* New York: Oxford University Press, 1997.
McWhiney, Grady, and Perry D. Jamieson, *Attack and Die: Civil War Military Tactics and the Southern Heritage.* Tuscaloosa: University of Alabama Press, 1982.

Meier, Kathryn Shively. *Nature's Civil War: Common Soldiers and the Environment in 1862 Virginia.* Chapel Hill: University of North Carolina Press, 2013.
Meyer, Howard N. *Colonel of the Black Regiment: The Life of Thomas Wentworth Higginson.* New York: W. W. Norton, 1967.
Miller, Brian Craig. "Confederate Amputees and the Women Who Loved (or Tried to Love) Them." In *Weirding the War: Stories from the Civil War's Ragged Edge,* edited by Steven W. Berry, 2:301–20. Athens: University of Georgia Press, 2011.
Miller, Richard. "Brahmins under Fire: Peer Courage and the Harvard Regiment." *Historical Journal of Massachusetts* 30, no. 1 (Winter 2002): 75–109.
Mitchell, Reid. *Civil War Soldiers.* New York: Viking, 1988.
———. *The Vacant Chair: The Northern Soldier Leaves Home.* New York: Viking, 1993.
Molloy, Peter Michael. "Technical Education and the Young Republic: West Point as America's École Polytechnique, 1802–1833." Ph.D. diss., Brown University, 1975.
Moore, Albert B. *Conscription and Conflict in the Confederacy.* New York: Macmillan, 1924.
Moran, Lord. *The Anatomy of Courage,* 1945. Reprint, Garden City Park, N.Y.: Avery, 1987.
Morgan, Edmund S. *The Birth of the Republic, 17463–89.* Chicago: University of Chicago Press, 1956.
———. *The Challenge of the American Revolution.* New York: W. W. Norton, 1976.
———. *Inventing the People: The Rise of Popular Sovereignty in England and America.* New York: W. W. Norton, 1989.
Morrison, James L. *"The Best School in the World": West Point, the Pre–Civil War Years, 1833–1866.* Kent, Ohio: Kent State University Press, 1986.
Morrison, Michael A. *Slavery and the American West: The Eclipse of Manifest Destiny and the Coming of the Civil War.* Chapel Hill: University of North Carolina Press, 1999.
Moseley, Thomas Vernon. "Evolution of the American Civil War Infantry Tactics." Ph.D. diss., University of North Carolina, 1967.
Moten, Matthew. *The Army Officers' Professional Ethic—Past, Present, and Future.* Carlisle, Pa.: Strategic Studies Institute, 2010.
———. *The Delafield Commission and the American Military Profession.* College Station: Texas A&M University Press, 2000.
Muir, Rory. *Tactics and the Experience of Battle in the Age of Napoleon.* New Haven, Conn.: Yale University Press, 1998.
Murdock, Eugene C. *One Million Men: The Civil War Draft in the North.* Madison: State Historical Society of Wisconsin, 1971.
Neem, Johann N. *Creating a Nation of Joiners: Democracy and Civil Society in Early National Massachusetts.* Cambridge, Mass.: Harvard University Press, 2008.

Newell, Clayton R., and Charles R. Shrader. *Of Duty Well and Faithfully Done: A History of the Regular Army in the Civil War*. Lincoln: University of Nebraska Press, 2011.

Noe, Kenneth W. *Reluctant Rebels: The Confederates Who Joined the Army after 1861*. Chapel Hill: University of North Carolina Press, 2010.

Noll, Mark A. *The Civil War as a Theological Crisis*. Chapel Hill: University of North Carolina Press, 2006.

Nosworthy, Brent. *The Bloody Crucible of Courage: Fighting Methods and Combat Experience of the Civil War*. New York: Basic Books, 2005.

———. *Roll Call to Destiny: The Soldier's Eye View of Civil War Battles*. New York: Basic Books, 2008.

Nye, Robert A. "Western Masculinities in War and Peace." *American Historical Review* 112 (April 2007): 417–38.

Nye, Roger H. *The Challenge of Command*. New York: Perigee, 1986.

Oakes, James. *The Ruling Race: A History of American Slaveowners*. New York: Vantage Books, 1982.

Onuf, Peter S. *Jefferson's Empire: The Language of American Nationhood*. Charlottesville: University Press of Virginia, 2000.

Orr, Timothy J. "'All Manner of Schemes and Rascalities': The Politics of Promotion in the Union Army." In *This Distracted and Anarchichal People: New Answers for Old Questions About the Civil War–Era North*, edited by Andrew L. Slap and Michael Thomas Smith, 81–103. New York: Fordham University Press, 2013.

Owsley, Frank L. *Plain Folk of the Old South*. 1949. Reprint, Baton Rouge: Louisiana State University Press, 1982.

Pace, Robert F. *Halls of Honor: College Men in the Old South*. Baton Rouge: Louisiana State University Press, 2004.

Patterson, Gerard A. *Rebels from West Point: The 306 U.S. Military Academy Graduates Who Fought for the Confederacy*. Mechanicsburg, Pa: Stackpole, 2002.

Perello, Christopher. *The Quest for Annihilation: The Role & Mechanics of Battle in the American Civil War*. Bakersfield, Calif.: Strategy & Tactics Press, 2009.

Peskin, Allan. *Winfield Scott and the Profession of Arms*. Kent, Ohio: Kent State University Press, 2003.

Pessen, Edward. "The Egalitarian Myth and the American Social Reality: Wealth, Mobility, and Equality in the 'Era of the Common Man.'" *American Historical Review* 76 (October 1971): 989–1034.

Pfanz, Harry W. *Gettysburg—Culp's Hill & Cemetery Hill*. Chapel Hill: University of North Carolina Press, 1993.

Phillips, Jason. "Battling Stereotypes: A Taxonomy of Common Soldiers in Civil War History." *History Compass* 6 (November 2008): 1407–25.

———. *Diehard Rebels: The Confederate Culture of Invincibility*. Athens: University of Georgia Press, 2007.

Pitcavage, Mark. "An Equitable Burden: The Decline of the State Militias, 1783–1858." Ph.D. diss., Ohio State University, 1995.
Pocock, J. G. A. "James Harrington and the Good Old Cause: A Study of the Ideological Context of His Writings." *Journal of British Studies* 10, no. 1 (November 1970): 30–48.
———. "Machiavelli, Harrington, and English Political Ideologies in the Eighteenth Century." *William and Mary Quarterly*, 3rd ser., 22 (October 1965): 549–83.
———. *The Machiavellian Moment: Florentine Political Thought and the Atlantic Republican Tradition*. Princeton, N.J.: Princeton University Press, 1975.
———. *Politics, Language, and Time: Essays on Political Thought and History*. New York: Metheun Young Books, 1972.
Power, J. Tracy. *Lee's Miserables: Life in the Army of Northern Virginia from the Wilderness to Appomattox*. Chapel Hill: University of North Carolina Press, 1998.
Price, Robert E. "Leadership in the Civil War: Officers of the Union Volunteer Army at Division Level and Below." M.A. thesis, U.S. Army Command and General Staff College, 1965.
Proctor, Nicholas W. *Bathed in Blood: Hunting and Mastery in the Old South*. Charlottesville: University Press of Virginia, 2002.
Prucha, Francis Paul. *The Sword of the Republic: The United States Army on the Frontier, 1783–1846*. New York: Macmillan, 1969.
Pugh, David. *Sons of Liberty: The Masculine Mind in Nineteenth-Century America*. Westport, Conn.: Greenwood, 1983.
Radley, Kenneth. *Rebel Watchdog: The Confederate States Army Provost Guard*. Baton Rouge: Louisiana State University Press, 1997.
Rahe, Paul A. *Inventions of Prudence: Constituting the American Regime*. Vol. 3 of *Republics Ancient and Modern*. Chapel Hill: University of North Carolina Press, 1994.
Ramold, Steven. *Baring the Iron Hand: Discipline in the Union Army*. DeKalb: Northern Illinois University Press, 2010.
Rhea, Gordon C. *The Battle of the Wilderness, May 5–6, 1864*. Baton Rouge: Louisiana State University Press, 2004.
———. *The Battles for Spotsylvania Court House and the Road to Yellow Tavern, May 7–12, 1864*. Baton Rouge: Louisiana State University Press, 2005.
———. *Cold Harbor: Grant and Lee, May 26–June 3, 1864*. Baton Rouge: Louisiana State University Press, 2007.
Richard, Carl J. *The Founders and the Classics: Greece, Rome, and the American Enlightenment*. Cambridge, Mass.: Harvard University Press, 1995.
Riker, William H. *Soldiers of the States: The Role of the National Guard in American Democracy*. Washington, D.C.: Public Affairs Press, 1957.
Rodgers, Daniel T. "Republicanism: The Career of a Concept." *Journal of American History* 79 (June 1992): 11–38.

Rood, Tim. *American Anabasis: Xenophon and the Idea of America from the Mexican War to Iraq.* New York: Overlook, 2011.

Rotundo, E. Anthony. *American Manhood: Transformations in Masculinity from the Revolution to the Modern Era.* New York: Basic Books, 1993.

Rowe, Mary Ellen. *Bulwark of the Republic: The American Militia in the Antebellum West.* Westport, Conn.: Praeger, 2003.

Royster, Charles. *The Destructive War: Stonewall Jackson, William Tecumseh Sherman, and the Americans.* New York: Vintage Books, 1993.

———. *A Revolutionary People at War: The Continental Army and American Character, 1775–1783.* Chapel Hill: University of North Carolina Press, 1979.

Ruffner, Kevin Conley. *Maryland's Blue & Gray: A Border State's Union and Confederate Junior Officer Corps.* Baton Rouge: Louisiana State University Press, 1997.

Ryan, Mary P. *Civic Wars: Democracy and Public Life in the American City during the Nineteenth Century.* Berkeley: University of California Press, 1997.

Samet, Elizabeth D. *Willing Obedience: Citizens, Soldiers, and the Progress of Consent in America, 1776–1898.* Stanford, Calif.: Stanford University Press, 2004.

Sandel, Michael. *Democracy's Discontent: America in Search of a Public Philosophy.* Cambridge, Mass.: Harvard University Press, 1996.

Scott, J. L. *45th Virginia Infantry.* Lynchburg, Va.: H. E. Howard, 1989.

Sears, Stephen W. *Chancellorsville.* New York: Mariner Books, 1998.

———. *Gettysburg.* New York: Mariner Books, 2004.

Selesky, Harold E. *War and Society in Colonial Connecticut.* New Haven, Conn.: Yale University Press, 1990.

Shaffer, Donald R. *After the Glory: The Struggles of Black Civil War Veterans.* Lawrence: University Press of Kansas, 2004.

Shannon, Fred Albert *The Organization and Administration of the Union Army, 1861–1865.* 2 vols. Cleveland, Ohio: Arthur H. Clark, 1928.

Shaw, William L. "The Confederate Conscription and Exemption Acts." *American Journal of Legal History* 6 (October 1962): 368–405.

Shea, William L., and Earl J. Hess. *Pea Ridge: Civil War Campaign in the West.* Chapel Hill: University of North Carolina Press, 1997.

Sheehan-Dean, Aaron. "The Blue and Gray in Black and White: Assessing the Scholarship on Civil War Soldiers." In *The View from the Ground: Experiences of Civil War Soldiers,* edited by Aaron Sheehan-Dean, 9–30. Lexington: University Press of Kentucky, 2007.

———. "Justice Has Something to Do with It: Class Relations and the Confederate Army." *Virginia Magazine of History and Biography* 113 (2005): 340–77.

———. *Why Confederates Fought: Family and Nation in Civil War Virginia.* Chapel Hill: University of North Carolina Press, 2007.

Shy, John W. *A People Numerous and Armed: Reflections on the Military Struggle for American Independence.* New York: Oxford University Press, 1990.

Sinha, Manisha. *The Counterrevolution of Slavery: Politics and Ideology in Antebellum South Carolina.* Chapel Hill: University of North Carolina Press, 2000.

Skeen, Charles. *Citizen Soldiers in the War of 1812.* Lexington: University Press of Kentucky, 1998.

Skelton, William B. *An American Profession of Arms: The Army Officer Corps, 1784–1861.* Lawrence: University Press of Kansas, 1992.

———. "The Commanding Generals and the Question of Civil Control in the Antebellum U.S. Army." *American Nineteenth-Century History* 7, no. 2 (June 2006): 153–72.

———. "West Point and Officer Professionalism, 1817–1877." In *West Point: Two Centuries and Beyond,* edited by Lance A. Betros, 22–37. Abilene, Tex.: McWhiney Foundation Press, 2004.

Smith, Adam I. P. *No Party Now: Politics in the Civil War North.* New York: Oxford University Press, 2006.

Smith, Derek. *The Gallant Dead: Union and Confederate Generals Killed in the Civil War.* Mechanicsburg, Pa.: Stackpole Books, 2005.

Smith, Kimberly K. *The Dominion of Voice: Riot, Reason, and Romance in Antebellum Politics.* Lawrence: University Press of Kansas, 1999.

Smith, Mark A. *Engineering Security: The Corps of Engineers and Third System Defense Policy, 1815–1861.* Tuscaloosa: University of Alabama Press, 2009.

Sommerville, Diane Miller. "'Will They Ever Be Able to Forget?': Confederate Soldiers and Mental Illness in the Defeated South." In *Weirding the War: Stories from the Civil War's Ragged Edge,* edited by Steven W. Berry, 2:321–39. Athens: University of Georgia Press, 2011.

Spiller, Ronald L. "From Hero to Leader: The Development of Nineteenth-Century American Military Leadership." Ph.D. diss., Texas A&M University, 1993.

Stagg, J. C. A. "Freedom and Subordination: Disciplinary Problems in the U.S. Army during the War of 1812." *Journal of Military History* 78, no. 2 (April 2014): 537–74.

Stauffer, Michael. "Volunteer or Uniformed Companies in the Antebellum Militia: A Checklist of Identified Companies, 1790–1859." *South Carolina Historical Magazine* 88 (April 1987): 108–16.

Stewart, George R. *Pickett's Charge: A Microhistory of the Final Attack at Gettysburg, July 3, 1863.* Boston: Houghton Mifflin, 1959.

Strayer, Larry M., and Richard A. Baumgartner, eds. *Echoes of Battle: The Atlanta Campaign.* Huntingdon, W.Va.: Blue Acorn, 2004.

Sword, Wiley *Courage under Fire: Profiles in Bravery from the Battlefields of the Civil War.* New York: St. Martin's, 2007.

Sydnor, Charles S. *American Revolutionaries in the Making: Political Practices in Washington's Virginia.* Chapel Hill: University of North Carolina Press, 1952.

Symonds, Craig L. "An Improvised Army at War, 1861–1865." In *Against All Enemies:*

Interpretations of American Military History from Colonial Times to the Present, edited by Kenneth J. Hagan and William R. Roberts, 155–71. Westport, Conn: Greenwood, 1986.

Thornton, J. Mills. *Politics in a Slave Society: Alabama, 1800–1860.* Baton Rouge: Louisiana State University Press, 1981.

Van Creveld, Martin. *Command in War.* Cambridge, Mass.: Harvard University Press, 1985.

Volk, Kyle G. "The Perils of 'Pure Democracy': Minority Rights, Liquor Politics, and Popular Sovereignty in Antebellum America." *Journal of the Early Republic* 29 (2009): 641–79.

Volpe, Vernon L. "The Origins of the Frémont Expeditions: John J. Abert and the Scientific Exploration of the Trans-Mississippi West." *Historian* 62 (Winter 2000): 245–63.

Voss-Hubbard, Mark. *Beyond Party: Cultures of Antipartisanship in Northern Politics before the Civil War.* Baltimore: Johns Hopkins University Press, 2002.

Wade, Arthur P. "Roads to the Top—An Analysis of General-Officer Selection in the United States Army, 1789–1898." *Military Affairs* 40, no. 4 (December 1976): 157–63.

Waldstreicher, David. *In the Midst of Perpetual Fetes: The Making of American Nationalism, 1776–1820.* Chapel Hill: University of North Carolina Press, 1997.

Walker, Scott. *Hell's Broke Loose in Georgia: Survival in a Civil War Regiment.* Athens: University of Georgia Press, 2007.

Warner, Ezra J. *Generals in Blue: Lives of the Union Commanders.* Baton Rouge: Louisiana State University Press, 1964.

———. *Generals in Gray: Lives of the Confederate Commanders.* Baton Rouge: Louisiana State University Press, 1959.

Watson, Harry L. *Liberty and Power: The Politics of Jacksonian America.* 2nd ed. New York: Hill and Wang, 2006.

Watson, Samuel J. "Continuity in Civil-Military Relations and Expertise: The U.S. Army during the Decade before the Civil War." *Journal of Military History* 75, no. 1 (January 2011): 221–50.

———. *Jackson's Sword: The Army Officer Corps on the American Frontier, 1810–1821.* Lawrence: University Press of Kansas, 2012.

———. "Manifest Destiny and Military Professionalism: Junior U.S. Army Officers' Attitudes toward War with Mexico, 1844–1846." *Southwestern Historical Quarterly* 99 (April 1996): 467–98.

———. *Peacekeepers and Conquerors: The Army Officer Corps on the American Frontier, 1821–1846.* Lawrence: University Press of Kansas, 2013.

———. "Professionalism, Social Attitudes, and Civil-Military Accountability in the United States Army Officer Corps, 1815–1846." Ph.D. diss., Rice University, 1996.

Waugh, John. *The Class of 1846: From West Point to Appomattox: Stonewall Jackson, George McClellan, and Their Brothers.* New York: Warner Books, 1994.

Weigley, Russell F. *The American Way of War: A History of United States Military Strategy and Policy.* New York: Macmillan, 1973.
———. *History of the United States Army.* Bloomington: Indiana University Press, 1984.
———. *Towards an American Army: Military Thought from Washington to Marshall.* New York: Columbia University Press, 1962.
Weinert. Richard P. *The Confederate Regular Army.* Shippensburg, Pa.: White Mane, 1991.
Weitz, Mark A. "Drill, Training, and the Combat Performance of the Civil War Soldier: Dispelling the Myth of the Poor Soldier, Great Fighter." *Journal of Military History* 62, no. 2 (April 1998): 263–89.
———. *More Damning Than Slaughter: Desertion in the Confederate Army.* Lincoln: University of Nebraska Press, 2005.
———. "Shoot Them All: Chivalry, Honour, and the Confederate Army Officer Corps." In *The Chivalric Ethos and the Development of Military Professionalism,* edited by D. J. B. Trim, 321–47. Leiden, The Netherlands: Brill, 2003.
Wettemann, Robert P., Jr. "A Part or Apart: The Alleged Isolation of Antebellum U.S. Army Officers." *American Nineteenth-Century History* 7, no. 2 (June 2006): 193–217.
———. *Privilege vs. Equality: Civil-Military Relations in the Jacksonian Era, 1815–1845.* Santa Barbara, Calif.: Praeger Security International, 2009.
Whisker, James B. *The Rise and Decline of the American Militia System.* Cranbury, N.J.: Associated University Presses, 1999.
White, Jonathan W. *Emancipation, the Union Army, and the Reelection of Abraham Lincoln.* Baton Rouge: Louisiana State University Press, 2014.
Wiley, Bell Irvin. *The Life of Billy Yank: The Common Soldier of the Union.* 1952. Rev. ed., Baton Rouge: Louisiana State University Press, 1992.
———. *The Life of Johnny Reb: The Common Soldier of the Confederacy.* 1943. Rev. ed., Baton Rouge: Louisiana State University Press, 2004.
Williams, T. Harry. "Badger Colonels and the Civil War Officer." *Wisconsin Magazine of History* 47 (Fall 1963): 35–46.
Wills, Garry. *Cincinnatus: George Washington and the Enlightenment.* New York: Doubleday, 1984.
Wilson, Mark. *The Business of Civil War: Military Mobilization and the State, 1861–1865.* Baltimore: Johns Hopkins University Press, 2006.
Wilson, Peter H. "Defining Military Culture." *Journal of Military History* 72, no. 1 (January 2008): 11–41.
Winders, Richard Bruce. *Mr. Polk's Army: The American Military Experience in the Mexican War.* College Station: Texas A&M University Press, 1997.
Wood, Gordon S. *The Creation of the American Republic, 1776–1787.* Chapel Hill: University of North Carolina Press, 1969.
———. *The Radicalism of the American Revolution.* New York: Knopf, 1992.

Wood, W. J. *Civil War Generalship: The Art of Command.* Cambridge, Mass.: Da Capo, 2000.

Woodward, Colin Edward. *Marching Masters: Slavery, Race, and the Confederate Army during the Civil War.* Chapel Hill: University of North Carolina Press, 2014.

Woodworth, Steven E. *Jefferson Davis and His Generals: The Failure of Confederate Command in the West.* Lawrence: University Press of Kansas, 1990.

Wooster, Robert *The American Military Frontiers: The United States Army in the West, 1783–1900.* Albuquerque: University of New Mexico Press, 2009.

Wright, John D. *The Language of the Civil War.* Westport, Conn.: Greenwood, 2001.

Wyatt-Brown, Bertram. *The Shaping of Southern Culture: Honor, Grace, and War, 1760s–1880s.* Chapel Hill: University of North Carolina Press, 2001.

———. *Southern Honor: Ethics and Behavior in the Old South.* New York: Oxford University Press, 1982.

INDEX

Abbott, Edwin Gardner, 176
Abbott, Henry Livermore, *following page 134,* 169, 186, 190
Abolitionism, 2, 59, 209–210
Accountability, 74
Adams, John, 7
Adjutants. *See* Staff officers
Administrative duties of officers, 48, 74, 107, 108–10
African American Civil War Memorial, 144
African American soldiers. *See* United States Colored Troops
Age, 40, 67, 70, 79, 85, 87, 89, 92, 93, 107, 116, 118, 135, 213, 228
Agriculture. *See* Farming
Aides-de-camp. *See* Staff officers
Alcohol. *See* Drunkenness
Allen, Ujanirtus, 126
Amateurism, 11, 18, 19, 30, 34, 65, 94–95, 105–6, 158–59, 182–83, 219–220
Ambition, 8–9, 13, 16, 25, 27, 39–40, 54–56, 58–60, 80–81, 103, 111–12, 146–47, 149, 211
American Revolution, x, 2, 3–4, 5–8, 10, 12–14, 24, 31–32, 129, 209
Anabasis (Xenophon), ix–x
Anderson, Robert, 22
Andrew, John A., 34
Andrews, C. C., 68–69, 87, 110, 191–92, 202–3
Antebellum army officer corps, 15–18, 23–24, 63–64, 94, 103, 108
Antietam, Battle of, 102, 152–53
Antimilitarism, 16
Appler, Jesse J., 139–42, 144
Appointments, 8, 10, 26–30, 32–36, 38, 43–50, 51–61, 67, 94, 97, 102, 122, 127, 173, 210
Appomattox Court House, 28, 150, 219
Areté (moral excellence), x, 7–9, 11, 23, 112–13

Aristocracy, 1, 5, 12–14, 16–17, 50, 58, 92–93, 129
Army of Mississippi, 45, 52, 140, 159, 170
Army of Northern Virginia, 64, 102, 104, 116, 121, 125, 149, 150,161, 173, 178, 185, 232
Army of Tennessee, 105, 108, 131, 184, 213, 215
Army of the Cumberland, 45
Army of the Potomac, 45, 80, 85, 104, 178, 202, 205
Army of the Tennessee, 139, 198
Arrogance, 93, 98, 106, 128, 131
Artaxerxes II, ix
Artillery. *See* Organization of armies
Atlanta Campaign, 91–92, 144, 184, 191, 197–98, 203
Attrition, 47, 159, 183–84, 185, 220, 223–225
Austin, Matthew S., 156
Authority, x–xii, 5, 8–10, 11, 16, 19, 22, 28, 32, 35–40, 60, 62, 64–65, 67–70, 72–78, 81, 83–84, 85–87, 90–92, 94–95, 97–100, 106, 108, 110, 116, 118, 121, 126–28, 133, 147–49, 157–58, 160, 162, 167, 175, 180, 193, 200, 207, 220–21
Ayling, Augustus D., 50–51

Babcock, Willoughby, 77, 82–83, 118
Bahnson, Charles Frederic, 38, 213
Ball's Bluff, Battle of, 151–52, 166
Barclay, Thomas, 13
Barralet, John J., 8
Bartlett, William Francis, 166
Bates, James C., 49–50
Battalion. *See* Organization of armies
Baugh, William Fielding, 156
Baxter, Eli H., 56–57
Baylor, George, 136–37
Beatty, John, 90–91

Bermuda Hundred Campaign, 192
Bierce, Ambrose G., 203–4
Big Bethel, Battle of, 154
Billings, John Davis, 174, 177
Billy Yank archetype, 10, 158
Black, John H., 212
Blake, Charles G., 119–20
Blakemore, George Thomas, 159
Boards of examination. *See* Examination of officers
Body servants. *See* Slaves and servants
Booker, John, 214–15
Bowen, George A., 187–88, 195–96, 203
Boyd, Cyrus F., 144–46
Bradwell, Isaac Gordon, 161, 219
Bragg, Braxton, 74, 170–71
Brevets, 16, 144, 211
Brewster, Charles Harvey, 181, 187, 188–89, 191
British army, 13, 16, 66, 161
Brooks, Charles E., 79
Brown, Alonzo 54–55, 56
Brown, Joseph E., 35
Browning, George W., 113–14, 119
Bruff, Joseph, 196–97
Buchanan, Samuel Thompson, 115
Buck, Henry A., 43–44
Buckland, Ralph Pomeroy, 141
Bull, Rice C., 79
Bumpus, Edgar L., 180–81
Bureaucracy and "red tape," 29, 59, 73, 105, 108, 109
Burgwyn, Henry, 51–52
Burgwyn, William H. S., 51–52, 192
Burkhalter, James L., 201–2
Butterfield, Daniel, 109
Byrnes, Richard, 88–89
Byron, George Gordon, Lord, 8

Cadets, 17, 67–68, 178
Calhoun, John C., 16
Campbell, John Quincy Adams, 74, 164–65
Canova, Antonio, 8
Capital punishment, 74
Careerism, 17, 71, 94, 103, 211
Carmichael, Peter S., 92, 213
Carter, Eugene, 138, 169–70
Carter, Robert, 86–87
Carter, Walter, 86–87
Cary, Richard D., 175–76
Casey, Silas, 108
Casualties, xii, 151, 159, 161–62, 167–69,
 176–77, 178, 181–85, 188, 198, 203, 205–6, 220, 223–25
Catlin, Isaac S., 83
Cavalry. *See* Organization of armies
Cedar Mountain, Battle of, 150, 151, 175
Ceracchi, Giuseppe, 8
Chamberlayne, John Hampden, 120–21
Chancellorsville, Battle of, 116–17, 149, 175, 181
Chandler, Charles L., 119–20
Chantilly, Battle of, 165–66
Chapin, Nelson, 53
Chaplains, 82
Chaplin, Daniel, 205–7
Character, 9, 33, 38–41, 45, 48, 55, 57, 61, 72, 99, 112–15, 147–48, 150, 161, 173, 177, 183, 186
Charisma. *See* Presence
Chattanooga Campaign, 183
Chickamauga, Battle of, 26, 194–95, 196
"Chicken guts." *See* Rank insignia
Chivalry, 111, 171
Christian virtue, 4, 111–12, 114–15, 150, 156, 180
Cincinnatus, Lucius Quinctius, 7–8, 11–12, 23, 129, 207
Citizenship, x, xii, 1–9, 12–15, 19, 23, 26, 31–32, 34, 58, 62–63, 67, 70, 75, 77–78, 94, 98–100, 133, 146, 155, 158, 174, 183, 207, 216
Citizen-soldier ethos, x–xiii, 2, 4–5, 7–10, 12–13, 15, 18–19, 23, 26–27, 29–30, 32–33, 39, 44, 46, 55, 59–61, 65–66, 75, 93–94, 97, 100, 103, 105–6, 116, 128, 158–60, 193, 217, 219–21
Civic virtue, 2, 4–7, 12, 15, 23, 32, 70, 100, 186, 221
Civilians, xiii, 5, 7, 11, 13, 16, 17, 18–20, 26, 30, 38, 41, 60, 62, 64–65, 70–71, 87–88, 95, 99–100, 104, 106, 121, 125, 130, 133, 147, 182, 185–86, 207, 212, 216, 219
Class, economic and social, xi, 29, 39–41, 78–79, 91–92, 111, 128–29, 229
Clayton, William Henry Harrison, 88, 96, 175
Cleburne, Patrick Ronayne, 181, 194
Clements, Stephen David, 114, 151
Cobb, Howell, 53
Coercion, 75–78, 99, 161, 169–72, 174, 176, 202–3
Coit, James B., 37–38
Cold Harbor, Battle of, 89, 189, 194, 202–3, 205
Coleman, E. L., 123–24
Combat, xi, 34, 37, 48, 63–64, 74, 79, 80, 89, 117, 134, 135–77, 178, 180, 182–83, 185–88,

190–94, 198, 200–205, 218, 220, 224
Comey, Henry Newton, 74–75
Command, ix, xi–xiii, 1–3, 8, 10, 13–14, 17–19, 22–23, 28, 30, 32–33, 35–36, 39–50, 52–53, 55–56, 58–72, 74–75, 77–98, 100, 102–5, 107–12, 115–19, 121, 127–28, 133–34, 137–44, 147–53, 155–57, 159–64, 167–78, 182–87, 190–91, 194–97, 199–200, 202, 204–6, 208, 211, 221
Commissions, xii, xiii, 25, 27, 35, 38–39, 42, 45, 47, 49, 50–52, 55–60, 62, 74, 81, 89, 92, 102, 104, 107–8, 110, 113, 118–22, 125, 127–28, 144, 151, 157, 163, 183–84, 185, 190, 211, 216, 223
"Commonwealth of Oceana, The" (Harrington), 5
Community and kinship, xii, 4, 9, 12–13, 15, 31, 34, 63, 70, 78–79, 86–87, 104, 121, 132, 158, 206
Company. *See* Organization of armies
Compassion, 167, 182, 190
Competence, x, 18–22, 34–35, 37, 39, 42, 44, 46–49, 51–53, 58, 61, 65, 67, 72–73, 76, 79–83, 85, 89, 100, 104–5, 134, 137, 139, 148, 158, 160, 173, 183, 190, 217, 219–20
Composure, 109–10, 150, 152–53, 158, 160–61, 165, 167, 177, 196, 198
Confederate units: Good-Douglas Battery, 118–19; Hampton Legion, 111; Purcell Battery, 102; Richmond Howitzers, 55; Rockbridge Artillery, 41
—Alabama: 6th Ala. Infantry, 96; 12th Ala. Infantry, 156, 190; 14th Ala. Infantry, 239–46; 18th Ala. Infantry, 154; 21st Ala. Infantry, 80; 47th Ala. Infantry, 239–46
—Arkansas: 3rd Ark. Infantry, 87, 239–46; 4th Ark. Infantry, 200, 239–46; 13th Ark. Infantry, 82
—Florida: 2nd Fla. Infantry, 239–46; 3rd Fla. Infantry, 79
—Georgia: 2nd Ga. Infantry Battalion, 38–39; 21st Ga. Infantry, 126, 239–46; 31st Ga. Infantry, 161, 219; 41st Ga. Infantry, 114, 154; 42nd Ga. Infantry, 198–99, 239–46
—Kentucky: 9th Ky. Cavalry (Confed.), 66; 5th Ky. Infantry (Confed.), 239–46
—Louisiana: 4th La. Infantry Battalion, 123; 3rd La. Infantry, 239–46; 14th La. Infantry, 31, 52
—Mississippi: 6th Miss. Infantry, 239–46; 16th Miss. Infantry, 159; 17th Miss. Infantry, 185; 43rd Miss. Infantry, 181
—North Carolina: 3rd N.C. Cavalry, 72; 3rd N.C. Infantry, 42–43, 126–27; 6th N.C. Infantry, 136; 22nd N.C. Infantry, 239–46; 26th N.C. Infantry, 51–52, 239–46; 35th N.C. Infantry, 52, 126, 192; 55th N.C. Infantry, 36, 123, 153
—South Carolina: 2nd S.C. Infantry, 113, 114; 3rd S.C. Infantry, 25–26; 10th S.C. Infantry, 239–46; 21st S.C. Infantry, 94
—Tennessee: 20th Tenn. Infantry, 184, 239–46; 23rd Tenn. Infantry, 159–60; 26th Tenn. Infantry, 74
—Texas: 9th Tex. Cavalry, 49; 28th Tex. Cavalry, 56; 4th Tex. Infantry, 76, 87; 5th Tex. Infantry, 81; 9th Tex. Infantry, 49
—Virginia: 1st Va. Howitzers, 112; 12th Va. Cavalry, 136–37; 2nd Va. Cavalry, 72; 4th Va. Infantry, 37; 17th Va. Infantry, 239–46; 18th Va. Infantry, 178; 38th Va. Infantry, 214–15; 45th Va. Infantry, 239–46; 48th Va. Infantry, 115; 61st Va. Infantry, 156
Confederate War Department, 35, 46–47, 105, 108
Confidence, 26, 33, 39, 45, 49, 51–53, 56, 58, 67–68, 79, 83–85, 88, 96, 99, 105, 128, 139, 148, 156–58, 166, 171, 183, 189, 200–201
Conflict, 18, 67, 68, 98–99, 109–10, 117–18
Conger, Arthur L., 133
Conscription, xiii, 8, 28–30, 46, 60, 185, 208, 219
Consent, 6, 18, 36, 55, 65–66, 78, 84, 98–99, 126, 175
Consistent leadership, 82, 101, 191
Continental Army, 1, 8, 10–11
Cooke, Chauncey H., 59
Cooper, James Litton, 184
Corbin, Richard W., 93, 97–98, 182, 189
Corruption, 2, 4–5, 10, 31, 37–40, 43–44, 46, 49, 55–58, 60, 89, 113, 115, 124
Courage, ix–xi, xiv, 17, 18, 21, 29, 37, 41, 48, 49, 55, 59, 63–64, 80, 87, 89, 91, 99–100, 115, 131, 134–35, 137, 138, 147–54, 156–57, 162, 164–69, 173–74, 176–77, 179, 183–84, 186, 189–92, 194, 201, 203–6, 211, 220
Courtesy, 78, 111, 112, 115
Courts-martial, 46–48, 56, 89, 170
Cowardice, xi, xiv, 74, 104, 123, 137–38, 139, 141, 149, 153–55, 157, 165, 168–69, 172, 174, 190–91, 208, 220
Craig, Cicero, 126–27
Craig, John B., 41–42
Craig, Samuel A., 66, 85
Crawford, William Harris, 16

Credibility, 148–49
Cress, Lawrence D., 5
Cruelty, xiv, 48, 76, 190
Culture, military, 16, 18, 58, 64, 70, 78, 95, 103–6, 111–13, 115–28, 220
Curtin, Andrew G., 34
Curtis, Newton Martin, 137, 138–39
Custer, George Armstrong, 211
Cyrus the Younger, ix

Dale, John Alexander, 72
Davis, James Cole, 41
Davis, Jefferson, 13–14, 29, 47–48, 182–83
Dawes, Ephraim Cutler, *following page 134*, 139–44
De Forest, John William, 106, 107, 124–25, 167–68, 192–93
Death, 19, 22, 26, 42, 50, 63, 74–75, 115, 135–36, 138, 143–46, 150–51, 155–58, 161–62, 164, 169, 170–71, 175–77, 178, 180–81, 182, 184, 188–91, 196–98, 201, 203, 219, 224
Defeat, xi, 147, 183, 202, 213–16, 221
Deism, 2
Democracy, xii, 2–3, 6–7, 8, 12–13, 15, 18, 23–24, 26, 30, 35–36, 43–44, 50, 52, 56, 58–59, 60- 61, 63, 66, 70, 78, 100, 128, 158, 193, 221
Democratic prerogatives. *See* Democracy
Dependence, 2, 4, 5, 9, 13, 26, 33–34, 36, 40, 52, 61, 62, 75, 98, 116, 158, 175, 220
DeRosset, William Lord, 42–43, 126–27
Desertion, 13, 50, 170, 174, 185, 214
Destruction, xiv, 4, 7, 9, 10, 21, 31, 32, 53, 60, 77, 81, 85–86, 119, 135–36, 137, 146, 148, 153, 157, 161–65, 176, 180–82, 186–87, 201, 206
Dickinson, Robert, 94
Discipline, ix, x, 9, 12, 15–16, 18–23, 30, 32–37, 42, 44, 46, 48, 51, 53–54, 60, 62, 65–67, 70, 74–76, 78–79, 86–87, 90–96, 99–101, 104–6, 108–12, 118, 127–28, 134, 138, 157–60, 167, 169–75, 177–78, 184, 189–90, 192–94, 200, 220
Disillusionment, 22, 56, 147, 181, 190–91
Disobedience. *See* Insubordination
Divine providence, 136, 150, 155–56, 180–81
Dobak, William A., 59
Doby, Alfred E., 113–14
Doctors. *See* Physicians
Donald, David Herbert, 158–59
Douglas, James P., 118–19
Drill, 18, 21, 54, 63–65, 68, 73–74, 79, 83, 85, 96–97, 99, 104, 106, 108–11, 118–19, 140–41, 144, 159–61, 163–64, 168–69, 193, 197, 211

Drunkenness, 19, 22, 23, 82, 87, 92, 93, 114, 116–17, 123, 189, 190
Dueling, 117–18
Duff, Levi Bird, 45, 65, 83, 96–97, 104–5, 116, 181–82, 209–210
Dungan, Robert H., 115
Dwight, Wilder, 35–36

Economic backgrounds of officers, 6, 12, 17, 29, 40–41, 54, 58, 126, 229
Education and training, xiii, 11, 12, 14, 16–18, 25, 27, 30, 40–41, 45–46, 48, 53, 58, 62–63, 65, 67–69, 70, 71, 73–75, 78–79, 92–93, 103–5, 107–9, 112, 114, 115, 118, 128, 138–39, 142, 144, 160–61, 165, 184–85, 219–20, 226–27
Efficiency, 6, 16, 18–19, 30, 32–33, 35, 45, 47–49, 59–60, 65–66, 94, 105, 118, 159, 162, 183, 220–21
Egalitarianism, 2–3, 12, 14, 15, 17–18, 23, 52, 58, 65, 100, 124, 128, 130, 132, 158, 193, 220
Elections of officers, 8, 10, 13–14, 25–30, 32–44, 46–53, 55, 57–61, 67, 72, 76, 78, 80–81, 93–94, 105, 127, 160, 219
Electioneering, 23, 33, 38–39, 40, 52–54, 57–60, 105
Elitism, 3, 12, 14–15, 50, 55, 80, 92–93, 111, 126–27, 129
Elliot, Isaac H., 43
Ellis, John S., 137
Emancipation, xi, 209–10
Empathy, x, 78, 87, 177, 208
Endurance. *See* Resiliency
Engineering officers, 28, 50, 98, 103, 115, 144, 203
English Opposition thought, 5
Entitlement, 11–12, 54, 82, 94–95, 116, 147–48, 179, 185
Equality, x, 3, 6, 9, 13–15, 19, 21, 36, 46, 59, 63, 66–67, 70, 75, 78, 82, 86, 94, 97–100, 109, 158, 161, 209
Etiquette, military, 66, 76, 86, 87, 105–7, 108–9, 117, 147, 214
Examination of officers, 42, 44–51, 59–60, 68–69, 84, 105, 160, 173, 183, 211
Example, leadership by, ix–x, 7–8, 11–12, 16, 21, 64, 66, 69, 82, 95, 96, 97, 103, 111–17, 147, 161, 164–65, 169, 176–77, 191, 200–201, 220–21
Expansible army, 11, 18
Experience, 34, 64, 74, 79, 104, 106, 137–39, 142, 145, 147–48, 157, 160, 181, 183, 186, 198, 200, 203, 205, 207, 215, 219
Ezra Church, Battle of, 230–31

Fair Oaks, Battle of, 156–57, 168–69, 182, 200
Fairness, x, 52–53, 55, 76, 78, 100
Familiarity between officers and men, 37–38, 88–89, 90, 91–92
Family, xi, 12, 21, 25–26, 40, 42, 50–51, 54, 79, 87, 93, 94, 115, 121, 125–26, 131–32, 149–50, 151, 154, 156, 179, 206, 207–8, 213, 216, 220, 229–30
Farming, 7, 14, 22, 40–41, 111, 127, 129–30, 216, 226–27
Fatalism, 180–82
Favill, Josiah Marshall, 52, 58, 94–95
Favoritism, 49, 52–53, 55–57, 81, 87
Fear, 23, 37, 45, 75, 82, 84, 114, 120, 136–38, 140–42, 144–45, 147, 149–50, 152–57, 158, 164–66, 168–69, 174, 176–77, 181–82, 187, 191–92, 201, 203, 208–9, 213
Featherstone, Mercer, 150
Federal units: Irish Brigade, 88–89, *following page 134*, 207; Iron Brigade, 185; 7th United States Cavalry, 211; 8th United States Infantry, 138; 43rd United States Colored Troops, 231–38; 1st United States Sharpshooters, 80
—Connecticut: 12th Conn. Infantry, 106, 167, 193, 207–8; 13th Conn. Infantry, 231–38; 14th Conn. Infantry, 37, 53, 102; 18th Conn. Infantry, 231–38; 21st Conn. Infantry, 122, 132
—Illinois: 7th Ill. Infantry, 231–38; 13th Ill. Infantry, 124; 17th Ill. Infantry, 142, 144; 33rd Ill. Infantry, 43, 80; 42nd Ill. Infantry, 165; 51st Ill. Infantry, 43–44; 86th Ill. Infantry, 201–2; 102nd Ill. Infantry, 39, 54, 79; 103rd Ill. Infantry, 197–98; 115th Ill. Infantry, 231–38
—Indiana: 10th Ind. Infantry, 231–38; 44th Ind. Infantry, 208; 57th Ind. Infantry, 76
—Iowa: 3rd Iowa Cavalry, 175; 5th Iowa Infantry, 74, 164; 15th Iowa Infantry, 144–46; 19th Iowa Infantry, 88; 26th Iowa Infantry, 131–32; 29th Iowa Infantry, 85, 88; 33rd Iowa Infantry, 231–38
—Kentucky: 3rd Ky. Infantry (Fed.), 198
—Maine: 1st Maine Heavy Artillery, 204–7; 16th Maine Infantry, 104, 152; 17th Maine Infantry, 149, 175; 18th Maine Infantry, 204; 19th Maine Infantry, 231–38
—Massachusetts: 10th Independent Battery, Mass. Light Artillery, 174; 2nd Mass. Infantry, 35, 42, 74, 85, 91, 117, 122, 151, 159, 174, 176, 231–38; 10th Mass. Infantry, 181, 188; 20th Mass. Infantry, 103, 154, 166, 168, 172, 186; 22nd Mass. Infantry, 86; 27th Mass. Infantry, 90; 28th Mass. Infantry, 88, 207; 29th Mass. Infantry, 50; 33rd Mass. Infantry, 180; 34th Mass. Infantry, 119; 35th Mass. Infantry, 105; 51st Mass. Infantry, 2; 55th Mass. Infantry (Colored), 218
—Michigan: 8th Mich. Cavalry, 115; 2nd and 5th Mich. Infantry, 160; 4th Mich. Infantry, 211; 10th Mich. Infantry, 199
—Minnesota: 1st Minn. Infantry, 231–38; 3rd Minn. Infantry, 191–92, 202; 4th Minn. Infantry, 54–55
—Missouri: 13th Mo. Cavalry (Fed.), 211; 21st Mo. Infantry (Fed.), 231–38; 45th Mo. Infantry (Fed.), 211
—New Hampshire: 4th N.H. Infantry, 82; 5th N.H. Infantry, 57; 13th N.H. Infantry, 64, 114, 124
—New Jersey: 5th N.J. Infantry, 156; 8th N.J. Infantry, 231–38; 12th N.J. Infantry, 187–88, 195–96; 33rd N.J. Infantry, 212
—New York: 6th N.Y. Infantry, 91; 16th N.Y. Infantry, 137; 34th N.Y. Infantry, 156; 40th N.Y. Infantry, 231–38; 51st N.Y. Infantry, 122, 165; 57th N.Y. Infantry, 52; 71st N.Y. Infantry, 95, 137; 72nd N.Y. Infantry, 172; 75th N.Y. Infantry, 77, 118; 85th N.Y. Infantry, 53; 123rd N.Y. Infantry, 79
—Ohio: 7th Ohio Cavalry, 113; 3rd Ohio Infantry, 90–91; 53rd Ohio Infantry, 139–44, 231–38; 54th Ohio Infantry, 113, 119; 74th Ohio Infantry, 191; 77th Ohio Infantry, 143; 101st Ohio Infantry, 58–59; 105th Ohio Infantry, 155, 194, 196; 115th Ohio Infantry, 133; 123rd Ohio Infantry, 128; 125th Ohio Infantry, 196–97
—Pennsylvania: 12th Pa. Cavalry, 31; 103rd Pa. Infantry, 231–38; 105th Pa. Infantry, 66, 209–10; 140th Pa. Infantry, 150–51
—Vermont: 2nd Vt. Infantry, 111, 130–31; 8th Vt. Infantry, 231–38
—Wisconsin: 6th Wisc. Infantry, 131, 185, 231–38; 18th Wisc. Infantry, 145, 146–47; 25th Wisc. Infantry, 59; 32nd Wisc. Infantry, 83, 212
Field, Charles W., 112
File closers, 153, 163, 170–74
Findley, Robert P., 191
First Bull Run, Battle of, 37, 95, 135–39, 144, 169–70, 219
Fisk, Wilbur, 111, 130–31

318 | Index

Fitzpatrick, Rene, 57
Five Forks, Battle of, 150
Fleharty, Stephen F., 39, 54, 79
Foote, Lorien, 78, 93
Formations, 163–64, 167, 194, 200–201
Fort Donelson, Battle of, 142
"Fragging" (assassination of officers), 174
Franklin, Battle of, 194
Fredericksburg, Battle of, 152
French army, 66
Friendship, xi, 31, 39, 44, 52, 53, 56–57, 76, 79, 80, 82, 104, 112, 115, 120–21, 124, 132–33, 142, 146–47, 150, 154, 169, 175–76, 180–81, 185, 212, 215–16
Frontal assaults, 178, 189, 194, 201
Frontier, 6–7, 11, 14, 16–17, 71, 107

Gambling, 23, 38, 92, 116
Garrett, Thomas M., 152–53
Gentility, 9, 12, 14, 17–18, 19, 40, 72, 81, 89, 93, 95, 99, 104, 111–15, 117, 119, 129, 131, 133, 151, 214
Gentlemanliness. *See* Gentility
George Washington's Resignation (engraving), 8
Gettysburg, Battle of, 84, 129–30, 163–64, 176–77, 178–79, 183, 190
Gibbon, John, 108
Giles, Val C., 76
Gillam, James H., 128
Glatthaar, Joseph T., 64, 116, 161, 193
Glendale, Battle of, 168
Glory, 9, 21, 25, 53, 63, 77, 91, 135, 151, 186, 212, 216
Goddard, Henry Perkins, 37–38, 53–54, 58, 102
Good, John J., 118–19
Goodwin, Richard Chapman, 176
Goree, Thomas J., 136, 137–38
Goss, Warren Lee, 124
Grand Review of the Armies of the Republic, 212
Grant, Ulysses S., 139, 186–87, 190, 202
Graves, Henry L., 38–39
Greece, ix–x, 5, 7, 55
Greed. *See* Selfishness
Griffin, James B., 111–12, 127
Grosvenor, Ira R., 168
Guard duty, 85, 104, 106, 110–11
Guernsey, Francis M., 83, 212

Habit of command. *See* Command
Hall, James A., 152

Hamilton, Alexander, 16
Hardee, William J., 108, 140
Hardship, xiv, 20–22, 31, 53, 78, 83, 87, 90, 95–96, 99, 118, 121, 123, 131, 135–36, 138, 146, 151, 155, 160, 169, 175, 177, 207, 209, 212
Harrington, A. L., 93
Harrington, James, 5
Harris, John W., 52, 131
"Harvard Regiment." *See under* Federal units
Hatred, 20, 213–14
Haughton, Andrew, 105
Henderson, Robert J., 199
Henricle, Jack, 143
Henry, Patrick, 7–8
Heth, Henry, 150
Hierarchy, 4, 14–15, 17, 60, 63, 70, 72–73, 97, 107, 126, 147, 157, 160, 177, 183, 217
Higginson, Thomas Wentworth, 2, 26, 59, 62–63, 65–66, 68, 70–71, 78, 98, 100
Hildebrand, Jesse, 139, 141–43
Hill, A. P., 121
Hill, Daniel Harvey, 19–20
Hindman, Thomas C., 171
Holmes, Oliver Wendell, Jr., 103–4, *following page 134*, 151–52, 168–69, 172
Holmes, Richard, 161
Honor, x, xi, 4, 12, 17, 21, 25, 34, 38, 41, 47, 52, 59, 60, 62, 76–77, 80, 99, 106, 114–16, 118, 120, 127, 129, 133, 149, 151, 153–54, 156, 175, 186, 191, 212, 220
Hooker, Joseph, 198
Horses, xi, 54, 59, 96, 97, 98, 110, 135, 138, 143, 146, 150, 152, 163, 171, 184, 188, 193, 198
Howard, Conway, 120–21
Hoyle, Joseph J., 36, 123
Hsieh, Wayne Wei-Siang, 202
Hunt, George B., 82
Hypocrisy, 21, 81–82

Incompetence. *See* Competence
Independence, 4, 5, 9, 26, 36, 40, 62, 75, 98, 123, 158, 220
Individualism, 18, 62, 65, 70
Inexperience. *See* Experience
Infantry. *See* Organization of armies
Inspections, 45, 46, 73–74, 110–11
Insubordination, 19, 21, 29, 38, 41, 46, 60, 64–65, 72–73, 75–77, 83, 85–86, 93, 98, 100, 106, 120, 123, 127, 134, 143, 158, 160, 170, 174, 193
Iuka, Battle of, 164–65

Jackson, Andrew, 12, 16
Jackson, Thomas J., 98, 112, 116–17

Jacksonian democracy, 12, 14, 17
Jefferson, Thomas, 14
Johnny Reb archetype, 10, 158
Johnston, Albert Sidney, 46
Johnston, Joseph E., 213
Johnston, William Preston, 46–47
Jones, Wells S., 142–44

Kautz, August V., 107–10, 116, 118, *following page 134*, 149
Keegan, John, 84, 128–29
Kellogg, Theodore Preston, 124
Kenly, John R., 21–22
Kennesaw Mountain, Battle of, 194, 201–2
Kettner, James H., 6
Kinzie, Arthur, 51
Kinzie, Juliette, 51

Laidley, Theodore, 20–21
Lalane, George M., 114–15
Lambert, William H., 212
Lane, Iverson, 56–57
Langhorne, James Henry, 37
Lasselle, Stanislaus, 21–22
Lavender, John W., 200–201
Lawyers, 16, 41, 45
Laziness, 22, 81–82, 94, 124
Lee, Charles F., 218
Lee, Edward, 90
Lee, Robert E., 33–34, 46–47, 173–74
Lewis, William Henry Harrison, 159, 186
Liberty, x, 1, 3–4, 6, 9–10, 13–15, 23, 26, 31, 62, 86, 100, 122, 123, 132, 209, 213, 216, 217
Lightfoot, James Newell, 96
Lightfoot, Thomas Reese, 77–78
Lincoln, Abraham, 4, 27, 34, 51, 209–10
Lincoln, William S., 119–20
Linderman, Gerald F., 78, 147–48
Little Bighorn, Battle of the, 211
Livingston, Albert, 79
Logan, John A., 217
Longstreet, James, 129–30, 136–38
Lost Cause of the Confederacy, 216–17
Lowe, Nathaniel, 57–58
Loyalty, 31, 49, 61, 75, 86, 90, 92, 96, 100, 111–12, 121, 127, 133, 174–75, 185, 209
Luxury, 54, 55, 124–26
Lyon, Henry C., 156–57
Lyster, Henry F., 160

Mahan, Dennis Hart, 103
Malvern Hill, Battle of, 172–73

Manhood, xi, 12, 54, 64, 119–20, 153
Manuals and military literature, 17, 45, 63, 64, 68–70, 85, 108, 161, 163–64, 171, 196
Marshall, Albert O., 36, 43, 80
Martin, Patrick H., 56
Martin, William Harrison, 87
Mason, George, 8–10, 12–13, 15
Matrau, Henry Clay, 131, 185, 211
Mattocks, Charles P., 149, 175
Maxey, Samuel B., 49
McCabe, William Gordon, 150
McCarthy, Carlton, 55
McClellan, George B., 20, 50
McClernand, John A., 143
McDowell, Irvin, 97
McKnight, William, 113
McPherson, J. A., 136
Meade, George Gordon, 18–19, 22–23, 33
Meares, Gaston, 42
Medical officers. *See* Physicians
Melton, Samuel W., 32–33, 48–49
Mercenaries, 5, 8, 182, 190
Mercer, George Anderson, 94
Merit, 11, 12, 16, 21, 32, 34, 54, 58, 65, 67, 109, 184
Mexican War (1846–48), 13, 15–24, 32, 33, 60
Miears, Lorenzo, 87
Militia, 2, 4–6, 8, 11–20, 23, 25, 35, 44, 69, 106, 139, 219
Miller, Robert H., 31, 52–53
Miller, William Bluffton, 73, 106, 155
Mills, Charles J., 132
Mitchell, J. T., 199
Mobilization, 27–28, 32
Moral excellence. *See* Areté (moral excellence)
Morale, xi, 9, 18, 31, 36–37, 45–46, 49–50, 52, 54, 58, 60, 77, 80, 86–88, 91, 97, 105, 109–10, 119–21, 124, 142, 147, 154, 156, 182, 200–202, 204, 213–14
Morfoot, Charles, 58–59
Morgan, John Hunt, 66–67
Motivation, xi, xiii, 23, 30, 42, 59, 67, 69, 75–77, 89–91, 155, 207, 214
Mount Vernon, 8
Mudge, Charles Redington, 174, 176–77
Musser, Charles O., 85–86, 88
Mutual obligation. *See* Dependence

Napoleon, 66, 157, 161
Nationalism. *See* Patriotism
Nelson, William Cowper, 185

Nepotism. *See* Favoritism
New Hope Church, Battle of, 196–97
New Orleans, Battle of, 16
Newburgh conspiracy, 11
Noncommissioned officers, 25, 26, 32, 33, 38, 39, 43, 51, 53, 54–55, 73, 75–77, 80–81, 88, 92, 99, 102, 104, 106, 110, 113, 119–20, 128, 129, 133, 142, 144–46, 152, 165, 171, 173, 175, 184, 187, 197
Norton, David, 165

Oakey, Daniel, 74–75, 91–92
Obedience, x, 4–5, 8–9, 13, 15, 35–36, 43, 49, 54–55, 65, 68–69, 73, 75–78, 79, 83–86, 90–91, 98, 100–101, 106, 110, 137, 140–41, 147–49, 161–62, 167, 169, 171–74, 185, 199–201, 204–6
Officers of the Day, 22, 92, 109–11
Officers' schools. *See* Education and training
Olmsted, Frederick Law, 44
Optimism, 83–84, 177, 207, 213–14
Ord, Edward, 104–5
Orderlies. *See* Slaves and servants
Ordnance officers, 50, 185
Organization of armies, 6, 8, 10–11, 20, 25, 27–30, 33–34, 43–44, 46–47, 62, 69–71, 75–76, 78, 80, 109, 139, 145, 157, 170, 192, 194, 196, 198, 204, 206, 219
Overland Campaign, 190–91, 202
Owen, Henry Thweatt, 178–80

Pace, Thomas, 175
Paine, Hannibal, 74
Park, Robert E., 83–84, 155–56, 190
Paternalism, 12, 92–94
Patriotism, xi, xiii, 2, 31, 39, 55, 71, 90–91, 124, 133, 160, 182–83, 207, 209, 211, 213–14, 216
Patronage, 2, 50–60
Pay, 10, 54, 82, 122–23, 132
Peale, Charles Wilson, 8
Pegram, William R. J., 102, 104, 112, 149–51
Pelham, John, *following page 134*, 135–36
Pendleton, Alexander Swift, 116–17, 125–26
Peninsula Campaign, 50
Percy, James R., 142, 144
Perkins, Stephen George, 176
Perry, Theophilus, 56–57
Persian army, ix
Personal connection, 86–92, 95–96, 148
Personal example, x, 82, 161, 169, 220
Persuasion, 69, 75, 78–79, 84, 86, 90, 147, 169–70, 172, 176, 214–15, 220

Petersburg, Siege of, 81, 93, 162, 173, 204–7
Physicians, 50, 173, 174
Pickett's Charge, 178–79
Pickett's Mill, Battle of, 181, 203–4
Pleasanton, Alfred, 211
Poague, William Thomas, 41–42
Pocock, J. G. A., 2
Politics, x, 2–5, 7, 11–18, 27, 34–35, 38–39, 42, 49, 53–58, 149, 189
Porter, John M., 66–67
Potter, Leander H., 80
Prairie Grove, Battle of, 171
Prayer, 114, 133, 145, 156, 189, 213
Presence, 11, 17, 39, 42, 66, 68, 70, 84–85, 86–88, 93, 98, 111, 117, 121, 127–28, 142, 148, 150, 162, 170, 220
Prestige, 41, 42, 122, 184
Prisoners of war, 43, 115, 129, 138, 183, 187, 196, 198, 205, 224
Privilege, xiii, 1, 5, 12, 14, 39, 48–49, 54–55, 78, 86, 92–93, 95, 116, 123–24, 126, 130–31, 190
Proctor's Creek, Battle of, 192
Professions of officers, 6, 16, 18, 40–41, 58, 111, 226–27
Professionalism, xiii, 2, 5, 8, 11–13, 15–23, 26, 49, 60, 63–66, 68–69, 71–72, 94–95, 100, 103–6, 108–9, 111–12, 115–16, 128, 134, 211, 219–20
Promotions, 16, 26, 29, 34, 42, 43, 47, 48, 50–51, 52, 53–54, 55–56, 57, 58, 60, 66–67, 77, 80–81, 87, 88–89, 96, 102, 106, 112, 113, 116, 118–19, 122, 126–27, 131, 132, 144, 164, 177, 183–85, 199, 237–38, 245–46
Prudence, 67, 86, 190–92, 220
Prussian army, 66
"Pumpkin rinds." *See* Rank insignia
Punishment, 56, 75–76, 78, 92, 106, 109–10, 172, 177
Puritanism, 2

Quince, William H., 42–43

Race, 1, 2, 5, 6, 13, 14–15, 22–23, 29, 59, 75, 77–78, 98, 122, 126, 209–10, 216
Ramey, William Neal, 56
Ramold, Steven, 116
Randal, Horace, 56
Rank insignia, 39, 53–55, 84, 102, 110–11, 128, 132–33, 149, 155, 162–63, 174, 191
Ranson, A. R. H., 72–73
Recklessness, 22, 54, 151, 153, 189–91
Reconciliationism, xiv, 216

Reconstruction, 216
Recruiting, 11, 16, 28, 32, 38, 51, 54–55, 59, 95, 107, 110, 139, 170
Reenlistment, 28–30, 77, 80, 208, 214–15
Regiment. *See* Organization of armies
Regular United States Army, xiii, xvi, 11, 13, 15–23, 27, 36, 44, 60, 63–64, 66–72, 87–88, 94–95, 97, 100–101, 103–9, 111–12, 123, 128–29, 134, 137–38, 158–59, 163–64, 169–70, 185, 193, 195, 197, 207, 210–11, 216–17, 219–21
Regularization, 105–6, 111, 134, 217, 220
Regulations, 17–18, 27–28, 36, 44–47, 56, 66–70, 97, 100, 103, 105, 108, 110–12, 126, 128, 131, 163, 175
Religion, xi, 2, 14, 102, 112, 114–15, 150, 155–57, 180–81, 210, 213
"Remarks on Annual Elections for the Fairfax Independent Company" (Mason), 8–10
Reorganization, 29–30, 32, 37–38, 42, 46, 49–50, 54, 60, 80–81, 160
Republican tradition, x, xiii, 1–11, 14–16, 19, 23, 26, 31, 47, 55–56, 60–61, 70, 100, 105, 124, 221
Reputation. *See* Honor
Resaca, Battle of, 181
Resignation, xiii, 7, 8, 27, 76, 80–81, 89, 118–19, 122, 127, 151, 183–84, 206, 208–9, 237–38, 245–46
Resiliency, x, 38, 59, 71, 76, 83, 90–91, 93, 98, 105, 146, 160, 169, 177, 181–86, 189–90, 193–94, 202–4, 208, 213–14
Resistance to authority. *See* Insubordination
Respect, 9, 17, 19, 27–28, 33, 40, 54–55, 67–68, 76, 78, 82, 87–88, 91, 97, 99–101, 106, 109, 120, 127–28, 131, 133, 148–49, 158, 166, 175
Revolutionary generation, 4, 7–8, 10, 12, 14
Rice, Ralsa C., 196–97
Richard, Carl J., 8
Richardson, Martin V. B., 82
Rocky Face Ridge, engagement at, 198–99
Rodgers, Thomas Blackburn, 129–30
Roe, Edward R., 43
Rome, 5, 7–8, 10, 55
Root, Elihu, 219
Royster, Charles, 11
Ruggles, Daniel, 52

Sacrifice, x, xiv, 2, 4, 8, 9, 11, 31, 32, 48, 55, 86, 95–96, 123, 137, 169, 176, 190, 206, 212, 214, 216, 220
Sashes. *See* Rank insignia

Scott, Sir Walter, 129
Scott, Winfield, 103
Secession, xiii, 2–4
Second Seminole War (1835–42), 16
Seddon, James A., 32–33, 35, 48–49
Selfishness, xiv, 5, 8, 9, 55, 89, 124, 191
Selflessness, 5, 7, 8, 11, 23, 72, 95, 100
Seniority, 16, 29, 34, 49, 52, 60, 137
Seven Days' Campaign, 126–27, 159, 172
Shame, 20, 30, 31, 55, 104, 122, 136, 137, 151, 154, 172, 191, 213, 218
Shannon, Fred Albert, 71
Shaw, Horace H., 235
Shaw, Robert Gould, 42, 44, 85, 95, 122, 154, 159, 174, 175–76
Sherman, William Tecumseh, 139–40
Shiloh, Battle of, 46, 139–44, 145–47, 170, 200, 219
Shirking, 31, 94, 174, 186
Shoulder straps. *See* Rank insignia
Simpson, Richard, 25–26
Simpson, Taliaferro N., 25–26
Skelton, William B., 17
Skilled artisans, 40–41, 226–27
Skirmishers, 163, 165, 197, 199
Slavery and slaveholding, x–xi, xvi, 2–4, 15, 208–10, 226–27
Slaves and servants, 4, 14, 76, 77, 117, 122, 125–26, 141, 215
Small, Abner R., 104, 152
Smith, Watson B., 115–16
Smither, John Mark, 81
Snipers and sharpshooters, 80, 94, 144, 162, 191, 192, 194, 206
Spanish-American War (1898), 217
Spotsylvania Court House, Battle of, 115, 187–88, 190, 194, 205
Squier, George W., 208–9
Staff officers, 38, 42, 50–52, 56–57, 71, 74, 93, 107, 108, 110, 116–17, 121, 122, 124–25, 129, 131, 132, 136, 139–44, 150, 170, 181–82, 184–85, 187, 189, 193, 195, 205–6, 211, 213–14
Stagg, J. C. A., 17
Standing armies, 2, 5–6, 11–12, 16, 20, 23
Stanton, Courtland G., 122, 132, 207–8
Stephenson, Philip Daingerfield, 82
Stephenson, William Blackford, 142, 144
Stiles, Robert Augustus, 112
Storrow, Samuel, 91–92, 117
Straggling, 141, 167, 169–71, 173, 198
Stubbs, John S., 199
Substitutes, xiii, 6

Sulokowski, Valery, 52–53
Sumner, Charles, 34
Sweet, Henry C., 155
Swords, 54, 102, 111, 119, 125, 128–33, 142, 145, 152, 155, 162, 172, 176, 193, 199, 207, 210
Sykes, Columbus, 181

Tactics, 45, 51, 64–65, 79, 83, 85, 95, 105, 108, 161, 163–65, 171, 194, 196, 198–200, 211, 220
Tapley, Frederick, 137
Taylor, Nelson, 172–73
Temperament, 51–52, 85, 97, 116, 153, 220
Temporariness of service, 1, 7–10, 18, 23, 62, 65–66, 86, 100, 193, 207
Tennyson, Alfred, Lord, 129, 212
Terrain, 194–97, 199–200
Thayer, Sylvanus, 103
Thompson, John J., 86–87
Thompson, M. Jeff, 43
Thompson, S. Millet, 64–65, 114
Thomson, Ruffin, 36
Thomson, T. P., 153
Tocqueville, Alexis de, 6–7
Tourgée, Albion W., 194–95
Training. *See* Education and training
Trauma, 144, 146, 175, 180, 182, 219
Trobriand, Philippe Régis de, 205–7
Trumbull, John, 8
Trust, 5, 13, 17, 26, 33–34, 39, 42, 49, 58, 60, 73, 78, 80, 83, 86–87, 90, 95, 96, 100, 116, 121, 148, 157–58, 162, 175, 185, 200, 212
Tuttle, John W., 198
Tyranny, 3, 6, 10, 13, 15, 17, 22, 70, 76, 93, 108, 124
Tyler, Robert C., 184

Uniforms and equipment, 71, 73, 90, 93, 96–97, 106, 122, 128, 131–32, 143, 150, 162–63, 166, 193, 212
United States Army. *See* Regular United States Army
United States Colored Troops, 59, 122, 144, 218, 224
United States Military Academy, 13, 17–18, 49, 66, 69, 71, 103, 104, 107, 112, 138–39, 220–21
United States War Department, 28, 45, 105, 108

Unskilled workers, 40–41, 226–27
Upton, Emory, 30, 44–45, 194, 218–19

Vicksburg, siege and campaign of, 131, 183
Virginia Military Institute, 178
Voluntariness of service, 6, 23, 46, 193
Voris, William M., 142, 144

Wade, John, 37
Walker, C. Irvine, 213–14, 215
Walker, R. Lindsay, 121
War for Independence (1775–1783), 5, 7, 10–11
War of 1812 (1812–15), 15, 16, 17, 108
Washington, George, 1, 5, 7–8, 11–12, 14, 16, 23, 129, 207
Watson, Samuel J., 63
Welsh, Peter, 88–89, 207
West Point. *See* United States Military Academy
Weston, George Washington, 131–32
Wharton, Charles Henry, 8
Wheeler, Harrison H., 106
Whig ideology, 5, 12
Whipple, Thomas J., 82
White-collar workers, 40–41, 226–27
Whiting, Nathaniel, 80–81
Whitman, George Washington, 122, 126, 133, 165–66
Wilderness, Battle of the, 186, 195–96, 205
Wilkerson, Simeon C., 154–55
Williams, James M., 80–81
Williams, John, 56
Williams, William B., 176
Willis, Martin, 82
Wills, Charles W., 197–98
Wilson, Henry, 34
Wilson, William, 91
Winchester, First Battle of, 159, 174
Winchester, Third Battle of, 193
Winthrop, Theodore, 154
"Wire-pulling." *See* Electioneering
Women, 14, 18, 53, 56–57, 81, 83, 88, 91, 106, 112–14, 118–19, 120, 122, 124–26, 128, 130–33, 154–56, 179, 181–82, 208–9, 212

Xenophon, ix–x, 221

Yates, George W., 211